VICTORIAN AFTE

We are things thrown in the air
alive in flight…
our rust the color of the chameleon.

Robert Lowell, 'Our Afterlife I'

Victorian Afterlives

The Shaping of Influence in Nineteenth-Century Literature

ROBERT DOUGLAS-FAIRHURST

OXFORD

UNIVERSITY PRESS

*This book has been printed digitally and produced in a standard specification
in order to ensure its continuing availability*

OXFORD
UNIVERSITY PRESS

Great Clarendon Street, Oxford OX2 6DP

Oxford University Press is a department of the University of Oxford.
It furthers the University's objective of excellence in research, scholarship,
and education by publishing worldwide in

Oxford New York

Auckland Cape Town Dar es Salaam Hong Kong Karachi
Kuala Lumpur Madrid Melbourne Mexico City Nairobi
New Delhi Shanghai Taipei Toronto
With offices in
Argentina Austria Brazil Chile Czech Republic France Greece
Guatemala Hungary Italy Japan South Korea Poland Portugal
Singapore Switzerland Thailand Turkey Ukraine Vietnam

Oxford is a registered trade mark of Oxford University Press
in the UK and in certain other countries

Published in the United States
by Oxford University Press Inc., New York

ISBN 978-0-19-926931-0

For MY PARENTS

Acknowledgements

THIS BOOK HAS taken a long time to complete. Without the help of many people it would have taken far longer.

I am especially grateful to Simon Christmas, Howard Erskine-Hill, Anne Henry, Tom Jones, Robert Macfarlane, Ruth Morse, Daniel Neill, Adrian Poole, Bharat Tandon, Barry Windeatt, and the readers appointed by Oxford University Press for commenting on earlier versions of this work with frankness and tact. Stephen Abell, Gillian Beer, Terri Beuthin, Jeremy Caddick, Dan Clarke, Adam Cork, Heather Glen, Ben Grange, Chris Greenwood, James Hendrickson, Simon James, Sean Matthews, John Ramster, Corinna Russell, Ian Sansom, Simon Schaffer, Anne Thwaite, Stephen Wainde, Ingrid Wassenaar, and Emma Widdis were generous with their ideas, encouragement, and advice. The librarians of Dorset County Museum, Trinity College Cambridge, Cambridge University Library, Ipswich Museum, and the Tennyson Research Centre in Lincoln made available manuscript collections and helped to track down elusive items. The efficient help offered by staff at the Whipple Library, Pembroke College Library, Fitzwilliam College Library, and Emmanuel College Library has also been greatly appreciated. Sophie Goldsworthy and Frances Whistler at OUP have been models of patient encouragement. I also owe a large debt to the three colleges of Cambridge University in which I worked on this project: Pembroke, Fitzwilliam, and Emmanuel.

My greatest debt is to Eric Griffiths, who started me writing this book and helped me finish it.

Contents

viii   *Contents*

List of Abbreviations

The following abbreviations are used for frequently cited works:

Agon	Harold Bloom, *Agon: Towards a theory of revisionism* (Oxford: Oxford University Press, 1982).
AI	Harold Bloom, *The Anxiety of Influence: A theory of poetry* (Oxford: Oxford University Press, 1973).
Allingham	*William Allingham: A diary, 1824–1889*, ed. by H. Allingham and D. Radford (1907, repr. Harmondsworth: Penguin, 1985).
BI	Jerome J. McGann, *The Beauty of Inflections: Literary Investigations in Historical Method and Theory* (Oxford: Clarendon Press, 1985, repr. 1998).
CMTC	Jerome J. McGann, *A Critique of Modern Textual Criticism* (Chicago: University of Chicago Press, 1983).
De Quincey	*The Works of Thomas De Quincey*, 16 vols. (Edinburgh: Adam and Charles Black, 1862–74).
EFGL	*The Letters of Edward FitzGerald*, ed. by Alfred McKinley and Annabelle Burdick Terhune, 4 vols. (Princeton: Princeton University Press, 1980).
EFGW	*The Variorum and Definitive Edition of the Poetical and Prose Works of Edward FitzGerald*, ed. by George Bentham, 7 vols. (New York: Phaeton Press, 1902, repr. 1967).
HL	*The Collected Letters of Thomas Hardy*, ed. by Richard Little Purdy and Michael Millgate, 7 vols. (Oxford: Clarendon Press, 1978–88).
Howe	*The Complete Works of William Hazlitt*, ed. by P. P. Howe, 21 vols. (London: J. M. Dent & Sons, 1930–4).
HP	*The Complete Poetical Works of Thomas Hardy*, ed. by Samuel Hynes, 5 vols. (Oxford: Clarendon Press, 1982–95).
Kabbalah	Harold Bloom, *Kabbalah and Criticism* (New York: Seabury Press, 1975).
KCH	*Keats: The critical heritage*, ed. by G. M. Matthews (London: Routledge, 1971).
Kintner	*The Letters of Robert Browning and Elizabeth Barrett Barrett, 1845–1846*, ed. by E. Kintner, 2 vols. (Cambridge, Mass.: Harvard University Press, 1969).

Kolb   *The Letters of Arthur Henry Hallam*, ed. by Jack Kolb (Col-
                umbus: Ohio State University Press, 1981).
KC   *The Keats Circle: Letters and Papers 1816–1878*, ed. by Hyder
                Edward Rollins, 2 vols. (Cambridge, Mass.: Harvard
                University Press, 1948, rev. 1965, repr. 1969).
KL   *The Letters of John Keats, 1814–1821*, ed. by Hyder Edward
                Rollins, 2 vols. (Cambridge, Mass.: Harvard University
                Press, 1958).
KP   *Keats: The complete poems*, ed. by Miriam Allott (Harlow:
                Longman, 1970).
Life   Florence Hardy, *The Early Life of Thomas Hardy, 1840–1891*
                (1928) and *The Later Years of Thomas Hardy, 1892–1928*,
                repr. as *The Life of Thomas Hardy*, 2 vols. (London: Studio
                Editions, 1994).
Memoir   Hallam Tennyson, *Alfred Lord Tennyson: A memoir*, 2 vols.
                (London: Macmillan, 1897).
MM   Harold Bloom, *A Map of Misreading* (Oxford: Oxford
                University Press, 1975).
Motter   *The Writings of Arthur Hallam*, ed. by T. H. Vail Motter
                (New York: Modern Language Association of America,
                1943).
OED   *The Oxford English Dictionary*, 2nd edn., ed. by J. A. Simpson
                and E. C. S. Weiner (Oxford: Oxford University Press,
                1989, repr. 1991).
Owen & Smyser   *The Prose Works of William Wordsworth*, ed. by W. J. B. Owen
                and Jane Worthington Smyser, 3 vols. (Oxford: Oxford
                University Press, 1974).
Page   *Tennyson: Interviews and recollections*, ed. by Norman Page
                (Basingstoke: Macmillan, 1983).
PR   Harold Bloom, *Poetry and Repression* (New Haven: Yale
                University Press, 1976).
RBP   *Robert Browning: The poems*, ed. by John Pettigrew, 2 vols.
                (Harmondsworth: Penguin, 1981, repr. 1996).
RT   Harold Bloom, *The Ringers in the Tower* (Chicago: Univer-
                sity of Chicago Press, 1971).
SM   Harold Bloom, *Shelley's Mythmaking* (New Haven: Yale
                University Press, 1959).
Strachey   *The Standard Edition of the Complete Psychological Works of
                Sigmund Freud*, ed. by James Strachey, 24 vols. (London:
                The Hogarth Press, 1953–74).
Super   *The Complete Prose Works of Matthew Arnold*, ed. by
                R. H. Super, 11 vols. (Ann Arbor: University of Michigan
                Press, 1960–77).

TA	*The Tennyson Archive*, ed. by Christopher Ricks and Aidan Day, 33 vols. (New York: Garland, 1987–93).
TC	Jerome J. McGann, *The Textual Condition* (Princeton: Princeton University Press, 1991).
TCH	*Tennyson: The critical heritage*, ed. by John D. Jump (London: Routledge, 1967).
TL	*The Letters of Alfred Lord Tennyson*, ed. by Cecil Y. Lang and Edgar F. Shannon, Jun., 3 vols. (Oxford: Clarendon Press, 1982–90).
TP	*The Poems of Tennyson*, 2nd edn., 3 vols., ed. by Christopher Ricks (Harlow: Longman, 1987).
WP	*William Wordsworth: The poems*, ed. by John O. Hayden, 2 vols. (Harmondsworth: Penguin, 1973, repr. 1989).

Manuscript sources are abbreviated as follows:

CUL	Cambridge University Library
Dorset	Dorset County Museum
Ipswich	Ipswich County Museum
Trinity	Trinity College, Cambridge University

Quotations from Dickens's novels refer by chapter to *The New Oxford Illustrated Dickens* (London: Oxford University Press, 1947–58); quotations from Shakespeare refer to *The Complete Oxford Shakespeare*, general editors Stanley Wells and Gary Taylor, 3 vols. (Oxford: Oxford University Press, 1987).

Further details of all other works referred to are listed in the Bibliography.

Introduction

If I listened to the words of my mouth, I might say that
someone else was speaking out of my mouth.
                        Wittgenstein, *Philosophical Investigations*

Writing in 1900, W. T. Stead celebrated the new 'spirit mysteries' of
the telephone, which had 'mounted sound upon the wire', and the
phonograph, which had permanently mounted sound in a way that
made possible its transmission by the wireless:

Countless generations mourning the dead have cried with vain longings to
hear the sound of the voice that is still. But in dreams alone or in those rare
visions vouchsafed to finer souls was the prayer ever granted. Now the very
sound and accent of the living words of the dead whose bodies are in the dust
have become the common inheritance of mankind.[1]

Stead's association of soundwaves and ghosts is itself a 'common
inheritance' of the nineteenth century.[2] Victorian scientific and spiritualist writings often overlapped when describing how voices might
linger beyond the grave, and the blurring of their vocabularies
infiltrated everyday speech, as when Tennyson explained that he
once stopped under a telegraph post 'to listen to the wail of the
wires, the souls of dead messages'.[3] But the way Stead chooses to
describe 'the sound of the voice that is still' also reveals a literary
inheritance which he and his readers shared; his interest in the
movement of sound across space and time adapts an earlier meditation upon larger, more visible, waves:

---

[1] Quoted in Asa Briggs, *Victorian Things* (1988), 395.
[2] See Gillian Beer, 'Wave Theory and the Rise of Literary Modernism', in *Open Fields: Science in Cultural Encounter* (1996); and Steven Connor, *Dumbstruck: A Cultural History of Ventriloquism* (2000), ch. 17: 'A Gramophone in Every Grave'.
[3] *Memoir*, II. 325; Tom Standage's *The Victorian Internet* (1998) explains what *Anecdotes of the Telegraph* (1848) had described as 'a very general but erroneous idea, even among the better order of folks ... that the humming aeolian harp-like effect of the wind on the suspended wire is caused by the messages passing' (66).

> Break, break, break,
>   On thy cold gray stones, O Sea!
> And I would that my tongue could utter
>   The thoughts that arise in me.
>
> ... But O for the touch of a vanished hand,
>   And the sound of a voice that is still![4]

By rhyming 'Sea' with 'me', Tennyson had hinted that the bereaved could feel haunted by more than one voice, as their sudden contact with death leaves them vulnerable to being swamped by what Freud was to describe as an 'oceanic' feeling of fellowship between the visible and invisible worlds.[5] But he was irritated by critics who assumed that his own poems were as haunted as the world they described: 'They allow me nothing ... For instance, "The deep moans round with many voices". "The deep", Byron; "moans", Horace; "many voices", Homer; and so on.'[6]

A number of later critics have been similarly reluctant to allow much to individual poets, choosing instead to concentrate on the overlapping forces (family, friends, editors, readers, other poets, ideological pressures, and so on) which can impinge upon the creation and revision of their work.[7] Harold Bloom, for example, who studies 'the life-cycle of the poet-as-poet',[8] concludes that what emerges from 'the deep | Moans round with many voices' are 'the inescapable accents of Keats, Tennyson's prime precursor'.[9] Jerome J. McGann, by contrast, attempts to listen in on the way that poems come to possess, and be possessed by, a lengthening reception history: '... readers, in those ghostly shapes we call critics and scholars, hear many voices in the texts they study. Like Tennyson's sea, what is literary "moans round" with many such voices.'[10] The theoretical models of Bloom and McGann offer mirror-reverses of the way

---

[4] 'Break, break, break', *TP*, II. 24.

[5] See *Civilisation and its Discontents* (1930), repr. in *Strachey*, XXI. 64–5; Freud is paraphrasing a letter from Romain Rolland, in which Rolland had attempted to locate 'the true source of religious sentiments' in 'a feeling which he would like to call a sensation of "eternity", a feeling as of something limitless, unbounded—as it were, "oceanic"'.

[6] Tennyson, as reported by H. D. Rawnsley, *Memories of the Tennysons* (1900), 71; the line is from 'Ulysses', *TP*, I. 619.

[7] An overview is provided in Jay Clayton and Eric Rothstein (ed.), *Influence and Intertextuality in Literary History* (1991).

[8] *AI*, 7.

[9] *MM*, 158.

[10] *TC*, 76.

'influence' has come to be understood in recent years. As McGann criticizes 'the artificially restricted geography of the individual person', so Bloom urges that 'We need to stop thinking of any poet as an autonomous ego.' For McGann, 'the artist writes in a dialectical relation to the objective world', and 'this relationship is fundamentally social rather than personal or psychological'; for Bloom, the fact that 'Every poet is a being caught up in a dialectical relationship' manifests itself chiefly as individual literary trauma.[11] Whereas McGann's poet is enmeshed by his 'social and historical filiations',[12] the 'filiations' of Bloom's poet are recoverable only by mapping out his trammels at the hands of his poetic father. Both produce detailed arguments to support the idea that writers and their texts are productively multiple and divided against themselves; both investigate the extent to which influence can form not only one of the conditions of writing but also one of its more or less explicit subjects.

The equal and opposite attentions which Bloom and McGann pay to 'influence' outline some of the problems involved in using such an indiscriminately accommodating term to account for a particular literary effect. As Ihab H. Hussan notes, influence is 'a rather furtive concept', forever threatening to give the slip to the unwieldy range of meanings and practices which it has attracted to itself over time.[13] Its applications include the impact of climate, locale, historical events, literary movements and conventions, social and cultural traditions, and individual writers or works; its forms include borrowings, forgeries, debts, and literary aftermaths, side-effects, and residues of many other kinds. Valéry's caution is instructive:

No word comes easier or oftener to the critic's pen than the word *influence*, and no vaguer notion can be found among all the vague notions that compose the phantom armory of aesthetics. Yet there is nothing in the critical field that should be of greater philosophical interest or prove more rewarding to analysis than the progressive modification of one mind by the work of another (to go deeper into the subject, we should also have to discuss the influence of a mind on itself and of a work on its author. But this is not the place).[14]

---

[11] *BI*, 49; *AI*, 91.
[12] *BI*, 5.
[13] 'The Problem of Influence in Literary History: Notes Towards a Definition', repr. in *Influx: Essays on Literary Influence*, ed. Ronald Primeau (1977), 35.
[14] 'Letter about Mallarmé', in *Leonardo, Poe, Mallarmé*, trans. Malcolm Cowley and James R. Lawler (1972), 241–2.

As Hussan points out, the fact that literary critics refer to 'influence' so often, and so variably, reveals that the problem of defining its bounds is 'at bottom a problem in relationships'.[15] Put another way, although the contingent sprawl of 'influence', as it promiscuously mingles different concepts of power, obligation, and persuasion, illustrates the inevitable difficulty in using a shared language to identify fine distinctions of human belief and behaviour, it also accurately reflects the potential richness and messiness of our relations with one another, both on and off the page. Ascribing some action to 'influence' can strike a balance between description and explanation; it can remove responsibility or attribute blame; it can weigh up what X does to Y against Y's receptivity to X. As a form of cultural shorthand for the diverse relationships which shape us, and the diversity of ways in which we put these relationships into words, 'influence' is not only something we might choose to think about; it is also, more indirectly, something we think with.[16]

During the nineteenth century, the vocabulary of influence developed a density in response to the variety and strength of the cultural pressures which were brought to bear upon it. The words and ideas which clustered around influence were central to the attempts of a number of disciplines, from psychology to sanitation reform, to create a shared cultural narrative which would account for the many ways in which people seemed able to move, interfere with, or control one another's minds and bodies. But because influence was too unstable and plural a concept, too prone to spillage and seepage, to be restrained by any one set of explanations, the same words and ideas also provided a discourse through which these disciplines were able to establish their own points of overlap and conflict. That is, the Victorian discourse of influence which I map out in this book was not homogeneous but homologous. In its passage between the human sciences, theological commentary, and literary endeavours, the language of influence was used to measure fluid exchanges between theories and vocabularies which were themselves unfixed and uncertain. While the rhetoric of influence often spoke of the need to believe that people were connected to one another in predictable and controllable ways, the self-divisions of the term also dramatized a

[15] 'The Problem of Influence', 35.

[16] I borrow this distinction from David Trotter's brilliant discussion of the attempts made by Victorian writers and artists to 'think *with* mess as well as about it'; see his *Cooking with Mud* (2000), 9.

complementary fear that people were becoming isolated, fragmented, at odds.

This study attempts to recover influence as a discourse which Victorian writers both recorded and actively helped to produce, whether explicitly (as an abstract idea) or implicitly (as a principle of composition). Take, as an example, Valéry's recognition that 'the progressive modification of one mind by the work of another' sometimes involves another state of the same mind rather than another mind altogether. Much Victorian writing is marked by a scrupulous and perplexed attention to the difficulties this could cause for some of the 'vague notions' we entertain about ourselves, such as an unexamined trust in the integrity of the self. As Lewis Carroll's Alice grows up, for instance, she does not feel quite herself. 'Let me think', she considers, '*was* I the same when I got up this morning?':

> 'I almost think I can remember feeling a little different. But if I'm not the same, the next question is "Who in the world am I?" Ah, *that's* the great puzzle!' And she began thinking over all the children she knew that were the same age as herself, to see if she could have been changed for any of them.[17]

In her tumble down the rabbit-hole, Alice is also going 'deeper into the subject' of 'progressive modification', and the questions she asks of herself and us are literary as well as ethical, as they are for Wilde when he remarks in *The Picture of Dorian Gray* that 'good form' is 'a method by which we can multiply our personalities'.[18] What the authors discussed in this book discover, through their methods of composition and revision, is that detecting another hand in one's writing raises awkward questions about what it means for one's self to be influenced, and therefore not one self only. In particular, their practical engagement with theories of influence in each case provides a set of opportunities to think about possible relations of 'mind' and 'work' which reach beyond the afterlife of an utterance, and into the empirical afterlife of its author.

The *OED* is reticent about the afterlife:

after-life. [AFTER—9.] 1. A subsequent or future life.
a. **1593** MARLOWE *Hero & Leander* (1598) (Ded.) sig. A2,
The impression of the man, that hath been deare unto us, living in an after life in our memorie, there putteth us in minde of farther obsequies.

---

[17] *Alice's Adventures in Wonderland* (1865), repr. in *The Complete Works of Lewis Carroll* (1982), 28.
[18] Ed. Isobel Murray (1974), 143.

2. The later period of one's life.

a. **1678** H. SCOUGAL *Life of God* (1726) 204 The lessons which afflictions teach us, are that we have the use of them in the conduct of our after lives.

The entry for 'afternoon' is approximately three times longer than that for 'afterlife'. This might seem neglectful, given that there are readers who believe that the afterlife will outlast an afternoon, although the interpretative strains which lurk between and within their illustrative quotations suggest that the *OED*'s editors are perhaps wise to avoid dwelling on definitions of what it is not given to us to know. Believers in Christian salvation, for instance, would expect 'the conduct of our after lives' to have an important bearing on a 'subsequent or future life', while the 'farther obsequies' of death and resurrection will not be brought to mind by remembering the dead, if 'an after life in our memorie' puts such thoughts out of our heads. The Victorians encountered similar difficulties in imagining the unknown shape of the future within the fixed shapes of their writing. In the hands of the best writers, however, the future represented not an unknowable void, a chaos of possibility, but rather a source of creative potential. For, although the Victorians wrote at length about death as an end to human life and its speculations, the energetic variety of their approaches to death and its aftermath shows how often it functioned as a means to an end; to confront death was also to confront those questions of change, continuity, and continuity-through-change which were actively embodied in their own methods of composition.

The responses of Bloom and McGann to Tennyson's description of the sea 'moan[ing] round with many voices' show that, despite the fundamental divergence of their theoretical claims, one premiss they share is that the only future which should concern writers is the future of their writing. Bloom explains that 'the poet's afterlife' can be 'prolonged' only if he revises his poetic father in his own image; McGann, similarly, concludes that only by 'continuous socialization' will the 'vaunted immortality sought after by the poetic impulse ... be achieved'.[19] It is certainly true that Tennyson's line has extended itself through the minds and poems of later writers, as when T. S. Eliot writes in *The Dry Salvages* that 'The sea has many voices', and thus associates the creative edges of his verse with the beaches it describes, where the sea 'tosses | Its hints of earlier and other

---

[19]   *TC*, 82; *AI*, 151.

creation'.[20] However, the conclusions of Bloom and McGann are more limited than the end which Tennyson imagines for himself, because his sea moans round with many voices other than those of earlier and other writers. One belongs to later Tennyson:

> Might I not say? 'Yet even here,
> But for one hour, O love, I strive
> To keep so sweet a thing alive:'
> But I should turn mine ears and hear
>
> The moanings of the homeless sea,
> The sound of streams that swift or slow
> Draw down Æonian hills, and sow
> The dust of continents to be ... [21]

John Churton Collins found several literary dwellings for 'The moanings of the homeless sea': 'This beautiful line is partly from Horace, *Odes*, II. xx.—*Visam gementis* littora *Bospori* (I shall go to see the shores of the moaning Bosporus), and partly from Shelley—*The thunder and the hiss | Of* homeless streams (*Alastor*).'[22] Christopher Ricks offers a different model: '*the homeless sea*: Shelley, *The Cyclops* 709'.[23] It would be hard to prove or disprove any of these as a source for Tennyson's lines, because a poem's sources need not be restricted to the poet's allusions; Tennyson's 'sea' could have been produced not in response to any particular sea, whether real or literary, but rather as an example of those 'minute perceptions' ('petites perceptions'), on or below the borderline of consciousness, which Leibniz described as being like the sound of the waves: innumerable moments of individual action and reaction which our ears hear only as an indistinguishable roar.[24] Tennyson explained to Knowles what else individual human ears would strain to hear in his sea: 'The vastness of the future—the enormity of the ages to come after your little life would act against that love.'[25] Literary source-study could not grasp this enormity, because although the echoes of Horace and Shelley alert us

---

[20] 'The Dry Salvages' (1941) ll. 17–24, repr. in *The Complete Poems and Plays of T. S. Eliot* (1969), 184.

[21] *IM*, XXXV, *TP*, II. 352.

[22] *Cornhill* (January 1880), repr. in Collins, *Illustrations of Tennyson* (1891), 102. Alongside this suggestion, Tennyson wrote 'Nonsense' (*TP*, II. 352n.).

[23] *TP*, II. 352n.

[24] Leibniz's 'petites perceptions' are discussed in Thomas McFarland's *Originality and Imagination* (1985), 36.

[25] *Nineteenth Century*, 33 (1893), quoted in *TP*, II. 352.

to how often Tennyson's thoughts of long persistence are expressed through the endurance of earlier poets, the echo of 'moanings' in 'Æonian' is also fed by a non-literary source: his thinking about the eternal.[26] As his lines suspend in their own movements a possible constancy of attitude towards the sea's restlessness ('moanings ... homeless ... Æonian'), so they sound out fragments from his writing career past and to come which do not 'act against that love', but reactivate it:

> ... the low
> Moan of an unknown sea ... [27]

> The phantom circle of a moaning sea ... [28]

> ... the waves that moan about the world ... [29]

On each occasion, the joining of 'sea' with 'moan' appears in a context of loss, and speaks of what can no longer speak for themselves: the voices of the dead. With each repetition, the line expresses how it is not only the sea which endures through alteration, and so establishes textually Tennyson's long-lasting interest in the idea that our loyalty to the dead provides a proper response to the loyalty of the dead, as they 'linger about the planet in which their earth-life was passed'.[30]

The 'many voices' of Tennyson's sea are remarkable, but in the context of his contemporaries they are not unusual. Indeed, it is the central argument of this book that to notice the frequency with which questions of influence stir the expressive surfaces and compositional depths of Victorian writing is also to become aware of another form of cultural 'frequency': it provides a way of tuning into the spirit of the age and turning up the volume.

---

[26] I discuss in Ch. 4 Tennyson's interest in 'Æonian' as a word and a concept.
[27] 'The Palace of Art' (pub. 1832), *TP*, I. 455.
[28] 'The Passing of Arthur' (pub. 1869), *TP*, III. 551.
[29] 'Demeter and Persephone' (pub. 1889), *TP*, III. 164.
[30] *Memoir*, II. 448.

1 Forms of Survival

Just before dawn on 26 February 1821, Keats's body was removed from 26 Piazza di Spagna, the lodgings in Rome which he had shared with Joseph Severn during the long weeks both had spent waiting for him to die. Keats's voice stayed with Severn:

Four days previous to his death—the change in him was so great that I passed each moment in dread—not knowing what the next would have—he was calm and firm at its approaches—to a most astonishing degree—he told [me] not to tremble for he did not think that he should be convulsed—he said—'did you ever see any one die' no—'well then I pity you poor Severn—what trouble and danger you have got into for me—now you must be firm for it will not last long—I shall soon be laid in the quiet grave—thank God for the quiet grave—O! I can feel the cold earth upon me—the daisies growing over me—O for this quiet—it will be my first'—when the morning light came and found him still alive—O how bitterly he grieved—I cannot bear his cries—

Each day he would look up in the doctors face to discover how long he should live—he would say—'how long will this posthumous life of mine last'—that look was more than we could ever bear—the extreme brightness of his eyes—with his poor pallid face—were not earthly—

These four nights I watch him—each night expecting his death—on the fifth day the doctor prepared me for it—23rd at 4 oclock afternoon—the poor fellow bade me lift him up in bed—he breathed with great difficulty—and seemed to lose the power of coughing up phlegm—an immense sweat came over him so that my breath felt cold to him—'don't breath on me—it comes like Ice'—he clasped my hand very fast as I held him in my arms—the mucus was boiling within him—it gurgled in his throat—this increased—but yet he seem'd without pain—his eyes look'd upon me with extreme sensibility but without pain—at 11 he died in my arms— ... On Sunday the second day Dr Clark and Dr Luby with an Italian Surgeon—opened the body—they thought it the worst possible Consumption—the lungs were intirely destroyed—the cells were quite gone—[1]

---

[1] Severn to Taylor (6 March 1821), *KC*, I. 224–5.

'How long will this posthumous life of mine last?' is a good question, and not only because, like many questions worth asking more than once, it cannot yet be answered. It was an especially far-sighted question to ask of Severn, because it was the publication of this letter to John Taylor which did so much to promote the later nineteenth-century image of Keats as a poet who was too unearthly to survive for long in this world, too frail to withstand the sneering of the critics, too ready to allow his physical body to be replaced by his literary remains.[2] As Elizabeth Barrett explained:

Keats was indeed a fine genius,—too finely tuned for the gross dampness of our atmosphere, the instrument breaking with its own music. As singers sing themselves out of breath, he sang himself out of life—interrupting with death, the perfection & unity of his cadence![3]

Death from tuberculosis is usually less lyrical than this description might suggest, as the sufferer's lungs slowly dissolve to create their own microclimate of 'gross dampness', flooding the body with itself. Barrett herself half-recognizes this with the phrase 'he sang himself out of life', which principally means 'he exhausted himself with his own eloquence', but also hints darkly at the mythical fate of the swan, said to sing herself to death, and perhaps too the watery fate of Ophelia, who accompanies herself with 'snatches of old tunes' as she drowns, 'like a creature native and endued | Unto that element'.[4] Yet although Barrett only obliquely alludes to the horrors Severn describes, her sense that Keats's voice was not altogether stopped by death, but merely interrupted by it, is true to the way Severn's report continues to echo Keats's dying words in his description of those words, as if seeking a verbal intimacy which could survive their physical separation. Consider Severn's 'poor fellow', which picks up and prolongs the sympathetic note of Keats's 'poor Severn', or Keats's longing to feel the 'cold earth' over him, which is returned to and retuned by Severn's guilty memory that 'my breath felt cold to him', or the unselfish advice 'now you must be firm for it will not last long', which is paralleled by Severn's report that Keats himself 'was calm and firm at [death's] approaches'. Like Severn's sudden lurches

---

[2] See Susan J. Wolfson, 'Keats Enters History: Autopsy, *Adonais*, and the Fame of Keats', in *Keats and History*, ed. Nicholas Roe (1995), 24.

[3] Barrett to Benjamin Robert Haydon (20 October 1842), repr. in *Invisible Friends: The Correspondence of Elizabeth Barrett Barrett and Benjamin Robert Haydon, 1842–1845*, ed. Willard Bissell Pope (1972), 5.

[4] *Hamlet* IV. vii. 152–5.

into the present tense ('I cannot bear his cries ... These four nights I watch him'), the sympathetic weave of his and Keats's words illustrates how long a deathbed can last for the one who lives on to report it. The increasingly breathless piling up of clauses ('the mucus was boiling within him—it gurgled in his throat—this increased') might then suggest a man racked with sobs, but might equally suggest a man breathing in sympathy with someone whose own breaths were quickening towards the last, and so ask for a further sympathy from his reader, as the rhythms of grief awkwardly encounter the rhythms of pain in the uneven rhythms of Severn's prose.

These points of imaginative contact between Keats and Severn provide some support for Keats's view that individuals who live in close proximity to one another start to merge:

Our bodies every seven years are completely fresh-materiald ... This is the reason why men who had been bosom friends, on being separated for any number of years, afterwards meet coldly, neither of them knowing why— The fact is they are both altered—Men who live together have a silent moulding and influencing power over each other—They interassimilate.[5]

The edges of two voices are often similarly blurred and blunted by their daily interaction, in which case the idea of Keats and Severn starting to sound alike within the confined air of the sickroom would be no odder than the way that lovers sometimes share the same mannerisms or finish one another's sentences. But it is difficult to hear Severn's and Keats's voices merging as neatly as the two halves of a compound word like 'interassimilate'. In the first place, Keats's last words cannot readily be disentangled from the inventive powers of a writer who, as his first biographer pointed out, 'had a capricious memory, and was at no time heedful of the exact verity of his statements'.[6] This was not Severn's first attempt to compose his memory of Keats's deathbed. Several phrases from this letter also appear in an earlier draft to Charles Brown, which trails off unfinished with the sketch of a mourning figure (Fig. 1) that could be interpreted equally as evidence of the writer's collapse into inarticulate grief, or his wish to rehearse an attitude towards loss before committing it to paper. Nor was the letter to Taylor Severn's final word on the scene. The observation that Keats's eyes were 'not earthly' already hints at the hazy Christian piety which would blur

[5] Keats to the George Keatses (21 September 1819), *KL*, II. 208.
[6] William Sharp, *The Life and Letters of Joseph Severn* (1892), xiii.

FIG. 1 Mourning figure, drawn by Joseph Severn on the unfinished draft of his letter to Charles Brown announcing the death of Keats. Reproduced in William Sharp, *The Life and Letters of Jospeh Severn* (1892).

the outlines of later accounts, just as Keats's remark that he could feel the daisies growing over him is elevated to the status of a prophecy, once it is associated with Severn's decision to have daisies planted on the grave in Rome; indeed, as it circulates between different Victorian accounts,[7] the anecdote is gradually reshaped into something like a floral tribute to Keats's prescient trust in his friend.

Even within the narrower timeframe of this letter to Taylor, there are clues that Keats's 'moulding and influencing power' upon Severn does not amount to a perfect meeting of minds or voices. Take Severn's self-reassuring conclusion that, while Keats slowly suffocated

[7] See, e.g., *KCH*, 307, *KC*, II. 36, and Elizabeth Barrett's letter to Mary Russell Mitford: 'Keats—yes—Keats—he WAS a poet ... from his first word to his last, when he said he 'felt the daisies growing over him' (26 October 1841), repr. in *The Letters of Elizabeth Barrett Browning to Mary Russell Mitford, 1836–1854* (3 vols., 1983), I. 297.

in his own blood and mucus, 'he seem'd without pain—
look'd upon me with extreme sensibility but without pain'
this gap between Keats's suffering and Severn's seeming disr
it can be attributed to the popular assumption that tuberculosis was,
in Thomas Browne's phrase, a 'soft Death',[8] a slow and decorative
wasting away of the flesh, and so one peculiarly suited to writers,
those creatures of refined sensibility who are forever thought to be
trying to escape the limitations of their bodies through the reach and
endurance of print. When Shelley attempted to console Keats with
the thought that 'this consumption is a disease particularly fond of
people who write such good verses as you have done',[9] he made wryly
explicit this lingering connection between the consumptive's physical
frailty and his or her creative resilience. Keats himself had written
that the last moments of his tubercular brother Tom 'were not so
painful, and his very last was without a pang',[10] so in this sense
Severn's remark reveals a shared convention of thought which also
kept them at a personal remove from one another; it signals a point of
imaginative exchange and sympathetic blockage. Another, less historically variable, assumption which may have contributed to
Severn's conclusion is that the pain of another person remains an
unbroachable secret even in our descriptions of it. To take up the title
of Elaine Scarry's remarkable book *The Body in Pain* (1985), to a
sufferer the body is *in* pain, as one might be in another country,
engulfed by a force that destroys the relationships of time and place
and language; to have pain is a model of what it means to have
certainty. But to an observer that pain is *in* the sufferer's body, the
unapproachable centre of his or her inner world; someone else's pain
is a model of what it means to have doubt. It is therefore impossible to
be both loyal to someone else's pain and to describe it, because
although pain invites the consolations of narrative, it also refuses
them; it erases a sense of structure, pattern, purpose; selfishly occupying the sufferer's full attention, it dissolves past and future into an
inescapable present tense.

Maria Gisborne recalled a meeting with Keats at Leigh Hunt's
during which singing was discussed; the Italian virtuoso Carlo Far-
inelli

---

[8] 'A Letter to a Friend, Upon Occasion of the Death of his Intimate Friend' (1657); see
Susan Sontag, *Illness as Metaphor* (1978, repr. 1991), 123–4.
[9] Ibid., 33.
[10] Keats to the George Keatses (16 December 1818), *KL*, II. 4.

... had the art of taking breath imperceptibly, while he continued to hold one single note, alternately swelling and diminishing the power of his voice like waves. Keats observed that this must in some degree be painful to the hearer; as when a diver descends into the hidden depths of the sea you feel an apprehension lest he may never rise again. These may not be his exact words as he spoke in a low tone.[11]

It is likely that Keats was speaking in a low tone because earlier that evening he had suffered another violent haemorrhage,[12] and this adds a private undercurrent of regret to his metaphor of drowning which remains 'in some degree painful to the hearer'. But whether or not these were his exact words, the idea of a single note 'alternately swelling and diminishing' accurately reflects the sustained modulations of Keats's own voice across his career, from the regular worries that he was 'treading out [of] my depth' in his verse,[13] to the nervous jokes about 'sinking' in his correspondence.[14] In particular, Keats's transference of the singer's failing breath to the pain of his listener is both typically generous and, in Gisborne's account, typically wary ('in *some* degree') of the limitations of such generosity. As Christopher Ricks has suggestively argued, much of Keats's writing is marked by his consciousness of the imagination's double responsibility: to find a voice for the many different worlds which are contained within our shared world, and to recognize that nothing about the pains or pleasures of these worlds can be assumed by the person without.[15] The poet who is forever 'infor—and filling some other Body'[16] is therefore confronted with the need both to expand the circumference of the self, and to observe its precious and precarious boundaries, just as the medium in which he or she works obliges him or her to reconcile the most intimate sharing of other people's experiences with a sense of their unapproachable otherness.

Many of Keats's poems are animated by a recognition that our words, like our bodies, are both private and public forms, our own

---

[11] Quoted in Walter Jackson Bate, *John Keats* (1963), 648.

[12] See Bate, ibid.

[13] Keats to Reynolds (3 May 1818), *KL*, I. 277.

[14] See, e.g., Keats to Bailey (13 March 1818), 'I have sunk twice in our Correspondence, have risen twice and been too idle, or something worse, to extricate myself—I have sunk the third time and just now risen again at this two of the clock P.M. and saved myself from utter perdition—by beginning this, all drench'd as I am and fresh from the Water ... ', *KL*, I. 240.

[15] See *Keats and Embarrassment* (1976) on the 'fundamental double truth which literature can prove upon our pulses ... that we are not other people, and so should never think that we can fully imagine their feelings, and yet that we can imagine others' feelings', 117.

[16] Keats to Woodhouse (27 October 1818), *KL*, I. 387.

and not our own, and so offer a helpful resource for investigating the sympathetic imagination's fluctuating movements of approach and recoil. His portrayal of the fallen Titans in *Hyperion* is both extraordinary and typical, as he describes how they are condemned to be

> ... pent in regions of labouring breath;
> Dungeoned in opaque element, to keep
> Their clenchèd teeth still clenched, and all their limbs
> Locked up like veins of metal, cramped and screwed;
> Without a motion, save of their big hearts
> Heaving in pain, and horribly convulsed
> With sanguine feverous boiling gurge of pulse.[17]

By this stage in his career, Keats had good private reasons to be attracted to the imaginative possibilities of drawing out 'labouring breath' on the page. He had already underlined a passage in his copy of *Paradise Lost* which described Satan entering the serpent:

Whose spirit does not ache at the smothering and confinement ... Whose head is not dizzy at the prosaible speculations of satan in the serpent prison—no passage of poetry ever can give a greater pain of suffocation.[18]

Many passages of his own poetry set out to challenge this claim, by containing natural patterns of breathing within forms which variously expand and contract the shape of the 'speculations' they carry. Keats was a breathless poet from the start, with *Endymion* his most breathless poem of all. Of his nine recorded usages of 'breathless', seven are in *Endymion*, but merely as a convenient poetic shorthand for the throbbings of desire: the 'breathless honey-feel of bliss', or 'breathless cups and chirping mirth'.[19] After his first mouthful of blood ('I know the colour of that blood;—it is arterial blood;—I cannot be deceived in that colour;—that drop of blood is my death-warrant;—I must die'),[20] Keats took breathlessness more seriously, from the 'panting' lovers of 'Ode on a Grecian Urn' (who, in a thoughtful pun, are 'All breathing human passion far above' because they are *on* a 'brede', not *about to* breed), to the sudden gasps and catches of *Otho the Great*:

---

[17] *KP*, 417–18.
[18] Keats's marginalia from his copy of *Paradise Lost* are repr. in *The Poetical Works and Other Writings of John Keats*, ed. H. Buxton Forman (8 vols., 1938–9), IV. 179–91.
[19] *Endymion*, I. 903, IV. 236 (*KP*, 160, 256).
[20] *KC*, II. 73.

> ... that the sword of some brave enemy
> Had put a sudden stop to my hot breath ...

> ... smother up this sound of labouring breath ...

> ... try
> Your oratory—your breath is not so hitch'd ... [21]

As a play, *Otho the Great* would enjoy a full-throated ease in performance whatever the state of Keats's own lungs, and his description of
the Titans similarly anticipates an extended life to come in the
mouths of its readers; the present tense is as much an appeal as a
method of description. In part this is because Keats's account of
'labouring breath', added in revision, is stretched out over a single
sentence, and so reminds its readers that this epic story of divinities
rising and falling requires the smaller scale rise and fall of their own
lungs; 'labouring breath' is what we must physically undergo as well
as imaginatively entertain. As these lines continue to exercise our
minds and bodies, Keats's lengthening reflections then form something like that 'physiology of style' which Benjamin heard in Proust's
asthmatic syntax; for the reader, as for the poet, they represent 'the
deep breath with which he shakes off the weight of memories'.[22] At
the same time, just as Keats found the range of his own sympathies
tested by his dying brother ('His identity presses on me so all day', he
complained, that he was forced to write in order 'to ease myself of his
countenance his voice and feebleness'),[23] so this passage from *Hyperion*
provides clues that the physical space we share can be mapped out
according to a more flexible human geography of perceived proximity and distance. Take the interpretative uncertainties of a line like 'all
their limbs | Locked up like veins of metal'. In one sense, this means
that each limb is clamped into place, like a seam of metal in rock, so
that the Titans' attention is focused upon what continues to move
even though it is kept in check: the blood still coursing through their
veins. In another sense, the line suggests that each Titan is no longer
sure how many limbs he possesses, as if the sensation of being racked
with pain could be experienced in a way that is as publicly mingled as
their groans, just as the half-rhyme on 'convulsed' and 'pulse' melts

---

[21] *Otho the Great* III. i. 4, V. i. 29, V. ii. 42 (*KP*, 576, 601, 603).
[22] 'The Image of Proust', repr. in Hannah Arendt (ed.), *Illuminations* (1970), 209.
[23] Keats to Dilke (21 September 1818), *KL*, I. 367.

away the individual aches and pains of their 'big hearts' into a single insistent metrical throb: 'sanguine feverous boiling gurge of pulse'. By observing these hidden movements in its own movements, Keats's line tests an abstract notion of sympathy against the actualities of the Titans' bodies, 'for axioms in philosophy are not axioms until they are proved upon our pulses',[24] but the supportive metrical pulse of this line cannot prevent the Titans' hearts from being '*horribly* convulsed': a word which brings together the Titans' horror at their state with the temptation of a witness to do for the Titans what they cannot do for themselves: avert their gaze. Like all truthful expressions of the sympathetic imagination, Keats's lines therefore acknowledge the necessary and desirable limits of our imaginings, as we are brought to understand not only that we cannot take the pains of other people for them or from them, but also that the most sympathetic response to the Titans could be a measured indifference to their fate, as we discover within the perpetual motion of their blood, fixed into the rhythms of printed verse, an imperturbability in the face of suffering to which they too must reconcile themselves.

It is Keats's lasting success in identifying the twin needs we have of art—to invite our participation in other lives, and to remind us of the unbroachable otherness of these lives—which also provided Severn with a way of coming to terms with Keats's last moments. For although Severn's references to his friend's 'calm' is a common theme of Keats's reviewers,[25] the way he chooses to characterize it ('the extreme brightness of his eyes—with his poor pallid face—were not earthly') reveals how far 'calm' can be an attitude in which a poem educates its readers:

> But for her eyes I should have fled away.
> They held me back with a benignant light,
> Soft-mitigated by divinest lids
> Half-closed, and visionless entire they seemed
> Of all external things—they saw me not,
> But in blank splendour beamed like the mild moon,
> Who comforts those she sees not, who knows not
> What eyes are upward cast.[26]

---

[24] Keats to Reynolds (3 May 1818), *KL*, I. 279.
[25] See *KCH*, 176, 216 on the 'calm beauty' and 'calm power' of his verse, and compare references to Keats's own calmness of demeanour in *KC*, I. 152–3, 165, 202, II. 73, 341.
[26] *The Fall of Hyperion*, I. 264–71, *KP*, 674.

Ricks has heard how much is retained in these lines:

The blank splendour of the moon is a type of the blank (not empty) splendour of art, which comforts those she sees not, and knows not what eyes are upward cast. The consolation which Keats here imagines, he at the same time provides; he comforts those he sees not, and this is of the essence of art.[27]

The same comfort may also be provided by one writer for another, as Severn's echo of *The Fall of Hyperion* discovers in Moneta a model of the patience to which he continued to mould his response to Keats's death. In 1848, he describes Keats's 'piercing supernatural eyes, which seem'd to encrease in life as his poor body decay'd';[28] as late as 1863, he is still caught in the beam of Keats's eyes: 'an unearthly brightness and a penetrating steadfastness that could not be looked at'.[29] The lasting consolation which Keats had imagined, he at the same time provided.

PERSONS AND POEMS

The lingering presence of Keats's verse in Severn's voice reflects one possible model of literature's workings. 'A great writer', Joseph Brodsky observes, 'is one who elongates the perspective of human sensibility, who shows a man at the end of his wits an opening, a pattern to follow.'[30] The act of reading is always likely to guide our eyes in this direction, because the events of a novel or poem are already organized into 'patterns' of plot and style. As we follow the patterning of a writer's ideas, his or her designs on the page, such texts offer both a description and an expiation of the contingencies and thwartings of real life; they simultaneously excite and control our desires; they afford us the temporary pleasures of occupying in imagination the sort of unchangeable world we could not easily inhabit in fact. At the same time, the 'pattern' of a literary work like *Hyperion* extends beyond its own covers. In speaking to us, the work speaks for us, as we become aware of thoughts and feelings that we recognize as our own, but might not have formulated on our own. Such works then 'elongate the perspective of human sensibility' still further by encouraging a reader to cultivate what William Empson characterized as a 'sense of proportion':

[27] *Keats and Embarrassment*, 191.
[28] Severn to Milnes (5 May 1848), *KC*, II. 234.
[29] 'On the Vicissitudes of Keats's Fame' (1863), repr. in *KCH*, 408.
[30] 'Catastrophes in the Air', repr. in *Less Than One: Selected Essays* (1986), 299.

... not the avoidance of emotion (which narrows understanding as much as pleasure) but a power to have strong emotions without forgetting the things he will value at other times, a power to know what his feelings will be under other circumstances so as not to be helplessly surprised by them when they come.[31]

Keats's description of Moneta, for example, is in many ways a surprising piece of writing, and some of the surprises it contains will allow us to prepare for those we have yet to experience outside the controlled conditions of reading. Some may even allow us to prepare for the surprises we encounter in our reading, because to read Keats's description with a due sense of proportion is to become aware that we will not always understand it in the way we do now, so allowing Moneta's indifferent stare to act as a measure of the more precarious nature of our human judgements. For its readers, as for its subjects, this is a poem about the need to come to terms with change.

'The interest of this production', Coventry Patmore observed of *Hyperion*, lies in its 'showing that Keats had begun to feel the necessity of looking to the future for his subject and inspiration'.[32] By this he probably meant no more than Keats's brilliant failure to accommodate the shape of his thinking to the fixed outline of his plot, as the sense of brooding expectation which is generated by his incomplete narrative sympathetically comes to echo the difficulties of his Titans in reconciling themselves to their fate. However, *Hyperion* also looks to its own future, because Keats's uneven diction, which repeatedly echoes the Titans' fall by engaging in its own local skirmishes of the old and the new (referring to the Titans' pain as 'sanguine', for example, keeps their situation expectantly poised between the Latinate sense of 'bloody' and the more recent sense of 'hopeful'),[33] implicitly concedes that even the most forward-thinking poem can contain the seeds of its own decay and abandonment. The evolutionary model of history which *Hyperion* hints at, therefore, it also threatens to embody; Keats's lines 'elongate the perspective of human sensibility' by stretching out into the future of his readers, but they also achieve a sense of perspective by organizing themselves around this future as their possible vanishing-point.

[31] 'Teaching Literature' (1934), repr. in *Argufying: Essays on Literature and Culture* (1987), 93.

[32] Review of R. M. Milnes, *Life, Letters and Literary Remains of John Keats* (1848), repr. in *KCH*, 337.

[33] 'Of persons and expectations, etc.: Hopeful or confident with reference to some particular issue' (*OED*, from 1673).

There is a long critical tradition which assumes that Keats's lasting success as a poet can be attributed in part to his social and literary ambition (Paul de Man remarked that the 'unfavourable circumstances of his birth' meant that Keats 'lived almost always oriented toward the future'),[34] and in part to his early death; 'by being the poet of youthfulness', W. M. Rossetti sighed, 'he was privileged to become and remain enduringly the poet of expectation and passionate delight'.[35] Andrew Bennett's recent investigation into the Romantic 'culture of posterity' has shown that Keats was not alone in hoping for a form of literary afterlife which would act as a 'redemptive supplement' to his present neglect.[36] A number of his contemporaries agreed that success, like posterity, can be thought of only in the future tense: only with death does the writer cease to be an obstacle to himself. 'The poet's cemetery is the human mind', Hazlitt declared, 'in which he sows the seeds of never-ending thought—his monument is to be found in his works.'[37] Hazlitt's indecision over which metaphor—static 'monument' or germinating 'seeds'—best characterizes the growing reputation of a literary work itself brings together old and new models of the writer's future life, as the familiar assumption, detailed in much classical and Renaissance verse, that present renown will be extended into the future, is gradually replaced by the idea that fame is a gift which is retained during the writer's life and bestowed at the discretion of posterity. However, as Bennett points out, despite the new energy and focus with which Romantic writers debated their chances of literary survival, the underlying worries over 'what is left of us when we leave' are as ancient as writing itself.[38] Writers have often expressed, with varying degrees of confidence, despair, and success, their wish to live on through their works. (Not all writers who trumpeted a lasting fame have lived up to their early promise.) The same writers have employed diverse tactics in their efforts to attract the eye of posterity, from the shaping of private sentiments into public forms, to the simpler business of providing the ephemera of experience with the permanent stamp of print. Yet although many of these writers might have welcomed Osip Mandelstam's question, 'To whom does the poet speak?', and agreed

---

[34] 'The Negative Road' (1966), repr. in Harold Bloom (ed.), *John Keats* (1985), 46.
[35] *Life of John Keats* (1887), 209.
[36] See his *Romantic Poets and the Culture of Posterity* (1999), especially pp. 11–64.
[37] *The Spirit of the Age* (1825), Howe, XI. 78.
[38] Op. cit., 13.

with his conclusion (itself a quotation), 'a reader in posterity',[39] it is also the case, as Mandelstam's experience of political repression sharply reminds us, that it will not always be possible or desirable to limit the 'works' of a writer to the extended life of words on the page.

The idea that we might survive our own deaths has been central to a number of recent attempts to investigate how far-reaching are our effects upon one another, and so how helpful are definitions of the self which consider each of us to be a unique and irreplaceable individual (from the Latin 'individuus': undivided), rather than a being who is more porous, more unfinished, more easily divided. Thomas Nagel argues one side of the problem in his discussion of 'Brain Bisection and the Unity of Consciousness':

> The natural conception of a single person controlled by a mind possessing a single visual field, individual faculties for each of the other senses, unitary systems of memory, desire, belief, and so forth, may come into conflict with the physiological facts when it is applied to ourselves.[40]

The slide in this sentence, from 'single person' to the more equivocal 'ourselves', neatly expresses Nagel's belief that the longer we think about the self, the readier we will be to think of it as a plural 'us' rather than a singular 'me'. Nagel's 'brain bisection' (in which he imagines the effects of slicing out parts of one person's brain, and replacing them with parts of a different person's brain) is a thought experiment typical of a strain of analytical philosophy which has grappled with the popular assumption that the self is, as Wittgenstein described it, 'something bodiless, which, however, has its seat in our body'.[41] According to this view, the various psychiatric and neuro-logical disorders in which individuals seem to divide (chronic memory loss, 'phantom limbs', possible disagreements between the left and right hemispheres of the brain, and so on) can be seen as extraordin-ary examples of ordinary lived experience. The closer we scrutinize 'unity of consciousness', it is claimed, the more we should recognize that the cases of split personality described by Jonathan Glover, 'where there is doubt about where one person ends and another perhaps begins',[42] are merely pathological variants of a condition which is as common as thinking.

---

[39] 'About an Interlocutor' (1913), repr. in *Selected Essays*, trans. Sidney Monas (1977), 58–9.
[40] *Mortal Questions* (1979), 164.
[41] *The Blue and Brown Books* (1958), 69.
[42] *I: The Philosophy and Psychology of Personal Identity* (1988), 21.

These epistemological enquiries into the location and limits of the self can appear to be, in more than one sense, of academic interest only. Whether or not I think of my self as identical with my body will perhaps not seem of much account when I reflect upon those much larger parts of the universe which are not contained within my own skin. However, recent work in environmental ethics has invested a new practical urgency into these traditional puzzles over how unstable and diffuse we should consider the circumference of the self to be, by pointing out that if I can no longer distinguish clearly what divides my self from other selves, I may decide that the line between selfishness and altruism is equally blurred.[43] Earlier discussions of individual integrity, such as Locke's chapter 'Of Identity and Diversity' in *An Essay Concerning Human Understanding*, pointed out the social and ethical consequences of assuming that someone was not the same from one moment to the next; how could one ascribe responsibility to a criminal who claimed that he was not to blame for the actions of his earlier self? A different account of these problems has been offered by Derek Parfit, who has made a persuasive case for thinking that questions of identity, whether or not they have a determinate answer, are less important than we think. What matters, he suggests, is not personal identity but survival, not absolute psychological 'continuity' but a looser form of psychological 'connectedness'. In Parfit's view, this should encourage us to think that our lives reach beyond their natural confines in space and time, and therefore to accept that the delayed outcome of our actions on other people will also have consequences for how we think about the relations between ourselves and other people. To think of my life as being unavoidably involved in other lives, he suggests, will produce a 'liberation from the self' which is also a liberation of the self, as I come to recognize, in a curious double movement of self-preservation and self-dissolution, that my intentions can be carried out by someone else in a way which is 'about as good' as if I carried them out myself. For this reason, Parfit concludes, even a fluid and incomplete self is not incompatible with moral agency; indeed, this expansion of our intentions into other lives should rather increase our sense of obligation to others, because acting from motives of self-interest will then also require us to take

---

[43] See Avner de-Shalit, *Why Posterity Matters: Environmental Policies and Future Generations* (1995); Michael Walzer, *Spheres of Justice: A Defence of Pluralism and Equality* (1983); and Ernest Partridge (ed.), *Responsibilities to Future Generations: Environmental Ethics* (1981).

account of our responsibilities to possible future selves. Helping other people requires less generosity if I may later merge with them:

Is the truth depressing? Some may find it so. But I find it liberating, and consoling.... After my death, there will be no one living who will be me. I can now redescribe this fact. Though there will later be many experiences, none of these experiences will be connected to my present experiences by chains of such direct connections as those involved in experience-memory, or in the carrying out of an earlier intention. Some of these future experiences may be related to my present experiences in less direct ways. There will later be some memories about my life. And there may later be thoughts that are influenced by mine, or things done as the result of my advice. My death will break the more direct relations between my present experiences and future experiences, but it will not break various other relations. This is all there is to the fact that there will be no one living who will be me. Now that I have seen this, my death seems to me less bad.[44]

The idea that I will continue to exercise influence after my death may indeed be 'consoling', as Parfit claims, but this prospect will not necessarily provide much comfort for the people who are left to mourn me. In his classic study *Attachment and Loss*, John Bowlby describes the importance of 'maintaining values and pursuing goals which... remain linked with [the lost person] and can without falsification continue to be maintained and pursued in reference to memory of him'. But he also points out the difficulties which the bereaved often encounter in reaching 'a state of mind in which they retain a strong sense of the continuing presence of [the dead] without the turmoils of hope and disappointment, search and frustration, anger and blame that are present earlier'.[45] It is this anguished ambivalence—loving the dead, and hating them for being dead—which haunts the introduction to Severn's letter on Keats's slow death: 'the recollection of poor Keats hangs dreadfully upon me—I see him at every glance— I cannot be alone now.'[46] More than one kind of regret speaks in 'I cannot be alone now'. Would Keats's death have seemed 'less bad', to Severn or to Keats, if the cry 'How long will this posthumous life of mine last' had been replaced with the more rational 'My death will break the more direct relations between my present experiences and future experiences, but it will not replace various other relations'?

[44] *Reasons and Persons* (1984, repr. 1987), 281.
[45] *Attachment and Loss* (3 vols., 1978–81), vol. 3: *Loss: Sadness and Depression* (1980, repr. 1998), 96.
[46] *KC*, I. 223.

The difficulties involved in this attempt to reconcile public reasoning and personal longings are not limited to Parfit's *Reasons and Persons*. It is one of the occupational hazards of being a philosopher to describe the sort of moral world which his or her readers would be reluctant or unable to live in; furthermore, the consolations of philosophy are likely never to be equal to the consolations we demand of it, because the reasons it provides cannot be adequate to those experiences, such as pain or grief, which challenge our capacity for rational thought. This problem is especially acute in assessing Parfit's model of psychological 'connectedness', because—as he admits—his replacement of individual integrity with a more dispersed form of identity goes against some of our most fundamental beliefs about, and ambitions for, our selves. Jonathan Glover explains the dissatisfaction which many people would feel in a world where, following Parfit, each of us no longer attempted to retrieve a sense of order and purpose from the flux of experience by constructing it into a personal narrative, 'in the way that an artist may want to create a unified work':[47]

Without the ego, the episodes of a life can seem like a heap of stones. Then perhaps death is less important. It does not much matter whether some extra stones are dumped on my pile or on some other one. But, if I see the stones as part of a building I am creating, being cut off with too few stones can ruin everything.[48]

There are writers for whom this abstract problem will also be a practical dilemma. Wordsworth, for instance, whose poems often lament the interrupted and forgotten lives which are marked on the landscape by a 'shapeless heap of stones',[49] and whose architectural metaphors disclose a lasting interest in the integrity of his own 'heap of stones': *The Prelude* and *The Recluse*, he declared, 'have the same relation to each other … as the ante-chapel has to the body of a Gothic church'.[50] The extended composition of *The Prelude* reveals how seriously he took the prospect of his personal 'continuity' dissolving into a looser form of psychological 'connectedness'; many of

---

[47] *Reasons and Persons*, 446.

[48] Op. cit., 106.

[49] 'For the Spot Where the Hermitage Stood on St Herbert's Island, Derwent-Water' (1800), *WP*, I. 442; compare the 'straggling heap of unhewn stones' which marks Michael's unfinished work ('Michael', *WP*, I. 456).

[50] Preface to *The Excursion* (1814); Zachary Leader makes the connection in his *Revision and Romantic Authorship* (1996), 11.

his revisions, in particular, critically test what Charles Taylor has described as 'the supposition that I could be two temporally succeeding selves':[51]

> ... so wide appears
> The vacancy between me and those days,
> Which yet have such self-presence in my mind
> That sometimes when I think of them I seem
> Two consciousnesses—conscious of myself,
> And of some other being.
>
> (1805, II. 28–33)

> ... so wide appears
> The vacancy between me and those days
> Which yet have such self-presence in my mind,
> That musing on them, often do I seem
> Two consciousnesses, conscious of myself
> And of some other Being.
>
> (1850, II. 28–33)[52]

On the page, the most significant vacancy in these lines is not an empty space, but an emptied space, because between 1805 and 1850 one of Wordsworth's smallest changes uncovers one of the largest hiding-places of his imagination, as he shifts the comma which follows 'days' to come after 'mind',[53] and so reconsiders the broken connections of his self through a form of 'after vacancy' which is already built into the structure of his verse.[54] Many of Wordsworth's textual revisions are similarly self-conscious about how strange a poet may appear to himself when confronted with evidence of his attempts to fix the workings of his mind by the movements of his hand, so that his poems of unexpected encounters can appear to be submerged commentaries on their own textual history, even if the same revisions are usually marked by their reluctance to admit that Wordsworth has substantially changed his mind or his tune. In its development from draft to draft, as in its narrative, *The Prelude* reveals 'The Growth of a Poet's Mind', but although Wordsworth's revisions alter the local

[51] *Sources of the Self: The Making of Modern Identity* (1989), 51.

[52] Jonathan Wordsworth, M. H. Abrams, and Stephen Gill (eds.), *The Prelude* (1979), 66–7.

[53] The change of punctuation is introduced in MS E (completed *c.*1839); see W. J. B. Owen (ed.), *The Fourteen-Book Prelude* (1985), 277.

[54] *The Borderers* (1797 manuscript), III. v. 62, ed. Robert Osborn (1982), 534.

acoustics of his 'ante-chapel', as they continue to test the private rhythms of his life against the public rhythms of his verse, they do not reshape this building into some other building. Instead, both as a person and a poet, he maps out that intimate topography which Taylor describes as 'the space of moral and spiritual orientation within which [our] most important defining relations are lived out'.[55]

Parfit attempts to explain why the prospect of being 'conscious of my self | And of some other being' should cause us more satisfaction than alarm. One of his thought experiments describes the effects of human 'fusion':

> We can imagine a world in which fusion was a natural process. Two people come together. While they are unconscious, their bodies grow into one. One person then wakes up....Any two people who fuse together would have different characteristics, different desires, and different intentions. How could these be combined?[56]

Like many of Parfit's 'imaginary cases', his vision of two people becoming one seems to be guided as much by imaginative zest as by philosophical rigour. This is not surprising, because the question of how different characteristics, desires, and intentions may be combined into the same physical form is also one which is central to the workings of imaginative literature, as when Keats describes how Madeline and Porphyro come together in 'The Eve of St Agnes':

> Beyond a mortal man impassioned far
> At these voluptuous accents, he arose,
> Ethereal, flushed, and like a throbbing star
> Seen mid the sapphire heaven's deep repose;
> Into her dream he melted, as the rose
> Blendeth its odour with the violet,
> Solution sweet—[57]

Solutions are a consequence of both solving and dissolving, so 'Solution sweet' not only refers to Porphyro's successful answer to the problem of charming his way into Madeline's bed, but also hints at their sticky pleasures in that bed, blurring the boundaries of their individual bodies in the same way that the stanza's unexpected meetings of diction ('throbbing star') and rhyme ('arose ... the rose') attempt to reconcile the poem's twin drives, towards romance and a teasing parody of romance. As so often, Keats's verse stays true to the

---

imaginative life of its subject in keeping itself quizzically open to wonder and distaste; suspended on the held breath of that dash, 'Solution sweet—' then holds out the different narrative possibilities for a union that could end in as many ways as Parfit's 'imaginary case': 'Fusions, like marriages, could be either great successes, or disasters.'[58] In this sense, Keats's poem, like all supple and accommodating pieces of writing, subjects to critical scrutiny what Schrödinger described as the 'unimaginable' idea that we can be more than one person at once: 'consciousness is never experienced in the plural, only in the singular'.[59] After all, however 'unimaginable' it is in theory to consider the world from two or more points of view at once, the pleasures and dangers of leading parallel lives on paper is precisely what the act of reading asks us imaginatively to entertain. But Keats's invitation to enter his lovers' minds and bodies in the act of reading is not the only way in which we can entertain thoughts of extending our lives beyond that of 'a mortal man'. For example, Parfit's distinction between personal 'continuity' and social 'connectedness' will not always be true to the ambitions which people have for themselves. It is certainly not true of the Victorian writers discussed in later chapters of this book, whose trust in their creative integrity is often braced by longings for a personal immortality, but whose writings are further shaped and permeated by earlier models of the utilitarian ethics which underpin Parfit's work. These continuities between Parfit's theories and his Victorian precursors go some way to supporting the idea that historical periods are no less divisible and porous than the people who live in them. They further suggest that we need a more flexible understanding of the afterlife than the one Parfit provides if we are to read Victorian writers in a spirit which is true to the way they approached their own writing.

'Disbelief in God', Parfit contends, 'openly admitted by a majority, is a recent event, not yet concluded.'[60] Leo Braudy is satisfied that this event has already taken place: 'In a secular civilisation', he argues, 'fame and the approval of posterity replace belief in an afterlife.'[61] The idea that one set of beliefs could simply 'replace' another is odd, but it was shared by a number of Victorians, notably those Positivist thinkers who argued that removing the prospect of immortality should encourage us to realize that 'human beings' did not cease to

---

[58] Op. cit., 299.
[59] Erwin Schrödinger, *Mind and Matter* (1967), 145.
[60] Op. cit., 453.
[61] *The Frenzy of Renown: Fame and its History* (1986), 28.

be merely because they were no longer around to witness the consequences of their actions.[62] For other Victorians, though, personal
continuity (the hope which is expressed in their writing) and social
connectedness (their hopes for this writing) do not present themselves
as competing ideas, but rather as wary and puzzled supplements to
one another. That these unsettled questions of belief and disbelief,
which generate and structure the work of so many Victorian writers,
continue to circle around one another in the minds of their readers,
suggests that 'the approval of posterity' has not wholly replaced
personal survival in our thoughts; announcements of the death of
immortality are at best premature. However, Braudy's account of the
turn away from the afterlife which has occurred over time clearly
marks him out as a critic of his own time, because what some current
theorists make of the Victorians is troublingly at odds with what the
Victorians made of themselves.

The most influential of these theorists is Harold Bloom.

INFLUENCE AND ANXIETY

It is not only Keats's imaginary characters in 'The Eve of St Agnes'
who are brought together in a 'solution sweet', because this phrase is
further thickened with Miltonic echoes (compare 'liquid sweet',
'intercession sweet', 'connection sweet', and 'nuptial embraces
sweet' in *Paradise Lost*),[63] and so blends Keats's voice with someone
else whose actions reach beyond those of a mortal man. The way
Milton's voice edges into Keats's poem then reminds us that writers
are likely to be especially alert to Parfit's conclusion that 'there may
later be thoughts that are influenced by mine'. Like Parfit's 'Eve' (the
fictitious amoeba-like creature in *Reasons and Persons* who reproduces
by a method of natural division), a writer like Milton might anticipate
having his voice drawn out through echo and allusion, and decide
that his relation to his increasingly split selves is 'about as good as
ordinary survival'.[64] It may not worry this writer that part of his work
will be taken up by later writers, like one of the stones Glover
describes being transferred between different heaps; it may not even
cross his mind that his own survival will perhaps pass without notice
once his stone is surrounded on the page by other stones, as Proust
remarks in *A la recherche* that 'a book is a great cemetery where on the

---

[62] See Ch. 2.   [63] V. 637, X. 228, X. 359, X. 994.   [64] Op. cit., 299–300.

majority of the tombs we can no longer read the effaced names'.[65] In this way, the blending of two or more voices within the same poem will produce another form of 'fusion', and—like the imaginary cases Parfit describes—such meetings on the page could be 'either great successes or disasters'.

The idea that one writer can take on another's influence as a 'solution sweet' to a particular literary problem, and that this solution could be a success rather than a disaster, is one that Harold Bloom has been writing against for many years. Bloom's theories need little rehearsal: the key word is 'after'. *The Anxiety of Influence* begins with aftermath ('After he knew that he had fallen ... '),[66] because for Bloom's post-Miltonic poet, pride can come only after a Satanic fall:

The motto to English poetry since Milton was stated by Keats: 'Life to him would be Death to me.'[67]

According to Bloom, the new poet broods resentfully on his inescapable 'burden' of influence, the pressure of literary forebears who stifle him in the struggle for breath, because a poem represents its poet's *psyche*, 'a breath [that] is at once a *word*, and a *stance* for uttering that word, a word and a stance *of one's own*'.[68] This 'stance' is both the poise for an embrace and the bracing of a warrior for battle. Even loving poets 'cannot breathe without ambivalence, and where there is ambivalence there can be war to the death', but by incorporating and revising the poetic father, the latecomer can attempt to substitute for this melancholy belatedness a sublime self-reliance.[69] Anxious about turning into his father, he turns away, through the distortions or 'willing errors' of literary tropes and psychic defences; the new poem then emerges as 'effectively the difference between the rival strengths of poetic father and poetic son'.[70]

One welcome consequence of Bloom's critical writings has been a redirection of 'influence' away from what the art historian Michael

---

[65] Proust's remark is discussed by Richard Macksey in his introduction to Proust's prefaces to *La Bible d'Amiens* and *Sésame et les Lys*, repr. as *On Reading Ruskin* (1987), xiv.

[66] *AI*, 3.

[67] *AI*, 32.

[68] *PR*, 1; italics original. Compare Freud's definition of anxiety as 'a manifestation of the self-preservative instinct' which repeats its source in the original birth trauma: 'The name "*Angst*"—"*angustiae*" [narrow place], "*Enge*" [straits]—emphasizes the characteristic of restriction in breathing which was then present as a consequence of the real situation and is now almost invariably reinstated in the affect', 'Anxiety', repr. in *Strachey*, XVI. 396–7.

[69] *Agon*, 30.

[70] *MM*, 88–9, 116.

Baxandall has called its 'wrong-headed grammatical prejudice'. If X influences Y, he points out, we should not think of X as the sole agent; Y can:

draw on, resort to, avail oneself of, appropriate from, have recourse to, adapt, misunderstand, refer to, pick up, take on, engage with, react to, differentiate oneself from, assimilate oneself to, assimilate, align oneself with, copy, address, paraphrase, absorb, make a variation on, revive, continue, remodel, ape, emulate, travesty, parody, extract from, distort, attend to, resist, simplify, reconstitute, elaborate on, develop, face up to, master, subvert, perpetuate, reduce, promote, respond to, transform, tackle X.[71]

This is sharply attentive to the sprawling range of literary relations which a poem can stage (not least because X and Y will sometimes be the same person, like Keats, returning to earlier work and turning it to new, 'self-influenced', ends),[72] and the generous scope of Baxandall's critical vocabulary highlights the narrower ambitions of Bloom's revisionary scheme. Part of this narrowness can be attributed to the influence of Freud. Like Bloom, Freud recognized that poetry and psychoanalysis are in some ways natural bedfellows in the search for therapeutic relief, whether from the present we live in, or from the past which stubbornly lives on in us. As Freud's tenderest and fiercest recent critic, Adam Phillips, has observed, on a simple and profound level, 'one goes to psychoanalysis, as one might go to poetry, for better words',[73] for discovering ways of making the world more bearable by our descriptions of it. And yet, because Bloom never critically examines Freud's status within his revisionary scheme, he also threatens to repeat in literary-critical terms what Frederic Crews has identified as the 'epistemic sieve' of Freudian hypothesis. Like other academic disciplines which, from flexible beginnings in hypothesis and experiment, end up settling their differences into a more or less coherent body of beliefs, psychoanalytic theory is, as Phillips notes, 'addicted to consensus'.[74] But as a means of gaining knowledge, Crews points out, psychoanalysis is also 'fatally contaminated by the inclusion, among its working assumptions and in its dialogue with patients, of the very ideas that supposedly get corroborated by clinical experience'.[75]

---

[71]   *Patterns of Intention* (1985), 59.

[72]   *Otho the Great*, I. iii. 107 (*KP*, 300).

[73]   'Poetry and Psychoanalysis', *Promises Promises* (2000), 4–5.

[74]   *The Beast in the Nursery* (1998), 38.

[75]   *The Memory Wars* (1995), 34; Crews is drawing on Adolf Grünbaum, *The Foundations of Psychoanalysis: A Philosophical Critique* (1984).

Freud's persistence with the Oedipus myth, say, could reveal far more about his uniquely productive combination of professional opportunism and stubbornness than it does more generally about the human psyche. As Jeffrey Masson and others have suggested,[76] many of the later case-histories, in particular, seem to be distinguished less by Freud's interest in understanding the haphazard and unpredictable course a human life can take, and more by his seeming reluctance to let the therapeutic needs of his patients get in the way of a good theory. Similarly, Bloom's returns to Freud seem to be motivated as much by the demands of theoretical consistency as they are by the variable requirements of the poets and poem he examines. To this extent, Bloom's use of Freud fulfils the promise held out by Freud's own teasing aside that, while a genuine psychological case-history 'can only serve to obscure and efface the outlines of [its] fine poetic conflict', its awkward edges 'would rightly fall a sacrifice to the censorship of a writer, for he, after all, simplifies and abstracts when he appears in the character of the psychologist'.[77] However, one central difficulty with Bloom's 'anxiety of influence' is that we are never told how the relations of 'writer' and 'psychologist' should be understood, whether between or within individual poets.

This is especially puzzling where Bloom discusses childhood: 'A new poem is not unlike a small child placed with a lot of other small children in a small playroom, with a limited number of toys, and no adult supervision whatever.'[78] Bloom is surprisingly cheerful about this miniature primal scene, but his mythical scheme never clearly explains how 'like' children poems are supposed to be, or indeed how they could be like children at all once the 'poet-as-poet' has been separated from the poet-as-person.[79] For Freud, childhood was not only the beginning of a human life, but its enduring centre; childhood represented the contingent pressures of the past which adult desires needed to develop away from, but could not altogether outgrow. Much the same attitude might be taken towards the history of psychoanalysis itself, which has struggled to work through the legacy

---

[76] See Jeffrey Masson, *Freud, The Assault on Truth* (1984).

[77] 'Fragment of an Analysis of a Case of Hysteria' (1905), repr. in *Strachey*, VII. 43. It has been widely noted that Freud's psychoanalytic and narrative treatment of Dora is less simple than he admits; a summary is provided in Lisa Appignanesi and John Forrester, *Freud's Women* (1992), 14–67.

[78] *Kabbalah*, 121.

[79] For this distinction, see *AI*, 7.

of Freud so often, and so publicly, that—to borrow Jonathan Lear's excellent conceit—the discipline has routinely put itself 'on the couch'.[80] However, Freud is not the only source of Bloom's interest in childhood. As the assumption that a poem is 'not unlike a small child' itself depends upon the not-unlike-ness of metaphor, its strange likenesses and like strangenesses, so it alerts us to the fact that Bloom is returning to something other than childhood which he shares with his readers—Northrop Frye's *Anatomy of Criticism*:

the new poem, like the new baby, is born into an already existing order of words, and is typical of the structure of poetry to which it is attached. The new baby *is* his own society appearing once again as a unit of individuality, and the new poem has a similar relation to its poetic society.[81]

As an attempt to describe poetry's affiliations with its living past, this is more reasoned and reasonable than Bloom's sketchy borrowings from Freud. Bloom never examines the possibility that using small children as a model for adult behaviour could lead to the very different observations of theorists such as Donald Winnicott or Melanie Klein;[82] nor does he pursue the question of how a person's Oedipal and poetic struggles relate to one another; nor how certain human actions emerge from a life without being fully representative of that life, as Freud's patients must work through the narrative of a pre-linguistic Oedipal fixation in the only system—a linguistic one— which is available for narrative. Yet although some of Bloom's narrowness of thinking can be attributed to Freud's influence, Freud cannot be held responsible for the uses to which Bloom puts him, not least because this narrowness often comes about as a result of Bloom's decision to adopt a theory of anxiety which is a curiously arrested version of Freud's thinking on the subject. When Bloom first wishes to make use of Freud's family romance, for example, a 'rather long passage of his darkest wisdom must be cited', which ends with the child's 'wish to be *the father of himself*'.[83] But here Bloom is chopping and changing, because Freud's paragraph continues by admitting that this is only partially true. 'A Special Type of Choice of Object

---

[80] *Love and its Place in Nature: A Philosophical Interpretation of Freudian Psychoanalysis* (1990), 18.

[81] Northrop Frye, *Anatomy of Criticism* (1957), 97.

[82] See, e.g., D. W. Winnicott, 'Aggression in Relation to Emotional Development', in *Through Paediatrics to Psychoanalysis* (1975); and Melanie Klein, 'Some Theoretical Conclusions Regarding the Emotional Life of the Child', in *Envy and Gratitude and Other Works* (1975).

[83] *AI*, 64.

Made by Men' cannot be made the type of all men, as 'Macduff of the Scottish legend, who was not born of his mother, but ripped from her womb, was for that reason unacquainted with anxiety.' Besides, it is also possible for the child to have 'a tender meaning contained in rescue-fantasies directed towards the father';[84] not only body-swerves, then, but points of contact. Similarly, Freud's essay on 'Family Romances' begins by boldly asserting that 'the whole progress of society rests upon the opposition between successive generations', but modulates into the lesser claim, better in keeping with his essay's emphasis on relative values, that with the adjustments of sublimation and substitution, the child's fantasy of replacing his father can also preserve the hope of returning him to the heart of the child's affections: 'the whole effort at replacing the real father by a superior one is only an expression of the child's longing for the happy, vanished days when his father seemed to him the noblest and strongest of men.'[85]

In their self-justifying repetitions, Bloom's citations of Freud acquire a scriptural authority, but they also disturb any clean distinction between real lives and the psychological life of verse: 'the strong dead return, *in poems as in our lives*'; 'the anxiety of influence, from which we all suffer, *whether we are poets or not*'; 'True poetic history is the story of how poets as poets have suffered other poets, *just as* any true biography is the story of how anyone suffered his own family.'[86] This sort of muddle could accurately represent a poet's desire to compare human and literary relations, as he or she discovers in his or her writing a model of the intimacy and constancy which ordinary family life cannot easily sustain. Thus, when Pope expresses the hope that he will prolong his mother's life through his skill in the 'lenient Arts' of the sickroom, he returns to rhymes which he had used several years earlier when further extending the literary life of the man he most often claimed as his poetic father, Homer:

> Me, let the tender Office long engage
> To rock the Cradle of reposing Age,
> With lenient Arts extend a Mother's breath,
> Make Languor smile, and smooth the Bed of Death ... [87]

---

[84] 'A Special Type of Choice of Object Made by Men', repr. in *Strachey*, XI. 173–4.

[85] *Strachey*, IX. 235–41, 237, 241. David Fite comments on Bloom's misreading of Freud in *Harold Bloom: The Rhetoric of Romantic Vision* (1985), 74–5.

[86] *AI*, 139, 56, 94 (my emphases).

[87] 'An Epistle from Mr. Pope, to Dr. Arbuthnot' (1735), *The Poems of Alexander Pope*, ed. John Butt (1965), 612; Pope's lines were originally enclosed in a letter sent to Aaron Hill on

> What cares his Mother's tender breast engage,
> And Sire, forsaken on the verge of age;
> Beneath the sun prolong they yet their breath,
> Or range the house of darkness and of death?[88]

All rhymes work as question and response, in the space opened up between anticipation and recollection, and Pope's retrieval of his rhymes here enlarges this principle to fit the shape of his career. As he contemplates the future death of his mother, whose 'tender breast' once kept him alive before his breaths were separate from hers, so he reaches back for support to the literary parent who continues to breathe through the 'tender Office' of his translator. Within and between these poems, then, Pope resolutely harbours an anxiety *for* influence, not an anxiety *of* influence.

As Pope's practice shows, not all forms of influence can be accommodated within Bloom's scheme, because his Oedipal model of menaced fathers and vengeful sons ignores the rich diversity of kinships, the imaginative lines of descent, which can be drawn out in a poem. For example, thinking of literary relations as an analogue of family ties asks us to recognize that, although it is tempting to take the institution of 'the family' as much for granted as we often do our own families, even the most stable family can be surprisingly flexible in character. T. S. Eliot's warning is suitably imprecise: 'it is advisable to remember that [the family] is a term that may vary in extension';[89] a family can shrink or expand not only in response to the regular punctuation of births and deaths, but also according to how into the past or future its definition is stretched. Much the same is true of the influences which work upon and through a poet. As Eliot observes elsewhere, 'A poet cannot help being influenced, therefore he should subject himself to as many influences as possible',[90] but these influences will not be sought out by the poet *en masse* at all times, any more than all the members of his family will be equally demanding or deserving of his attention. For the young poet, especially, some influences will appear 'like distant ancestors who have

---

3 September 1731 from his mother's sickbed; see *The Correspondence of Alexander Pope*, ed. George Sherburn (5 vols., 1956), III. 226–7.

[88] Pope's translation of Homer's *Odyssey* (1725–6), XV. 370–3; I quote from Maynard Mack's edition (1967), 87.

[89] *Notes Towards the Definition of Culture* (1948, repr. 1962), 43.

[90] From a 1936 lecture, quoted by Christopher Ricks in his edition of *Inventions of the March Hare: Poems 1909–1917 by T. S. Eliot* (1996), xxix.

been almost deified; whereas the smaller poet, who has directed one's first steps, is more like an admired elder brother'.[91] However, the variety of literary relations which a poet can entertain or suffer, like the variety of ways in which a poem can present itself as an act of achieved disobedience towards its forebears, rarely seems as important in Bloom's account of influence as it is in the thinking of his subjects. Instead, in the 'densely overpopulated world of literary language',[92] Bloom presents himself as a critical Malthus, cutting wasteful relations down to size by reading Victorian poetry only as an '*aftering*' of Romanticism, an Oedipus who must come to terms with the earlier accomplishment of his desires.[93] The way Bloom argues for a narrowing literary tradition, within the tightening coils of his own theoretical system, then takes full account of Freud's warning, in his account of 'Anxiety', that a writer 'cannot reproduce the stuff of reality unchanged, but must isolate portions of it, remove disturbing associations, tone down the whole, and fill in what is missing. These are the privileges of what is known as "poetic licence".'[94] Yet although Bloom's critical prose often borrows its licence from nineteenth-century writers, as when he echoes Wilde in noting that 'We must see the object, the poem, as in itself it really is not, because we must see not only what is missing in it, but why the poem had to exclude what is missing',[95] it is in his selective appropriations of these writers that Bloom also draws attention to the alternative models of influence which are largely missing (or excluded) from his account.

Pater was attracted to *Measure for Measure* because here Shakespeare 'has refashioned ... materials already at hand, so that the relics of other men's poetry are incorporated'.[96] Bloom extends 'incorporation' into cannibalism: the god of poets is 'not Apollo, who lives in the rhythm of recurrence, but the bald gnome Error', who sneaks out of his cave 'to feast upon the mighty dead'.[97] Like a number of Bloom's more startling claims, this is announced with a relish that does not seem to take itself entirely seriously, perhaps even a wistfulness for the sort of

[91] 'What Dante Means to Me' (1950), repr. in *To Criticise the Critic* (1965), 126.

[92] Jonathan Culler, *The Pursuit of Signs* (1981), 107.

[93] *PR*, 4.

[94] 'A Special Type of Choice of Object Made by Men' (1910), repr. in *Strachey*, XI. 165.

[95] *Agon*, 18, paraphrasing Wilde's turn on Arnold: 'the primary aim of the critic is to see the object as in itself it really is not', 'The Critic as Artist' (1889), repr. in Richard Ellmann (ed.), *The Artist as Critic* (1968), 369.

[96] *Appreciations* (1889), 182.

[97] *AI*, 78; compare *RT*, 9.

decisive action that literary critics tend to be better at discussing on paper than carrying out in person. But Bloom's own feasting leads to some indigestion in his prose. 'As literary history lengthens, all poetry necessarily become verse-criticism, just as all criticism becomes prose-poetry.'[98] And as this critical history lengthens, so Bloom shortens. There is his decision to ignore the changing dimensions of 'influence', as a concept and an explanatory term, as it has been understood and practised in different periods of literary history.[99] There is his loyal adherence to a select group of earlier authorities, as the same swatches of Emerson, Freud, and Nietzsche are repeatedly wheeled out. There is his exclusion of others: Bloom has no room for De Quincey's 'literature of power' as an alternative to 'strong poetry', for example, presumably because for De Quincey, 'the mode of [Milton's] influence' is felt in what a reader owes to his '*power*—that is, exercise and expansion to your own latent capacity of sympathy with the infinite, where every pulse and each separate influx is a step upwards',[100] not a fall downwards. Most tellingly, there is his habit of extracting each quotation as a narrow core of authority, while shying away from the context which originally surrounded and questioned it.

Quotations will offer a significant resource for any practical investigation into the growth or decay of literature because they can be read as equally convincing evidence of the redemptive power of art or the vanity of art. That passionate collector of quotations, Walter Benjamin, had a darkly persuasive explanation for modern attempts to substitute the citability of the past for its authority: the quotation is born out of a despair of the present, and a desire to engage the past with 'not the strength to preserve but to cleanse, to tear out of context, to destroy'.[101] This is more aggressive than other descriptions of literature's ongoing engagement with itself, such as Frank Kermode's proposal that the 'Classics' possess 'an openness to accommodation which keeps them alive under endlessly varying dispositions'.[102] Kermode's 'accommodation' has a reassuringly cosy feel to it, but where classic

---

[98] *MM*, 3.

[99] On changes in the understanding of influence, see W. T. J. Mitchell, 'Influence, Autobiography, and Literary History: Rousseau's *Confessions* and Wordsworth's *The Prelude*', *English Literary History*, 57 (1990), 643–64.

[100] 'The Literature of Knowledge and the Literature of Power' (1848), repr. in *De Quincey*, II. 302–6; De Quincey's distinction between 'Power' and 'Knowledge' itself owes much to Wordsworth: see D. D. Devlin, *De Quincey, Wordsworth, and the Art of Prose* (1983), 77.

[101] *Illuminations*, 43.

[102] *The Classic* (1975), 44.

texts themselves are opened up piecemeal by a later writer, and where each piece is further loosened from its historical moorings, as in Bloom's thickly allusive but unfootnoted works, the quotation can act in more antisocial ways: as a time-bomb, or a depth-charge.

Benjamin puts the point well: 'In the quotation that both saves and chastises, language proves the matrix of justice. It summons the word by its name, wrenches it destructively from its context, but precisely thereby calls it back to its origin.'[103] A quotation has hidden depths, but also hidden widths; it resonates in its new context, saved, but its outline is also pressed against, chastized, by what remains behind. This is often the case with Bloom's use of quotation. A misreading, Freud argues, occurs when 'Whatever interests and concerns us puts itself in the place of what is strange and still uninteresting. After-images of [old] thoughts trouble new perceptions.'[104] One of the tasks of psychoanalysis, as Freud described it, was to make the world of its patients both strange and interesting, by breaking the patterns of behaviour, the emotional stuttering, which had stalled their lives. Once the past had been put in its place, the present could be made surprising again. But, as Freud also recognized, just as it may be seductively easy to describe past hurts without understanding them, as the encounter of analyst and patient organizes the stubbornly unpredictable events of a life into the pleasingly coherent shapes of narrative, so our seeming mastery of a text may not prevent unsettled ghosts from rising up to question the fiction of control which reading promotes. In reading, as in other forms of human behaviour, mistakes can lead to misgivings, and it is in Bloom's misreading of earlier writers on influence that the stifling one-sidedness of his theories is most apparent.

Emerson's stance in *Self-Reliance*, for example, with its denial of belatedness, becomes for Bloom the 'Primal Lie' at the heart of a strong American Romanticism;[105] but this prophet of 'antagonism' also considered the poet's reliance on origins which are not only his: 'There never was an original writer. Each is a link in an endless chain. To receive and to impart are the talents of the poet and he ought to possess both in equal degrees.'[106] Emerson's metaphor of chains joins

---

[103] Quoted in David Bromwich, *Hazlitt: The Mind of a Critic* (1983), 436n.
[104] 'Parapraxes', repr. in *Strachey*, XV. 71.
[105] *PR*, 287; compare *Agon*, 145, and *MM*, ch.9.
[106] Stephen E. Whicher and Robert E. Spiller (ed.), *The Early Lectures of Ralph Waldo Emerson* (1966), I. 284–5.

him to later theorists, such as John Hollander, who have also attempted to discriminate between the broad sweep and local effects of one writer's influence upon another:

A poem treats another one as if it posed a question, and answers it, interprets it, glosses it, revises it in poetry's own way of saying, 'In other words...' In these terms, the whole history of poetry may be said to constitute a chain of answers to the first texts—Homer and Genesis—which themselves become questions for successive generations of answerers... Intertextual answer can often be the minute matter of a single word or scheme taken up by another writer and used significantly, particularly with respect to its original use.[107]

'Intertextual answer' suggests the ghost of a rather different model of literary connections hovering in the cracks of Hollander's argument, because if textual glossing is not limited to one voice answering one other voice, his account could not explain how influence had come to constitute a 'chain'. Despite this theoretical hiccup, though, the idea that we answer for other people as well as to them, through 'the minute matter of a single word or scheme taken up by another writer', is clearly announced in Hollander's own writing, because his 'chain of answers' casts its own link back to Shelley's defence of poetic influence:

The sacred links of that chain have never been entirely disjointed, which descending through the minds of many men is attached to those great minds, whence as from a magnet the invisible effluence is sent forth, which at once connects, animates, and sustains the life of all... [108]

The metaphor stretches back further still to Plato's description of a 'long chain' of poetic inspiration in the *Ion*,[109] so its appearance in Hollander's account then forms a literary-critical version of the trope he has described elsewhere as 'transumption': 'as if the Latin word were a portmanteau of transcending and summing up'.[110] But although 'with respect to' suggests a tactful revision of Bloom, whose ephebe answers his poetic father back with neither precision nor

---

[107] *Melodious Guile* (1988), 56.

[108] David Lee Clark (ed.), *Shelley's Prose* (1988), 286–7.

[109] See Shelley's fragment translated from Plato's *Ion*: 'Thus a poet, being [him]self divinely inspired, communicates this inspiration to others, until a long chain is made, every link of which is a human spirit and the first <link> of which is attached to that of the poet', quoted in P. M. S. Dawson, 'Shelley and the *Improvisatore* Sgricci: An Unpublished Review', in *Keats–Shelley Memorial Bulletin*, 32 (1981), 22–3.

[110] John Hollander, *The Figure of Echo* (1981), 120.

regard,[111] 'poetic answers' is still uncomfortably close to Bloom's oddest theoretical premiss, which is that poems never answer to anything but poems.

Bloom assumes Hazlitt's 'conviction' of 'the love of power' by citing him on *Coriolanus*: 'The language of poetry naturally falls in with the language of power.'[112] By removing this phrase from the questioning pressures of Hazlitt's context, and glossing 'power' as 'the power of usurpation', Bloom's revisionary swerve goes some way to creating its own safety-net: it does what it says.[113] This does not prevent his borrowing from sitting uneasily with Hazlitt's declared aims for literature:

I wish to show how it is that books have an influence over manners, and tend to reform the maxims and business of common life, and to bring the excesses of lordly power, and the assumptions of personal consequence, into discredit and disuse.[114]

That an 'influence over manners' could be achieved by books is not an issue which ever arises for Bloom, because his understanding of composition as private trauma bypasses not only those forms of memory which are willing to confront the truth of antecedents without revisionary flinching, but also the 'common life' of what is composed. It is surprising that Bloom should ignore this 'common life', because as his 'Fall of Poetic Influence' taps into a shared progress myth of the Fall from Innocence into Theory,[115] so his rhetoric relies upon many of the pragmatic and literary presuppositions which his theory sets out to deny. True to the spirit of strong criticism, Bloom takes Arnold's words out of his mouth ('The function of criticism at the present time, as I conceive it'),[116] and speaks in tough locutions (figures of speech murder, poetry assaults, texts are broken into, readers 'will' and misreadings 'must be');[117] even the pumped-up 'strong' sets up a determined rhythm in his prose, like a flexing bodybuilder. But although critics who 'love continuities' are

[111] Compare Hollander's claim, in a parallel discussion, that Bloom attempts to treat the poet's family romance 'with an analogue of psychoanalytic respect'; John Hollander (ed.), *Poetics of Influence: Harold Bloom* (1988), xvi.

[112] *Agon*, 17; *Howe*, IV. 214; compare similar remarks at XI. 59; VII. 317; XII. 348; XX. 47.

[113] *Agon*, 17.

[114] 'The Influence of Books on the Progress of Manners' (1828), repr. in *Howe*, XVII. 325.

[115] *AI*, 71; see Christopher Ricks, *Essays in Appreciation* (1996), 319–20.

[116] *PR*, 270.

[117] See M. H. Abrams, *Doing Things With Texts* (1989), 289.

pushed aside in favour of those who are haunted by a 'desperate insistence upon priority',[118] Bloom's own relish for continuity speaks on almost every page. The descent of poetry since Milton is described through name-dropping: 'as Nietzsche said', 'in the Freudian sense', 'We know, as Blake did'.[119] His revisionary ratios 'carry on from various traditions that have been central to Western imaginative life'.[120] As early as *Shelley's Mythmaking*, Bloom claims to be 'looting [Buber's] work ... for my own purposes',[121] but his later writing does not only loot. It also invests, in a shared vocabulary of debt and inheritance, as we read of 'the legacy of melancholy', or 'anxieties of indebtedness', but also of 'the gift of a language'; Shelley is 'the disciple and heir of Rousseau'; *Alastor* is 'a stepchild of *The Excursion*'; *The Fall of Hyperion* is 'a marvelously eloquent imaginative testament'; Tennyson is 'legitimately the heir of Keats'; and so on.[122]

Bloom's vocabulary is often better than his theory at remaining in imaginative contact with the assumptions and practices of his chosen poets. When the Romantics were attacked for lacking 'subject matter',[123] for example, Tennyson was quick to respond:

he does not take sufficiently into consideration the peculiar strength evolved by such writers as Byron and Shelley which however mistaken they may be did yet give the world another heart and new pulses—and so are we kept going. Blessed be those that grease the wheels of the old world, insomuch as to move on is better than to stand still.[124]

Byron and Shelley transferred their pulses to the world, and so to Tennyson, 'and so are we kept going', as 'another heart and new pulses' recalls the poet whom Bloom reads as Tennyson's strongest precursor, Keats.[125] Tennyson's 'Blessed be those' further eludes Bloom's conflation of poetic authority with personal priority by drawing both poets together through *The Book of Common Prayer*. 'Blessed is the man whose strength is in thee: in whose heart are thy ways.... They will go from strength to strength.'[126] The 'ways' of poetry are not always the ways of history, which is why Coleridge could claim, when struggling to make sense of his awkwardly uneven

---

[118] *AI*, 78, 13.   [119] *Agon*, viii; *AI*, 29.   [120] *AI*, 11.   [121] *SM*, 3.
[122] *AI*, 27, 5, 25; *RT*, 134, 133, 113, 91, 114, 146.
[123] Sir Henry Taylor, *Philip Van Artevelde: A Dramatic Romance* (2 vols., 1834), I. xii.
[124] Letter to James Spedding (October 1834), *TL*, I. 120.
[125] Keats's early sonnet to Haydon (discussed below) describes the 'spirits' of his contemporaries who 'will give the world another heart, | And other pulses', *KP*, 36.
[126] Psalms 84: 5–7; compare Revelation 18: 3.

literary relationship with Wordsworth, that the 'visible space' of the printed page transcended the demands of chronology, and so bypassed the assumption that literature develops only in straight lines:

> The truly great
> Have all one age, and from one visible space
> Shed influence! ...
> O Friend! My comforter and guide!
> Strong in thyself, and powerful to give strength![127]

When Wordsworth himself finds 'strength in what remains behind',[128] his self-reliance is similarly strengthened by what else has remained behind to act as a model for his private revelations, namely the line 'Be watchful, and strengthen the things which remain, that are ready to die.'[129] However, as with Tennyson's echo of *The Book of Common Prayer*, it is difficult to see how this could provoke a personal *agon*, since it does not represent the personal challenge of an original poet, but the lasting consequence of translation by committee.

The conviction that poetry finds strength in what is past, or sets out to strengthen that past, provides an especially forceful challenge to Bloom's central assumption, which is that only in the midst of death can the strong poet bring himself fully to imaginative life: although readers devote their attention to 'straining to hear the dead sing',[130] Bloom argues, poets spend their creative lives struggling to drown out the dead with their songs. By the time his final revisionary ratio of *apophrades* is reached (the return of the dead to their old houses), Bloom is warning dolefully that even elegists 'subvert the immortality of their precursors, as though any one poet's afterlife could be metaphorically prolonged at the expense of another's'.[131] The idea that surviving another person's death may make the living feel more alive is an important half-truth; Theodora Bosanquet records how invigorated Henry James became as he described his brother William's death: 'dreadful as was the tale he unfolded his cheek took on a healthier tint while he did so, and by the end he was quite

---

[127] 'To William Wordsworth' (1807), repr. in *The Oxford Authors Coleridge*, ed. H. J. Jackson (1985), 126–7.
[128] 'Ode: Intimations of Immortality from Recollections of Early Childhood' (1807), *WP*, I. 523.
[129] Revelation 3: 2.
[130] *AI*, 65.
[131] *AI*, 151.

blooming'.[132] Bloom never explores the other half of the truth, which is that an 'anxiety' provoked by learning that '*the dead poet lives in one*' may manifest itself as solicitude for the dead rather than distress at their presence; nor does he explain to what extent this 'afterlife' is a matter of accident or design: whether the poetic father is 'the voice that cannot die because already it has survived death', or whether having acknowledged poetic sequence, and so mortality, 'a poem is written to escape dying', survival not being the same thing as escape.[133] However, a more fundamental objection to Bloom's 'poetry of loss' is that elegies do not respond only to poetic losses.[134] 'A philosophy of composition ... is a genealogy of imagination necessarily, a study of the only guilt that matters to a poet, the guilt of indebtedness ... '.[135] But poets have many debts, not all of them poetic, and a debt which exacts its effects upon a poem need not come only from a poem, any more than a 'grief of influence' will cancel out the other griefs to which a poem bears witness.[136]

Much of Bloom's argument concerning the poet's competitive stance towards the past is adapted from Walter Jackson Bate's meditation on the 'accumulating anxiety' to which writers since Milton have been subject, as literature continues to refine itself out of existence, and so continues to present writers with different versions of the same question: '*What is there left to do?*'[137] This is not only a literary question. Bernard Williams, writing about regret and the desire to make amends, has observed that cases exist where

there is no room for any appropriate action at all. Then only the desire to make reparation remains, with the painful consciousness that nothing can be done about it; some other action, perhaps less directed to the victims, may come to express this.[138]

As Peter Robinson points out, one activity which can be prompted by a sense of there being no 'appropriate action' of a direct kind is the writing and revision of a poem, to stand as a public emblem for acts of reparation directed towards victims for whom we are not solely or

---

[132] Diary entry for 20 October 1912, quoted in Michael Millgate, *Testamentary Acts* (1992), 97.

[133] *MM*, 19.

[134] *AI*, 33.

[135] *AI*, 117.

[136] *AI*, 141.

[137] *The Burden of the Past and the English Poet* (1971), 3.

[138] *Moral Luck* (1981), 29.

directly responsible. This writing will have two interdependent aims: 'it will try to inhabit the circumstances of the irreparable, to describe its "painful consciousness that nothing can be done", and it will attempt, through the attributes of poems themselves, to perform a "reparative action or substitute for it".'[139] One example of this process, which also provides a significant counter-example to Bloom's 'anxiety of influence', can be heard working its way through Hardy's 'Poems of 1912–13', because although Bloom justifies his theory of belatedness with the truism 'two poems are not the same poem, any more than two lives can be the same life',[140] what Hardy's elegies for his dead wife discover, to his relief and distress, is that lives can overlap in poems when they no longer can in life.

When Emma Hardy died, not only did she become Hardy's late wife but in his state of grief and guilt he also became a late husband to her, as his writing confronted how years of marriage had dulled his ears to a woman whose voice he could now hear only in his own. His elegies respond by mourning a past which is 'past amend | Unchangeable';[141] at the same time, they are shaped into an act of atonement for the very belatedness with which they listen for this voice:

Some of them I rather shrink from printing—those I wrote just after Emma died, when I looked back at her as she had originally been, & when I felt miserable lest I had not treated her considerately in her later life. However I shall publish them as the only amends I can make, if it were so.[142]

For Bloom, poems represent imaginative strangleholds; for Hardy, they are lifelines.

*

Hardy is one of Bloom's strongest poets.[143] 'He Resolves To Say No More', for example, the last poem of *Winter Words* (1928), is for Bloom a paradigm of *apophrades*, or 'deep poetic influence in its final phase', because here Hardy is said to rewrite Shelley, 'as though Hardy were

---

[139] *In the Circumstances* (1992), 1. Robinson notes that Williams is drawing on Melanie Klein's 1929 paper 'Infantile Anxiety-Situations Reflected in a Work of Art and in the Creative Impulse', repr. in *Love, Guilt and Reparation* (1975).
[140] *AI*, 94.
[141] 'The Going', *HP*, II. 47.
[142] *HL*, V. 37.
[143] See *Kabbalah*, 67.

Shelley's ancestor, the dark father whom the revolutionary idealist failed to cast out'.[144] In effect, failure forms the shadowy heart of Bloom's entire *agon*, 'for what strong maker desires the realization that he has failed to create himself?'[145] Here Bloom's use of Hardy does not rest comfortably with the creative allegiances Hardy claimed for himself:

January 1. New Year's thought. A perception of the FAILURE of THINGS to be what they are meant to be, lends them, in place of the intended interest, a new and greater interest of an unintended kind.[146]

This represents more than a consolation for those things which are anticipated without being intended, such as the breaking of new year's resolutions. Much of Hardy's fiction and poetry lives in the haunted gap between 'intended' and 'unintended', as his writing debates how far we can be held responsible for our failings, whether of one another or ourselves. His lyric 'The Lacking Sense', for example, describes how nature's disregard for her creatures handicaps the 'would-be perfect' world, and Hardy's lines sadly and typically strain between two forms of 'lacking sense' which unavoidably press on one another: nature's blind rule over the 'unfulfilments' of our desires, and our own mournful consciousness of these wants.[147]

The idea that we possess a 'lacking sense' as a supplement to our existing senses, a ghostly sixth sense which responds to what is now beyond them, is one Emma Hardy might have strongly supported, given her keen sense of the unhappy course her married life had taken. In 1899, Elspeth Grahame wrote to Emma Hardy to ask for advice on dealing with her new husband. Emma tackled her brief with grim relish:

Keeping separate a good deal is a wise plan in crises— ... Love interest— adoration, & all that kind of thing is usually a *failure—complete*—some one comes by & upsets your pail of milk in the end. If he belongs to the public in any way, years of devotion count for nothing. Influence can seldom be retained as years go by, & *hundreds* of wives go through a phase of disillusion,—it is really a pity to have any ideals in the first place.[148]

The claim that '*hundreds* of wives go through a phase of disillusion' is typical of this letter's nervy knots of tact and self-justification, imply-

---

[144] *MM*, 23.   [145] *AI*, 5.   [146] *Life*, I. 163.   [147] *HP*, I. 151.
[148] Michael Millgate (ed.), *Letters of Emma and Florence Hardy* (1996), 15–16 (hereafter cited as *LEFH*).

ing as it does the twin faces of solidarity in distress: 'I sympathize with
you', but also, 'why should you escape when I could not?' That
homely metaphor 'pail of milk' then casts a wary eye on the way
that a sudden household upset could sharply concentrate the gradual
decline of a marriage into mutual disappointment and recrimination;
like Proust's Albertine letting slip the vulgarism 'casser le pot', it opens
a keyhole onto a previously unbroached domestic world.[149] However, one difficulty with Emma's conviction, that the original 'happy
state' of marriage is an ideal to which actual marriages can 'occasionally' return, is that the person one married may not be the same as the
person to whom one is still married. Given how many 'phases' a
married couple could go through, individually and together, it is quite
possible that both partners will decide to 'keep separate' in order to
avoid the mutual awkwardness of approaching one another with a
caution usually accorded strangers. For, as Hardy noted, where being
taken for granted is exactly what one partner cannot do to another,
apprehensiveness always threatens to slide into misapprehension:

January 6. Misapprehension. The shrinking soul thinks its weak place is
going to be laid bare, and shows its thought by a suddenly clipped manner.
The other shrinking soul thinks the clipped manner of the first to be the
result of weakness in some way, not of its strength, and shows its fear also by
its constrained air! So they withdraw from one another and misunderstand.[150]

When James Richardson judges that 'Hardy's poems are written at
the moment when conventions are *strongest*, the moment when it is
clear both that they are "merely" habits and that mere habit rules the
universe',[151] he brings to mind the way that a couple's withdrawals
from one another could be detected as the visible chinks not only in
their own marriage but also in the conjugal ideal which is being
fractured against their everyday actualities. One social form which
takes measured account of both the ideal and the actual is poetic
form, because a poem can attend to the shifting demands of social
customs and particular human relations over time by measuring
individual utterances against the conventions which are preserved
in its own time, in its rhythmic and stanzaic patterns of expectation

---

[149] See Roland Barthes, *Fragments d'un discours amoureux* (1977) trans. Richard Howard as
A Lover's Discourse (1979), 25–8.
[150] *Life*, I. 232.
[151] *Thomas Hardy: The Poetry of Necessity* (1977), 89.

and fulfilment. Being a model of these conventions as well as a distinctive expression of them, a poem is likely to prove an especially effective medium for drawing attention to the way that a speaker relaxes into 'mere' habits, or guards against their unthinking repetition, as the settling of his or her speech into predictable measures comes to represent the regulating of a first fine rapture into loving routines, or its grimmer petrification into a parody of marital ideals.[152] The relative tightness of fit between established form and expressed sentiment will then test how 'the FAILURE of THINGS to be what they are meant to be' has been perceived by the speaker and observed in his or her verse. John Bayley is not quite right, therefore, when he glosses Hardy's remark, 'I do not promise overmuch', with the complaint that the poems themselves show little promise: 'Hardy is never seen striving to rise to the height of an ideal conception, nor failing to bring such a thing off.'[153] Hardy came closer to explaining his true aims, with a somewhat cack-handed compliment to Sir George Douglas on the collection which was to appear as *Poems of a Country Gentleman* (1897): 'It sometimes occurs to me that it is better to fail in poetry than to succeed in prose.'[154] For despite Hardy's regular and remorseful complaints that his verse had failed to realize his ambitions,[155] he also failed *in* his verse, as Browning's Pacchiarotto worked *in* distemper; rather than striving but failing, he strives *to* fail, his disappointment as deliberate and predictable a pursuit as the foreplay he describes in *Tess*: 'Lotis attempting to elude Priapus, and always failing.'[156]

Many of Hardy's poems describe the failure of some ideal conception in two mutually informing ways: in their lines of narrative, and in the formal shapes against which his cadences chafe and collapse. In this, the patterning of his verse responds to an aspect of ethical thought which he also detected in other artistic forms:

He knew that in architecture cunning irregularity is of enormous worth, and it is obvious that he carried on into his verse, perhaps in part unconsciously, the Gothic art-principle in which he had been trained—the principle of

---

[152] Compare Eric Griffiths's discussion of Victorian marital and poetic ideals in *The Printed Voice of Victorian Poetry* (1989), ch. 3.

[153] *An Essay on Hardy* (1978), 11.

[154] *HL*, I. 182.

[155] See, e.g., his warning in 1899 that *Wessex Poems* will 'sadly disappoint': 'I do not cease to feel the smallness of what I have brought to you beside that which I ought to have brought but have feebly left behind', *HL*, II. 204, 221.

[156] Ch.10.

spontaneity, found in mouldings, tracery, and such like—resulting in the 'unforeseen' (as it has been called) character of his metres and stanzas, that of stress rather than of syllable, poetic texture rather than poetic veneer.[157]

That well-timed parenthesis dividing 'unforeseen' and 'character' indicates how, as Peter Robinson expresses it, 'the "unforeseen" becomes the preconceived',[158] as Hardy abstracts the uneven imperfections of genuine Gothic into the '*cunning* irregularity' of Victorian mock-Gothic, random felicities into a '*principle* of spontaneity' (my emphases). Besides mutely confessing how individual humans succeed one another without necessarily becoming more successful, a further application of the Gothic as an emblem of poetic form inheres in the fact that a church carries the marks of the different hands and periods that went into its construction, and can be visited by the same person at different times. Hardy refers to the 'compound influence' of churches upon regular worshippers,[159] and a similar encounter of direct experience and the mediations of memory is true of the way his stanzas too keep time, as they measure the succession of one moment by another, and then brood over the unsuccesses which these changes reveal. It is this 'compound influence' of social and literary institutions upon the events of a life which Hardy's 'Poems of 1912–13' investigate with such care. For, although Hardy's expressions of belatedness involve some rewriting of what no longer answers to him, such as his wife, his stanzaic forms not only admit to what had been 'unforeseen'—'I have been full of regrets that I did not at all foresee the possibility of her passing away like this, but merely thought her few days of illness a temporary ailment which I need not be anxious about'[160]—but also reproduce it, as the speaker's regrets create rhythmic aftershocks, formal and ethical contortions, which tug against the 'compound influence' generated by the metrical patterns of his verse.

Emma Hardy died of 'heart failure from some internal perforation'.[161] Hardy remembered how, only weeks before her death, and having 'complained of her heart at times', she 'one day suddenly sat down to the piano and played a long series of her favourite old tunes,

---

[157] *Life*, II. 78–9.
[158] *In the Circumstances*, 59–60.
[159] 'Memories of Church Restoration', repr. in *Thomas Hardy's Personal Writings*, ed. Harold Orel (1967), 215.
[160] *HL*, IV. 239.
[161] *HL*, IV. 246.

saying at the end that she would never play any more'.[162] The first stanza of 'Lost Love' harps on these old tunes:

> I play my sweet old airs—
> 　　The airs he knew
> 　　When our love was true—
> But he does not balk
> 　　His determined walk,
> And passes up the stairs.[163]

All lyric verse puts the events it describes into perspective, by organizing the chances and surprises of human experience into its own controlled structures of space and time. 'Lost Love' stretches out this process, and invests it with a characteristically self-suspicious ethical inflection, as the timing of Hardy's thought negotiates between reliving the past and relieving himself of it, of recollection and calling himself to account. The poem starts lightly, airily even, so that our ears quickly become attuned to the singsong: 'I play my sweet old airs— | The airs he knew | When our love was true'. And so it goes on, with resigned good humour, 'But he does not baulk | His determined walk, | And passes up the stairs': the predictable tread of the verse mimics the predictable path her husband always takes, and uses its own reluctance to pause for thought to echo both his thoughtlessness and her own affected disregard for such a routine slight. But he could have done otherwise, of course, as we hear in the echo of another 'old air', Barnes's 'The Wife A-Lost', which begins 'Since I noo mwore do zee your feäce, | Up steäirs or down below',[164] and in the yearning counter-rhythms which replay the scene through Hardy's new accents of self-blame and self-pity: 'But *he* does *not* baulk ... As *if* he *would* stay'.

In 1922, Hardy copied into his notebook some comments by Robert Bridges on free verse:

The main effectual difference between the rhythms of the old metrical verse & of fine prose is that in the verse you have a greater *expectancy* of the rhythm ... & the poet's art was to vary the expected rhythm as much as he could without disagreeably baulking the expectation.[165]

[162] *Life*, II. 153.
[163] *HP*, II. 24.
[164] *The Poems of William Barnes*, ed. Bernard Jones (2 vols., 1962), I. 333.
[165] 'Humdrum and Harum Scarum: A Paper on Free Verse', *London Mercury*, 7 (November 1922), 55, repr. in Richard H. Taylor (ed.), *The Personal Notebooks of Thomas Hardy* (1978), 62–3.

'Lost Love' depends equally upon expectation and its baulking, and in Hardy's hands this is an aspect of good form which stretches beyond his manner of address. Coventry Patmore explained one way in which the 'integrity' of literary form and human character should be brought together in reading:

When ... some familiarity with the poet's work has assured you that, though his speech may be unequal and sometimes inadequate, it is never false; that he has always something to say, even when he fails in saying it: then you will not only believe in and be moved by what he says well; but when the form is imperfect you will be carried over such passages, as over thin ice, by the formative power of passion or feeling which quickens the whole ... [166]

This is encouraging advice, for poets as well as for their readers, but Patmore's own connections between 'moved', 'carried over', and 'quickens' are too brisk for his model of reading to be applied successfully to 'Lost Love', because what moves Hardy's lines is both the quick and the dead. Just as the *Life* imagines that to adjudge between the relative 'strength' or 'weakness' of shrinking souls could depend upon a significant delay between the moment of misapprehension and the moment it is understood, so 'Lost Love' makes the distribution of 'strong' and 'weak' stresses depend less upon a fixed metrical form than upon the different occasions imagined for the poem's utterance. In their insistent metrical shape, their 'expectations', Hardy's lines are a model of events which are past, and so beyond amend. At the same time, the pauses and counter-rhythms, the 'baulking', which bring these events to life in a speaker's voice, carry a central self-rebuke for the way Emma's voice was passed over: not because it was 'unequal', but because Hardy was then unequal to it. In this way, whereas Bloom's 'strong' poet must come to terms with the way 'the precursor went wrong by failing to swerve' poetically,[167] Hardy's lines are marked by his knowledge that verse, itself a structure of visible 'turns' on the page,[168] is equally accomplished at dramatizing the human errors which it describes. As reversed metrical feet assert lost opportunities for reversing human footfalls, so 'Lost Love' registers the shocking unpredictability of the past which results from Hardy's revised understanding of his walk as

---

[166] 'Poetical Integrity', *Principle in Art* (1889), 48–9.
[167] *AI*, 85.
[168] 'Verse', from the Latin *versus*: 'turn of the plough, furrow, line, row, line of writing, verse' (*OED*).

'determined' in the sense of 'bloody-minded', not as 'irrevocably ordained'. Embodying and enacting his new ethical priorities, Hardy's metrical variations take the measure of his remorse.

One excuse Hardy might have claimed for pacing briskly upstairs to his study in 1912 is that he was at the time correcting proofs for the 1912–13 Wessex Edition of his works. The only novel Hardy continued to revise after this edition was *A Pair of Blue Eyes*, the work in which the romance of Elfride and Stephen had reflected upon Hardy's own experience of meeting Emma while drawing up plans to restore the church at St Juliot. The 1920 Mellstock Edition of *A Pair of Blue Eyes* adds a musical interlude to Elfride and Stephen's blossoming romance:

Selecting from the canterbury some old family ditties, that in years gone by had been played and sung by her mother, Elfride sat down to the pianoforte, and began "Twas on the evening of a winter's day,' in a pretty contralto voice. Next she took 'Should he upbraid,' which suited her exquisitely both in voice and mien.

'Do you like that old thing, Mr, Smith?' she said at the end.

'Yes, I do much,' said Stephen—words he would have uttered, and sincerely, to anything on earth, from glee to requiem, that she might have chosen.[169]

Prospect and retrospect, in fiction and in life, are touchingly balanced in this addition, as Hardy discovers how 'the music ... Rose again from where it seem'd to fail.'[170] 'Should he upbraid' was, claims the *Life*, 'the most marvellous old song in English music in its power of touching an audience.' Hardy continues:

'*March* 18. End of the Sturminster Newton idyll ... ' [The following is written in later] 'Our happiest time.'[171]

The addition of 'Should he upbraid' to *A Pair of Blue Eyes* fulfils the same function as Hardy's self-interruption in his journal, as he shows how drawing out a dead voice need not clog up the surviving writer's private imaginative space, as Bloom claims, but rather console him or her for the non-literary discontinuities and ruptures, the wounds of grief, which bereavement has opened up in this space. Like his literal

---

[169] Ch.3; see Alan Manford, 'Thomas Hardy's Later Revisions in *A Pair of Blue Eyes*', *PBSA*, 76: 2 (1982), 209–20.

[170] Tennyson, 'The Vision of Sin', *TP*, II. 158.

[171] *Life*, I. 156.

and elegiac returns to Cornwall, Hardy's revision restores his wife to her former self, effecting an accord between his old consideration of the past and a new consideration for this past. It also responds to one of the saddest features of 'Poems of 1912–13', which is that although the poet and his dead wife repeatedly confirm one another's presence by speaking, they never speak to one another. And yet, 'Lost Love' shows how it is not only textual revision which brings together Hardy's loss and recovery of his wife's presence, as he composes his 'lack of foresight' and pained hindsight in the balance of individual lines. 'I play my sweet old airs': there is a sudden thickening of the voice on 'my sweet', because only now does he hear that she could have been playing *old* airs to recall her husband, 'my sweet', to the time when she had first sung for him. (Elfride's 'that old thing' similarly slips between an affected carelessness—'oh, *that* old thing'—and the former fondness which this song now calls to mind.) Only now, as he projects her voice through his own, is he brought to wonder whether the singer had remained as constant to him as his own favourite songs.

*

Rather than think of such moments, with Bloom, as 'wrestling with the mighty dead',[172] we can better consider them, with Hazlitt, as 'conversing with the mighty dead': 'By conversing with the mighty dead, we imbibe sentiment with knowledge; we become strongly attached to those who can no longer either hurt or serve us, except through the influence which they exert over the mind.'[173] This sentiment need not collapse into sentimentality. (In *The Dynasts*, Sergeant Young remembers how he lost his girl: in the rough draft, he 'was a good deal upset about it at the time'; in the British Museum MS, he adds, 'But one gets over things!', and remembers a song.)[174] Although Hardy is alert to the lapses of attention through which he mistook his wife, he is equally alert to her own habit of slipping off into a different world, particularly when it existed for her only on paper, as she must now for him. It is, then, especially in their quiet incorporation of fragments from Emma's own writings that Hardy's

---

172 *AI*, 71.
173 'On Classical Education', repr. in *Howe*, IV. 5.
174 Walter F. Wright, *The Shaping of 'The Dynasts'* (1967), 112.

elegies seek atonement for the irreparable fact that time 'wrought division',[175] because the joining of her words to her husband's shows how the influence which one writer exerts over the mind of another can reflect upon, and reproduce, strong attachments which are not only textual.

Emma's *Some Recollections* (1911) are largely structured around a superstitious faith in her husband's journey to St Juliot as predestined, a conjugal convergence of the twain, which proved that 'an Unseen Power of great benevolence directs my ways.'[176] 'Way' and 'ways' are charged words in 'Poems of 1912–13', hovering guiltily between the speaker's description of their bad old habits and his new pursuit of Emma's flitting ghost. Given his wife's sense of future and past as equally inevitable, the fixed brackets around a world of seeming chance, it is then not surprising that Hardy's elegies should also engage with her 'ardent belief in … the life beyond this present one',[177] as set out in her privately-printed religious tract, *Spaces*:

> The doomed, probably, certainly are not in hell immediately after death as their bodies are not changed, and soul and body must go together at last. There is a general belief of spirits being restless until the Judgment Day, giving us occasionally slight intimations of their existence though viewless. The 'rest' of God's people is not for them.[178]

The eccentric tone of this, as it veers unpredictably between self-assurance and hectoring (a whole shift of doctrine is invested in the comma which separates 'probably, certainly'), suggests that the voices of the living can be as 'restless' as the spirits of the dead. Hardy himself seems to have recognized this, because when he tracks his wife's flitting presence ('Hereto I come to view a voiceless ghost'), or appeals to it directly ('Can it be you that I hear? Let me view you, then'), his choice of 'view' is haunted by the older sense of 'interview', and so concedes that, underlying the sheer fact of Emma's absence, what is most missed is the sound of her voice.[179] In one draft of 'The Voice', 'view' was originally 'interview', and Hardy's final choice expresses the personal remorse which has come to be heard in the

---

[175] 'After a Journey', *HP*, II. 59.

[176] *Life*, I. 96; Robinson (*In the Circumstances*, 71–7) notes the principal allusions.

[177] *Life*, I. 96.

[178] *Spaces* (MS, n.d.), 10; 'viewless', set so close to immortal 'intimations', may be recalling Wordsworth, 'viewless as the buried dead' (*Poems Dedicated to National Independence and Liberty*, XXX).

[179] 'After a Journey', *HP*, II. 59; 'The Voice', *HP*, II. 56.

dictionary's neutral information that the sense of 'view' as 'interview' is now '*obs*';[180] as R. C. Trench observed in 1851, when describing the changeable state of a living language, 'How deep an insight into the failings of the human heart is implied in many words.'[181] However, the solemnity is spiked with sly humour, because the dramatic situation and vocabulary alike suggest that the speaker of 'The Voice' is also responding to Emma's firm opinion that the only 'viewless' dead we could sense about us are 'Satan's myridoms [*sic*] doing his bidding in his service and "blown with restless violence about the pendent world".' After all, should Hardy have taken his wife at her word, his epigraph to 'Poems of 1912–13', 'Veteris vestigia flammae', could have provided not only a Virgilian model for the 'old flame' of his wife and his marriage, but also a warning of 'The New Element of Fire' which Emma describes, with enthusiastic vagueness, as the stuff of Hell which restless spirits must 'breathe in or love in, somehow'.[182]

It is unlikely that Hardy would have taken this entirely seriously. It is equally unlikely that he could have taken it entirely unseriously, given that more or less 'rest' was central to his self-rebuking response to Emma's death: 'a lack of insight, which, if I had had it, might have enabled me to prolong her life a little by assiduous attention, & insistence on her taking more rest'.[183] Compare what husband and wife each makes of 'rest':

> Wholly possessed
> By an infinite rest! [184]

Before every other change after death comes rest complete. Muscles, nerves, brain, in a state of rest, sweetest of all rests, never had in life ... [185]

Hardy's uses of 'view', or 'rest', like his strained but jaunty rhythms in 'Lost Love', supply glimpses of a literary form which Bloom's agonistic scheme repeatedly gestures towards, but could not accommodate: parody. Like the elegist, the parodist is often moved to observe the passing of forms which have gone dead, but thereby discovers in his original an innocence of its fate to which his work must also accustom itself if it is to be, like the best jokes, instinct with what it condemns. The parody assumes that it knows more about its target than the target does about itself, but comes to recognize that its superior understanding has grown out of the very poem it is trying creatively

---

[180] *OED* 2c.   [181] *On the Study of Words* (1851), 37.   [182] *Spaces*, 9–10.
[183] *HL*, IV. 240.   [184] 'Lament', *HP*, II. 54.   [185] *Spaces*, 3.

to shrug off.[186] Here, for example, we notice how Hardy reinvests Emma's voice with an intermittent quirkiness which is oblivious of its hardening into predictable absurdity, but also how the formal constraints of the verse in which he sets this voice allow his writing to crackle with the parodist's managed reconciliation of affection and repudiation, nostalgia and reproof:

> When shall I leave off doing these things?—
> When I hear
> You have dropped your dusty cloak and taken you
> wondrous wings
> To another sphere,
> Where no pain is.[187]

THE HIGH DELIGHTS OF HEAVEN

Our capabilities will be increased richly to enjoy everything that will be there … Highest knowledge as known to angels, and special comprehension of the former perplexities about our earthly existence. Lightness of body and ease of locomotion—whether by wings or otherwise—no weight, no trouble of the flesh; … Evil being abolished absolutely of every kind, so also will all pain.[188]

What emerges from these glancing points of contact is not Hardy's single-minded drive to expel Emma's writings on the future from the poetic afterlife into which they have been summoned. Rather, they attend to the warning implicit in all good parody, that it too could come to sound seriously mistaken about itself, the parodist parodied. For if our ability to outstrip the past does not end with death, then the dead may already be laughing, on the other side, at what we face:

The amusement of the dead—at our errors, or our wanting to live on … [189]

MULTIVERSES

A dissatisfaction with the rapid attachments and detachments of desire is one thing Hardy and his wife could agree on:

… persons are successively various persons, according as each special strand in their character is brought uppermost by circumstances.[190]

---

[186] See Ch. 3 for a fuller discussion of parody as a form of attenuated literary afterlife.
[187] 'Why do I?', *HP*, III. 157.   [188] *Spaces*, 2.
[189] Hardy's 1890 note for a poem, quoted in Michael Millgate, *Thomas Hardy: A Biography* (1982), 411.
[190] *Life*, I. 301.

I can hardly think that love proper, and enduring, is in the nature of Man ... characters change so greatly with time, and circumstance.[191]

Parfit explains why this sort of self-division could also distance us from other people:

It may be clear to some couple that they love each other. But if they ask whether they are still *in love with* each other, they may find this question perplexing. It may still seem to them that they are in love, yet their behaviour towards each other, and their feelings in each other's presence, may seem not to bear this out. If they distinguished between successive selves, their perplexity might be resolved. They might see that they love each other, and are in love with each other's earlier self.[192]

This is a philosophical rather than a practical solution to the problem of our desires breaking up and dispersing along with the selves they once stirred. Thus, to recognize, with Proust, that 'We are incapable, while we are in love, of acting as fit predecessors of the next persons who, when we are in love no longer, we shall presently have become',[193] might encourage us better to understand our dread of losses to come, and so to make better sense of grief as a form of thinking which can be directed as much by anticipation as by memory. But it is unlikely to remove the circumstantiality of fondness, any more than Hardy and his wife were reconciled to one another in their later years merely because they were both unhappy at the changes their marriage had undergone.

Writing records these dilemmas, but it can also enact them, because as I suggested earlier in this chapter, Parfit's argument for the self's partial survival in the thoughts and actions of its survivors is often visibly realized in the composition and endurance of a printed text. For example, when P. B. Shelley called *Frankenstein* 'one of the most original and complete productions of the day', no doubt he was shiftily aware of his own part (some 4,000 words) in its achieved completeness, as he acted the Frankenstein to his wife's Walton:

... he asked to see [my notes] and then himself corrected and augmented them in many places ... 'Since you have preserved my narration,' said he, 'I would not that a mutilated one should go down to posterity.'[194]

191 Emma Hardy to Elspeth Grahame, *LEFH*, 15.

192 *Reasons and Persons*, 305.

193 *A l'ombre des jeunes filles en fleurs*, quoted by Parfit, ibid.

194 Charles E. Robinson (ed.), *The Frankenstein Notebooks* (2 vols., 1996), I. xciii; II. 607. Hereafter I abbreviate Percy Bysshe Shelley to PBS and Mary Wollstonecraft Shelley to MWS.

The shaping of Frankenstein's story was rehearsed in the composition of *Frankenstein*, as husband and wife passed the manuscript back and forth, each drawing on the other in a tactful conversation on the page:

Yet ~~one feeling~~ he enjoys,
            offspring
one comfort, the ~~sourse~~ of solitude
& delirium—he ~~tho~~ believed that when
                              holds converse with
& derives from   in dreams he ~~saw~~ his friends, ~~who consoled~~
that communion   *excitement*   *his*
consolation for   his miseries or ~~instigated him~~ to vengeance
                              are   ∧
                    that they ~~were~~ not the creations of his
                    fancy but the real beings ~~that he saw~~
            ~~beheld and conversed with~~
who visit
him from
the regions
of a remoter world [195]

With PBS's intervention, 'sourse of solitude' becomes 'offspring of solitude' ('sourse' suggests 'spring'; 'spring' provides 'offspring'), as *Frankenstein*'s textual transmission comes to reflect the narrator's occasional misgivings over other human lines of descent, such as the submerged warning about the need for two parents. But the circumstances of the novel's authors were not always in perfect accord with the circumstances of their writing. Even after her husband's death, MWS generously preserved his changes in subsequent versions of the novel, and so continued to raise his voice into the patchwork creation of their 'hideous progeny'. Her revisions between the first (1818) and third (1831) editions, then, like Hardy's revisions to *A Pair of Blue Eyes*, are not the result of a separate intention, but the achievement of a textual *intention* (*OED* 10: 'the joining of severed tissues') made necessary by her separation from one who could then be embraced only in the figurative space of the page.

The extended composition of *Frankenstein* should encourage us to pause over Parfit's remark on the difficulties involved in retaining

[195] Draft (1816–17) in MWS's hand (reproduced in plain text) with alterations by PBS (in italics), ibid., II. 607–9; the language is echoed in MWS's essay 'On Ghosts', *London Magazine*, 9 (March 1824), 253–6.

feelings of affection 'in the presence' of the person who formerly excited them, because revision raises similar questions over how far the person who originally wrote a text is still present in it. Hardy's ideal was 'freshness':

'Why!' he said, 'I have never in my life taken more than three, or perhaps four drafts for a poem. I am afraid of it losing its freshness.'[196]

I have a faculty … for burying an emotion in my heart or brain for forty years, and exhuming it at the end of that time as fresh as when interred.[197]

These comments are not contradictory, because many of Hardy's drafts were separated by periods of years or decades, and his replies to requests from journals often picture himself burrowing mole-like through sheaves of incomplete poems to bring his earlier impulses and impressions to light. Such searching and stretching of intention, stringent time-spanning, produces publications which are, like his punningly-titled collection from *Time's Laughingstocks* (1909), 'Poems Occasional and Various', each poem varied in its occasions even before it prompted a further variety of published forms. Yet, as Hardy also knew, even if a poem sets out to retain a loved voice, no work can remain entirely under its author's control once it is released into the public world of print, and so into what Jonathan Miller has described as the 'undulating curve of estrangements and rapprochements' which any artwork will produce in its passage through the 'unforeseen hereafter'.[198] Hardy's lyric 'Her Immortality' imagines an encounter between a mourner and the ghost of his departed lover:

> I said: 'My days are lonely here;
>   I need thy smile alway:
> I'll use this night my ball or blade,
>   And join thee ere the day.'
>
> A tremor stirred her tender lips,
>   Which parted to dissuade:
> 'That cannot be, o friend,' she cried;
>   'Think, I am but a Shade!
>
> 'A Shade but in its mindful ones
>   Has immortality;

---

[196] Quoted in Robert Graves, *Goodbye to All That* (1929), 377.

[197] *Life*, II. 178.

[198] *Subsequent Performances* (1986), 32, paraphrasing the work of the Warburg Institute on the 'afterlife of the antique'.

> By living, me you keep alive,
> By dying you slay me.[']

> ... When I surcease,
> Through whom alone lives she,
> Her spirit ends its living lease,
> Never again to be![199]

Hardy's lines invite a more cheering conclusion, which is that the page will fix the voice of this Shade more enduringly than the speaker's mind ever could, thereby reconciling in neutral print what time and circumstance have split apart. In this sense, the lines anticipate redeeming their sad pun on 'alone' by hinting that although what they describe is 'Her Immortality', what they achieve is something more like 'Their Immortality'. As with Shakespeare's *Sonnets*, the speaker's survival is intimately bound up with the quality of attention which is directed towards his listener. But Hardy's lines also appear more suspicious of their claims to permanence, as if they had anticipated Yeats's remark that 'A poem comes right with a click like a closing box',[200] and then provided it with a deadly new gloss, by wondering aloud how soon a poem could turn out to be a final rather than a temporary resting-place for its speaker's words. Given its unpredictable and cautionary collapses into archaism, there are clues that 'Her Immortality' might be as ephemeral as the life of its subject.

Hardy was keen on the imaginative possibilities of folding the future back into present experience:

For my part, if there is any way of getting a melancholy satisfaction out of life it lies in dying, so to speak, before one is out of the flesh; by which I mean putting on the manners of ghosts, wandering in their haunts, and taking their views of surrounding things. To think of life as passing away is a sadness; to think of it as past is at least tolerable.[201]

Like many of Hardy's poems which put on the manners of ghosts, in their subject-matter and style alike, 'Her Immortality' is expectantly charged by the imaginative overlap of 'out of life' and 'out of the flesh', as if recognizing that although all poems emerge from a living speaker, their ability to outlast this speaker will largely depend upon

---

[199] *HP*, I. 73–4.

[200] Letter to Dorothy Wellesley, quoted in Geoffrey Hill, 'Poetry as "Menace" and "Atonement"', *The Lords of Limit: Essays on Literature and Ideas* (1984), 2.

[201] *Life*, I. 218.

the nature of the 'satisfaction' offered to their readers: the extent to which the poem's conclusion works as a self-renewing invitation or a self-fulfilling prophecy. But the Shade's worried accent on 'mindful' ('A Shade but in its mindful ones | Has immortality') suggests a further problem for the idea that human lives can extend themselves through the supplementary afterlife of writing. Because the transmission of a text is only as accurate as the eyes of its printers and readers, and depends upon the shifting state of the language which passes it on, a poem will suffer as much from the pressures of circumstance as its author. Just as individuals can be thought of as the more slippery and contingent beings Parfit labels 'successive selves', their writing too can be considered as a set of flexible responses to the world rather than a fixed part of it, as if at a fundamental level every literary work was a work in progress.

*

Not all critics have been enthusiastic about the afterlife of writing as a developing social encounter between a work and its successive readers. The Greg–Bowers model of critical editing, for example, takes a strong line on the need to guard against foreign incursions into an author's text:

Only a practising critic and bibliographer knows the remorseless corrupting influence that eats away at a text during the course of its transmission. The most important concern of the textual bibliographer is to guard the purity of the important basic documents of our literature and culture. This is a matter of principle on which there can be no compromise.[202]

Following nineteenth-century principles laid down by Lachmann and the Higher Criticism, the New Bibliography traces textual descent as an exemplary narrative of fall and recovery, corruption and atonement. The editor's task is doubly one of repair: by tracing texts back to an uncontaminated state, the editor restores or reconstructs authorial intentions which have been clouded by the successive interference of publishers or printers; by working out errors, his reforms uphold the principle which textual transmission shares with other forms of cultural passage, that 'Purity', in Mary Douglas's terms, 'is the enemy of change, of ambiguity and compromise'.[203] Bowers gives

---

202 Fredson Bowers, *Textual and Literary Criticism* (1959), 8.
203 Mary Douglas, *Purity and Danger* (1966), 162.

an example from the Constable Standard Edition of Melville's *White-Jacket*, as the speaker falls overboard:

> I wondered whether I was yet dead or still dying. But of a sudden some fashionless form brushed my side—some inert, soiled fish of the sea; the thrill of being alive again tingled in my nerves, and the strong shunning of death shocked me through.[204]

Melville wrote 'coiled fish', not 'soiled fish'. Bowers suggests that for 'a scholar of depth', to 'guard against a proof-reader's error' like this is to brace bibliography with ethics, because to excuse as 'just a little corruption' the substitution of 'soiled fish' for 'coiled fish' (or any other misprint: 'boiled fish', 'foiled fish', and so on) is like admitting 'just a little sin' into Eden; a text cannot be 'almost' pure, any more than someone could accurately describe himself or herself as 'almost' a virgin.[205] Naturally, Bowers's slide between description and appraisal does not sufficiently allow for the place of unexpected felicities in transmission, such as the typist's error in 'Journey to Iceland' of 'port' for 'poet' ('every port has its name for the sea'), which Auden chose to print as one of 'the gifts of language, tradition and pure accident' occasionally granted a writer.[206] Nor could it countenance editorial methods which seek to rescue an author's intentions from the ruins he is thought to have made of them, as Empson and Pirie's printing of 'The Rime of the Ancient Mariner' removes the marginal glosses Coleridge added to later editions, on the grounds that although he had 'managed to convince himself that he was surrounded by the comforting angels of an orthodoxly Christian universe', his poem did not 'admit more than a marginal invasion by such aliens'.[207]

   Where Bowers casts editors as vigilant security-guards, patrolling 'our literary and historical monuments' on the lookout for cultural trespassers and graffiti, a number of later theorists have argued that the many hands and voices which a literary work retains in its bibliographical history should be a matter for celebration as well as regret. Like James Thorpe, who celebrates the poem's 'collaborative status',[208] and Hans Zeller, who replaces the principle of an ancestral

[204] Quoted in Bowers, 30.

[205] Ibid., 8.

[206] Auden, 'A Literary Transference', *Southern Review*, 6 (1940), 85; the poem's composition is discussed in John G. Blair, *The Poetic Art of W. H. Auden* (1965), 152.

[207] Note by Pirie, in William Empson and David Pirie (ed.), *Coleridge's Verse: A Selection* (1972), 212.

[208] *Principles of Textual Criticism* (1972), 48.

series of texts with one of textual versions,[209] Jerome McGann points out that 'alien influences' are already present within any edition, even one purged of error by the New Bibliographer;[210] in terms he borrows from information theory, 'whenever information is mediated some contamination results'.[211] It is a process that begins with the author's mediation of the influences which unavoidably press in upon any act of writing:

biographical analysis falters because it maintains the poem, and the poetic analysis, in the artificially restricted geography of the individual person. Such a criticism is aware that the artist writes in a dialectical relation to the objective world, but it often seems unaware that this relationship is fundamentally social rather than personal or psychological, and hence that object-ive history exerts a shaping influence upon the poetry.[212]

For an author to have 'entered the world' of print,[213] McGann argues, proves that his or her text has already been broached by that world. Because 'objective history exerts a shaping influence upon the poetry', each new edition of the poem will contribute to 'the influence of the work's own production history on the work itself': a set of reciprocal cultural pressures which creates the conditions for the poem's ongoing 'socialization'.[214] Certain effects of a work's publication, such as the actual or anticipated responses of its readers, may be detectable in the pressure-points of particular textual changes; others will not, such as the way in which individual acts of reading add a little extra 'thickness' and 'noise' to the work's developing social life. The author, then, is not dead, as was once thought, nor is he or she left lingering in a serenely uninterrupted afterlife, but is instead as porous and shifty in print as some philosophers of identity consider each of us to be in person: 'Authors themselves do not have, as authors, singular identities; an author is a plural identity and more resembles what William James liked to call the human world at large; a multiverse.'[215]

McGann's theoretical model provides a broad and varied justifica-tion of the need to map out what he calls 'the double helix of a work's

---

[209] See 'A New Approach to the Critical Constitution of Literary Texts', in *Studies in Bibliography*, 28 (1975), 231–64.
[210] *Textual and Literary Criticism*, 10; *CMTC*, 102.
[211] *CMTC*, 102.
[212] *BI*, 49.
[213] *CMTC*, 53.
[214] *BI*, 83.
[215] *TC*, 75.

reception history and its production history',[216] and his writing has contributed to some welcome emphases in recent literary criticism: a focus on the physical appearance of the book as a carrier of meaning, or even as a form of literary allusion; an insistence on the inevitable overlaps and slippages between editorial and critical endeavours; a recognition of the exemplary stamina and flexibility of the best literary works, as they continue to adapt themselves to new conditions of reading; a reminder that literature is as much an active intervention in history as a detached response to its events. However, the central assumption of this model, that literature will always overleap what McGann calls 'the artificially restricted geography of the individual person', also raises doubts over whether it can ever be as 'comprehensive' as he claims. One leading aim of McGann's critical method is to restore 'the social relationships which gave [an author's works] their lives (including their "textual" lives) in the first place, and which sustain them through their future life in society': the expanding 'multiverse' of a writer's literary personality.[217] But his 'first place' is often not early enough. The echoes of Emma Hardy's voice in 'Poems of 1912–13' show how a poet's verses too can be multiverses, acting not as a 'medium of uniqueness',[218] but more like the mediums William James knew from his séances, as the author recognizes the influence of particular individuals on his or her writing, and seeks to draw it out: as persistence, foundation, or disturbance. Even social acts can have personal significances. In particular, McGann's 'distinction between point of origin and point of reception [as] fundamental to any historical analysis' is too tidy a distinction to account for the experience of the revising author, as he or she engages in a form of historical analysis which is also an exercise of literary judgement.[219]

Consider Keats's explanation of his creative development:

I may write independently & *with judgment* hereafter. The Genius of Poetry … cannot be matured by law & precept, but by sensation & watchfulness in itself—That which is creative must create itself.[220]

Wordsworth had argued that an ambitious author should set himself 'the task of *creating* the taste by which he is to be enjoyed', by employing his 'genius … in such a manner as to produce effects

---

[216] *TC*, 16.   [217] *CMTC*, 81.   [218] *BI*, 182.
[219] *BI*, 23.   [220] *KL*, I. 374.

hitherto unknown'.[221] Many of Keats's textual revisions demonstrate that the effects of a poem could include more private side-effects or after-effects, as his changes to individual poems, such as *Hyperion*, come to reflect self-consciously upon those ideas of endurance and alteration which the narratives of these poems explicitly describe. Richard Woodhouse remembered Keats being 'impatient of correcting':

'My judgment, (he says,) is as active while I am actually writing as my imagin^n['] ... he has said, that he has often not been aware of the beauty of some thought or expr^n until after he has composed & written it down—It has then struck him with astonishm^t—& seemed rather the prod^n of another person than his own ... This was the case with the descr^n of Apollo in the 3 b. of Hyp^n white melodious throat.[222]

Keats's description reads:

> —Apollo then,
> With sudden scrutiny and gloomless eyes,
> Thus answered, while his white melodious throat
> Throbbed with the syllables.[223]

The 'poetical character', which is 'continually in for—and filling some other Body', here imagines Apollo as somehow a foreign body to himself, as we hear in the sudden double-take on 'throat | Throbbed', and the colouring of 'while' with 'white', which allow the uneasy self-divisions of Keats's lines to discover a poetic shape for that experience of being beside one's self which Baudelaire was to characterize as the philosopher's self-consciousness: 'la puissance d'être à la fois soi et un autre'.[224] This feeling of self-alienation is likely to be of more than passing interest to a poet, not only because of the tradition that imagines literary composition emerging from a fine frenzy of inspiration, but also because writing involves the separation of a voice from the body which first gave it life. According to McGann, it is this detachment of the poem from the poet which forms the first stage of its 'socialization'; as he puts it in his essay on 'Keats and the Historical Method in Literary Criticism', citing Bakhtin, 'Every concrete utterance is a social Act', a conversational word whose 'individual reality is already not that of a physical body, but the reality of a historical

[221] 'Essay, Supplementary to the Preface', repr. in *Owen & Smyser*, III. 80, 82.
[222] *KC*, I. 129.
[223] *Hyperion*, III. 79–82; *KP*, 438.
[224] *Œuvres* (12 vols., 1931–50), I. 524.

phenomenon.'[225] Keats might have been surprised by the assumption that 'a physical body' is not itself 'a historical phenomenon', particularly after the sore throat which 'haunted [him] at intervals' had started to sharpen his thinking about how far a 'melodious throat' could project its voice beyond the speaker's death.[226] He might have been equally surprised by the idea that a poem's 'point of origin' (its writer) could be so easily separated from its 'point of reception' (its reader), given the methods of composition—such as his return in *Lamia* to the subject of Apollo's throbbing throat[227]— through which he gave literary expression to what one Victorian critic described as his 'habitual self-contemplation'.[228] In Keats's revisions and self-borrowings, 'point of origin' and 'point of reception' come together with the contact of his pen on the page; the rhythms of his hand measure the creative through-lines of his career.

McGann makes some startling claims for the self-divisions a poet will suffer once his work successfully passes into multiple editions and readings:

No poem can exist outside of a textual state any more than a human being can exist outside of a human biological organism. But just as a person is not identical to a particular human body, so neither is a poem equal to its text.[229]

This comparison of a poem (in McGann's terms, the total number of a work's possible textual states) and a person (by implication, the sum of his or her possible physical frames) accurately reflects the parallels which Keats seems to have drawn between his creative integrity and his personal identity, but it disregards how different the life of a poem is from our lives. Poems, like people, have beginnings and ends, but their life-spans are usually longer than ours; their time is slower. McGann's claim is not helped by the ambiguity at work within the idea that a poem can never be 'equal to its text', which risks idealizing the writer's material forms just as crudely as some earlier critics had idealized the writer's intentions. However, the central difficulty with this theoretical model is that, just as philosophical arguments for the

---

[225] Quoted in *BI*, 19.

[226] Keats to Fanny Keats (11 February 1819), *KL*, II. 38.

[227] 'Not even Apollo when he sang alone, | Deaf to his throbbing throat's long, long melodious moan', *Lamia*, I. 74–5, *KP*, 343.

[228] Unsigned review of R. M. Milnes's *Life, Letters and Literary Remains of John Keats* (1848), repr. in *KCH*, 334.

[229] *BI*, 22.

self as a fluid and contingent set of responses to the world sometimes find it difficult to explain how each loose bundle of impulses could be thought of as the same human being, so McGann's arguments for the material rootedness of all poems in their textual states never make clear the exact relation between a particular 'text' and the abstract ideal of the 'poem':

The enabling principle is that if a work arrives to our view as a unique order of unique appearances, then a grid of the poem's social and historical filiations ... should help to elucidate the poem's orders of uniqueness.[230]

That is, 'the historically specific character of all poetry' will be revealed by a bibliographer who recovers 'whatever in a poem is most concrete, local, and particular to it' in each of its published forms.[231] As stated, this would constitute a fair analogy for earlier models of cultural development, such as John Morley's 'Historic Method', which sought to explain an idea or belief in its current form 'by connecting [its existing parts] with corresponding parts in some earlier frame; in the identification of present forms in the past, and past forms in the present'.[232] But it could not be true of McGann's 'historical method', because a critic who adopted his most radical criteria for reading would not be given grounds for tracing the continuities which would allow each of a poem's textual states to be understood as contributing towards its historical identity as one and the same poem, remaining uniquely itself throughout its multiple changes of address. For example, when he points out that the authorized and pirated texts of Byron's *Don Juan* Cantos I–II are 'identical in all essential verbal features', it is not clear how the poem's 'complete, social particularity' is to be recovered if it is also true, as he claims, that in each bibliographical environment 'the "meaning" was radically different'.[233] It is hard to square this with McGann's insistence that poems, like all other human utterances, are rooted in the real world of their readers, because his identity-criteria seem to assume that each printed form is a different type of utterance, rather than a different token of the same type. Applied to the pragmatics of everyday situations, these criteria would work against conventions

---

[230] *BI*, 5.
[231] *BI*, 131.
[232] *On Compromise* (1877), 29.
[233] *BI*, 22, 85; compare *BI*, 117: 'different texts, in the bibliographical sense, embody different poems (in the aesthetic sense)'.

of interpretation which are learned and reapplied in recognizably similar circumstances, as the driver of a car acts on the assumption that a 'STOP—CHILDREN' sign always means 'stop to allow children to cross the road', and not sometimes, 'prevent children from crossing the road by running them over'. Applied to literary interpretation, the same criteria would not allow us truthfully to claim that we had read, for instance, *The Giaour*, or *The Beauty of Inflections*, if the meaning was in each case 'radically different'. Instead, we would need to say, 'I've read one of these *Giaours* before', or 'How many *Beauties of Inflection* have you read?' McGann's appeals to a poem's unique 'appearances' in print can therefore seem as suspicious of what underpins each appearance ('the event of it and the physique of it alike')[234] as is a philosopher like F. H. Bradley regarding the evasive 'identity of character' which would allow an observer to abstract *what* something is, in places and times other than those immediately present, from the fact *that* it is, here and now.[235]

At its bluntest, McGann's historical method 'takes for its subject the idea of "context" and tries to explain the special relevance of this for poetry',[236] but asks that a critic in search of relevant context begin by admitting into his or her account the state and situation of all editions of a poem, whether or not he or she is aware of their existence, and this seems a lot to ask. The occasional strangeness of McGann's claims is increased if we read them with a more rigorous model of contextual dependence in mind, such as J. L. Austin's distinction between the illocutionary and locutionary dimensions of a linguistic exchange, or 'the performance of an act *in* saying something as opposed to performance of an act *of* saying something':

for some years we have been realizing more and more clearly that the occasion of an utterance matters seriously, and that the words used are to some extent to be 'explained' by the 'context' in which they are 'designed' to be or have actually been spoken in a linguistic exchange.[237]

Although Austin's reservations ('to some extent'; the wary pincering of 'explained', 'context', and 'designed') are attentive to the equally serious matter of an utterance not being fully explained by its occasion, his discussion of 'illocutionary force' helps to clarify McGann's understanding of a work's successive 'appearances' in print, because it reminds us that the same locutionary act may have

---

[234] *BI*, 41.   [235] *Appearance and Reality* (1893), 62.   [236] *BI*, 31.
[237] *How to Do Things with Words*, ed. J. O. Urmson (1962), 100.

various illocutionary forces. Applied to McGann's historical method, the bibliographer's task would then be not only to establish which locutionary acts have been performed, but also to situate and individuate the illocutionary force present in each edition of a particular locutionary act. He would then be better able to distinguish what was meant by the poem on *this* occasion rather than on any other.

Austin's warning that the clues for establishing illocutionary force 'are over-rich: they lend themselves to equivocation and inadequate discrimination' is at least as true of written utterances as it is of speech. This is not simply because certain resources of speech 'are not readily reproducible in written language' (Austin instances tone of voice, cadence, emphasis, and so on), nor because the imaginative work of 'writing poetry' provides for the suspension of 'normal conditions of reference' (so that 'if I say "Go and catch a falling star", it may be quite clear what both the meaning and the force of my utterance is', although without ever resolving how seriously the utterance is intended).[238] In the first place, a theory which is impressed by the context-dependency of meaning also needs to consider the meaning-dependency of context, given that the circumstances of a piece of writing will tell us little unless we can recover what these circumstances meant to the person writing. Knowledge of the audience for whom a writer publishes, for example, will not always amount to full knowledge of the audience for whom he or she writes, either because of the unpredictable wants of the market-place ('The English Rubaiyat', notes Pound, 'was still-born | In those days'),[239] or because of a desire to write for posterity (as Wordsworth distinguished between the 'factitious influence' of a transitory reading 'Public' and the more lasting judgement of the 'People ... which the Deity inspires').[240] Furthermore, the readers of a text can establish historical contexts over and above, and sometimes contrary to, the facts of its publication. To know the context of a Shakespeare sonnet, say, might require historical knowledge of many kinds (conventions of anonymous publication, laws and attitudes concerning sex and sexuality, and so on), but much of what was present at the time of writing is not reproduced in that writing (bear-baiting, potatoes, and more), and few of these public contexts will be as significant as the sonnet's more immediate surroundings, because it forms one of a sequence, and

---

[238] Ibid., 76, 104.
[239] 'Yeux Glauques', *Selected Poems, 1908–1959* (1975), 101.
[240] 'Essay, Supplementary to the Preface', repr. in *Owen & Smyser*, III. 84.

these poems touch upon one another in the proximity of their concerns, in addition to being pressed upon by the contingent world of events in which they take their place. It is true that writers who move in the thick of human circumstance may use it to thicken their writing, as Shakespeare sets out to measure the idealisms of love against the abstract form of the sonnet. But it is also true that they may choose to dislocate or absolve their writing from this circumstance, as love sonnets are not always written by people in love. As Barbara Everett explains, for a poem to be of a more than documentary interest, something other than a sign of the times, it will need to contain features which escape the prejudices of its age: 'any good poet can focus for us [a] vivid sense of the life of his own time', but '[a] poet will, however, embody his time for us only if we read him as a poet and not as a crypto-historian—and give due attention to matters that can seem as contingent as Marvell's metres or Browning's syntax or Larkin's imagery.'[241] This reminds us that there are some literary contexts which are as self-evolved as any other feature of writing, but Everett's reference to Marvell's metres also valuably reminds us that there are some literary contexts which will be marked by their time without being restricted to it, given that a poem, like other forms of social speech, can show in its details one working out of general rules which could also be applied in other settings.

Geoffrey Hill's revival of the term 'contexture' provides a practical solution to the need for a critical approach which can discriminate between the circumstances *of* a piece of writing (the place and time of its production) and the circumstances *in* that writing (the other worlds which it conjures into itself).[242] Poised between 'context' and 'texture', 'contexture' is a suitably compound word to suggest 'the field of brokerage, negotiation, and compromise' which surrounds and informs the writer's voice.[243] Given that lines of print can calibrate these pressures without submitting to them, a critic who sets out to be true to the unique contexture of a poem will therefore need to be responsive to those places where the poet's private accents are braced or warped by the coercive force of the public language in and against which he or she moves, but also to those features of thought or style which differ from, or are simply indifferent to, prevailing currents of

[241] *Poets in their Time: Essays on English Poetry from Donne to Larkin* (1986), vii.
[242] See *The Enemy's Country: Words, Contexture, and other Circumstances of Language* (1991).
[243] Ibid., 11.

political or literary opinion. This is the type of criticism which Hill's final sonnet in the 'Funeral Music' sequence invites:

> Not as we are but as we must appear,
> Contractual ghosts of pity; not as we
> Desire life but as they would have us live,
> Set apart in timeless colloquy.
> So it is required; so we bear witness,
> Despite ourselves, to what is beyond us,
> Each distant sphere of humanity forever
> Poised, unanswerable.[244]

There are a number of ways in which a poet might draw out 'what is beyond us' for his or her readers: by describing concepts which are incomprehensible to us; by making us aware that our shared reactions to a piece of writing can dissolve some of the differences which usually divide us from one another; by reminding us that there are some questions, such as those concerning the future, which are likely to remain 'forever | Poised, unanswerable'. Because Hill's poem admits of these possibilities evenly, it invites us to measure them against each other, and against ourselves, in any attempt to think about 'what is beyond us'. That these possibilities are resolved into a line of printed verse further suggests that even dreams of the transcendent will always be rooted in the dreamer's more material world. But the fact that the poem itself is in some measure 'Set apart in timeless colloquy' means that it also acts as a figure of its readers' capacities to imagine an existence which is not limited by constraints of either time or understanding.

It is partly because the English language is, to borrow McGann's terms, so 'thick' and 'noisy', so richly saturated with both expressions of belief and empty echoes of those beliefs, that its speakers can bear witness to what is beyond them in these multiple and potentially self-contradictory ways. McGann provides one example of this process with his claim, in a chapter of *The Beauty of Inflections* entitled 'Shall These Bones Live?', that we 'raise up the past life of literary works in order to clarify or reveal the nature of our present experience'.[245] The analogy of reading and resurrection is not unusual; Proust, similarly, describes in the preface to his translation of *The Bible of Amiens* how Ruskin's prose succeeds in bringing to life a tiny crumbling figure carved on the face of Rouen cathedral: 'like the dead,

---

[244] *Collected Poems* (1985), 77.   [245] *BI*, 90–110. The source is Ezekiel 37: 3.

whom, not far away, the tympanum represents awakening at the sound of the archangel's trumpet ... the figurine is now alive again and has recovered its look, and the Judge has said, "You have survived; you will live".'[246] The use of the same Biblical metaphor in different accounts suggests that it is not only 'the past life of *literary works*' which can 'clarify or reveal the nature of our present experience'. It further suggests that present forms of understanding cannot readily be separated from the past life of the language in which this understanding is expressed: a form of historical self-consciousness which, like metaphor itself, involves unstable negotiations between sameness and difference, sharing and remaining distinct.

Compare some historical placings of the phrase 'mighty working'. Nicholas Rowe (1706):

ANTINOUS: The King return'd? So long conceal'd in *Ithaca*?
            Aethon the King? What words can speak my Wonder?
TELEMACHUS: Yes, my *Antinous*, 'tis most amazing,
            'Tis all the mighty Working of the Gods,
            Unreachable and dark to human Eyes.[247]

John Keats (1818):

And other spirits there are standing apart
    Upon the forehead of the age to come;
These, these will give the world another heart,
    And other pulses. Hear ye not the hum
Of mighty workings?——
    Listen awhile ye nations, and be dumb.[248]

Thomas Hardy (1917):

'According to the Mighty Working'

Peace, this hid riot, Change,
    This revel of quick-cued mumming,
    This never truly being,
    This evermore becoming,
    This spinner's wheel onfleeing
Outside perception's range.[249]

---

[246] *On Reading Ruskin*, 46.
[247] *Ulysses* (1706), IV. i. 1–5.
[248] Sonnet to Haydon (untitled), *KP*, 36; Haydon heard and replied: the ellipsis was his suggestion.
[249] *HP*, II. 336.

In each case, the writer's approach to questions of concealment and revelation reflects upon a single text, the Order for the Burial of the Dead:

... earth to earth, ashes to ashes, dust to dust, in sure and certain hope of the Resurrection to eternal life, through our Lord Jesus Christ; who shall change our vile body, that it may be like unto his glorious body, according to the mighty working, whereby he is able to subdue all things to himself.[250]

'Mighty working' is similarly successful in subduing change to itself, as the same fragment of the burial service is flexibly turned in different directions by its successive speakers, and so goes some way to justifying Keats's faith in the 'grand march of Intellect' which 'proves that a mighty providence subdues the mightiest Minds to the service of the time being'.[251] In all three contexts, 'might' suggests possibility as well as strength: Rowe anticipates possible objections to pagan heroics in the way he returns Telemachus to the newly-revived English stage, since he alludes to a Christian faith in resurrection which was necessarily dark to Homer's eyes; Keats takes a text which imagines sudden physical transformations, and adapts it to consider the progress of poetry in a mechanical age ('mighty workings' suggests the repetitive throb of heavy industry); Hardy retunes 'mighty working' to his life and times in order to produce a stereoscopic vision of the events it describes, given that the long-delayed end of the First World War is suspended between the poem's writing (1917) and its publication (1919). Each utterance of 'mighty working' could then be said to enact William Empson's understanding of the poet as a 'go-between':

Large societies need to include a variety of groups with different moral codes or scales of value, and it is part of the business of a writer to act as a go-between; so their differences are liable to become a conflict within himself.[252]

These differences often take time to reveal themselves, making the writer's response to his society not just immediate, as McGann often argues, but an act of timely mediation. As Rowe, Keats, and Hardy each responds to this fragment of the burial service, so their lines critically investigate how far the questions of change, continuity, and continuity-through-change which are asked of the individual believer

---

250 *The Book of Common Prayer*, 331.
251 *KL*, I. 282.
252 Introduction to *Coleridge's Verse: A Selection*, 39.

in resurrection will also be asked of his or her beliefs, as they are
stretched and trimmed to fit the variable demands of historical and
literary circumstance.

According to McGann, though, even the most adaptable of beliefs
will be staled by repetition; even the most forward-looking ideas will
come to sound backward:

> Poetry does not triumph over its times by arriving at a 'vision' or idea of the
> Truth, whether religious or otherwise; it triumphs when it reveals, once
> again, the local and human origin of all particular and historical events.
> Hence it is that poetry only maintains its life in later ages and cultures when it
> preserves its integrity, when it confronts those later ages and cultures with a
> human world which is important to other human worlds precisely because it
> is different, local, limited.... [Christina G. Rossetti's] poetry contains a
> forcible and persistent reminder that the themes of Christian poetry—even
> the greatest of such themes, like those of guilt and redemption, of resurrec-
> tion, of incarnation—are time- and place-specific, that they have had a
> beginning, and a middle, and that they will finally have an end as well.[253]

McGann's concern for the preservation of 'integrity' is puzzling. For
example, it is hard to see how a critic could remain imaginatively in
tune with Christina G. Rossetti's poetry, and at the same time assume
that it reveals 'the local and human origin of all particular and
historical events', when Rossetti herself understands resurrection to
be a theme which 'will finally have an end' in an event which occupies
such a 'forcible and persistent' place in her poetic meditations, and in
the thoughts of the person writing them, precisely because its origin is
not local or human.[254] Nor does the assumption that poetry attracts
its readers to a world which is 'different, local, limited' accurately
reflect the way many poems are composed and understood, as Rowe,
Keats, and Hardy each incorporates a common rhythmic shape into
his work (the resolute trochaics of 'mighty working(s)') and, by abstracting his writing into a time which is greater than that of any one
writer, briefly entertains the idea that, as D. G. Rossetti remarked of
The House of Life, 'The "life" involved is neither my life nor your
life, but life representative.'[255] This is not a possibility which
McGann's uncompromising claims for specificity can admit; his
historical method must therefore discount the beliefs held by some

---

[253] *BI*, 251–2.
[254] See Jan Marsh, *Christina Rossetti: A Literary Biography* (1994), 57.
[255] William M. Rossetti (ed.), *The Works of Dante Gabriel Rossetti* (1911), 638.

historical individuals, such as those Victorians who were convinced of the limitations of the particular.

To this extent, Wittgenstein's assessment of Frazer's *The Golden Bough* also largely holds true for the form of critical anthropology practised by McGann: 'What narrowness of life we find in Frazer! And as a result: how impossible for him to understand a different way of life from the English one of his time!'[256] It is especially surprising that McGann should stress 'the survival of that which is specific and therefore obsolete',[257] given how often he arrives at the same conclusions about different authors, thereby allowing his critical method a satisfying consistency of approach which is denied the 'different, local, limited' objects of its enquiry. And yet, this occasional sense of strain in his writing is perfectly in tune with a second current of Victorian thinking, which concerns itself with precisely these questions of how far old ideas of the future should be preserved or ignored; how far poetry should retain an 'Ideal' status and style;[258] how far individuals were capable of resisting what Carlyle referred to, with the raised eyebrows of his quotation marks, as 'the "force of circumstance"',[259] and so whether their writing could engage with those compromises which the world forced upon them without itself being compromised. In particular, this current of thinking is concerned with how far development—whether of a species, an individual, or a set of cultural beliefs—could be marked as much by resurgence and renewal as by the 'different, local, limited'. Put another way, although McGann claims that his 'historical method' develops nineteenth-century principles,[260] the relativism of his method also exposes how many of these principles were not consistent in themselves or their application, but were instead the source of diverse and fertile disagreement over what we should read, how we should read it, and why we should bother.

Even McGann's belief that a study of religious writing will invariably prove the 'different, local, limited' objects of all human enquiry has its own echoes in Victorian criticism. In 1865, J. S. Mill described Comte's ideas of social development with the true zeal of the disillusioned convert:

---

[256] *Remarks on Frazer's 'Golden Bough'*, trans. A. C. Miles, ed. Rush Rhees (1979), 5e.
[257] *BI*, 252.
[258] Aubrey de Vere (1849); see Isobel Armstrong, *Victorian Scrutinies* (1972), 13.
[259] 'Signs of the Times' (1829), repr. in *Critical and Miscellaneous Essays* (5 vols., 1838), II. 75.
[260] See *CMTC*, 117.

After the ample evidence he has brought forward of the slow growth of the sciences ... it yet appears as if, to his mind the mere institution of a positive science of sociology were tantamount to its completion; as if all the diversities of opinion on the subject, which set mankind at variance, were solely owing to its having been studied in the theological or the metaphysical manner, and as if when the positive method which has raised up real sciences on other subjects of knowledge, is similarly employed on this, divergence would at once cease, and the entire body of positive social inquirers would exhibit as much agreement in their doctrines as those who cultivate any of the sciences of inorganic life. Happy would be the prospects of mankind if this were so.[261]

This is magnificently arch, carefully suspended between a patient reproduction and an irritated parody of Comte's views; Mill's split tone is then resolved into the studiedly neutral 'Happy would be the prospects of mankind if this were so', in which the 'diversities of opinion' he has just described can suddenly be heard squabbling for the reader's attention, and reminding us that Comte's confident anticipation of social agreement sidesteps the more rapid and temporary sequences of belief to which many individuals are subject. Even our doubts can come to seem doubtful. However, not all Mill's contemporaries were convinced that 'diversities of opinion' would necessarily 'set mankind at variance', particularly if 'mankind' was understood in a more generous sense than merely 'Victorian people'. In 1857, Arnold reflected on the 'modern':

Horace warms himself before the transient fire of human animation and human pleasure while he can, and is only serious when he reflects that the fire must soon go out:—

> 'Damna tamen celeres reparant cœlestia lunæ:
> Nos, ubi decidimus—'

'For nature there is renovation, but for man there is none!'—it is exquisite, but it is not interpretive and fortifying.[262]

Nor is Horace 'modern', at least as Arnold understands the term, because in his eyes one mark of the modern is an ability to fortify and be fortified by those earlier ages which achieved modernity in their turn. This is tellingly at odds with Pater's version of the 'modern spirit', which restricts the 'transient fire' of public values (fortified, in Arnold's account, with echoes of the Virgilian tradition that Roman

---

[261] *Auguste Comte and Positivism* (1865, repr. 1968), 121.
[262] 'On the Modern Element in Literature' (1857), repr. in *Super*, I. 36.

civilization rose up, phoenix-like, from the flames of Troy) to the 'hard, gem-like flame' of private impressions which are 'unstable, flickering, inconsistent'.[263] Arnold is not the only Victorian writer who sensed that modernity has its own history. When Carlyle heard a secret voice urging him to yoke his writing to the present ('Thou, behold, thou too art of it—thou must be of it!'),[264] one reasonable question might have been 'What is "it"?' at a time of so much revivalism in behaviour and speech: the Catholic revival yielding 'neo-Catholic' (1842, the first such 'neo-' neologism cited by the *OED*); the Hellenic revival, 'neo-Hellenic' (1869); the Gothic revival, 'neo-Gothic' (1892); and so on.[265] So much of what Christina G. Rossetti's contemporaries talked about, and talked with, draws on the insistences of the past, that 'The action or fact of rising again from sleep, decay, disuse; revival; restoration' (*OED* 3, 'resurrection') often provides Victorian speakers with both a 'theme' and the means of its expression. Arnold's remarks concentrate this active interest in what passes with time, and what remains, because they include a translation, and so go some way to supporting his idea that civilization should be understood not as an ongoing competition between different cultures, a set of historical squabbles, but rather as the sum of their responses to one another. Indeed, McGann's notion of the 'different, local, limited' nature of literary expression is challenged with particular force by a translation's capacity to break from one spatio-temporal context into another, thereby bearing witness to the encounter of two geographically distinct individuals, and at the same time providing what Boris Pasternak has described as 'a medium for the age-old communion of cultures and peoples': passages of writing as passageways between readers.[266]

Consider T. S. Eliot's skill in bringing together some different forms of human and literary resurrection:

> I am the Resurrection and the Life
> I am the things that stay, and those that flow ... [267]

'I am the Resurrection and the Life' is John 11: 25, but Valerie Eliot's note to this unpublished fragment cites another scripture: 'This little

---

[263] Conclusion to *Studies in the History of the Renaissance* (1873), 248.

[264] Quoted in Buckley, *The Triumph of Time* (1967), 124.

[265] All examples drawn from *OED*; compare 'neo-Christian' (1882), 'neo-Darwinian' (1895), 'neo-Kantian' (1881), 'neo-medieval' (1878), and others.

[266] *Pasternak on Art and Creativity*, ed. Angela Livingstone (1985), 187.

[267] Valerie Eliot (ed.), *The Waste Land, A Facsimile and Transcript* (1971), 111.

poem was influenced by *The Bhagavad-Gita*.'[268] Eliot's lines have a plural religious context, part-Christian and part-Hindu, and the joining of these two translations also combines two distinct forms of the afterlife. A belief in the resurrection of the body or in the transmigration of the soul each assumes that there are unchanging features of the self ('things that stay') which endure through changes of form ('things that flow'), and Eliot assumes both beliefs into 'the things that stay, and those that flow' of translation:[269] resurrection by the revival of a Biblical fragment in this new poetic frame, unchanged through change, and transmigration by the more diffuse inspiration of *The Bhagavad-Gita* working through his lines. Committed to neither view, but shifting between both, Eliot's verse provides a model of religious tolerance. By entertaining the alternative convictions of his readers, Eliot suggests that these convictions could be as multiple and contrary as the sources of a poem; by drawing attention to the shadowy transformation of one source into another, he raises the possibility that religious beliefs can be as unfixed and permeable as the people who hold them.

This need to accommodate different points of view into a single stretch of writing has been responded to by many authors, and in relation to many subjects, as when Empson attempts to reconcile Marvell's critics to the intellectual tussles which his verse successfully contains: 'The poetry does say ... that the human creature in the world is inherently puzzled or betrayed; but a reader of the poetry is granted, for the time, a more lofty viewpoint.'[270] However, a decision like Eliot's, to turn lines of print into lines of ethical perspective, is likely to be especially true of poetic approaches to the afterlife. This is not only because the same individuals often have differing views concerning the prospect of personal immortality, as Tennyson wistfully told Allingham that although he believed he would rise up after death to everlasting life, 'Sometimes I have doubts, of a morning'.[271] Even if the 'lofty viewpoint' of a poem rehearses an attitude which would be expected of less timebound beings, such as the dead, to respond to the puzzled questions which are left unresolved in its lines is also to recognize that ideas of survival themselves alter unpredictably over time; the future is always framed in a provisional tense.

[268] Valerie Eliot (ed.), *The Waste Land*, 130.
[269] Daniel Neill suggested this to me.
[270] 'Other People's Views', repr. in *Using Biography* (1984), 39.
[271] (3 April 1867), *Allingham*, 151.

As I pointed out earlier in this chapter, the act of writing is likely to concentrate a poet's attention on this problem, because capturing a voice on the page entails throwing that voice into the future; by fixing the poet's words, a poem provides them with a means of transport in time and space. A poet might then use the resources of verse to investigate the afterlife in a number of ways. Taking on someone else's words can allow the poet to question how far a literary afterlife is as socially dependent as the human life from which it emerges, and so whether it can be prepared for in advance by writing in such a way that a poem's appeal will live up to the sheer persistence of its printed form. Alternatively, an argument for personal immortality might be expressed with an intellectual and stylistic coherence which supported its claims for the integrity of the person writing. Or, borrowing the characteristic vocal inflections and stylistic tics of an earlier writer would allow two poems to be lined up against one another in order to test and confirm a view of the future they share. And so on.

This is clearer if we consider another of Eliot's translations. 'One of the reasons for learning at least one language well', Eliot observed, 'is that we acquire a kind of supplementary personality; one of the reasons for not acquiring a new language *instead* of our own is that most of us do not want to become a different person.'[272] I have already argued that the threat or promise of becoming a different person is one which influence raises with particular force, and which individual writers have responded to with varying degrees of enthusiasm or dread. It is possible to speculate on the reasons why Eliot may have been especially sensitive to becoming a different person, ranging from the dislocated existence in the United States, France, and England which so permanently marked his voice,[273] to the thesis on F. H. Bradley which so regularly haunts his verse. Perhaps this is why Eliot was so attracted to the idea and practice of translation, because the translator is committed to entertaining a supplementary personality while resisting the prospect of becoming a different person. In his essay on Dante, for example, Eliot argues that 'it is the allegory which makes it possible for the reader who is not even a good Italian scholar to enjoy Dante. Speech varies, but our eyes are all the same.'[274] In one sense, this ignores the different shapes, as well

---

[272] 'The Social Function of Poetry', *On Poetry and Poets* (1957), 19.
[273] See Christopher Ricks, *T. S. Eliot and Prejudice* (1994), 154–203.
[274] 'Dante' (1929), repr. in *Selected Prose*, 210.

as the different sounds, which Italian and English make on the page; *terza rima*, in particular, has a flow and persistence which no English form can exactly reproduce. But Eliot's remark is perfectly in accord with his willingness to use English forms of verse to train his reader's eyes in the same direction as Dante's:

> Unreal City,
> Under the brown fog of a winter dawn,
> A crowd flowed over London Bridge, so many,
> I had not thought death had undone so many.[275]

> si lunga tratta
> di gente, ch'io non averei creduto
> che morte tanta n'avesse disfatta[276]

'So many' is not a rhyme for 'so many' as 'tratta' is for 'disfatta', and so fails to express as deftly as Dante's Italian the union of sameness and difference which someone lost in a crowd might experience. Similarly, whereas Dante's lines flow onward past the line break ('si lunga tratta | di gente'—'such a long stream of people'), Eliot's choppily circle back on themselves, as if warning that the fine distinctions of language must break down when confronted with the undifferentiated mass of the dead; stuck in the rut of 'so many', his words appear reluctant to do what the crowd cannot but do: move on. But as 'Under' flows into 'London', and both words combine to become 'undone', Eliot's internal rhymes succeed in discovering, within the forms available to him, a parallel version of Dante's description of crowds being drawn together and split apart, and so prove that the lines of a poem can also rehearse the forms of human contact they describe. To read these accounts side by side, therefore, is to recognize how unsatisfactory it would be to describe the fluid mingling of their verse as Dante's 'influence' on Eliot, or even (following the model of 'Tradition and the Individual Talent') Eliot's 'influence' on Dante. It is, rather, a confluence, as Dante and Eliot move towards one another on the page, but keep in mind, and retain in their verse, the prospect of a common goal towards which each is moving independently. After all, as both Dante and Eliot knew, there may be some forms of translation which are still beyond even the very best poets.

---

[275] *The Waste Land* (1922), repr. in *The Complete Poems and Plays of T. S. Eliot*, 62.
[276] *Inferno*, II. 55–7; the allusion is discussed by Ricks in *T. S. Eliot and Prejudice*, 137–41.

'...A DISTANT RINGING HUM ...'

Jerome McGann is impatient with critics who refuse to pay close attention to 'the specific and concrete forms' in which literary works are produced and read:

> Human beings are not angels. Part of what it means to be human is to have a body, to occupy physical space, and to move in real time. In the same way the products of literature, which are in all cases human products, are not disembodied processes.[277]

This is valuable as a reminder that literary works are written by real people before they are abstracted into genres and discourses, and persuasive as a warning that, given the material conditions of publication, proper study of 'the words on the page' should involve close inspection of the page as well as the words. But if 'the products of literature ... are in all cases human products', any account of literary composition which is to be true to the writer's understanding of these processes will also need to recognize that there are some humans for whom the prospect of translating their handwriting into print will not be altogether a cause for celebration. Coventry Patmore, for instance, whose revisions to *Angel in the House* answered his wife's death by gradually removing the presence of one whom 'every page is more or less indebted for such truth and grace as it may have',[278] as he responded to the latent elegiac charge of his title by recognizing that becoming an angel need not be only a *domestic* ideal. Or Kafka, who once complained 'I feel so loose inside my skin that it would only have needed someone to give it a shake for me to lose myself completely.'[279] Ashamed of taking up so much space even on paper, and convinced that his narrative style was like his body in being 'too long for its weakness',[280] Kafka's last work, a short story about a singing mouse, asked a question which reflected a lifelong ambivalence over how little he was as a writer: 'Is it her singing that charms us or isn't it rather the solemn stillness that surrounds the feeble little voice?'[281] It might be argued that Kafka's fascinated loathing of his

---

[277] *BI*, 95.

[278] Prologue to *The Betrothed* (1854), 7.

[279] See Ronald Hayman, *K.: A Biography of Kafka* (1981), 158.

[280] Ibid., 122; compare Gabriel Josipovici on Kafka's interest in the idea that 'Writing reinforces our belief in our own immortality by helping us to avoid the acceptance of our bodies', *Writing and the Body* (1982), 111.

[281] 'Josefine die Sängerin oder Das Völk der Mäuse' ('Josefine the Singer or the Mouse People', 1924), quoted in Hayman, 298.

body and its visible after-effects in print is too strange to trouble us as fully as it troubled him and his writing. It might better be argued that this very strangeness should remind us of how often the physical space of the page has been employed to reflect on the possibility that although, as McGann argues, 'Part of what it means to be human is to have a body', another part of what it means to be human will be to not have a body, or at least not the body to which we have become accustomed; the contact of pen on paper is an embodied process which can be used to investigate processes of disembodiment.

Writing 'On the Feeling of Immortality in Youth', Hazlitt sadly explained that people do not die all at once, but instead slowly moulder away over the course of their adult lives: 'faculty after faculty, attachment after attachment, we are torn from ourselves piece-meal while living'. Increasingly ignored in our passage through the world, the final erosion of our physical space ('trampled to dust, or dispersed into air') merely confirms the gradual diminishment of the room we take up in other people's minds. Like those mythical beings who are granted immortal life but not eternal youth (Tennyson's Tithonus, say, or Swift's Struldbruggs in *Gulliver's Travels*), all of us are doomed to 'outlive ourselves, and dwindle into nothing'.[282] But even the prospect of dwindling into nothing can animate a piece of writing sufficiently for the prospect of 'outliving ourselves' to be what the writing itself abidingly confirms. Charles Cowden Clarke records how Keats responded to Shakespeare's moving description of Post-humus's departure:

Once, when reading the *Cymbeline* aloud, I saw his eyes fill with tears, and for some moments he was unable to proceed, when he came to the departure of Posthumus, and Imogen's saying she would have watched him

> till the diminution
> Of space had pointed him sharp as my needle;
> Nay, followed him till he had *melted from*
> *The smallness of a gnat to air;* and then
> Have *turn'd mine eye and wept.*[283]

Reading through his poems in 1817, Keats complained that, compared to the monumental achievement of Shakespeare, what he had created so far was a mere 'Pin's Point'.[284] And yet, the mourning

---

[282] *Howe*, XVII. 198–9.
[283] 'Recollections of Keats' (1861), repr. in *KCH*, 389 (Cowden Clarke's emphases).
[284] Keats to Leigh Hunt (10 May 1817), *KL*, I. 139.

cadences of 'To Autumn' would show how successfully Keats followed Shakespeare's example, as he attempts to reconcile human expressions of loss to the indifferent sounds of the natural world. Autumn's music has a dying fall:

> Then in a wailful quire the small gnats mourn
> Among the river sallows, borne aloft
> Or sinking as the light wind lives and dies;[285]

Keats advised Shelley to ' "load every rift" of your subject with ore'.[286] Writing 'To Autumn', he follows his own advice by richly investing his lines with 'or', as 'mourn', 'borne', and 'Or' form a path of sounds to echo the faintly heard passage of gnats through the air. The rhythms of this description then show Keats's skill in exercising his 'poetical Character' (a character equally willing to enter into the life of 'high or low ... mean or elevated') in order to dwell on creatures larger than a gnat,[287] because 'or' is one of the 'pure' vowel sounds, supposedly uncorrupted by the later life of the English language, which Bailey tells us Keats identified as the 'great charm' of Chatterton's poetry.[288] By joining the 'music' of Autumn to Chatterton's 'native music',[289] 'To Autumn' therefore uses the gnats' rise and fall in space to reflect, with pity and self-pity, on how short and insignificant the life of a poet's songs could be. But although Keats himself would later be lamented as a writer who was 'suffered to rise and pass away almost without a notice', and Shelley's Preface to *Adonais* would swat *Endymion* as a droning 'gnat' of a poem,[290] his success in drawing out Chatterton's voice, turning 'To Autumn' into a 'brotherhood in song',[291] would prove that departing bodies can be preserved in the suspended animation of print far longer than they can in the human eye; even a pin's point can make a lasting impression.

Keats was attracted to the idea that the printed page, by extending the writer's voice at one remove from his or her body, provided a way

---

285 *KP*, 653–4.
286 Keats to Shelley (16 August 1820), *KL*, II. 323.
287 Keats to Woodhouse (27 October 1818), *KL*, I. 387.
288 'Methinks I now hear him recite, or rather *chant*, in his peculiar manner, the following stanza of the "Roundelay sung by the minstrels of Ella": "*Come with acorn cup & thorn*" ... The first line to his ear possessed the great charm', *KC*, II. 277.
289 For Keats's remarks on Chatterton's 'native music', see *KL*, II. 212.
290 Obituary notice, signed 'L', in *London Magazine* (April 1821), repr. in *KCH*, 241; Shelley's comment is repr. in *KCH*, 126.
291 'To George Felton Matthew', l. 2, speaking of Chatterton (*KP*, 14).

of imagining an afterlife in which communication would be freed from the hesitations and misunderstandings of human speech and, perhaps of more significance for one who chose to explain this idea in a letter to George and Georgiana Keats in America, freed too from the inevitable time-lag of writing. As he explains:

... sometimes I feel a immense separation, and sometimes, as at present, a direct communication of spirit with you. That will be one of the grandeurs of immortality—there will be no space and consequently the only commerce between spirits will be by their intelligence of each other—when they will completely understand each other—[292]

It is a common hope, even if Keats is characteristically forward-thinking in wanting to rehearse what it might feel and sound like, with his appeal to a 'you' which does not distinguish between the two intended readers of his letter. In the years that followed Keats's expression of this hope, traditional models of immortality continued to exercise the minds and mouths of Victorian readers. At the same time, the arguments which came to surround these models produced the more awkward situation of speakers who set out to explain their faith in the existence of an afterlife in which they and their antagonists would 'completely understand each other', but were regularly forced by the intellectual squabbles and feuds provoked by their explanations into the recognition that such an afterlife seemed as much an alternative to this life as an extension of it. Victorian writers were especially drawn to the competing claims of theologians, for whom the 'mighty working' of resurrection would change each 'vile body' into a 'glorious body', and Positivists, who retorted that the only immortality possible would be a dispersal of the individual consciousness through later lives. The range of literary responses they produced then reveal the difficulties any group of individuals might experience in trying to agree on answers to these questions, or even in trying to agree on what the questions should be. The same responses also reveal how often the afterlife concentrated the attention of Victorian writers on the experience of 'moving in real time', and how fully their writing supported attempts to think about moving beyond time altogether.

[292] Journal-letter to George and Georgiana Keats (16 December 1818–4 January 1819), *KL*, II. 5; compare *Endymion*, I. 777–81, on the 'clear religion of heaven': 'Wherein lies happiness? In that which becks | Our ready minds to fellowship divine, | A fellowship with essence, till we shine | Full alchemized, and free of space', *KP*, 154.

Tennyson concludes *In Memoriam* by looking forward to eternal companionship with

> That friend of mine who lives in God,

> That God, which ever lives and loves,
> One God, one law, one element,
> And one far-off divine event,
> To which the whole creation moves.[293]

Literary survival comes together with hope for a personal afterlife in Tennyson's recollection of Arthur Hallam's own lines on 'The Love, | Toward which all being solemnly doth move',[294] themselves recalling Dante's 'l'amor che move il sole e l'altre stelle'[295]. Dante, Hallam, and Tennyson: three lasting intelligences occupying the same space; literary allusion as a model of immortality. In listening for his friend's voice across years of possible interference, Tennyson demonstrates how seriously some writers would have taken Keats's casual remark that reading offers 'a nice way of filling up intervals'.[296] He also offers a model of good critical practice, because as Dominick LaCapra points out, study of literary history requires similarly patient ears:

Even if one accepts the metaphor that presents interpretation as the 'voice' of the historical reader in the 'dialogue' with the past, it must be actively recognised that the past has its own 'voices' that must be respected, especially when they resist or qualify the interpretations we would like to place on them. A text is a network of resistances, and a dialogue is a two-way affair; a good reader is also an attentive and patient listener.[297]

If we are to listen to Victorian writers in the way they listened in upon one another, we first need to attune our ears to what Lionel Trilling once described as the 'huge, unrecorded hum of implication' which surrounds and situates a writer's distinct voice.[298] It is a need to which Trilling's own remark responds. In *Bleak House*, as the moon gazes steadfastly down upon the tangled lives of Dickens's characters, 'a solitude and stillness seem to proceed from her, that influence even crowded places full of life'. It is not only cities in Dickens

---

293 *IM*, Epilogue, *TP*, III. 458–9.
294 'On the Picture of the Three Fates', *Motter*, 3.
295 *Paradiso*, XXXIII. 145.
296 Keats to the George Keatses (24 September 1819), *KL*, II. 212.
297 *Rethinking Intellectual History* (1983), 64.
298 Quoted in Ronald Primeau (ed.), *Influx: Essays on Literary Influence*, 42.

which are crowded. The air too is full of life, as the sounds of London drift into the sky until 'every noise is merged, this moonlight night, into a distant ringing hum, as if the city were a vast glass, vibrating ... '.[299]

[299] *Bleak House,* ch. 48.

2   *Voices in the Air*

'... A DISTINCT SPECK ...'

Towards the end of *Great Expectations*, as Magwitch is sentenced to death, he is described by Pip in a way that leaves his eventual fate still hanging in the air:

The sun was striking in at the great windows of the court, through the glittering drops of rain upon the glass, and it made a broad shaft of light between the two-and-thirty and the Judge, linking both together, and perhaps reminding some among the audience, how both were passing on, with absolute equality, to the greater Judgment that knoweth all things and cannot err. Rising for a moment, a distinct speck of face in this way of light, the prisoner said, 'My Lord, I have received my sentence of Death from the Almighty, but I bow to yours,' and sat down again. There was some hushing, and the Judge went on with what he had to say to the rest (ch. 57).

Dickens's reference to 'the greater Judgment that knoweth all things and cannot err' might usefully encourage feelings of modesty in professions other than the judiciary. Literary critics, for example, are not always distinguished by their humility; like the judge in Dickens's courtroom, they tend to be better at pronouncing verdicts upon what comes before them than they are at recognizing the necessary and desirable limitations of their sentences. This is perhaps surprising, given how easily a literary work absorbs supplementary critical versions of itself, and how rarely it is completed or replaced by them. Since our human eyes do not look at the world or its creations from a position of timeless authority, *sub specie aeternitatis*, even the most complete and up-to-date interpretation is destined to be superseded; in this sense, expectation is both the subject of Pip's narrative and the very mode of its existence. But the same would be true of any literary work, because it is in the nature of a writer to be a type of escape-artist, for whom no contextual bonds are strong enough to prevent his or her work from wriggling free and asserting its independence. As Roland Barthes puts it, the work is '*something else* than its history, the sum of its sources, influences, or models'; in any attempt to pin it down, 'the work *escapes*'.[1]

Not all critics have concluded from this that the protracted evasiveness of a literary work should be met with a corresponding critical restraint. I have already discussed Jerome McGann's generous attempts to redeem the reputation of those textual scholars (occasionally sneered at as 'dryasdust' pedants by colleagues who move in the more exciting, or excitable, world of literary theory) who have asserted that a literary work can be critically examined as, if not reduced to, 'the sum of its sources, influences, or models'.[2] His method has a confidence and sweep that is often repeated in critical attempts to retrieve a writer's entire literary 'environment',[3] such as the efforts of Browning scholars Philip Kelley and Betty A. Coley to track down 'any article which might have influenced Robert or Elizabeth Browning; any work which they created, possessed or presented; and items which indicated the breadth of their influence on others.'[4] It would be an extraordinary catalogue indeed that could achieve this aim, not least because one defining feature of a literary achievement like the Brownings' is that the influence of their books is still underway, so that 'the breadth of their influence on others' could not be indicated within the fixed dimensions of another book, no matter how many pages it had. However, even the smaller dimensions of this passage from *Great Expectations* should give similar pause to a critic who decided to reconstruct its original 'environment', because on closer inspection it too appears to be full of passages: the corridors, detours, and blind alleys of Dickens's imaginative wandering.

Consider the cultural bearings of Pip's 'distinct speck', which forms the smallest of the memories that interrupt his confession, but thereby shows up what would otherwise remain invisible in the events which this confession struggles to retrieve and understand, like dust caught in a shaft of sunlight.[5] Many possible environments could be reconstituted for this literary mite, from the proximate histories of literature, science, and language. For instance, Dickens claimed that 'the man

---

[1] *On Racine,* trans. Richard Howard (1983), 154–5.

[2] For McGann's remarks on 'dryasdust' scholarship, see *BI*, 90–110.

[3] See *BI*, 85.

[4] *The Browning Collections: A Reconstruction with Other Memorabilia* (1984), ix.

[5] Kate Flint provides a wide range of examples of the Victorian interest in dust in *The Victorians and the Visual Imagination* (2000), 40–63.

who had most influenced him was Thomas Carlyle',[6] but he often makes Carlyle's coinage 'environment' ('the sum-total of influences which modify and determine the development of life or character', 1827) a more personal affair.[7] We are environed by other people, Dickens notes, but we also physically environ them, as we breathe in floating particles from those most intimate of Victorian dust-heaps: the dead.[8] Writing in *The Uncommercial Traveller* about his visits to churches, Dickens observes with interest how the congregation coughs and sneezes as 'a strong kind of invisible snuff' drifts up from the pulverized corpses stored in the vaults (ch. 9), while in *Oliver Twist*, Mr Sowerberry has as a snuff-box 'an ingenious little model of a patent coffin' (ch. 4). This enthusiasm for dirty air as both substantial and immaterial, thick with floating relics of the past and hints of the future, coincides with experiments which were to prove that our absorption of the dead need not be deliberate. In 1871, Tyndall noted that half the dust caked onto the walls of the British Museum was inorganic matter, and concluded that 'the visible particles floating in the air of London rooms' were more likely to be the dry flakes of skin which we shed in our movements through the world. Even before we die, we create clouds of dust. Once these particles have been 'winnowed from the heavier matter' by air currents, Tyndall suggests, they will be concentrated in or diffused by other bodies, as they seep into the lungs of the living or are propelled by them into the atmosphere:[9]

However ordinary daylight may permit it to disguise itself, a sufficiently powerful beam causes dust suspended in air to appear almost as a semi-solid. Nobody could, in the first instance, without repugnance, place the mouth at the illuminated focus of the electric beam and inhale the thickly-massed dust revealed there. Nor is the repugnance abolished by the reflection that, although we do not see the floating particles, we are taking them into our lungs every hour and minute of our lives.[10]

As if the thought of breathing in bits of other people's dandruff and dried scabs were not unpleasant enough, Tyndall notes that Kircher's

---

[6] Harry Dickens, quoted in Michael Goldberg, *Carlyle and Dickens* (1972), 2.

[7] On 'environment' in Carlyle, see John D. Rosenberg, *Carlyle and the Burden of History* (1985), 35–7.

[8] Jonathan Arac, *Commissioned Spirits* (1979), 97, discusses the introduction into sociology and fiction of the biological concept of 'milieu', whereby 'microcosmic relations of part and whole were once again intellectually respectable in theories of "atmospheric influence".'

[9] John Tyndall, 'On Dust and Disease', repr. in *Fragments of Science for Unscientific People* (1871), I. 293.

[10] Ibid., 300.

and Linnaeus's work in epidemiology had proved that 'epidemic diseases are due to germs which float in the atmosphere, enter the body, and produce disturbance by the development within the body of parasitic life'.[11] This too stirs Pip's speck at the level of metaphor, because describing someone as a 'speck' successfully brings to our attention how little we tend to regard most of the people who surround us in the world, as thickly massed and invisible as dust in the air. Like particles of dust, these germs might have been intercepted before they took possession of our lungs, if only a strong enough light had illuminated them in time. Similarly, Pip might have noticed Magwitch's disturbing influence on his life before it took hold, if only a clear-sighted vision of his true place in the world had not already been blocked by the small but stubborn obstacle of his own pride. As George Eliot observes in *Middlemarch*: 'Will not a tiny speck very close to our vision blot out the glory of the world, and leave only a margin by which we see the blot? I know no speck so troublesome as self.'[12] The specks which represent our flawed perception of other people can be less troublesome. Victorian medical opinion, wary of a possible 'contagion' of insanity, warns darkly and often of the vigilance required to regulate our contact with other minds: 'the smallest speck on the edge of the horizon ought to be regarded with awe, as portending, if not speedily dispersed, an universal and impenetrable gloom'.[13] And yet, the year before Pip's chastened return to Joe's forge, the Uncommercial Traveller had been encouraged to retrace the trajectory of his life, after bumping into a childhood friend who 'illuminated Dullborough with the rays of interest that I wanted and should otherwise have missed in it, and linked its present to its past, with a highly agreeable chain' (ch. 12). His name was Joe Specks.

Pip's 'speck' is carried further into fields of ethical enquiry by the cultural freight and momentum of the word itself, as it accommodates a new slang sense of 'damaged goods'.[14] In 'Merlin and Vivien' (1859), Tennyson refers to the corrupting 'little pitted speck in garnered fruit': the spreading rottenness that perverts healthy development after suffering an impact from some foreign body.[15] As with

---

[11] John Tyndall, 'On Dust and Disease', repr. in *Fragments of Science for Unscientific People* (1871), I. 302.
[12] *Middlemarch* (1871–2), ch. 42.
[13] John Reid, *Essays on Hypochondriasis* (1821), 316.
[14] *OED* 3b (from 1851).
[15] *TP*, III. 406.

fruit, we might think, so with Pip, still feeling the convict's dirty touch. (The last of Dickens's memoranda for *Great Expectations* reads: 'The one good thing he did in his prosperity, the only thing that endures and bears good fruit',[16] because it is by becoming Herbert Pocket's anonymous overseas benefactor that Pip sets out to atone for the events which blighted his own youth.) His use of 'speck' could then be understood to reproduce broader period concerns at the way social life develops through the inheritance of words as well as money. For as a number of Victorian commentators pointed out, 'influence' is unlikely to be experienced as the free flow of ideas from one person to another once these ideas have been translated into a living language, given that the language in which social beings appeal to, describe, or understand one another will usually be experienced not as a single and constant force, but instead as a much looser accumulation of vocabularies and practices that mingle and quarrel in promiscuous disarray.

Victorian philology sets itself to chart the propagation and impact of individual words and speakers upon one another. In several accounts, it is an uneasily short step from noticing the multiple inflections which a shared language inevitably suffers, to wondering whether the descent of language will manifest itself as a moral decline. In R. C. Trench's Hericlitean terms:

it is the essential character of a living language to be in flux and flow, to be gaining and losing, the words which constitute it as little continuing exactly the same, or in the same relations to one another, as do the atoms which at any one moment make up our bodies.

To understand what words mean, we must first know where they have been: 'the date and place of their birth, the successive stages of their subsequent history, the company which they have kept, all the road which they have travelled, and what has brought them to the point at which now we find them'.[17] Given how well-travelled a language could be, our responsibilities as speakers will therefore include standing by our words, recognizing that we are standing by other people's words, and taking account of the fact that words, like people, rarely stand still. For Trench, it is the speaker's lot to give inherited words his or her individual 'stamp'; 'language is ever needing to be recalled, minted and issued anew, cast into novel forms':[18]

---

[16] Harry Stone (ed.), *Dickens' Working Notes for his Novels* (1987), 323.

[17] *English: Past and Present* (1855), 75, 159–60.

[18] *Notes on the Parables of Our Lord* (1840), 25.

How great a part of true wisdom it is to be able to separate between things seemingly, but not really alike ... this power of exactly saying what we mean, and neither more or less than we mean ... has a moral meaning as well. It is nearly allied to morality, inasmuch as it is nearly connected with truthfulness.[19]

The distinctions made by Trench's vocabulary and syntax have a powerful ring of confidence about them, but he could be trusting too far in the unambiguous ability of a printed argument 'to separate between things seemingly, but not really alike'. Given the unpredictable ways in which a piece of writing is likely to be 'issued anew' from the mouths of particular speakers and speech communities, even the assertive stance of Trench's prose cannot altogether discount the possibility that 'nearly allied' and 'nearly connected', coming from a more jaded observer, might be reduced from proud intimacy to apologetic near-miss.

A similar friction generates and structures *Great Expectations*, as Pip's mysterious distinction between the circulation of 'clean' and 'dirty' money is echoed in the strained narrative links through which he attempts to justify a persistent feeling that everything joining him to other people is contaminated, diseased, forged. As reported, even his first exercise in writing broods over mistakes other than spelling mistakes:

MI DEER JO i OPE U R KRWITE WELL i OPE i SHAL SON B HABELL 4 2 TEEDGE U JO AN THEN WE SHORL B SO GLODD AN WEN i M PRENGTD 2 U JO WOT LARX AN BLEVE ME INF XN PIP. (ch. 7)

Pip's 'i OPE i SHAL SON B HABELL 4 2 TEEDGE U JO' brings together the scrawled carelessness of his young self (the hope that he will 'soon be able' to improve Joe) with the measured carefulness of his older, sadder self (the belated recognition that, as the unwitting 'son of Abel' Magwitch, there was more than one foster-father leading his hopes on); 'BLEVE ME INF XN PIP' then compacts 'IN AFFECTION' with the warning that he is a walking health-hazard, 'INFECTION', as he retraces the steps of the romance plot which he had been convinced was organized around himself as its hero: 'IN FICTION'.

We could go on multiplying and mapping out more or less convincing 'environments' for Dickens's speck, just as we could make lists of

---

[19] *On the Study of Words* (1851), 114–17.

the diverse sources of decomposition which go towards the composition of dust itself.[20] However, this activity would not of itself achieve
McGann's goal of 'particularity'. According to McGann, '[I]t should
be evident that to establish the pertinence of historical method to the
field of literary analysis is tantamount to establishing the hegemony of
historical method to literary studies in general.'[21] This is a tempting
theoretical aim, but not one which will be uncomplicatedly supported
by what is 'evident' from practical attempts at historical analysis,
because however purposefully a critic sets out to map out the valency
and spread of literature within a broader cultural field ('A region in
which a body experiences a force as the result of the presence of some
other body or bodies ... a method of representing the way in which
bodies are able to influence each other'),[22] success in locating the co-
ordinates and drift of this field's constituent particles is likely to prove
more elusive. Even situating individual cultural fragments within the
loose structure which Thomas McFarland has called 'anteriority of
field' ('anterior' because literary history assumes an object of enquiry
which also establishes many of the conditions for this enquiry) could
not of itself reveal which contexts a piece of writing feeds off, and
which it fends off; when it settles into well-worn Victorian commonplaces, and when it jumps out of these cultural grooves, like the
needle on an old record.[23] Historical criticism which is not to be
spoilt by choice might then need to begin by plotting the currents and
progressions from which the fixed constellations of a culture are
abstracted: the translations between literary and non-literary forms
of invention, which could be directed as much by the assumptions of
vocabulary as they are by the assertions of argument; the spliced
discoveries of logical enquiry and metaphor; the shadows of one

[20] A number of books and articles in the period sought to categorize the changeable
ingredients of dust. Robert Brudenell Carter notes with Dickensian relish that the dust
which settles in our homes contains 'particles of every description of decaying animal and
vegetable matter. The droppings of horses and other animals, the entrails of fish, the outer
leaves of cabbages, the bodies of dead cats, and the miscellaneous contents of dust-bins
generally, all contribute their quota to the savoury compound', 'Lighting', in *Our Homes, and
How to Make Them Healthy* (1883–5), 397–8; compare John Capper's article 'Important
Rubbish' in *Household Words*, 11 (19 May 1855), 376–9; and H. P. Malet, *Incidents in the
Biography of Dust* (1877).

[21] *BI*, 62–3.

[22] *Oxford Concise Science Dictionary*, quoted in Gillian Beer, *Open Fields* (1996), x. Nicola
Luckhurst makes a helpfully cautious attempt to rehabilitate the idea of 'atmosphere' as 'the
set of epistemological possibilities available' to a writer, in *Science and Structure in Proust's 'A la
recherche du temps perdu'* (2000), 69.

[23] See *Originality and Imagination* (1985), 31–59.

discipline which fall across another without establishing causal links. A study of the influences which affect Victorian literature compounds these complex cultural shifts and dislocations, not only because the same term, 'influence', cannot readily discriminate between effects which have been achieved and those which are still underway, but also because in the mouths of its nineteenth-century speakers this term is often as slippery and unstable as the concepts it is taken to represent. As I shall be showing in later sections of this chapter, writers who try to account for influence are equally attracted to metaphors of cohesion and dispersal, proximity and distance, orderly transmission and chaotic sprawl. Repeated in diverse contexts, the word becomes a form of shared cultural shorthand for the desire to make connections as well as to describe them, because for many writers to present an account of influence is also to provide a way of exploring what joins the often discrete vocabularies we use to divide up the world; it allows the circulation and flow of ideas to be charted as they create and resist alliances with one another; in the hands of its most self-conscious practitioners, it forms a tool for probing the question of how we understand understanding itself.

Dickens provides a valuable focus for this sort of enquiry, because the sprawling connections made by his plots, between types of sub-ject-matter and people which many of his contemporaries struggled to keep at a distance from one another, is compounded by the accumulative drive of a narrative style which, as Steven Connor has pointed out, 'manifests itself in the problematic overflowing of cat-egories, the blurring of boundaries, and the promiscuous commin-gling of what official ideologies wish to promote as naturally distinct'.[24] I suggested in the previous chapter that 'influence', be-cause it is unstably situated between ideas of action and reaction, the effects of X upon Y and the simultaneous reshaping of Y by X, provides a model of the difficulties involved in distinguishing between the objective pushes and pulls of the world upon us, and the cognitive shapes which we impose upon the world. Dickens's career draws out and tests the practical scope of this model because, as Connor's choice of active participles ('overflowing', blurring', 'commingling') helpfully reminds us, his busy interest in process cannot easily be disentangled from his own imaginative development. Like other Victorian writers who use discussions of influence to test their period's

---

[24] Steven Connor (ed.), *Charles Dickens* (1996), 28.

complex movements of cultural pressure, Dickens's novels work through his recognition that he cannot neutrally register these movements, like a form of literary barometer, when his own writing forms a significant part of the intellectual and social trends it describes. However, while there is some truth in the claim that influence is too plural and variable a concept to be permanently fixed by any single critical definition, this could not represent the whole truth, because it does not follow from the fact that we cannot describe everything that we cannot describe anything. As Hegel remarked in the *Wissenschaft der Logik*, to suggest that a 'determinate or finite being' can be understood only in relation to all other beings, and that the world can therefore be seen in a *Stäubchen* (little piece of dust), is to 'make the assertion (which is really a tautology) that if the least grain of dust was destroyed, the whole universe must collapse'.[25] That it has not, yet, while not preventing certain forms of abstract epistemological scepticism, should then encourage us to pay closer attention to those writers who set out to retrieve a sense of order and proportion from the flux of human affairs by first checking the implications of their own writing.

Henry James outlines the problem, and hints at a solution, when he explains in his preface to *Roderick Hudson* that a good novel, like a good conversation, relies on the art of knowing what not to say:

Where, for the complete expression of one's subject, does a particular relation stop—giving way to some other not concerned in that expression?

Really, universally, relations stop nowhere, and the exquisite problem of the artist is eternally but to draw, by a geometry of his own, the circle within which they shall happily *appear* to do so. He is in the perpetual predicament that the continuity of things is the whole matter, for him, of comedy and tragedy; that this continuity is never, by the space of an instant or an inch, broken, and that, to do anything at all, he has at once intensely to consult and intensely to ignore it.[26]

For James, novels concentrate ethical questions which are raised by more than writing alone, such as the permanent dilemma over where we should draw the line between our own concerns and other people's concerns, given that one of the things we most concern ourselves with is one another. All writing is doubly partial: shaped

[25] Quoted in McFarland, *Originality and Imagination*, 56.
[26] Preface to *Roderick Hudson* (1876), repr. in Roger Gard (ed.), *The Critical Muse: Selected Literary Criticism* (1987), 452; compare James's 'neat figure of a circle' in the Preface to *The Awkward Age* (ibid., 528).

by the writer's desires, it is full of the haunted absences and silences which drive these desires, a form of achieved forgetting. But reading involves similar questions of scale and proportion, which encourage us to echo in our responses what James calls the author's 'difficult, dire process of selection and comparison, of surrender and sacrifice'.[27] This is not only because a novel which appears small on the shelf will reveal itself to be rangy and expansive when opened up to be read, but also because each act of reading will model itself upon the testing combination of decisions and doubts which are already built into the work by and towards which our attention is directed. James's preface, for example, is both a critical conclusion to the work he has completed, and an introductory set of clues to the work we are about to read, and so provides a practical guide to reading the novel in a way which is true to James's own struggle to realize his original intentions in the density of a medium which he finds both obligingly compliant and awkwardly resistant. To read this preface closely then means attuning our ears to James's characteristic style, at once commanding and cajoling, and so learning how to discriminate between the local details of each page in a way that acknowledges their place within the 'complete expression' of his ideas. The pressures of James's historical period are especially brought to bear upon the timing of his thought, as the cautious advance of his syntax studiously consults and steadfastly ignores the possibility of his line of thought breaking down, by negotiating its passage across the moments of pausing and checking, the 'stopping', which are provided by his punctuation: 'this continuity is never, by the space of an instant or an inch, broken'. By investing his 'expression' with his convictions, James describes the 'continuity of things' as one might describe a circle, and so answers that central Victorian worry over the unchecked sprawl of relations by confining it to the more controlled relations of his prose; like all good writers, he provides a literary shape which attends simultaneously to the forms we impose upon experience and its resistance to these forms.

James is not unusual in thinking that there are some historical predicaments of the writer which are intimate with the more immediate predicaments of his writing. Particles, for example, are for much of the nineteenth century 'in the air' not only literally, but also as they

---

[27] Preface to *Roderick Hudson* (1876), repr. in Roger Gard (ed.), *The Critical Muse: Selected Literary Criticism* (1987), 452.

contribute towards an intellectual climate, or 'ethos',[28] which is largely shaped by ideas of physical and moral influence. James taps this set of ideas in 'The Art of Fiction' when he argues that the writer's experience forms a large and growing web, 'suspended in the chamber of consciousness, and catching every air-borne particle in its tissue', because he is drawing upon a number of unsettled, and potentially unsettling, ideas that also structured the thinking of his contemporaries and the forms in which they 'caught' these ideas on the page. In particular, James's metaphor richly concentrates a number of questions concerning the effects of influence upon what he refers to as the 'atmosphere of the mind'.[29] During the period which shaped and stirred James's imagination, close attention to 'influence' forms a significant part of the atmosphere of individual writers' minds, and an equally significant part of the pervasive atmosphere of cultural debate, the flow of the current, in and against which these writers moved. (The use of 'atmosphere' to mean 'prevailing psychological climate; pervading tone or mood' is itself a characteristic nineteenth-century development.)[30] Victorian scientists and moralists frequently point out the difficulties we are likely to encounter in any attempt to distinguish between the local impacts of particular deeds and utterances, and the unlocatable effects of a social environment which exerts a pressure as even and constant as the air upon our bodies. It is the loose and baggy nature of influence which then brings to their attention the importance for many lives of human influences—such as marriage or friendship—which are simultaneously cumulative *and* surprising, general *and* particular. Here literary texts provide a key resource for writers who wish to reflect on the relative importance of different kinds of influence, because it is in the nature of these texts to measure the demands of particular turns of plot or phrase against the larger demands of the form in which these moments are resolved. It is for this reason that Victorian literature still provides practical scrutiny of the period's most far-reaching and contested theories of influence, because the same questions of chance and design, the visible and the invisible, the responsibilities of individuals and groups, which are such an important feature of the era's

[28] *OED*: 'The characteristic spirit, prevalent tone of sentiment, of a people or community' (from 1851).
[29] 'The Art of Fiction' (1884), repr. in *Henry James's Literary Criticism*, ed. Leon Edel (2 vols., 1984), I. 52.
[30] *OED* 4a.

social and ethical thinking, are also among the questions which individual authors self-consciously investigate in their own practice: the literary after-effects and by-products which linger on in so much Victorian writing as a presence as well as a theme.

Specifically, restoring Dickens's 'speck' to its place in a complex and shifting set of literary relations, like a form of cultural Brownian motion, locates popular doubts and perplexities over what many believers in resurrection would consider most individual, most 'particular', about themselves: their bodies. These are not exclusively Victorian concerns, but they often cluster anxiously around arguments which are: the debates between Positivists and their theological opponents over the sort of afterlife we should expect or produce for ourselves. By the end of the century, one apologist declared, 'the positive spirit was as pervasive as the air'.[31] It is a reasonable claim. Indeed, so often and so diffusely are its assumptions brought into Victorian writing that Positivism has some claim to the title of that most fluid and unlocatable of cultural phenomena: 'the spirit of the age'. And yet, the metaphor chosen implicitly concedes that Positivist arguments could be disordered or diluted by their circulation in an intellectual atmosphere which was far thicker and noisier than could be produced by any one spirit or age. With so many rival theories contending for space and attention, even Positivists might not be entirely sure about who or what had influenced their ideas, any more than they could observe the atoms of the air they breathed.

'... ONE VAST LIBRARY ...'

Speaking in 1869 to the annual inaugural meeting of the Birmingham and Midland Institute, Dickens urged his appreciative working-class audience to cultivate 'the beauties of self-improvement'. Such beauties, he claimed, are more than a matter of pride in one's own showing in life. They are catching. The Institute sends out shockwaves of 'interest and sympathy' to the community from which it is 'inseparable', like a drop of water sending ripples across a pond:

I do not strain the truth. [*Applause.*] It was suggested by Mr. Babbage, in his *Ninth Bridgewater Treatise*, that a mere spoken word—a mere syllable thrown into the air—may go on reverberating through illimitable space for ever and

---

[31] Lucien Lévy-Bruhl (1898), quoted in T. R. Wright, *The Religion of Humanity* (1978), 273.

ever, seeing that there is no rim against which it can strike: no boundary at which it can possibly arrive. Similarly it may be said—not as an ingenious speculation, but as a steadfast and absolute fact—that human calculation cannot limit the influence of one atom of wholesome knowledge patiently acquired, modestly possessed, and faithfully used [*Applause.*]

Each atom of knowledge, he continues, can be compared with a planet in one of the 'innumerable solar systems besides ours', and the force of 'besides' will shift from a proximity in thought ('as well as') to a neighbourly influence ('next to') when we consider how planets are like people:

[I]t is certain that every man, however obscure, however far removed from the general recognition, is one of a group of men impressible for good and impressible for evil, and that it is in the eternal nature of things that he cannot really improve himself without in some degree improving other men. [*Hear, hear.*][32]

Clearly Dickens had been impressed by Charles Babbage's argument, 'On the Permanent Impression of Our Words and Actions on the Globe We Inhabit', in *The Ninth Bridgewater Treatise, A Fragment* (1837). The fragment itself reverberates through his fiction, from the air 'full of phantoms' in *Bleak House* (ch. 32), back to the storyteller in *Master Humphrey's Clock*, who hears 'voices congregate around me', and is unable to resist the gravitational pull of 'a paved courtyard so full of echoes, that sometimes I am tempted to believe that faint responses to the noises of old times linger there yet, and that these ghosts of sound haunt my footsteps as I pace it up and down' (ch. 1). According to Babbage, we cannot walk away from such sounds even if we no longer hear them, because '[t]he pulsations of the air, once set in motion by the human voice, cease not to exist with the sounds to which they gave rise.' Rather, the 'aerial pulses' from each utterance continue to move inaudibly across the surface of the earth (Babbage calculates that a girdle of sound is put round about the globe in less than twenty hours) until 'every atom of its atmosphere takes up the altered movement', and will forever 'continue to influence its path throughout its future existence', like endless billiard-balls absorbing and redirecting waves of shock:

[32] Kenneth Fielding (ed.), *The Speeches of Charles Dickens* (1960), 399. Dickens was a regular guest at Babbage's *soirées*; there are several letters from Dickens to Babbage, repr. in *The Letters of Charles Dickens*, ed. Graham Storey, *et al.* (1965–), II. 307; III. 477; IV. 134; V. 251; VI. 283, 295.

Thus considered, what a strange chaos is this wide atmosphere we breathe! Every atom impressed with good and with ill, retains at once the motions which philosophers and sages have imparted to it, mixed and combined in ten thousand ways with all that is worthless and base. The air itself is one vast library, on whose pages are for ever written all that man has ever said or even whispered. There, in their mutable but unerring characters, mixed with the earliest, as well as the latest sighs of mortality, stand for ever recorded, vows unredeemed, promises unfulfilled, perpetuating in the united movements of each particle, the testimony of man's changeful will.[33]

Babbage's library is an oracle as well as an archive. If an action's elusive reverberations could be arrested in mid-air, he suggests, we might then 'distinctly foresee and might absolutely predict for any, even the remotest period of time, the circumstances and future history of every particle of that atmosphere'; were we to plot the trajectories of a sufficient number of these particles, we could then produce mathematical equations for working out something we do not usually imagine counting on: the future (p. 111).

Babbage's figure of the air's 'pages', permanently criss-crossed with the ghosts of time past and to come, is richly echoed in the reaches of his own volume, which goes some way to proving that it is not only theoretical physics that is involved with lines and fields of force. As the local impact of this 'Fragment' on later social theory comes to confirm its central premiss that 'every fragment of the material world' has delayed knock-on effects (p. xv),[34] so its own 'united movements' of argument and metaphor are in turn stirred by the emergence of a dense intellectual atmosphere which passes on and through his writing. One current of this atmosphere draws on research into acoustics. By the time of Dickens's speech, the irreversible dissipation of 'sound waves',[35] together with waves of light and heat, had been given popular expression by Tyndall and Müller.[36] Both draw on Helmholtz's work on acoustics, whose analogies in turn draw

---

[33] *The Ninth Bridgewater Treatise, A Fragment* (1837), 112–13; further page references are given in the text. Babbage's images of a particle's 'pulsations' draw on Pierre de Laplace's *Théorie analytique des probabilités*; the idea that each atom *retains* its 'impressions' mixes two emerging fields of enquiry—fluid mechanics and germ theory—in a 'strange chaos' of his own.

[34] See, e.g., the paraphrase of Babbage by 'T. H.', 'The Sphere of Human Influence', in *The Christian Examiner and Religious Miscellany*, 45: 6 (September 1846), 213–16, and 45: 13 (November 1848), 424–7.

[35] The *OED* cites 1848 as the first recorded use. By 1867, Tyndall's *Sound* refers to the metaphorical 'sound wave' as a 'sound-wave': the transplant has taken.

[36] John Tyndall, *Sound* (1867); F. Max Müller, *Lectures on the Science of Language* (1864).

on the earlier researches into the wave physics which drive Babbage's thought. Compare:

… when a point in a surface of still water is agitated—as by throwing in a stone—the motion thus caused is propagated in the form of waves, which spread in rings over the surface of the water. The circles of waves continue to increase even after rest has been restored to the point first affected.[37]

Every one who has thrown a pebble into the still waters of a sheltered pool, has seen the circles it has raised gradually expanding in size, and as uniformly diminishing in distinctness … The waves of the air, although in many instances perceptible to the organs of hearing, are only rendered visible to the eye by peculiar contrivances.[38]

Babbage's reference to 'peculiar contrivances' also glances at the shapes of things to come, by hinting at the untapped potential of those new human productions for registering the 'united movements' of the air: machines for seeing sound.[39] More pressingly, Babbage's fantasy of the air as an invisible research library serves as one blueprint for the unfinished but chunkily visible storage system which he was experimenting with in the 1830s: the 'Difference Engine'.[40] His treatise returns to the subject with a rhythmic glint of ambition, because the 'Difference Engine' was only a prototype of the larger 'Analytical Engine', which was designed to store its own computations and use them to predict future numerical movements. The regular clocking-up of natural numbers, Babbage reasoned, as they combined and recombined into new forms, would gradually reveal the underlying operation of mathematical laws until then known only to the programmer. Once unpredictable leaps of numerical sequence could be revealed as programmed discontinuities, the engine's steady stockpiling of data would allow its makers to analyse the divinely reckoned structural principles on which both they and their mathematics depended: theodicy worked by steam.

---

[37] H. von Helmholtz, 'On the Physiological Causes of Harmony in Music' (1857), repr. in *Popular Lectures on Scientific Subjects*, trans. E. Atkinson (1884), 61–2.

[38] *The Ninth Bridgewater Treatise*, 113.

[39] On the nineteenth-century developments in acoustical research which lay behind Edison's phonograph, from Chladni's *Klangfiguren* to Edouard-Léon Scott de Martinville's *l'écriture acoustique*, see Thomas L. Hankins and Robert J. Silverman, *Instruments and the Imagination* (1995), ch. 6.

[40] My information is drawn from Anthony Hyman, *Charles Babbage: Pioneer of the Computer* (1982); and Francis Spufford and Jenny Uglow (eds.), *Cultural Babbage: Technology, Time and Invention* (1996).

In his 1869 speech, Dickens's 'human calculation' nods courteously towards the massive ambition of Babbage's pistons and wheels, but stresses that people too can calculate the consequences of their actions, and develops Babbage's idea that Newton's laws of '[t]he principle of the equality of action and reaction' have certain 'unexpected consequences', by turning to evidence of the sorts of attraction Newton left out (p. 108). Rather than rest content with our perpetual bombardment by undifferentiated and fleeting 'particles', Dickens considers human capacities for distinguishing, dwelling on, and redirecting the particular, and leads by example, as he retains Babbage's word 'atom', but settles it into the new associations and discriminations of his own sequence: 'the influence of one atom of *wholesome* knowledge *patiently* acquired, *modestly* possessed, and *faithfully* used' (my emphases).

Dickens's cautious use of Babbage alerts us to a second and more significant current of the Victorian atmosphere which they shared: the web of affinities joining material and moral influence. The ancient connection between human affairs and the 'influence' of the air had already undergone scientific and philosophical scrutiny. In 1818, William Roscoe was arguing that 'instead of attributing the progress or decline of letters and arts to the influence of climate ... we are to seek for them in the unceasing operation of moral causes, in the relations of society, and the dispositions and propensities of the human mind'.[41] As scientists increasingly urge that 'education ought to teach us to see the invisible as well as the visible in nature; to picture with the eye of the mind those operations which entirely elude the eye of the body',[42] even the (as yet) invisible collisions of atoms are used to prod social consciences. For Babbage, these tiny material shifts confirm the existence of a First Cause guiding the 'unceasing operation of moral causes', because although the impact of one atom on another creates only local and temporary 'impressions', each movement is underwritten by divine laws which are 'impressed in indelible characters' (p. xv) upon the physical world.

---

[41] *On the Origin and Vicissitudes of Literature, Science, and Art, and their Influence on the Present State of Society* (1818), 11. See also Robert Hunt, *The Poetry of Science* (1848). The career of Thomas Forster provides an example of the gradual shift in discussion from physical to moral influence. In 1817, he cites Lucretius and Virgil as support for his claim that there is 'a local influence on the body' which can be ascribed to 'the state of the atmosphere' (*Observations on the Casual and Periodical Influence of Particular States of the Atmosphere on Human Health and Diseases*, 14); by 1844 he has switched to 'the influence of example' (*A Collection of Letters on Early Education, and its Influence in the Prevention of Crime*, 6).

[42] Tyndall, *Sound*, 5.

James Clerk Maxwell writes of 'molecules' rather than 'atoms', but he too sees God in these little things:

They continue to this day as they were created, perfect in number and measure and weight, and from the ineffaceable characters impressed on them we may learn that those aspirations after accuracy in measurement, truth in statement, and justice in action, which we reckon among our noblest attributes as men, are ours because they are essential constituents of the image of Him Who in the beginning created, not only the heaven and the earth, but the materials of which heaven and earth consist.[43]

The 'ineffaceable characters' of molecules, which have been recombining into new forms without material alteration of themselves since the beginning of time, makes of their discovery and explanation an up-to-date revelation of the Word. Maxwell's prose tests and supports this claim, because the question of what is changed by the impact of one body upon another, and what remains, can be heard working its way through 'in the beginning': a phrase which has drifted away from its Biblical origins, unchanged through change, into the new frame of his argument. A page earlier, Maxwell also adopts Tennyson's 'Lucretius', itself a loose reworking of Lucretius's *De Rerum Natura:*

> ... and I saw the flaring atom-streams
> And torrents of her myriad universe,
> Ruining along the illimitable inane,
> Fly on to clash together again, and make
> Another and another frame of things
> For ever:[44]

Not 'Running along', but 'Ruining along'. The local slippage allows Tennyson to admit into his own verse the conceit of literature as a further history of gradual and relentless drift, and the very looseness of his adaptation provides corroborating evidence that the older the 'frame of things', the more likely it is to crumble under a modern touch. At the same time, the re-placing of Lucretius in Maxwell's account situates historically one general claim which I made in the previous chapter, that for a writer to make 'another frame of things' need not be a Bloomian patching-up operation after a ruinous 'clash'. It could be a considered and welcome meeting of minds.

*

[43] James Clerk Maxwell, 'Molecules', in *Nature*, 8 (1873), 441.
[44] Ibid., 440; *TP*, II. 710.

It is likely that Babbage was especially in Dickens's mind a year before he began to serialize *Great Expectations*. In 1859 (the *OED* cites this year as the first recorded use of 'influenceable') Samuel Smiles quoted Babbage in his *Self-Help*, as evidence to support the important second part of his title: *with Illustrations of Conduct and Perseverance*. Like *Great Expectations*, which begins with a reference to the 'universal struggle' in 'getting a living' (ch. 1), Smiles's title makes ethical what in Darwin's *Origin of Species* (1859) is purely statistical. It also answers to a broader Victorian interest in the impact of the self on what follows it which is detectable in the sheer number of words newly prefaced by 'self'. Some of these can be understood as lexical aftershocks of a slightly earlier debate over Romantic 'ego-' compounds which, as Stephen Bygrave has pointed out, disclose in the development of the language 'a clear progression in the contraries of retirement from and engagement with late eighteenth-century English society which can be seen "in little" in the words in which it describes itself'.[45] In a word like 'egotism', associated with both commendable autonomy and suspect pride, these extremes meet. A similar ambivalence over the necessary independence and equally necessary interdependence of selves can be heard working its way through the Victorian interest in 'self-', as Carlyle's coinage 'self-help' (*Sartor Resartus*, 1831) establishes the pattern for other 'self-' conjunctions to weigh up how self-interest could serve less competitive desires, like that 'sublime repression of himself', willed rather than unconscious, which Tennyson saw in Prince Albert.[46]

The spreading offshoots of 'self' show how alternative ideas of adaptation and inheritance were being exercised in the popular imagination as much as in the earlier evolutionary theories of

---

[45] *Coleridge and the Self: Romantic Egotism* (1986), 9.

[46] 'Dedication' to *Idylls of the King* (pub. 1862), l. 18, *TP*, III. 264. Other conjunctions include: self-absorption (1862), self-analysis (1860), self-changing (1865), self-criticism (1857), self-effacement (1866), self-estimate (1837), self-estrangement (1878), self-evolution (1857), Darwin's 'self-fertile' (1859), self-forgetful (1848), self-hatred (1865), self-identical (1877), self-induced (1886), selfless (1825), self-limitation (1847), self-observation (1832), self-perfecting (1883), self-reliance (1833), self-repression (1870), self-revelation (1852), self-similar (1867), and a number of inventions like 'self-raising' flour (1854). Often these compounds attract one another into solemn triumvirates: 'self-denial, self-control, and self-sacrifice' (F. W. Newman, *Life after death? Palinodia* (1886), 34); 'self-discipline, self-control, and self-reliance' (W. H. Davenport Adams, *Woman's Work and Worth in Girlhood, Maidenhood, and Wifehood* (1880), xvii; compare Revd Ephraim Peabody, 'Methods of Influence', in *The Monthly Religious Magazine*, 11: 1 (January 1854), 2); 'Self-reverence, self-knowledge, self-control' (Tennyson, 'Oenone', *TP*, I. 428).

Lamarck which had stressed intention, habit, memory.[47] In 1831, John Stuart Mill justified the new self-consciousness about *Zeitgeist*, the 'force of circumstances' which circulates through social relations, by remarking that 'it is only through the present that it is in our power to influence that which is to come'.[48] He then took heed of his own warning by praising Comtian Positivism in the *System of Logic* (1843). Comte had urged that we live for others in life, and in others after death. Like an atom in the physicist's sound-wave, the individual citizen receives a pulse of energy (birth), is moved by it (life), and returns to a point of rest (death), and so fulfils his part in the 'ever-widening circles' of altruism, through which he simultaneously confirms his predecessors' 'immortality of influence' and achieves his own.[49] In a world of continuous change, Comte seemed to show how transience could be made integral to our sense of ourselves as creatures capable of living beyond the present; endings could be infinitely extended; losses could be redeemed. However, the concentric pulse implied by 'circles' is too tidy a model for Comte's own impact on Victorian patterns of thought. Even as his secular elevation of works above faith continued to exercise later writers directly (George Eliot's first original work was to have been called *The Idea of a Future Life*), the edges of his thought were being disturbed by currents sent out by alternative models of descent: genealogy, cultural transmission, inheritance.

Smiles's writings often dramatize these encounters between older and newer models of influence. Much of *Self-Help* is devoted to explaining that we shall best help ourselves by being aware that our conduct perseveres through a 'system of mutual dependencies':

There is, indeed, an essence of immortality in the life of man, even in this world. No individual in the universe stands alone; he is a component part of a system of mutual dependencies; and by his several acts he either increases or diminishes the sum of human good now and for ever. As the present is rooted in the past, and the lives and examples of our forefathers still to a great extent influence us, so are we by our daily acts contributing to form the condition and character of the future ... No man's acts die utterly; and

47 See Beer, *Darwin's Plots: Evolutionary Narrative in Darwin, George Eliot and Nineteenth-Century Fiction* (1983), 24–6.

48 'The Spirit of the Age' (1831), repr. in Gertrude Himmelfarb (ed.), *Essays on Politics and Culture* (1963), 2.

49 Frederic Harrison, 'The Soul and Future Life', in *The Nineteenth Century*, 1: 4–5 (June–July 1877), 520–37, 832–56 (p. 839); further page references are given in the main text.

though his body may resolve into dust and air, his good or his bad deeds will still be bringing forth fruit after their kind, and influencing future generations for all time to come. It is in this momentous and solemn fact that the great peril and responsibility of human existence lies.[50]

This reinforces an ethical framework for social life which Darwin's rather different understanding of a 'system of mutual dependencies' was to put under such intense—and for some, intolerable—strain. Carlyle was typically forthright in pointing out that if Darwin's theories were true, then even seemingly generous human sentiments like sympathy and compassion could be traits which had proved favourable to the survival of the race, and so be nothing more than a shared form of selfishness. Moral life might have no moral purpose.[51] In Smiles's account of 'mutual dependencies', however, a stress on influence works to recuperate moral values from this otherwise mechanistic and indifferent world. By reconsidering the world of 'because' on a human scale, Smiles critically investigates the hope that within subsequence consequence is to be found.

According to Smiles, no individual stands alone even when nobody else is present, because the spirits of the dead 'still live and walk abroad among us' through the lingering traces of their actions.[52] (Smiles's reference to the decisions which are 'still... bringing forth fruit after their kind', like Dickens's description of the good deed 'that endures and bears good fruit', recovers a rhetorical shape for its belief from the language and cadences of the Biblical creation myth.)[53] Crucially, this afterlife includes the effects upon ourselves of our earlier selves. In *Character* (1878), Smiles cites Ruskin on the way that 'every past effort of my life... is with me now';[54] in *Self-Help*, he warns that each word uttered or act performed 'insensibly influences the lives of those about us', and that our conduct also 'exercises an inevitable influence upon all the acts of our future life':[55] 'Example in conduct... even in apparently trivial matters, is of no light moment, inasmuch as it is constantly becoming interwoven with the lives of others, and contributing to form their natures for better or

[50] *Self-Help* (1859), 343–4.

[51] Carlyle's attitudes are discussed in James Froude, *Thomas Carlyle. A History of his Life in London, 1834–1881* (2 vols., 1884), II. 259.

[52] *Self-Help*, 343.

[53] Genesis I: 11 refers to 'the fruit tree yielding fruit, whose seed was in itself, after his kind'.

[54] *Character* (1878, repr. 1888), 10.

[55] *Self-Help*, 345.

for worse.'[56] The echo of the marriage service carries Smiles's concern for the special responsibilities of parents in setting a pattern of 'good examples' before their offspring, in order that the 'chain of example is carried down through time in an endless succession of links'.[57] Married couples promise to stay together 'for better *and* for worse', suggesting that the strength of their bond will see them through good times *and* bad. Smiles's 'for better *or* for worse' emphasizes instead the moral choices which a couple take together, and the lasting effects of these choices on the lives they create together. For Smiles, children are the sum of their parents, their shared future, in ways that reinvest a traditional moral urgency into newer theories of physical inheritance.[58] We take after our parents, growing up like a visible memory of their own growth, and they take after us, both in the usual way that children tend to reshape their parents' lives, and because we continue to be their 'future state' even after they no longer have any direct control over our lives, just as we do not stop being our parents' children when we stop being children.[59] 'Childhood is like a mirror, which reflects in after-life the images first presented to it': this is why Smiles, like Dickens in his 1869 speech, celebrates those 'poor students' who 'have only been able to snatch an atom of knowledge here and there at intervals'.[60] Education repeats the lessons of the nursery, because it is 'from this little central spot' in a household, a spot of space which is also a spot of time, that 'the human sympathies may extend in an ever widening circle, until the world is embraced'.[61] To read Smiles, therefore, is to confront at the level of argument a moral dilemma which more often makes its presence felt when we stop reading: in our responses begin responsibilities.[62]

Because attention in these and similar accounts of the period is focused so strongly upon the consequences of our actions, the definition of an action is expanded. Events do not only happen once,

[56] Ibid., 57, 342.

[57] Ibid., 353.

[58] These theories are summarized by François Jacob, *The Logic of Living Systems: A History of Heredity*, trans. B. E. Spillmann (1974); and Goldie Morgentaler, *Dickens and Heredity: When Like Begets Like* (2000).

[59] *Self-Help*, 342.

[60] *Character*, 34.

[61] *Self-Help*, 329, 342.

[62] Compare the guarded promise, printed on a pack of cards, that phrenology can be family fun: 'By MORAL INFLUENCE is meant, the tendency of each faculty' to increase the sum of human knowledge and happiness, but only '*when well directed and governed*', *Phrenology; And The Moral Influence of Phrenology* (1835; italics original).

but continue to happen; the cognitive shape of an incident is swollen by its active aftermath. In careful hands, the idea that our present-tense speech reverberates with the lingering traces of past utterances can stimulate thoughtful reflections on the writer's need to respond to earlier voices without hollowly echoing them; in more slapdash hands, the same idea can also stifle thought, by seeming to justify the writer's collapse into commonplaces and stereotypes. Mrs Brereton's *Woman's Influence*, Mrs Brookfield's *Influence*, and Grace Aguilar's *Home Influence*, for example, each provides a female protagonist who must learn to replace good advice with good examples;[63] each does little more than give a motto the shape of a plot. But there is nothing a writer can abuse that another writer cannot responsibly use, and the lasting value of these cliché-ridden novels lies in their ability to draw attention to the skill with which other writers give cliché the slip. Thus, Catherine D. Bell's cloyingly inept *Unconscious Influence; or, Horace and May* (1855) depicts the struggles of May ('a kind, helping little puss', who enjoys ruling lines on paper and making clothing for destitute orphans) to persuade her headstrong brother to see that 'Must' is 'both a strong and a strength-giving word', but only when said to one's self.[64] Dickens's *Bleak House* (1852) had depicted, among so much else, the struggles of Esther to make cousin Richard 'conquer what was amiss in himself', by rendering 'what kind services I could, to those immediately about me; and to try to let that circle of duty gradually and naturally expand itself' (ch. 8). Both suggest the need to temper overt persuasion with the hidden work of domestic influence; only Dickens's version of the fable continues to expand its own circle of influence.

On a smaller literary scale, echoes and allusions draw attention to healthy influence in action,[65] and are garnered into bestselling collections ('The Wit and Wisdom of X', or 'Beauties of Y').[66] Words are

---

[63] Respectively, 3 vols., 1845; 2 vols., 1871; 2 vols., 1847 (24 editions up to 1869). On the popular assumption that women's domestic influence provided men with an uplifting combination of purification and inspiration, see Leonore Davidoff and Catherine Hall, *Family Fortunes: Men and Women of the English Middle Class, 1780–1850* (1987), 149, 183.

[64] pp. 151, 1. Bell's chapter titles give a flavour of this connection between influence and self-influence: 'She Who Would Help Others Must Learn to Control Herself', 'She Who Would Help Others Must Be Self-Denying And Self-Watchful'.

[65] Amariah Brigham quotes Falstaff's warning that 'either wise bearing or ignorant carriage is caught, as men take disease', in *Remarks on the Influence of Mental Cultivation* (1833), 90n.

[66] See, e.g., Alexander Main's best-selling collection, *Wise, Witty and Tender Sayings in Prose and Verse Selected from the Works of George Eliot* (1872).

bonds which tie the speaker to his or her past and to other people, and where it exercises influence, speech is action. Smiles refers to 'eloquent acts' and to 'visible rhetoric'; 'the best books are those which most resemble good actions'.[67] Biographies provide an especially potent example of the way that 'the lives and examples of our forefathers still to a great extent influence us', because they helpfully collapse 'lives' and 'examples' into a single literary form. As a moral guide which will 'hold us by the hand' every time we pick it up, a biography is a 'forefather' which encourages its readers 'to reproduce life anew, and to illustrate his character in other forms':[68] 'It is a still living voice; it is an intellect. To use Milton's words, "It is the precious life-blood of a master spirit, embalmed and treasured up on purpose to a life beyond life".'[69] Once a human voice is preserved in the stilled life of print, a good book, like a good friend, 'will never change'. However, its ink is more than embalming-fluid. When Smiles read Milton, the book formed 'a bond of union', and the same bond which allows the subject of a biography to enjoy 'a life beyond life' allows the more dispersed community of its readers to move beyond the confines of their individual lives: they 'live in him together, and he in them'.[70] To some extent, therefore, Smiles's use of Milton does what it says. As a piece of cultural capital which has been 'treasured up on purpose', the quotation represents an enduring proof of the profitable ease with which ideas, like other forms of capital, can be transferred between accounts. By abstracting Milton's remark into an example of the healthy circulation of ideas between 'intellects' widely separated in space and time, Smiles briefly explores the possibility that writers can help to produce the ideal conditions of influence that they describe. But because Smiles's purposes in borrowing this line are not identical with Milton's purposes in writing it, the quotation also represents a lurking threat to the conservative notion that lines of writing embody invariable lines of descent. Victor Hugo puts the problem well when he points out that 'all great writers create two œuvres, one deliberate, the other involuntary',[71] because his comment draws attention to the possible futures of a literary work which a writer might occasion but not anticipate. For Smiles, a biographical Life represents the circumference of a circle of activity which spreads

---

[67] *Self-Help*, 346; *Character*, 72, 295.
[68] *Self-Help*, 350–1.   [69] *Character*, 351.   [70] Ibid.
[71] Letter to Adèle Hugo (January 1853), quoted in Graham Robb, *Victor Hugo* (1997), 76.

until its centre is no longer visible: like the dispersed atoms of his or her body, the biographical subject is everywhere and nowhere. But as a number of Smiles's contemporaries pointed out, because circles of influence cannot be contained as easily as words between the covers of a book, many writers' afterlives will be marked as much by whim and accident as by loyal extensions of the 'purpose' which they store up in their work.

   When Florence Hardy read Samuel Butler's biography, she found the clinching lesson of its final pages to be less cheering than Smiles might have expected: 'We have finished the biography of S. Butler, which is depressing at the end as all biographies must be—decay, disillusion, death.'[72] Her remark shows that she was more alert than Smiles to the way that a reader's thoughts can be turned in new directions, as they follow the shape of a piece of writing, without providing these thoughts with more than a temporary home. She was equally alert to the way that a biographical Life, like the life of its subject, may fray towards the end, as the thud of the anticipated full-stop sends shockwaves of inevitability and retrospective irony back into the description of events which seemed to have been finished with on paper as fully as they had been in person. It is likely that this sensitivity was sharpened by the knowledge of her ageing husband's ambition to record his own biography, and the corresponding dread that this would become a genuine biography only when his decline and death made it necessary for her to complete the book in a way that would be true both to the living voice registered on its pages, and to her mourning of that voice. But her suspicion of the commonplace pieties surrounding Victorian 'Lives', while reflecting upon the awkward peculiarities of her own situation, also reflects a more widespread caution surrounding the idea that, whether in our actions or our descriptions of these actions, the abstract ideals of influence described by writers like Smiles could ever be true to the messy actualities of human behaviour.

*

A sustained enquiry into this problem is provided by the Brownings' courtship correspondence. Take Elizabeth Barrett's reply to the fear,

---

[72] Florence Hardy to Cockerell (27 December 1919), *Friends of a Lifetime: Letters to Sydney Carlyle Cockerell*, ed. Viola Meynell (1940), 305–6.

expressed by Robert Browning in a previous letter, that her dedication to him and his writing might force her to neglect her own literary
career:

> If it were possible that you could do me harm in the way of work, (but it isn't)
> it would be possible, not through writing letters & reading manuscripts, but
> because of a reason to be drawn from your own great line
>
> 'What man is strong until he stands alone?'
>
> What man ... what woman? For have I not felt twenty times the desolate
> advantage of being insulated here & of not minding anybody when I made
> my poems?—of living a little like a disembodied spirit, & caring less for
> supposititious criticism than for the black fly buzzing in the pane?—*That*
> made me what dear Mr. Kenyon calls 'insolent,'—untimid, & unconven-
> tional in my degree; and not so much by strength, you see, as by separ-
> ation—
> ... Still ... when all is changed for me now, & different, it is not possible
> ... that I should not be better & stronger for being within your influences &
> sympathies, in this way of writing as in other ways. We shall see—you will
> see.[73]

That tender shift from 'We shall see' to 'you will see' is entirely
characteristic of EBB's growing recognition of how much she could
take for granted from her reader, and so how a letter sent at this stage
of their relationship—the one hundred and forty-ninth in their correspondence—could lightly touch upon matters which earlier letters
had investigated with such scrupulous care. Her reference to 'the
black fly buzzing in the pane', for example, shows how keen she was
to preserve the private mythology of herself as one who had been
trapped in her room like Tennyson's Mariana,[74] waiting for a lover
who would never come, and so the mingled disappointment and relief
which was generated by her new lover's willingness to visit her on
paper more often than he did in person. Similarly, 'living a little like a
disembodied spirit' forms part of the related self-image of one who
had spent long years suspended in a curious social limbo, issuing forth
into the world only in the form of her publications, and so part of the
gradual change in her self-descriptions from lament to celebration, as

---

[73] EBB to RB (10 November 1845), *Kintner*, 263; hereafter I abbreviate Elizabeth Barrett
Browning to EBB in the main text.
[74] Compare *Kintner*, 87: 'I am like Mariana in the moated grange and sit listening too
often to the mouse in the wainscot' (6 June 1845); and 152: 'Do *you* conjecture sometimes
that I live all alone here like Mariana in the moated Grange?' (11 August 1845).

her letters set out to thank Browning for interrupting the deadening sameness of her existence and recalling her to life.[75]

One way in which EBB tests the claim that she is no longer suffering from the idiosyncrasies caused by social and literary 'separation' can be heard in the emphatic echoes of Browning's voice which her letter incorporates into itself. Thus, the allegation that she is 'better & stronger for being within your influences & sympathies' also quietly admits that she can now at least entertain the assumption which Browning held, and which provided an early and persistent source of disagreement between them, that the person who writes and the literary personality which he or she projects are one and the same, because 'better & stronger' does not clearly distinguish between a diagnosis of her physical condition (many of their letters dwell lovingly on one another's medical symptoms)[76] and an assessment of her poetic powers. But EBB's references to 'strength' here represent more than a set of complimentary reflections upon the quotation 'What man is strong until he stands alone?' (actually a misquotation,[77] as if EBB's habit of suggesting revisions to Browning's poems was now too engrained to need any encouragement). 'Strong' is also a key word in Browning's critical vocabulary, where it forms a central expression of his ambivalent attitude towards the will as a site of conflict in which, as Daniel Karlin has noted, 'the spirit of mastery wrestles with the spirit of submission'.[78] And yet, because EBB, too, was keen that her will should be subject to the irresistible force of another, trembling on a pivot between choice and surrender, their correspondence circles around the vocabulary of 'strength' much as they and their letters circled around each other, in a form of competitive abjection, a flirtation with the fantasy of losing themselves in the other person:

When grief came upon grief, I never was tempted to ask 'How have I deserved this of God,' as sufferers sometimes do: I always felt that there must be cause enough ... weakness enough, needing strengthening ...

---

[75] Daniel Karlin explores 'the shift of perspective by which Elizabeth Barrett invested in earthly passion the values she had formerly attributed to the transcendent after-life', in *The Courtship of Robert Browning and Elizabeth Barrett* (1985), 270.

[76] See, e.g., EBB to RB (16 June 1845): 'I am behaving very well in going out into the noise,—not quite out of doors yet, on account of the heat—& am getting better as you say, without any doubt at all, & stronger' (*Kintner*, 97).

[77] The correct line (*Colombe's Birthday*, III. 231) is 'When is man strong until he feels alone?'

[78] *The Courtship of Robert Browning and Elizabeth Barrett*, 140.

You were stronger than I from the beginning, & I felt the mastery in you by the first word and first look.

What do you expect this letter will be about, my own dearest? Those which I write on the mornings after our days seem naturally to answer any strong point brought out in the previous discourse and not then completely disposed of... so they generally run in the vile fashion of a disputatious 'last word'; 'one word yet'—do not they?[79]

Although J. S. Mill complained that Browning's writing revealed his personality's 'self-seeking and self-worshipping state',[80] this final 'do not they?', poised between the bluntness of a rhetorical question and the pointed affection of an invitation, shows how some writing will involve a process of 'self-seeking' which is more investigative and tentative. As Browning offers himself up to his beloved, he does so partly in the hope that her response will show him the identity of the self he has surrendered. And yet, the way he chose to reveal himself, in the shifting dimensions of a shared correspondence, also threatened to blur the identity that his letters gradually bring into focus, because this vocabulary of 'strength' is not limited to its self-reinforcing appearances in their 'previous discourse'. It also forms part of a larger set of attempts to investigate what Daniel Pick has identified as 'the indeterminate border', in much writing of the period, 'between covert command and creative collaboration, inspiration and interference, partnership and possession'.[81]

According to Smiles, the 'strength' of living writers depends upon the number of weaker talents they can support: 'If they are stronger than ourselves, we become participators in their strength';[82] if they are dead, the 'renewed strength' of example they bequeath relieves our self-reliance from 'the bondage of self'.[83] The author of an anonymous article on 'Influence', similarly, analyses in steely Carlylean fashion 'the influence which a strong mind will ever have over a weak one', and concludes that we desire in other people what we lack in our selves; in both senses, we choose our influences to satisfy what

---

[79] EBB to RB (17 November 1845), EBB to RB (19 May 1846), RB to EBB (10 September 1846), *Kintner*, 275, 714, 1058.

[80] Marginal note in Mill's copy of *Pauline*, quoted in Christopher Ricks (ed.), *The Brownings: Letters and Poetry* (1970), 28.

[81] *Svengali's Web: The Alien Enchanter in Modern Culture* (2000), 64.

[82] *Character*, 67.

[83] Ibid., 86; compare Smiles's discussions of 'strength' on pp. 16, 18, 36–7, 66, 268f.

we want.[84] Edward Dowden, in a more explicitly Positivist vein, asks 'Do we desire to be strong?', and answers that we shall be so only on condition that 'we resolve to draw for strength upon the common fund of thought and feeling and instinct stored, within us and without us, by the race'.[85] One of Browning's early letters to EBB had concluded with a wary flourish: 'if these words were but my own, and fresh-minted for this moment's use!'[86] Yet it is because the vocabulary of 'strength' is not his own, and is associated with both general and particular examples of inspiring action, that he and EBB seem to have found it such a helpful tool in testing the flexibility and durability of their most intimate forms of self-expression. As their letters probe and appeal to one another's 'strength', with a good-humoured mix-ture of defiance and deference, so they measure an abstract model of social relations against the changing actualities of their relationship. As this shared vocabulary of 'strength' gradually adopts the private inflections of their correspondence, so they recover a unique and loving accent from the anonymous contours of public speech.

The need to find shadings of intimate significance within a shared vocabulary will be true of any developing relationship, particularly one which, like the Brownings' romance, was conducted at an awk-ward angle to the social world. Lovers' individual expressions of affection often threaten to sound hollowed out by repetition, whether by turning their own declarations into shabby and self-conscious parodies of earlier lovers' vows, or by hitting a rhetorical pitch which elevates the beloved into an idealized figure which ordinary human relations cannot easily sustain. These dangers were particu-larly acute for lovers whose physical meetings supplemented the regular arrival and departure of letters which, from the start, had blurred the line between literary appreciation and personal affection. (Browning's letters, in particular, were letters about love long before they became love letters: 'I do, as I say, love these books with all my heart', he had claimed in his first approach to EBB, before continu-ing, prophetically, 'and I love you too.')[87] Although the shuttling back and forth of their letters tactfully mapped out what Patmore was to describe as 'the space which makes attraction felt',[88] the words which

[84] *Chambers' Edinburgh Journal,* n.s., 15 (January 1851), 8–9.
[85] *Studies in Literature 1789–1877* (1878), 266.
[86] RB to EBB (11 March 1845), *Kintner,* 39.
[87] RB to EBB (10 January 1845), *Kintner,* 3.
[88] *The Angel in the House,* repr. in *The Poems of Coventry Patmore,* ed. F. Page (1949), 128.

traverse this space are just as often marked by the dread that they would remain forever distant from the person who received them. EBB's remark, 'Anguish has instructed me in joy—and solitude in society',[89] could then receive an unhappy new emphasis from letters which had lost full imaginative contact with their reader, meaning not just that she had learned about the pleasures of company from the times she was alone, but that she had come to understand the sadness of feeling most isolated when in the society of those who were nearest and dearest to her.

Consider Browning's reply to a letter which seems to have been prompted by a meeting during which, perhaps impatient at EBB's reluctance to leave the country with him, he wondered aloud whether she might be persuaded by her family to convalesce in Italy if he were to die:

… if in drawing you, all of you, closer to my heart, I hurt you whom I would—*outlive*… yes,—I cannot speak here—forgive me, Ba.

My Ba, you are to consider now for me: your health, your strength—it is all wonderful; that is not my dream, you know—but what all see: now, steadily care for us both—take time, take counsel if you choose; but at the end tell me what you will do for your part—thinking of me as utterly devoted, soul and body, to you, living wholly in your life, seeing good and ill, only as you see,—being yours as your hand is,—or as your Flush, rather.[90]

Mastery and submission are teasingly at odds here. Claiming that he is 'yours as your hand is,—or as your Flush, rather', Browning's tone hovers indecisively between possessiveness and self-sacrifice, servile proximity and sexual control, as 'Flush', placed so close to 'hand', hints at 'flesh', but also glows in expectation of the desire and embarrassment which such a thought might conjure up in his reader's mind. Not being privy to the squabble that prompted this letter, it is hard to know whether EBB would have understood 'living wholly in your life' as a promise or a threat, just as it is hard to know how seriously she was expected to take Browning's attempt to cheer her up by alleging that, rather than make her unhappy by dying, he intends to outlive her. The very difficulties we now have in grasping the tone of this letter, as it lurches between flattery and scolding, cajolery and earnestness, reflect Browning's success in fashioning it for its intended

---

[89] EBB to RB (5 March 1845), *Kintner*, 35.
[90] RB to EBB (15 January 1846), *Kintner*, 388.

reader. A love letter is always a delicately reciprocal affair: offered as a revelation of love, the letter is also a request for love, because it trusts in the reader's ability to complete its halting blanks and unpick its knots of ambiguity in a way that will prove how in tune with, true to, the writer he or she is. This can still faintly be heard in the tender pressure of thought that moves Browning's letter from the tongue-tied '—I cannot speak here—forgive me, Ba' to the restored confidence of 'My Ba', as it can in the way that EBB, in a later letter, showed that she had considered the possibility of Browning being 'your Flush' seriously enough for her to turn it into a shared joke: 'It seems to me that you and I are *at one* upon the whole question,—only that *I* am *your* Flush, and *he* is mine.'[91]

Earlier in their correspondence, however, the possibility of this reciprocity had repeatedly come under threat. When Browning asked EBB not to express 'gratitude' for his 'kindness', for instance, on the prematurely boastful grounds that they need not sink to using words already rubbed smooth by too much handling, her reply struck a note of caution: 'you are so restricting our vocabulary, as to be ominous of silence in a full sense, presently'.[92] Browning's attempt to tighten the meaning of their discourse also threatened its very exist-ence, because at this stage in their relationship—a friendship that could hint at a romance only through the occasional ambiguity of their written appeals to one another—common words like 'kindness' or 'gratitude' were a necessary, if debased, point of contact. Their removal could produce an impassable void in communication. The way their correspondence develops then demonstrates lexically what they were also to discover physically: that, as Browning put it, 'all love is but a passionate *drawing closer*'.[93] As they grow more accustomed to one another's presence, and better at filling in the gaps within and between one another's words, even misunderstandings are incorpor-ated into the deliberate and fond teasing of their letters, left on the page like traps. However cautiously EBB responded to Browning's promptings of marriage, so tenderly imbued with his presence are her replies, her hand joined with his on paper as permanently as he wanted it to be in person, that each letter leaving Wimpole Street could rehearse an event which the very existence of the letter also deferred: literary exercises in elopement.

91 EBB to RB (5 September 1846), *Kintner*, 1046.
92 EBB to RB (21 May 1845), *Kintner*, 71.
93 RB to EBB (6–7 January 1846), *Kintner*, 365.

As EBB and Browning repeatedly warned one another, only by no longer needing to write these letters could they prove that their love was more than a set of conventional literary gestures. The way their correspondence tackles this problem, by discovering a range of private significances within the words of common speech, then shows how far they set out to achieve a fuller sense of 'correspondence': physical distances bridged by intimacies of style. 'Seeing', for example, slowly alters its meaning in their letters from descriptions of physical sight to promises of perfect understanding. References to 'halves', similarly, become less worried about the limitations of the self, and more interested in the way that attentive lovers strive perfectly to meet one another's needs. Above all, the changing dimensions of 'influence' register a struggle at the heart of their romance, between the need to create a world of private intimacy without interference from outside forces, and the need for their love not to be so removed from the world of public speech that it could not be detached from the charged air of Wimpole Street without shivering into pieces:

Can you, speaking for yourself, separate the results in you from the external influences at work around you, that you say so boldly that you get nothing from the world? You do not *directly*, I know—but you do indirectly & by a rebound. Whatever acts upon you, becomes *you* ... [94]

I will never fail to you from any human influence whatever—*that*, I have promised ... [95]

I dare say you have asked yourself sometimes, why it was that I never managed to draw you into the house here, so that you might make your own way. Now *that* is one of the things impossible to me. I have not influence for *that*.[96]

I have my own thoughts of course ... & you have yours ... & the worst is that a third person looking down on us from some snow-capped height, & free from personal influences, would have *his* thoughts too ... [97]

The Brownings' success in discovering an idiolect of love within a sociolect of influence can be heard in a much later letter, in which Browning attempts to come to terms with his wife's death:

My life is fixed and sure now. I shall live out the remainder in her direct influence ... I shall live in the presence of her, in every sense, I hope and

[94] EBB to RB (17 April 1845), *Kintner*, 48.
[95] EBB to RB (17 October 1845), *Kintner*, 240.
[96] EBB to RB (26–7 January 1846), *Kintner*, 423.
[97] EBB to RB (26 February 1846), *Kintner*, 494.

believe—so that so far my loss is not irreparable— ... Pen has been perfect to me: he sate all yesterday with his arms round me; said things like her to me ... Don't be in any concern for me, I have some of her strength, really, added to mine.[98]

When the Brownings' love letters were published by their son, 'Pen' Browning, he explained that his parents never wrote to one another again, 'for after their marriage they were never separated'.[99] We hear in this letter how closely his parents' voices continued to be involved in one another even after their separation by death, as Browning returns once again to their shared vocabulary of 'strength' and 'influence'. The morning after EBB had finally promised to leave with him, Browning wrote to her of the 'hundred deepest reasons for gratitude and love which I could write about but which my after life shall prove I have never forgotten'.[100] Now, after her death, he finds strength in what remains behind in his dark promise to live through Pen ('his arms round me'), but also by drawing out his wife's dying words through his description of them. His account of EBB's final moments shows how he had been prepared to recover the accents of a loved voice he could now hear only in his own:

She put her arms round me 'God bless you' repeatedly—kissing me with such vehemence that when I laid her down she continued to kiss the air with her lips, and several times raised her own hands and kissed them; I said 'Are you comfortable?' 'Beautiful.'[101]

A love that began with the exchange of letters is preserved with faint echoes of them, as Browning's compliment to his son ('Pen has been perfect to me') repeats the final postscript of EBB's final letter to her husband-to-be ('Wilson has been perfect to me'),[102] and she dies as she once used to sign off her letters, with a heartfelt 'God bless you'. It is, then, both fitting and touching that Browning chooses to end this letter with one word more from his wife, an expression of gratitude and love he is not yet finished with: 'How she looks now—how perfectly beautiful!'

---

[98] RB to Sarianna Browning (30 June 1861), repr. in Thurman L. Hood (ed.), *Letters of Robert Browning Collected by Thomas J. Wise* (1973), 62–3.

[99] Preface to the first volume of Robert Wiedemann Barrett Browning (ed.), *The Letters of Robert Browning and Elizabeth Barrett Barrett, 1845–1846* (2 vols., 1899).

[100] RB to EBB (10 September 1846), *Kintner*, 1059.

[101] Hood, *Letters of Robert Browning*, 62.

[102] EBB to RB (18 September 1846), *Kintner*, 1087.

'... THE MORAL ATMOSPHERE ...'

'I shall live in the presence of her': Browning's words illuminate J. S. Mill's description of the poet's 'power':

... that which enables us, by a voluntary effort, to conceive the absent as if it were present, the imaginary as if it were real, and to clothe it in the feelings which, if it were indeed real, it would bring along with it. This is the power by which one human being enters into the mind and circumstances of another.[103]

The cautious advance of Mill's syntax is fully alive to the differing weights which could be placed on those 'as if's, from willed illusion to haunted delusion. After all, as Mill also recognized when attempting to explain how the idea of history as teleological development had been diffused throughout nineteenth-century France, it is not only by 'voluntary effort' that one person 'enters into the mind and circumstances of another':

Certain conceptions of history considered as a whole, some notions of a progressive unfolding of the capabilities of humanity—of a tendency of man and society towards some distant result—of a *destination*, as it were, of humanity—pervade, in its whole extent, the popular literature of France. Every newspaper, every literary review or magazine, bears witness of such notions. They are always turning up accidentally, when the writer is ostensibly engaged with something else; or showing themselves as a background behind the opinions which he is immediately maintaining. When the writer's mind is not of a high order, these notions are crude and vague; but they are evidentiary of a tone of thought which has prevailed so long among the superior intellects, as to have spread from them to others, and become the general property of the nation.[104]

This spreading 'tone of thought', which provides a means of cultural self-definition too pervasive and shifty to be traced to any single origin, makes its own presence felt in Mill's description, because it is echoed in Arnold's later praise for the source of a writer's habitual 'self-control' in 'the tone of the city, of the centre, the tone which always aims at a spiritual and intellectual effect'.[105] So regular are Arnold's returns to this 'tone' in his cultural criticism that he goes some way to providing a practical demonstration of the model of

---

[103] 'Bentham', repr. in F. R. Leavis (ed.), *Mill on Bentham and Coleridge* (1950), 61–2.
[104] J. S. Mill, 'Guizot's Essays and Lectures on History' (1845), repr. in *Dissertations and Discussions Political, Philosophical and Historical* (4 vols., 3rd edn., 1875), II. 221.
[105] 'The Literary Influence of Academies' (1865), repr. in *Super*, III. 241–54.

influence Mill describes: a prevailing mode of elevated thought and expression to which Arnold's own writing responds as both diagnosis and therapy. However, to draw upon a shared discourse of influence, as both writers do when explaining what silently tells upon our voices, is also to disclose how much of what we say is directed through intellectual currents which are usually hidden behind and between our words, and so to restore to conscious speech how intimately we are involved in one another's silent imaginative worlds. The common use which Mill and Arnold make of 'tone', like the Brownings' passionate scrutiny of the public idiom which their letters worked within and worked against, then provides a self-conscious illustration of a widespread habit in Victorian writing: adapting a shared vocabulary of influence to investigate the intellectual affinities, proximities, and crossing-points which invisibly join people and ideas.

Butler's Mr Pontifex, in *The Way of All Flesh*, expresses the hope that naming his son Ernest 'might, like his having been baptised in water from the Jordan, have a permanent effect upon the boy's character, and influence him for good during the more critical periods of his life'.[106] His remark provides a keen parody of more simple-minded versions of Smiles's ideas, such as the assumption that individual wills can be invariably moulded to the shape of the same moral examples—an assumption which was also to sharpen Wilde's satirical edge. The unresolved ambiguity over whether influencing somebody 'for good' will involve effects which are morally improving, or merely permanent, draws attention to the self-consciousness with which any writer could approach these questions regarding the power of example to be both preserved and diffused by particular actions. The shape of a poem, say, might show how the writer's thinking proceeds by falling in and out of step with borrowed patterns of thought, and so stage the competing tugs upon his voice of development and reversion: the need for independent speech to move away from the frames which guide it, and the anxiety that speech which is altogether freed of its attachment to these frames might also be cut loose from the audience to whose ears particular forms have gradually attuned themselves. By subjecting the 'critical periods' of influence upon the poet's voice to the controlled periodicities of his verse, this poem would then provide a detailed enquiry into how he has come to speak with a voice which is both intimately his own and not

---

[106]   *The Way of All Flesh* (1903, repr. 1933), 87.

his own. Furthermore, as Butler reminds us by linking 'influence' with a quick smack at baptism, because this voice will be indelibly marked by traces of the intellectual disputes which have preoccupied and shaped our shared language, the way it is organized on the page can also be used to examine the Victorian era as a far larger 'critical period' in the long and ongoing history of literature's gradual emancipation from other social institutions, such as religious authority or political patronage.

Reflecting on her life, in 1859, George Eliot recognized that it was not just the past which exercised its cumulative pressures on present conduct: 'The weight of my future life exerts an almost paralysing effect.'[107] Caught between a wholly unalterable past and an infinitely malleable future, her comment is curiously suspended between anticipation and mourning, as if wondering whether our most painful losses could be those we have yet to suffer. Eliot was unusual in her ability to release these feelings of paralysis into the structure of her novels, so many of which inhabit the growing gap which is opened up between the future her characters imagine for themselves, and the one her narrative provides for them, that together they form one of the period's most finely worked sets of literary experiments in the production of disappointment. But she was not unusual in recognizing that the burden of the future could encourage a self-consciousness as crippling for the Victorians as that central worry, identified by Walter Jackson Bate, around which so much eighteenth-century writing painstakingly revolves: 'the burden of the past'. 'We are crushed', wrote F. D. Maurice in 1833, 'by the spirit of this world, by the horrible Babylonian oppression … of contradictory opinions, strifes, divisions, heresies, selfishness. We feel this spirit around us, above us, within us.'[108] Maurice was writing a year after the disputed passage of the Reform Act, so he might have added that this spirit was also before him: the anxiety that a system of government rooted in the wrangling of opposed political parties risked the creation of fresh divisions with every attempt at consensus or compromise. The debates of the years that followed added a particular strain to this anxiety by pointing out that, within a developing parliamentary democracy, each voter's voice was less likely to be of equal weight than it was to be combined into the uneven and unstable pressures of

---

[107] Gordon S. Haight (ed.), *The George Eliot Letters* (9 vols., 1954–78), III. 170.
[108] Quoted in Walter E. Houghton, *The Victorian Frame of Mind*, 72.

factional self-interest. In Disraeli's *Coningsby* (1844), set against the turbulent political activity of 1832, Eustace Lyle confesses that he too feels 'confused, perplexed, harassed. I know that I have public duties to perform; I am, in fact, every day of my life solicited by all parties to throw the weight of my influence in one scale or another; but I am paralysed' (ch. 23). Faced with endless and conflicting demands upon his attention, the politician's 'public duties' become impossibly plural, and action is suspended in the pause for reflection which separates each appeal. These demands raise important questions relating to political representation. How should elected politicians exercise their delegated powers in ways which are both fair and effective? How can a democracy function without elevating the wishes of some voters above others? Should parliamentary representatives follow the urgings of their own consciences, or those of the constituents whose views they are elected to represent? The same demands raise equally important questions relating to literary representation, because as the ambivalent status of Lyle's speech suggests—the dilemma over what he should do is left unfinished as an argument, but forms part of an achieved piece of fiction— Victorian theories concerning the mutual responsibilities of the individual and the group find their most urgent application in the 'public duties' which are exercised on and in the voice of the published writer.[109]

Joseph Brodsky's remarks on the relationship between literature and democracy provide a suggestive sketch of the writer's predicament:

A writer ... is a democrat by definition, and the poet always hopes for some parallelism between the processes taking place in his own work and those in the consciousness of the reader.[110]

... we should bear in mind that art is not a democratic enterprise, even the art of prose, which has an air about it of everybody being able to master it as well as to judge it.[111]

To a critic these remarks could seem contradictory. To a writer they are more likely to be complementary: the dialectical opposition of ideas out of which a literary work evolves its singular life. The precise

---

[109] Eric Griffiths has explored the implications of this idea in *The Printed Voice of Victorian Poetry*, 78–80.
[110] 'Footnote to a Poem', *Less Than One*, 200.
[111] 'Catastrophes in the Air', ibid., 302.

form taken by this life will to a large extent be determined by the way it responds to a further set of questions. Should the writer present himself or herself as an active leader of the reading public, or as its neutral mouthpiece? Should the style and dissemination of his or her work reflect social divisions, or seek to heal them? Should he or she record the present state of the world, or use the inevitable time-lag which is built into publication to do what Hazlitt accused Bentham of doing: setting down ideas which 'legislated for future times'?[112] These and similar questions, constantly present even if rarely asked, are likely to confront all writers who are influenced by the variable needs of the literary marketplace. They form an especially acute problem for Victorian writers, for whom the gradual collapse of a coherent reading public threatened to replace the imaginative reciprocity of author and audience with a series of pathological alternatives.[113] The growth of sociology during the 1880s and 1890s would attempt to describe forms of collective behaviour, from the suggestibility of crowds to the development of social crazes, which revealed what Daniel Pick has described as 'a shadowy world of social communication and mutual psychic entanglement' running alongside, and occasionally running into, the more visible world of conscious human relationships.[114] Like empirical psychology, from which it emerged as a parallel attempt to explain those parts of our lives which forever threaten to escape our notice, sociology provided both a set of solutions and a fresh set of problems, because it seemed to show that people were being most themselves when they were behaving most like one another. Visiting the Great Exhibition in 1851, Charlotte Brontë described how 'The multitude filling the great aisles seemed ruled and subdued by some invisible influence', drifting past the surprising sights of the Crystal Palace, with the cool imperturbability of fish in a glass tank, as if controlled by 'superhuman hands'.[115] The tone of her account, uneasily suspended between mirth and fear, reproduces a standard ambivalence about the ability of the mesmerist to use his hands as organs of seduction and coercion, exerting his will over his subjects and so freeing them from the responsibility of choice. It also resonates

[112] *The Spirit of the Age, Howe*, XI. 5.

[113] On the early stirrings of this collapse as 'one of the most far-reaching influences of modern times', see Bertrand Harris Bronson, *Facets of the Enlightenment: Studies in English Literature and its Contexts* (1968), 299.

[114] *Svengali's Web*, 81.

[115] Letter to her father (October 1851), quoted in Alison Winter, *Mesmerised: Powers of Mind in Victorian Britain* (1998), 26–7.

self-consciously with the idea that the hand of the writer was similarly associated with establishing conditions of control over suggestible groups of people. Sceptics pointed out that anyone who believed, with the more wide-eyed enthusiasts of mesmerism, that somebody 'under the influence of mesmerism could read a book in the next room', was 'labouring under a delusion'.[116] However, even where the impact of mesmerism was diluted from the affirmations of belief to the assumptions of vocabulary, the idea that readers formed a collective body which could be gripped by the same piece of writing, nerves jumping and pulses racing as one, slipped easily into discussions of the writer's influence, because the notion that influence was at its strongest where it was exercised indirectly, through a dispersed communion of readers, already formed a sharp focus of Victorian critical debate.

Leslie Stephen asked in 1876:

> How is it that a tacit intellectual cooperation is established between minds placed far apart in the scale of culture and natural acuteness? How is it that the thought of the intellectual leaders is obscurely reflected by so many darkened mirrors?[117]

One answer to these questions is suggested by John Henry Newman's warning that what his countrymen celebrated as their 'private judgment' on religious questions often meant nothing more than 'passive impression':

> Most men in this country like opinions to be brought to them, rather than to be at the pains to go out and seek for them. They like to be waited on, they like to be consulted for, they like to be their own centre.... Hence the extreme influence of periodical publications at this day [which] teach the multitude of men what to think and what to say...In good faith and in sincerity of heart [the Englishman] measures all things in heaven and earth by the floating opinions which have been drifted into his mind.[118]

A pointed literary echo (Hamlet's 'There are more things in heaven and earth, Horatio, | Than are dreamt of in our philosophy') reminds Newman's readers how much of what they have to think about and think with comes from a 'tacit intellectual cooperation' working below their full consciousness.[119] Even if the average Englishman's

---

[116] John Ashburner, 'Facts in Clairvoyance', *The Zoist*, 6 (1848–9), 96.

[117] Quoted in Walter E. Houghton, *The Victorian Frame of Mind*, xvi.

[118] 'Christ Upon the Waters' (1850), repr. in *Sermons Preached Upon Several Occasions* (3rd edn., 1870), 148–51.

[119] *Hamlet*, I. v. 174–5.

head contains what Newman characterizes as 'an accidental collection of tenets',[120] intellectual odds and ends picked up here and there, the repeated efforts of periodical writers to influence these tenets (notice the unexpected appearance of 'been' in 'have *been* drifted into his mind') show how some accidents can be planned for, some chances made more likely than others. What is less clear, however, is whether these 'floating opinions' might also drift more indirectly into their minds and mouths, spreading—like Leslie Stephen's Biblical fragment—with that anonymous stealth which Coleridge beautifully described, in the account of frost which opens 'Frost at Midnight', as nature's 'silent ministry'.

Darwin provides a good description of this process of indirect influence when he warns his son George not to submit an article to *The Contemporary Review* on 'future reward and punishments', by reminding him of Voltaire's discovery that 'direct attacks on Christianity ... produce little permanent effects', and that 'good seems only to follow from slow & silent side attacks'.[121] Tell the truth but tell it slant, seems to be the advice; avoid the head-on assault of argument, and instead fall back on the oblique but steady moulding of public opinion which Matthew Arnold associated with the moderating effects of the clerisy:

... we have told silently upon the mind of the country, we have prepared currents of feeling which sap our adversaries' position when it seems gained, we have kept up our own communications with the future. Look at the course of the great movement which shook Oxford some thirty years ago! It was directed ... against what in one word may be called 'Liberalism'. Liberalism prevailed; it was the appointed force to do the work of the hour ... [122]

Describing liberalism as an 'appointed force' muddles socio-political and religious vocabularies in a way which leaves it characteristically (and for Arnold perhaps necessarily) unclear whether liberal opinion prevailed because the machinery of government, organized around an intricate network of democratic representation and unofficial patronage, worked to sway public feeling in favour of established values, or because the crisis had proved beyond reasonable doubt that God was a supporter of the Church of England. However, what

---

[120] 'Christ Upon the Waters', 151.

[121] See Adrian Desmond and James Moore, *Darwin* (1991), 602–3.

[122] *Culture and Anarchy*, repr. in *Super*, V. 106. Ben Knights sets Arnold into the context of Victorian debates over the role and responsibilities of the clerisy in *The Idea of the Clerisy in the Nineteenth Century* (1978), 100–39.

links Arnold with Newman and Darwin, in many ways a surprising meeting of minds, is precisely this understanding that what distinguishes influence from persuasion or sheer coercion is its ability to 'tell silently', providing supplementary routes of communication to those we use to approach one another more directly.

A conviction that 'the power by which one human being enters into the mind and circumstances of another' includes these invisible and cumulative social pressures is richly supported in the period by a range of writings which struggle to come to terms with the variable and untidy workings of influence.[123] Such writings often rely less upon explicit argument than upon the assumptions which are carried by their rhetoric: the extension of syntax to insinuate the spread of ideas; the use of metaphor to suggest how influence blurs self and other, sameness and difference. And, like the notions of progress which Mill describes in his account of a nation's characteristic 'tone of thought', these rhetorical gambits 'are always turning up accidentally, when the writer is ostensibly engaged with something else; or showing themselves as a background behind the opinions which he is immediately maintaining'.

The idea that our acts and words can be compared with a stone dropped into a pond, for example, ripples through a number of accounts to create a characteristic tone, at once scientific and homely, for attempts to consider how far our influence stretches. 'The Lounger in Society' describes the 'constantly increasing circle' of 'Our Influence on One Another'; the anonymous author of *The Wives of England* argues for 'the influence of individual character upon a surrounding circle ... from which will radiate good or evil influence extending onwards, in the same manner, to the end of all things'; earnest churchmen like Asa Saxe grapple with the question 'Why does not a wave of influence go out from the central spirit and make creation clean?'[124] Taken together, these accounts suggest an idealized form of social influence, which extends from a set of fixed centres (the self, family, religion) towards the periphery of other people and institutions. At the same time, the indiscriminate

---

[123] Compare R. H. Hutton's argument that even Positivists could be affected by 'the constant influence of a religion by which, nevertheless, they were only imperfectly penetrated', 'Mr. Coter Morison on "The Service of Man"', repr. in *Criticisms on Contemporary Thought and Thinkers* (2 vols., 1898), I. 278.

[124] [W. H. Davenport Adams], *The Glass of Fashion* (1881), 325; Anon., *The Wives of England* (1843), 344–5; Revd Asa Saxe, 'Influence', *The Universalist Quarterly and General Review*, 47 (1890), 36.

reappearance of their shared metaphor reveals how easily this sort of orderly spread could be disrupted: there is always the possibility of an unexpected turn of thought or phrase becoming familiar through diffusion, of the eccentric becoming concentric. Arnold's own contrast between the 'wholesome restraining influences' of the cultural centre, and the cramping of style a writer suffers if confined to the margin or periphery, relies on a vocabulary ('check', 'force') which works between many of these metaphors, creating a hovering question mark over whether our impact on one another is insubstantial (like a tone), or leaves evidence of its form and pressure (like a stone). So, when George Eliot writes on 'The Influence of Rationalism', she cheers the 'great historical collisions' which are creating 'railways, steamships, and electric telegraphs, which are demonstrating the interdependence of all human interests, and making self-interest a duct for sympathy'; W. E. H. Lecky's book shows how these 'sequences of things … press themselves upon us like bars of iron'. And yet, although Eliot confesses herself 'strongly impressed' by Lecky, her language is also gripped by the less comforting thought that if 'external Reason' spreads and connects like metal railway-tracks, it might weigh as heavy as the tortures Lecky describes:[125]

The first was a kind of thumb-screw; the second was a frame in which the leg was inserted, and in which it was broken by wedges, driven in by a hammer; the third was also an iron frame for the leg, which was from time to time heated over a brazier.[126]

Eliot's anxieties over the 'impressions' of influence are shared by other writers, as they consider possible connections between the older sense of 'influence' as the external government of behaviour, and this enriched sense of moral and psychological hold.[127] Hands, for example, are described repeatedly and at length, because they represent the expressive extremities of our bodies which also threaten to cross the boundaries which separate one body from another. In *Great Expectations*, Jaggers demonstrates his control over Estella's mother by taking her by the hand:

He took his hand from hers, and turned that wrist up on the table. She brought her other hand from behind her, and held the two out side by side.

---

[125] Review of Lecky, *History of the Rise and Influence of the Spirit of Rationalism in Europe* (2 vols., 1865), repr. in Nathan Sheppard (ed.), *The Essays of George Eliot* (1883), 261, 270–1.

[126] *History of the Rise and Influence of the Spirit of Rationalism in Europe*, I. 142.

[127] See Steven Mintz, *A Prison of Expectations* (1983), 27–39.

The last wrist was much disfigured—deeply scarred and scarred across and across.... 'There's power here,' said Mr. Jaggers, coolly tracing out the sinews with his forefinger. 'Very few men have the power of wrist that this woman has. It's remarkable what mere force of grip there is in these hands.'   (ch. 26)

This is an extraordinary and creepy piece of writing, as the cool discussion about 'force of grip' plays across Jaggers's power over that grip, and the tiny pulse of his forefinger rubs against the surface swelling of another hand's veins and sinews. But however 'remarkable' Molly's grip, hers are not the only hands which retain a hold on Pip's imagination. His view of the world is abruptly and permanently refocused through Estella's scorn for his 'coarse hands':

I had never thought of being ashamed of my hands before; but I began to consider them a very indifferent pair. Her contempt was so strong, that it became infectious, and I caught it.   (ch. 8)

Ashamed of his hands as 'vulgar appendages' (ch. 7), body parts which are attached to him without seeming fully to belong to him, Pip diligently attends to other people's hands: Jaggers's hand, for example, which 'smelt of scented soap' (ch. 11); or Biddy's hands, which 'always wanted washing' when young (ch. 7), but then seem to be 'always clean' (ch. 17). Both offer a mute reproach to Pip's own hands, which emblematically busy themselves in '[writing] my name with my finger several times in the dirt of every pane in the window' (ch. 21), as if keen to express their owner's latent suspicion that his good name in society, his personal and financial credit, has already been underwritten by Magwitch's dirty hands.

Great Expectations returns repeatedly to the rich vocabulary of human touch, like a thesaurus entry spread out through the novel, because in its narrator's eyes and voice other people's hands seem to function both as metonymic fragments of the body and signatures of personality: Magwitch's 'large brown veinous hands' (ch. 39); Miss Havisham's 'wasting hands' (ch. 38); Estella's 'taunting hand' (ch. 9); Mrs Joe's 'hard and heavy hand' (ch. 2). Even when they are expressing intentions for future conduct—as with those pivotal moments in Pip's narrative where a handshake signifies a decision made or a friendship affirmed—hands point towards origins. The way Pip's narrative broods, with appalled fascination, over details which it seemed to have lightly touched upon and abandoned, then produces one of Dickens's most sympathetic investigations into the way that children can be so easily and lastingly impressed, and so easily and unpredictably bored. As the frequency of his returns to hands invests the formal tenderness of Victorian social relations into the character-istic rhythms of his voice, its narrative pulse, so the suddenness of their reappearance comes to suggest our limited ability to control the past and its effects on present behaviour: 'It is not possible to know how far the influence of any amiable honest-hearted duty-doing man flies out into the world; but it is very possible to know how it has touched one's self in going by ...' (ch. 14). Pip's choice of metaphor brings into unsettled equilibrium an inevitable self-consciousness and the equally inevitable limits of self-knowledge, because it is true both to the way that certain pairs of hands have permanently 'touched' the way he sees and describes the world, and to the more anonymous inflections of a shared language which cannot be traced to any particular speaker. After all, it is not only shameful individuals like Pip to whom hands represent such a compelling invitation and threat to self-expression. Like the irregular aftershocks of an event which '[fly] out into the world', writing about hands is in the air.

Popularizers of mesmerism frequently pointed out that the mys-terious flow of magnetic spirit from the mesmerist's fingertips allowed him to bridge physical distances and gaps of understanding. In the strange and estranging communion of mesmerism, the mesmerist's delayed touch disclosed that minds could be manipulated as easily as bodies. A similar vocabulary filters into less exotic descriptions of personal influence, where it functions as a convenient shorthand for debates over how far it is possible to 'move' or 'grasp' the behaviour of other people even when they are beyond our physical reach. The presence of hands in a piece of writing, then, often conveys an attempt to discover points of contact between ideas and vocabularies from both established and emerging fields of enquiry, such as ethics, sociology, and psychology. As hands can signify in concentrated form the meaning of diverse social encounters, from the clinching hand-shake of a business deal to the tender pressures of lovers' hands, so the way they are described can represent in equally concentrated form a range of possible encounters between different models of influence.

An 1851 article on 'Influence' argues that, observing 'a strong mind', and conscious of our own deficiencies, 'we involuntarily seek to imbibe by contact, and, as it were, strengthen a weak part'.[128] By 1871, the author of 'The Influence of Externals' is worrying that, in a

---

[128] *Chambers' Edinburgh Journal*, 15 (January 1851), 8.

mob, 'imitation supplants self-rule', but also noticing how contact can be avoided even in 'the confusion of a great city'. A match-girl can walk 'but a few arms-lengths from a nobleman's daughter passing by in her carriage', but if 'no kindly human hand is stretched forth to lead her into sober duties', her own calloused hand will remain an untouched record of 'the power of home-culture':

> The influence of externals has great power in modifying the hand: you may form some idea of a person's training, work, habits, and even phase of mind, from the hand. That poor match-girl's hand has nothing attractive in it, being probably (though not of necessity) dumpy, ill-grained, rough, and dirty, with nails not to be mentioned; whereas our young lady's hand is probably clean, smooth, fine-grained, with delicate, pleasing nails.[129]

This lingeringly detailed description has a Jaggers-like coolness of tone, with references to the hand's 'grain' and 'nails' which make it seem as if the author, so keen to assert that anatomy is destiny, would be happier describing a match-girl's hand which was made out of a substance more durable and compliant than flesh, such as wood. Yet this oddly fetishistic attention to hands resonates, in its self-doubts and self-qualifications ('probably ... not of necessity ... probably'), with more mainstream concerns over the extent to which 'the influence of externals' can overpower the influence of heredity, and the extent to which social class, by revealing the variable sway of these influences, provides a way of calibrating the dialectical set of struggles between family and environment which largely shape human development.

*

What these writers share, and reflect in the shape of their writing, is the understanding that to judge how far we can influence the 'mind and circumstances' of another person will ask us to consider the relevant circumstances of each mind: the encounters of necessity and accident, strategy and improvization, physical surroundings and moral reflection which punctuate and structure our shared passage through the world. Smiles cites approvingly the 'personal influence' of one mother:

> When she entered a room it had the effect of immediately raising the tone of the conversation, and as if purifying the moral atmosphere—all seeming to

---

[129] 'H. P.', 'The Influence of Externals', in *Dublin University Magazine*, 78 (July 1871), 77.

breathe more freely, and stand more erectly. 'In her presence', says the daughter, 'I became for the time transformed into another person.' So much does the moral health depend upon the moral atmosphere that is breathed.[130]

It is the pleasure and duty of being transformed into another person, and breathing in sympathy, which the moment of reading also offers. Yet, as Smiles concedes with a later reference to the 'manners [which] are about us everywhere, pervading society like the air we breathe',[131] the prospect of being 'transformed into another person' will not always be a matter of choice or a source of unalloyed pleasure.

The spreading associations made by Victorian metaphors of breath, for example, reveal how it is possible to be profoundly, even terminally, affected by other people without ever having met them. The author of 'The Influence of Externals' explains that, unlike a 'poor child of evil influences and unwholesome dwelling', a girl raised in an 'atmosphere of comparative purity and airiness' will continue to be surrounded by the 'fragrance of a sweet life'.[132] This idea that moral effects have physical causes ('airiness' measures a breezy confidence in the power of good example against the more basic need for well-ventilated living conditions),[133] and that it might therefore be possible to live within a private 'atmosphere' wholly unaffected by broader environmental pressures, was an attractive one to Dickens, whose characters often seem to carry personal microclimates around with them. When David Copperfield is going to bed, he feels the Murdstones coming into the house like 'a blast of cold air'; Scrooge 'carried his own low temperature always about with him', and 'didn't thaw it one degree at Christmas'; in *Bleak House*, Mrs Pardiggle 'seemed to come in like cold weather, and to make the little Pardiggles blue as they followed', while Mr Vholes is described riding on top of a stage-coach, with his shadow 'passing over all the sunny landscape' and 'chilling the seed in the ground as it glided along'.[134] The assumption that cold personalities will produce suitably chilly

---

130 *Self-Help*, 343.

131 Ibid., 367.

132 'The Influence of Externals', 77.

133 Compare Felix's worry in Patmore's *The Angel in the House* that his sweetheart Honoria will return 'alter'd' from the 'harmful influence' of London, 'having caught | The foolish, fashionable air | Of knowing all, and feeling nought' (*The Poems of Coventry Patmore*, 115).

134 I am indebted for these examples to John Carey's *The Violent Effigy: A Study of Dickens' Imagination* (1973), 134–5.

atmospheric effects is a minor Dickensian obsession, but when in *Dombey and Son* he describes Carker's 'daily breath', from which 'issues forth some subtle portion of himself, which gives a vague expression of himself to everything about him' (ch. 33), or invites his readers to follow the clergyman or doctor descending into the dens of the poor, 'with his life imperilled at every breath' (ch. 42), he also taps into the more orthodox Victorian idea that, whatever else we decide to keep to ourselves, the air which we share is no respector of physical boundaries or moral distinctions:

We reflect that the air ... is the fluid in which rich and poor are equally immersed—that it is a commonwealth in which all are born, live, and die equal ... a subject in which every member of the community is self-interested.[135]

As a 'commonwealth' which floats over and around our less democratic earthly communities, the air reminds us that worries over social 'origins' or 'mobility' cannot be restricted to physical location or economic ambition. After all, where tainted air is freely circulating between different areas of housing and classes of people (like the 'pestilential gas' of the slums in *Bleak House* which, in Dickens's ominously vague description, 'propagates infection and contagion elsewhere', ch. 16), an 'atmosphere of comparative purity and airiness' will be about as much help to the girl wafting around in it as burning sweet-smelling herbs was to sufferers of the plague. In this way, the spread of contagion provided a vengeful double for images of the radiating circles of influence, warning Victorian readers that they affected one another as much by their failures to act as by what they chose to do. Just as the air mixed up what they tried to keep physically separate, so metaphors of influence showed how shifty and reversible attitudes could be towards who or what was 'still breathing fresh life into men'.[136]

One key difficulty in writing about influence to which metaphor answered was that influence seems both to require narrative, by drawing on ideas of transition and change, and to refuse it, by implicitly conceding how many of its effects are unfinished or unplottable. Metaphor holds likeness and unlikeness in uneasy equipoise; it provided Victorian writers with a rhetorical framework which could support both sets of ideas at once, particularly when assessing how far

---

[135] *Quarterly Review*, 71 (1843), 421.
[136] *Self-Help*, 350.

influence could invisibly cross borders of sex, class, and education. Whether they relaxed into commonplaces or stiffened into questions metaphors of the shared air in particular allowed these writers to test how far we should welcome having another person's life breathed into our own. Just as the physical atmosphere contains the circulation and mingling of our breaths, so the idea of the atmosphere, its shifting dimensions on the page, became a site of speculative connections between different attempts to explain the limits of self-determination, sounding out their agreements and quarrels through overlaps of vocabulary or well-placed turns of phrase. As a term which describes what flows between people and ideas, 'influence' is regularly used in these accounts to observe the split loyalties which join us to many of our most cherished social beliefs. For example, there is a reasonable view of philosophical activity, largely deriving from Kant, which holds that morality is a form of pure disinterestedness far removed from such features of the everyday world as sewers and privies. (This ignores the less abstract attitude which many philosophers, including Kant, have taken towards the embodied nature of their own reflections.) There is an equally reasonable view which holds that this disinterestedness cannot be achieved through the conflicting demands of practical reasoning, not least because, as Bernard Williams points out, 'its insistence on abstracting the moral consciousness from other kinds of emotional reaction or social influence, conceals not only the means by which it deals with deviant members of its community, but also the virtues of those means'.[137] But the discourse of influence which Victorian writers tapped and extended offered a middle ground between these alternatives, an imaginative space in which their readers could weigh up the desire to construct a moral ideal which transcended local variations of habitat and class, against the equally necessary desire to recognize that moral reasoning, as a product of human consciousness, is no more immune from the inescapable forces of environment and accident than any other form of social behaviour.

A good example of this way of thinking and writing can be seen in Victorian accounts of criminal behaviour. Because criminals were often described in pathological terms as an incurable disease of the social body, descriptions of their activities are especially haunted by the fear that the moral blight which they represented would spread beyond control:

---

[137] *Ethics and the Limits of Philosophy* (1985, repr. 1993), 195.

It is clear that we have not yet found out what to do with our criminals. We neither reform them, nor hang them, nor do we keep them under lock and key, nor ship them off to the Antipodes. Our moral sewage is neither deodorised nor floated out to sea, but remains in the midst of us polluting and poisoning our air.[138]

However clearly criminals embody a nuisance and a puzzle to this reporter, it is less clear precisely what form of threat they represent. Written during a period still coming to terms with the implications of a new continental strain of criminal anthropology, which promised to reveal that criminals were a distinct species of mankind,[139] the report tests this foreign hypothesis by subjecting it to the sympathetic and suspicious attentions of its own language. The connotations of 'moral sewage', for example, spread into forms of speculation that allow the writer to exercise a caution which his argument seems to reject, because the phrase expresses the idea that criminals are both separate from us and part of us; they carry the threat of contamination, and represent the natural by-product of a healthily functioning social organism; they are the waste-matter we can do without but, like most of what we waste, they can be redeemed. (As sanitation campaigners were keen to point out, when arguing that the city's sticky deposits of dung should be recycled as agricultural fertilizer, even sewage can contribute to the economic health of the nation if it is properly treated.)[140] In this way, the writer amplifies on a rhetorical level worries over the possibility of autonomous action which his theoretical vocabulary is not yet advanced enough to articulate more explicitly. But by adapting for this new sociological context a phrase which appears so regularly elsewhere (Dickens, in *Our Mutual Friend*, refers to the banks of the River Thames as a place 'where accumulated scum of humanity seemed to be washed from higher grounds, like so much moral sewage', ch. 3), his report also shows how emergent intellectual disciplines were busy moulding expressions from a shared discourse of influence into their own likeness, in order to establish a distinct identity for themselves on the page.

---

[138] 'Ticket-of-leave men', *Saturday Review*, 14 (1862), 241–2.

[139] Daniel Pick offers a summary of these debates in *Faces of Degeneration: A European Disorder, c.1848–c.1918* (1989, repr. 1993), 178–88.

[140] This overlap of economic and ethical vocabularies is a commonplace feature of Victorian writing on waste management; see, e.g., 'Dust; or Ugliness Redeemed', in *Household Words*, 16 (13 July 1850), 379–84.

Waste offers an especially rich set of possibilities for writers interested in this translation of ideas between different professional communities and their distinctive idioms, because it has unmatched capacities for accumulation and transformation. As material waste brings together heterogeneous elements into the organized chaos of a single location, like a rubbish-tip or a dung-hill, so the concept of waste attracts and mingles heterogeneous ideas. Here Edwin Chadwick's influential *Report on the Sanitary Condition of the Labouring Population of Great Britain* (1842) sets the pattern for later writings on environmental reform, in the energetic efforts which it makes to retrieve principles of order and causality from the bewildering mess of overcrowded slums, and the equally energetic muddle which it makes of these principles in the self-enriching slippages of its own prose. For example, one of the *Report*'s most prominent and revealing words is 'nuisance', which frequently provides a pursed-lipped attempt to describe particular blackspots of human excrement and filth, but cannot always restrain itself from ascribing blame to the people who create them. Filtered through the language of 'nuisances', a messy pavement represents both the signature of contingency and the scene of a crime. Several contributors to the *Report* make the connection only implicitly, as they describe 'cleansing the town and removing nuisances', or complain that 'the city is surrounded with such nuisances'.[141] Others free up the link with more explicit condemnations of poor hygiene, as they explain that 'the streets in this neighbourhood have for many years been an intolerable nuisance to the town at large', or argue that 'the nuisance of so many congregating' makes the stench of their unventilated homes a health hazard to the wider community.[142] Structured by these crossed lines of argument and assumption, the *Report*'s accounts of choking waste matter shift between description and explanation; narrative threatens to become plot; accident is reimagined as symptom or symbol. 'Nuisance' carries the sound of these conceptual shunts and skids with particular force, because it is uneasily situated between metaphor and metonymy: the poor produce nuisances, therefore they are nuisances. Focused through a language of dirt and decay which has a foot in both the physical and moral worlds, description is repeatedly invested with judgement, so when we read that certain foul-smelling

[141] Edwin Chadwick, *Report on the Sanitary Condition of the Labouring Population of Great Britain* (1842) ed. M. W. Flinn (1965), 87, 95.
[142] Ibid., 412, 415.

lodging houses are located 'in the midst of nuisances giving rise to malaria',[143] the confusion over whether these 'nuisances' come from humans, or simply are humans, detonates an unresolved ambiguity which runs through the whole *Report*. This unsteady set of exchanges between literal and figurative senses of 'cleanliness' is solidified by Chadwick's conclusion, which argues that a population left to rot in its own sewage 'is less susceptible to moral influences':

... the removal of noxious physical circumstances, and the promotion of civic, household, and personal cleanliness, are necessary to the improvement of the moral condition of the population; for that sound morality and refinement in manners and health are not long found co-existent with filthy habits among any class of the community.[144]

The collision of 'physical circumstances' and 'moral condition' in 'filthy habits' finally reconciles two strands of thought that the *Report* has twisted together into a suggestive explanation of the inextricably 'co-existent' sources of human behaviour, the double helix of our social DNA, which are to be found in the environment and our responses to it.

Chadwick and his contributors are not the only writers in the period attracted to the fertile imaginative possibilities of 'filth'. In 1849, a newspaper investigation into slum living conditions explains how the reporter 'went from room to room, and from house to house—not to witness an endless repetition of filth and degradation, but in each house to see some additional wretchedness'.[145] As the account continues, the physical business of moving from room to room, and seeing the same messy misery in house after house, is mapped out in a suitably self-generating style, because as with the metaphoric loops and shimmies which Chadwick's *Report* makes between its subjects, filth is always seen to breed more filth,[146] just as it is forever threatening to clog up our capacities to describe it on paper. Like any form of muddle or clutter, to the writer this sort of mess represents what David Trotter has acutely identified as 'both a

---

[143] *Report*, 414.

[144] Ibid., 370.

[145] *The Times* (9 July 1849), 3. I am grateful to Dan Clarke for drawing this example to my attention.

[146] See Christopher Hamlin's survey 'Providence and Putrefaction: Victorian Sanitation and the Natural Theology of Health and Disease', *Victorian Studies*, 28: 3 (Spring 1985), 381–411.

source of invention and a thwarting'.[147] The *Report*'s uses of 'influence' and its cognates ('effluence', 'effluvia', 'influenza', and so on) are even more powerfully charged by these 'co-existent' ideas surrounding the effects which human beings and their world can have on one another, because the word's appearance in descriptions of open sewers or overflowing privies suffers from analogous processes to the ones it describes. In the same way that human beings lose their physical and moral distinction through the mingled waste matter they produce, so 'influence' generates fertile categories of semantic spillage and flux.

To some extent, this instability of 'influence' as an explanatory term reflects broader shifts in Victorian science. Writing in 1847 of the urgent need for further sanitation reform, the report of public health inspector William Farr shivers with an indignation which is typical of the growing agreement in medical circles that disease was transmitted by invisible clouds of 'miasma':

This disease-mist, arising from the breath of two millions of people, from open sewers and cess-pools, graves and slaughter-houses, is continually kept up and undergoing changes; in one season it is pervaded by cholera, in another by influenza; at one time it bears smallpox, measles, scarlatina, and whooping-cough among your children; at another it carries fever on its wings. Like an angel of death, it has hovered for centuries over London. But it may be driven away by legislation.[148]

The miasmatic theory of disease would itself be driven away in the 1870s and 1880s by the development of bacteriology, but for much of the Victorian period it exerted a powerful sway over the popular and literary imagination. It emerges sporadically in a disgusted fascin-ation with the smells of poverty, as Chadwick's *Report* wrinkles its nose at the 'atmosphere of gin, brimstone, onions and disease' which the poor generate around themselves,[149] or as *Aurora Leigh* describes how the crowds from St Giles's slum 'ooze' into church in a 'dark slow stream', poisoning the 'unaccustomed air' with their 'hideous inter-fusion'.[150] It generates Charles Kingsley's 1869 lecture 'The Two Breaths', which warns gloomily that

Those who habitually take in the breath which has been breathed out by themselves, or any other living creatures, will certainly grow up, if they grow

---

[147] *Cooking With Mud*, 8.
[148] William Farr, *Tenth Annual Report of the Registrar-General* (1847), xvii.
[149] *Report*, 411.
[150] Elizabeth Barrett Browning, *Aurora Leigh* (1856), ed. Cora Kaplan (1978), 172.

up at all, small, weak, pale nervous, depressed, unfit for work, and tempted continually to resort to stimulants, and become drunkards.[151]

It even helps to structure the writing career of Dickens, for whom, as Humphrey House pointed out, 'In *Pickwick* a bad smell was a bad smell; in *Our Mutual Friend* it is a problem.'[152]

Dickens's preoccupation with smells lingers, leaving its character-istic trace in the atmosphere of his writing, thereby allowing descriptions of even the most chaotic of structures and fluid of forms, from stinking dung-hills to disease-breeding slime, to contribute to his own orderly imaginative growth. For other writers of the period, though, smells produced a worrying air of contingency around human development, in particular the chance that diseased air could lead to our being 'transformed into another person'. Smells are invisible accidents, the messes we make but cannot clear up, because wherever the air touches us, some part of us is airborne. Like the 'disease-mist' which Farr describes, we are forever 'undergoing changes' as a result of the air we share; our bodies stubbornly insist on having meetings with one another that we cannot predict or control. It is because smells sensibly remind us that we cannot help releasing small parts of ourselves into other people's noses and lungs that they are especially good at alerting us to what invisibly flows between people, and to the medium of that flow. Similarly, because a shared discourse of influence provided Victorian writers with a flexible set of concepts to describe what was happening between them, it also provided a creative resource to account for other forms of individual and cultural in-between-ness.

In *David Copperfield*, for example, one of Uriah Heep's more un-pleasant habits is breathing into a horse's nostrils, 'and immediately covering them with his hand, as if he were putting some spell upon him' (ch. 15). The queasy juxtaposition of modern medical lore and folk magic, while being imaginatively true to the narrator's way of refracting his story through a double focus of the new and the old, is also historically true to similar overlaps in other forms of writing, as they adapt the developing conceptual contours of 'influence' to the

---

[151] *Sanitary and Social Lectures and Essays* (1892), 50. The same volume contains his essay 'Great Cities and their Influence for Good and Evil', which similarly collapses pathology and morality into a single vision of the 'influence' that crosses geographical and social divides: 'remember that these physical influences of great cities, physically depressing and morally degrading, influence, though to a less extent, the classes above the lowest stratum' (205).

[152] *The Dickens World* (2nd edn., 1942), 135.

established notion that our social environment (living conditions) could have effects on human behaviour just as grave as our natural environment (atmospheric conditions). One of Chadwick's investigators reports that he had to retreat to the open door of a particularly disgusting hovel to write his notes, 'as I found the stench and close atmosphere produce a sickening sensation which, on one occasion, terminated in vomiting'.[153] In the context of miasmatic contagion, his 'sickening sensation' represents both an instant recoil from the scene and the anxiety that he has already been infected by it. The experiments of medical researchers like Foy had sought to reproduce the earlier success with smallpox, by arguing that immunity from cholera could be achieved by 'inoculating [ourselves] with blood taken from the veins of cholera victims, in breathing their exhalations, and in tasting ... vomited liquids',[154] so one further implication of the observer's 'sickening sensation' is that, physiologically as well as psychologically, he would control his feelings of sickness rather better if only he could stop flinching from the stink and ooze of the poor.

These local oddities in Chadwick's *Report* provide idiosyncratic examples of a mainstream pattern in Victorian thinking: the process of cultural self-definition which Steven Connor has identified as 'experience becoming explanation'.[155] As a set of ideas and an activity, influence provided a vocabulary of flow and alteration to explain theories which were unstably situated between fields of enquiry, or changing too rapidly to be pinned down in a fixed set of terms. As it moved between speakers, this shared discourse of influence investigated what joined people and what kept them apart; as it repeatedly failed to come into clear focus, so the ongoing redefinition of its terms reflected the changeable processes that it was describing. In its anonymous circulation, it could make sense of the worry that human connections were invisible and unpredictable; in its regular reappearances within the structured world of print, it expressed the competing hope that these connections could be plotted and controlled.

*

[153] *Report*, 282.

[154] F. Foy, *Du choléra-morbus de Pologne* (1832), quoted in François Delaporte, *Disease and Civilisation: The Cholera in Paris, 1832*, trans. Arthur Goldhammer (1986), 165.

[155] 'Culture is neither experience on the one hand, nor explanation on the other; it is experience becoming explanation'; Connor's remark is discussed in David Trotter, *Cooking With Mud*, 9.

Victorian case-studies of moral development were especially attracted to the multiple associations spawned by this discourse, not least because they allowed the writer to express some solidarity with his or her subject: both were confronted with the practical dilemma of choice, and haunted by the worry that these choices were not altogether under their control. In *Self-Help*, Smiles tells his readers of a studious individual who ' "caught the infection" of self-improvement' from his friends;[156] in *Great Expectations*, when Pip asks Biddy how she manages to improve herself through education, she quietly replies, 'I suppose I must catch it—like a cough' (ch. 17). In both cases, descriptions of moral influence inoculate themselves, like a lexical equivalent of tasting diseased vomit, against the threat of being taken over by alien forces which was usually carried by a vocabulary of physical contagion. No writing in the period is entirely immune from this commingling of vocabularies, because as a number of Victorian critics pointed out, just as some corpses infected the physical atmosphere shared by everyone who breathes, so to open a book was to come into contact with a foreign body which threatened to infect the 'moral atmosphere' shared by everyone who reads. The circulation of words was potentially as damaging to the reading public's moral health as tainted matter was to their bodies.

Browning hints at the problem when he describes the 'effluence' of Shelley:

... what he produces will be less a work than an effluence. That effluence cannot be easily considered in abstraction from his personality—being indeed the very radiance and aroma of his personality, projected from it but not separated.[157]

There is a suggestion here that to be 'transformed into another person' through the processes of reading will require us temporarily to share not only the imaginative workings of the poet, his intellectual stance, but also the physiological patterns of pulse and breathing, those lingering traces of the poet's body, which are inescapably written into his verse. When the Revd John Trodd warns his readers to 'Beware of Bad Books', his attack on Byron tightens the connection:

---

[156] *Self-Help*, 349.
[157] 'An Essay on Percy Bysshe Shelley' (1852), repr. in *The Poetical Works of Robert Browning*, ed. Ian Jack *et al.* (7 vols., 1983–95), IV. 426.

Is he a benefactor to his species, who, here and there, throws out a beautiful thought, or a poetic image, but as you stoop to pick it up, chains upon you a putrid carcase, which you can never throw off?[158]

Ruskin's defence of Byron turns the same vocabulary in the opposite direction:

... we are clasped in the arms of the poetry as if borne away on the wings of an archangel, and our rapture is illimitable, and we are elevated and purified and ennobled by the mightiness of the influence that overshadows us.[159]

Although it is hard to take this strain of rhetoric as seriously as it takes itself, Ruskin's hope that 'hours whose wings were loaded with odours so soft, and tinted with colours so gay, may not be pronounced to have left ... pestilence in the air they have enchanted' helpfully reminds us of the extremes of self-consciousness which Victorian writers regularly threatened to reach once they recognized that 'influence' was both the subject and activity of their work. As the producers of objects which could have both physical and moral effects upon their readers, they were unavoidably inhabiting and extending the very problems they described.[160]

Between the first (1837) and second (1838) editions of his treatise, Babbage added a long coda to the chapter 'On the Permanent Impression of Our Words and Actions on the Globe We Inhabit', in which he explained what, other than stones, was routinely dropped into the sea: slaves.

The master having a large cargo of these human beings chained together, with more humanity than his fellows, permitted some of them to come on deck, but still chained together, for the benefit of the air; when they immediately commenced jumping overboard, hand in hand, and drowning in couples; and, continuing the person (relating the circumstance), 'without any cause whatever'.... The men are chained in pairs; and, as a proof they are intended so to remain to the end of the voyage, their fetters are not locked, but rivetted by the blacksmith, and as deaths are frequently occurring living men are often for a length of time confined to dead bodies; the living man cannot be released till the blacksmith has performed the operation of cutting the clench of the rivet with his chisel ... [161]

---

[158] Quoted in Ruskin's 'Essay on Literature' (1836), repr. in the *Collected Works*, ed. E. T. Cook and A. D. O. Wedderburn (39 vols., 1902–12), I. 358.

[159] Ibid., 374.

[160] Ibid., 358.

[161] Babbage, *The Ninth Bridgewater Treatise*, 117–18, citing a report by Captain Hayes to the Admiralty printed in the *Quarterly Review* (December 1835).

The catalogue of miseries described here is appalling, but equally appalling is the blithe indifference shown for them by 'the person (relating the circumstance)'. Babbage derives a certain comfort from the thought that in an 'after stage of existence', every quivering particle of the air and sea will give evidence of the slave-trader's orders and 'the last gurgle of the waters which closed over the head of his dying victim', but he also hints that it might not be only the slaves who are shackled together. Even the act of reading about this event risks swelling the parenthesis which pincers the phrase '(relating the circumstance)': it may not be possible to relate this story without relating oneself to it.

There are grounds for thinking that any description of man's routine inhumanity will need to be similarly divided between indignation and complicity. As Disraeli observed, in a speech about Jewish emancipation which thoughtfully turned on the idea that influence sometimes exerted its prejudicial pressures from a position below conscious thought:

You are influenced by the darkest superstitions of the darkest ages that ever existed in this country. It is this feeling that has been kept out of the debate; indeed that has been secret in yourselves—enlightened as you are—and that is unknowingly influencing you as it is influencing others abroad.[162]

That is, influence need not be as benignly forward-looking as theorists like Comte or Smiles assumed; it could equally represent the atavistic drag of the past, 'dark' secrets which an 'enlightened' human race largely keeps from itself. Any account of human progress will then need to measure its hopes for the future against a drawn-out version of Prospero's sigh: 'This thing of darkness I acknowledge mine.' What Babbage's account recognizes, however, is that it is through the narrative shapes which it retrieves from history that a culture endeavours to make sense out of the suffering it has produced in the course of its development. Although the slave-trader's actions add another link to the murderous chain which stretches back to Cain, the brackets around 'relating the circumstance' therefore suggest that the way these actions are described will also form one in a long line of this culture's efforts to shackle the physical facts of its history to their moral significance, to recover meaning from what seems to destroy it.

---

[162] *Hansard* (1847), quoted in Daniel Pick, *Svengali's Web*, 149.

Even where nobody else is present, whether directly (like the 'personal influence' of the mother described by Smiles) or indirectly (like the more impersonal influence of diseased air drifitng across from the slums), to be 'transformed into another person' could be an unsettling prospect, particularly for someone who is still coming to terms with what it is to be himself. '[F]irst impressions, you know, often last a long time, and go a long way': Dickens's enthusiasm for Babbage's notion that the mind can be physically 'impressed' with— and so for—good or evil, draws particularly upon the idea that the consequences of past actions last longer than the body which acted.[163] In *Great Expectations*, when the adult Pip returns to the ruined garden of Satis House, his body remembers:

I turned my head to look back. A childish association revived with wonderful force in the moment of the slight action, and I fancied that I saw Miss Havisham hanging to the beam (ch. 49).

Here Pip is looking back in time as well as space, so the 'wonderful force' of this sudden return to childhood perception includes a belated celebration of the child's unwitting skill in imaginative transformation, his readiness to reshape the world to fit his own desires. The ambivalent tone of 'wonderful force' also suggests Pip's rueful knowledge that it is only adults who possess the historical self-consciousness which would make this capacity for wonder into something 'wonderful'. As Arthur Hallam observed in his review of Tennyson's early fantasy, 'Recollections of the Arabian Nights', when we read again the stories which once thrilled our eyes, 'That happy ductility of childhood returns for a moment, and yet there is a latent knowledge, which heightens the pleasure, that to our change from really childish thought we owe the capacities by which we enjoy the recollection.'[164] However, Pip's imagination is not the only part of him which has changed, because his adult head is no longer the same as the child's head which had earlier been turned by such a fancy, subject not only to visible growth and change but also to what Walter Pater described as 'that continual vanishing away, that strange, perpetual weaving and unweaving of ourselves'.[165] For Babbage, though, the consequences of our actions endure even if our bodies

[163] *Martin Chuzzlewit*, ch. 5.

[164] Unsigned review of *Poems, Chiefly Lyrical* (1830), *Englishman's Magazine* (August 1831), repr. in *Motter*, 193.

[165] Harold Bloom (ed.), *Selected Writings* (1982), 60.

are no longer our own, and these actions also link our selves to other selves:

If the Almighty stamped on the brow of the earliest murderer,—the indelible and visible mark of his guilt,—he has also established laws by which every succeeding criminal is not less irrevocably chained to the testimony of his crime; for every atom of his mortal frame, through whatever changes its severed particles may migrate, will still retain, adhering to it through every combination, some movement derived from that very muscular effort, by which the crime itself was perpetrated.[166]

Tennyson's Ulysses could wander away from the scene of his actions and claim that 'I am a part of all that I have met.'[167] Babbage's Cain is even more stuck in the past: all that he has met is a part of him. Babbage's conviction over the slow migration of individual bodies emerges in his overlapping syntax: 'every ... irrevocably ... every ... whatever ... severed' strings a single idea across the page, preserving a continuity of thought through the shifting combinations of his syntax; but is the referent of 'his' ('chained to the testimony of his crime') a present-day malefactor, or does the chain stretch back further to Cain and 'his guilt'? The second 'his' snags on both possibilities, because given Babbage's premiss we cannot know how much of Cain (or Abel) survives in each of us.

   This speculative interest in the tainting afterlife of others' crimes finds an imaginative reception in Dickens, whose fictional children often have to atone for their 'inheritance of shame'.[168] He remembered his own boyhood self after his father's arrest for debt: '(small Cain that I was, except that I had never done harm to anyone)'.[169] As the parenthesis rotates around that measured pause which separates 'I was' and 'except', it forms a concentrated space of time in which Dickens suddenly grows up, and allows his adult self to perform an indignant double-take on the child whose situation should have provoked shame in others rather than in himself. The *cordon sanitaire* of the parenthesis sustains equally measured comparisons with *Great Expectation*'s Compeyson, who slouches out 'like Cain or the Wandering Jew' (ch. 15). Compeyson is the darkest double of erring Pip:

---

[166] Babbage, *The Ninth Bridgewater Treatise*, 116–17.
[167] *TP*, I. 616.
[168] *Bleak House*, ch. 44.
[169] John Forster, *The Life of Charles Dickens* (1874), 19; compare the 'young Cain' of *Dombey and Son*'s workshy Biler, ch. 22.

That was a memorable day to me, for it made great changes in me. But it is the same with any life. Imagine one selected day struck out of it, and think how different its course would have been. Pause you who read this, and think for a moment of the long chain of iron or gold, of thorns or flowers, that would never have bound you, but for the formation of the first link on one memorable day (ch. 9).

This 'moment' discovers an enriched echo in the later 'moment' of the turned head, because it might be only in retrospect that we distinguish what was of moment from what was merely of the moment. The child's freeing of 'my convict' (the possessive pronoun is disturbing, a possession being something we can suffer from as well as seize upon) then casts its own link, binding him to Abel Magwitch throughout his own body's changes of size and address, just as Babbage's prose is haunted by the fear that 'Cain' will always be hidden in 'chain', and 'chain' in 'change', as more than lurking puns.

Dickens was uneasily drawn to images of chains, conscious that days bound each to each can produce what De Quincey described with simmering understatement as 'subtle links of suffering',[170] but conscious too that these links cannot be cut out without disfiguring the self they bind together, as Redlaw, his 'Haunted Man', tries to destroy the 'golden links' of his 'intertwisted chain of feelings and associations, each in its turn dependent on, and nourished by ... recollections' (ch. 1). Coleridge's description of the processes of composition should make us wary of claiming that these anxieties form a characteristic signature only of Victorian literature:

Even your writing desk with its blank paper and all its other implements will appear as a chain of flowers, capable of linking your feelings as well as thoughts to events and characters past or to come; not a chain of iron which binds you down to think of the future and the remote by recalling the claims and feelings of the peremptory present.[171]

Similar metaphors are commonplace in earlier philosophical accounts of the mind's activities (notably those of Locke and his followers) which concern themselves with what succeeds in escaping our memories, and what we are bound to recall. Furthermore, it is not only published authors who might be self-conscious about contemplating the possible after-effects of their words, as Babbage's

---

[170] *Confessions of an English Opium-Eater* (1821), repr. in *De Quincey*, I. 13.
[171] J. Shawcross (ed.), *Biographia Literaria* (1979), II. 153–4.

description of the slave-trader proves. Later in his treatise Babbage expands on these ideas, and pushes them forward, by wondering how each of us will look back on our lives in the hereafter, as the 'last great day of human account' forcibly brings to mind all the moral pluses and minuses which have contributed to the final figure that we present (p. 116). Freed from the effects of time, he argues, memory will exist as a condition of total and simultaneous recall, as we recapture our words, or they catch up with us:

If we imagine the soul in an after stage of existence, connected with a bodily organ of hearing so sensitive, as to vibrate with motions of the air, even of infinitesimal force, and if it be still within the precincts of its ancient abode, all the accumulated words pronounced from the creation of mankind, will fall at once on that ear. Imagine, in addition, a power of directing the attention of that organ entirely to any one class of those vibrations: then will the apparent confusion vanish at once; and the punished offender may hear still vibrating on his ear the very words uttered, perhaps, thousands of centuries before, which at once caused and registered his own condemnation (p. 148).

It may well be, as Babbage claims, that there is no place for confusion in heaven, but there are certainly blurred edges to his earthly account of it. It is not clear, for instance, what sort of celestial ear-trumpet could 'connect' an immaterial soul with a 'bodily organ of hearing', nor how it would transfer vibrations to what is beyond them. It may be that Babbage has in mind some variation on the invisible 'ether' which earlier scientists had understood to act as a medium between mind and matter, such as Newton's notion of a physiological fluid that filled the nervous system, and linked volition with action by vibrating from the brain along to the muscles.[172] Nineteenth-century physicists, with a wary eye on spiritualism, were to develop this theory by appealing to an ether which would properly 'connect' mortal body and immortal soul. Oliver Lodge, for example, claimed that on death the 'spiritual body' referred to in I Corinthians 15: 44 ('There is a natural body, and there is a spiritual body') was released into the atmospheric ether of which it is composed. 'Our spiritual and real home is in the ether of space', and because this ether is a substance which differs equally from physical matter and 'spirit', but is able to interact with both, the participants at a séance would bear witness to the way that the ethereal body which carries the soul of a departed

---

[172] *Opticks* (2nd edn., 1718), 328.

person affects not only material objects, like tables, but also material subjects, like themselves.[173]

A more substantial shortcoming in Babbage's argument, however, is that our earthly ears might also want to perform these acts of ethical self-scrutiny, and they already possess a means for plotting out and brooding over a particular 'class of vibrations': writing.

'... SNATCHES OF OLD TUNES ...'

In 1866, a reader looking for Ophelia's death in the Cambridge Shakespeare edition of *Hamlet* would have found this:

> Her clothes spread wide,
> And mermaid-like awhile they bore her up:
> Which time she chanted snatches of old tunes,
> As one incapable of her own distress,
> Or like a creature native and indued
> Unto that element ... [174]

Like Ophelia, the Cambridge editors were interested in testing the acoustics of 'old tunes' in new settings. The reading text of their *Hamlet* richly answers this interest, because it offers a conflation of Quarto and Folio versions of the play, with the aim of reproducing 'as near as may be, the work as it was originally written by Shakespeare, or rather as finally retouched by him',[175] while their notes supplement this evidence of authorial revision by showing how Ophelia's speech has accumulated further 'old tunes' of textual corruption and editorial emendation since she first sang herself to death: 'remnants' (Q1676) as a possible alternative to 'snatches', 'bear' (F4) for 'bore', 'laudes' (Q2, Q3, Q4) or 'lauds' (Q5, Q6) for 'tunes', and for 'indued' a range of 'indewed' (Q2–5), 'deduced' (F2–4), and the plausible but unlikely 'inured' and 'reduced' of two earlier editors. Following Edmund Malone's argument in 1778 that Shakespeare had revised his own plays as well as 'new-modelled' existing ones, the issue of authorial versus editorial alteration had resurfaced in Collier's edition

---

[173] Quoted by G. N. Cantor, 'The theological significance of ethers', in G. N. Cantor and M. J. S. Hodge (eds.), *Conceptions of Ether* (1981), 146.

[174] W. G. Clark and W. A. Wright (eds.), *The Works of William Shakespeare* (9 vols., 1863–6), VIII. 149.

[175] Ibid., ix.

of 1842–4. Variorum editions provided one response to this debate, because they revealed the layers of authorial revision usually hidden between different editions, as well as the editorial commentary which traditionally surrounded a page of the classics.[176] Writing of these new editions, the Shakespeare scholar Charles Knight expressed his gratitude for 'the opportunity which they afford of studying the growth … of [Shakespeare's] profound philosophy, his wonderful penetration into what is most hidden and most obscure in men's characters and motives'.[177] While Knight found in *Hamlet* a play-wright whose self-conscious investigations and delayed achievement had grown to resemble the irresolutions of his hero, his contemporaries found in variorum texts a suitable means for revealing this 'penetration'. Every page of the Cambridge Shakespeare *Hamlet* offered a measured slice through the play's textual history. By printing variants on the same page as the reading-text, and identifying those editions in which certain readings appeared or died out, it documented 'a textual continuum, which demonstrated that certain fossils appeared only in certain strata'.[178] Each revision could then be recovered like one of Lyell's geological finds.

The controlling rationale behind printed variorums, to make visible the shifts and steadinesses of an author's intentions over time, is paralleled in other nineteenth-century attempts to explain why the mind itself often delivers, in Babbage's terms, 'testimony of man's changeful will'. De Quincey tells the story of a 9-year old who fell into 'a solitary brook'. As her lungs began to fill with water,

… a blow seemed to strike her, phosphoric radiance sprang forth from her eyeballs; and immediately a mighty theatre expanded within her brain. In a moment, in the twinkling of an eye, every act, every design of her past life, lived again, arraying themselves not as a succession, but as parts of a coexistence.[179]

---

[176] The *OED* gives the first use of 'variorum' as a noun to denote a critical edition as 1955, but notes that the adjectival sense, 'obtained or collected from various books or sources', dates from 1850.

[177] Quoted in Gary Taylor, *Reinventing Shakespeare* (1989), 180. Editions of Q1, Q2, and Q3 of *Hamlet* were published respectively in 1858, 1859 (both ed. Payne Collier), and 1860 (ed. James O. Halliwell); a full variorum *Hamlet* was published in 1877, ed. Horace H. Furness (2 vols.).

[178] Taylor, *Reinventing Shakespeare*, 188; see also Grace Ioppolo, *Revising Shakespeare* (1991), 1–43.

[179] 'The Palimpsest of the Human Brain', in *Suspiria de Profundis* (1849), repr. in *De Quincey*, XVI. 20.

The child is to be renewed not beyond death but in it, as her past 'acts' emerge from the shadows of forgetfulness into the 'mighty theatre' of her memory. Unlike Ophelia's 'snatches of old tunes', this *tableau mourant* is not one which could ever be reproduced for a larger audience, because it is silently held in the child's head. Yet although the 'designs' of her life are concealed from De Quincey, he can still offer her as a living model for the powers of recall she shares with his readers, because in describing the private resurgence of her past he also raises an allusion which is etched into their own habits of thought. 'In a moment, in the twinkling of an eye' adopts for the secular afterlife of memory St Paul's remarks on resurrection:

We shall not all sleep, but we shall all be changed,
   In a moment, in the twinkling of an eye, at the last trump: for the trumpet shall sound, and we shall be raised incorruptible, and we shall be changed.[180]

De Quincey's allusion offers a perfect illustration of the argument he is using the child's near-drowning to advance. The mind works like a palimpsest: 'A parchment or other writing-material written upon twice, the original writing having been rubbed out to make place for the second.'[181] But this definition lacks a clear sense of how a palimpsest differs from, say, a wax tablet: scientific and paleographic advance in the late eighteenth century made the original, over-written, writing on the parchment for the first time *recoverable*, so that a chemical wash had the same effect as watching invisible (or 'sympathetic') ink reappear. This excited De Quincey: 'the monkish chemist' of the Middle Ages finally succeeded in finding a way of cleansing a manuscript of its text, he writes, 'but not so radically as to prevent us, their posterity, from *un*doing it'. Enshrined for future restoration, the 'spirits of a departed literature' could be made to rise:[182]

The traces of each successive handwriting, regularly effaced, as had been imagined, have, in the inverse order, been regularly called back: the footsteps of the game pursued, wolf or stag, in each several chase, have been unlinked, and hunted back through all their doubles; and as the chorus of the Athenian

[180] I Corinthians 15: 51–2.
[181] *OED* 2a, with figurative senses from 1845; the *OED* does not cite Carlyle's essay 'On History' (1830), which represents history as a palimpsest prophetically illuminating present and future time.
[182] C. W. Russell, 'Palimpsest Literature and its Editor, Cardinal Angelo Mai', in *Afternoon Lectures on Literature and Art* (1867), 110.

stage unwove through the antistrophe every step that had been mystically woven through the strophe, so, by our modern conjurations of science, secrets of ages remote from each other have been exorcised from the accumulated shadows of centuries.[183]

In a moment of transformation, the accumulated writings of the palimpsest are linked together in time and space, 'exorcised' here meaning not 'banishment to the shades' but 'citation *from* the shades'.[184] De Quincey's pleasure in the chemist's cohering touch is shown in the patternings of his prose, as he invites the reader to follow his own weaving and hunting from 'stag' to 'stage' to 'ages', because reading, like writing, depends upon the palimpsest structure of the brain itself. Through our ability to impress experience upon memory, the direction of time described in Locke's *tabula rasa* can be reversed:[185]

Yes, reader, countless are the mysterious hand-writings of grief or joy which have inscribed themselves successively upon the palimpsest of your brain; ... But by the hour of death, but by fever, but by the searchings of opium, all these can revive in strength. They are not dead, but sleeping.[186]

During the nineteenth century, the figure of the palimpsest becomes the self-reflexive home for diverse models of psychological, historical, and social integration, and poetic shorthand for a shadowy archaeology of memory and desire:

> Hidden long from sight
> Within the pale leaves of a palimpsest,
> Ev'n as a ghost not wholly laid to rest
> Moves shadowy in a house of living men,
> So the blurred script may now be read again
> Athwart the faded lines of later writ.[187]

Individual poets add metaphorical extensions: 'that convenient palimpsest the heart'; 'The rest | Of our life' as 'a palimpsest— | The old writing written there the best'; 'the unread | And polyglot palimpsest of this body'; the world as 'a witless palimpsest'; the soul not as 'a clean white paper' but 'A palimpsest, a prophet's holograph | Defiled,

---

[183] 'The Palimpsest of the Human Brain', 16.

[184] Ibid.

[185] See, e.g., John Gideon Millingen, *Mind and Matter* (1847), 151–5.

[186] *De Quincey*, XVI. 20–1; 'They are not dead, but sleeping' adapts Matthew 9: 24 on the recalling to life of Jairus's daughter: 'the maid is not dead, but sleepeth'.

[187] F. W. Bourdillon, 'Prelude: On Beachy Head', *Preludes and Romances* (1908), 3–4.

erased and covered by a monk's'; even, self-consciously, the palimpsest operations of the poetic mind.[188] In 1828, Coleridge added a
preface to his incomplete prose work, 'The Wanderings of Cain': 'I
have in vain tried to recover the lines from the palimpsest tablet of my
memory: and I can only offer the introductory stanza, which has been
committed to writing.'[189] 'Committed to writing' glances bashfully at
'committed to memory' even as it announces the writer's firmness of
purpose, and Coleridge's absent-mindedness, while true to his own
dilatory methods of composition, alerts us to more widespread
qualms about the palimpsest's perfectly even restoration of the past,
such as its removal of the discriminations which could arise from
historical distance, or the possible uses of forgetting.

As a number of Victorian writers pointed out, a consideration of
what is read between the lines of our thought could lead to a pleasure
in the ease with which the present falls into line with the past, as the
erased lines of writing on the surface of the palimpsest work like
tramlines to settle new ideas into their old grooves. Others remained
more troubled by the idea that a life would form a recognizable
pattern only after we became aware of the hand which had invisibly
guided it, especially if the path it was set upon turned out to be more
like a faultline; *suspiria de profundis* might end up being sighs of regret.
Furthermore, as Victor Hugo discovered, when he attempted to
describe Paris in a letter of 1833, if one worry is that the individual
could be unduly influenced by factors outside himself, a no less
serious worry is that he could be unduly influenced by himself:

> Poor old Paris continues to be very boring ... Dead calm and sunny. It's very
> tiresome. No crowds in the street, no clouds in the sky.—Excuse me, I'm
> wrong: yesterday it poured with rain. That's what happens when you have a
> mania for writing symmetrical sentences.[190]

Where the writer carries around a private 'atmosphere' of grammatical tics and quirks, the currents of his writing will always threaten to

---

[188] Alfred Austin, 'A Dialogue at Fiesole', *Love's Widowhood: And Other Poems* (1889), 61;
'Michael Field' [K. H. Bradley and E. E. Cooper], 'A Palimpsest', *Wild Honey from Various
Thyme* (1908), 30; Sydney Dobell, *Balder. Part the First, The Poetical Works of Sydney Dobell* (1875),
217; Lionel Johnson, 'To C. K. P.', *The Poetical Works of Lionel Johnson* (1915), 95;
E. B. Browning, *Aurora Leigh*, I. 826, *The Poetical Works of Elizabeth Barrett Browning* (1897),
363; 'Henry Browne' [Henry Ellison], 'Seizures and Inspirations', *Stones from the Quarry*
(1875), 312.

[189] H. J. Jackson (ed.), *The Oxford Authors: Samuel Taylor Coleridge* (1985), 41.

[190] Victor Hugo, *Correspondance familiale et écrits intimes*, ed. Jean Gaudon, Sheila Gaudon,
and Bernard Leuilliot (1988–), II. 123; see Graham Robb, *Victor Hugo*, 170.

pass across the world without being seriously disturbed by it, flattening out the landscape of fact to fit the individual contours of his unique verbal imagination. Comte's decision to regularize his syntax, for example, allowed him to look forward to the spread of Positivism in a way that made the development of the human race sound as orderly and predictable as the destination of each sentence.[191] (Mill pointed out, in a sharp set of criticisms, the startling self-contradictions of an intellectual system which trumpeted the idea that 'nothing should remain arbitrary', but did so in prose which busied itself in elevating Comte's private grammatical prejudices to the status of inflexible moral principles.)[192] However, when G. H. Lewes describes how history 'unrolls the palimpsest of mental evolution',[193] his theories of psychological inheritance and social incorporation raise important questions over the possibility of independent speech. Given that the 'blurred script' and 'later writ' of a textual palimpsest could belong to the same or to different writers, a single mind is just as likely to give testimony of *Man's* changeful will as of one man's will. 'Our perceptions are evolutions':[194] the argument from recapitulation (in Ernst Haeckel's neat summary, 'ontogeny recapitulates phylogeny')[195] would later be echoed by Freud's claim that individual decisions overlay and are moved by shared cultural residua, because 'in mental life nothing which has once been formed can perish'.[196] What Lewes and Freud share, in their approaches to this problem, is the idea that the invisible web of affinities which joins us to one another is historical as well as spatial. Freud's hypothesis that telepathy was 'the original, archaic communication between individuals', and his argument that this sort of direct psychological transference can be reactivated under certain social conditions, 'for instance in passionately excited mobs',[197] reflects an advancing nineteenth-century fear that the unpredictable behaviour of people in crowds shows sudden surges of primitive impulses, an atavistic backwash, as they make mental

[191] The rules which Comte imposed upon himself (and others) included the requirement that no sentence should exceed two lines of his manuscript (approximately five lines of print); no paragraph should exceed seven sentences; no sentence or consecutive sentences should use the same word twice; and so on.

[192] See J. S. Mill, *Auguste Comte and Positivism* (1865, repr. 1968), 196–9.

[193] *The Study of Psychology, Its Object, Scope and Method* (1879), 153.

[194] Ibid., 170.

[195] See Stephen Jay Gould, *The Mismeasure of Man* (1981), 142.

[196] *Civilisation and its Discontents* (1930), repr. in *Strachey*, XXI. 65.

[197] See Freud's discussion of dreams and occultism in the *New Introductory Lectures*, repr. in *Strachey*, XX. 3–182.

links with that much larger crowd whose growth has been staggered by the historical accidents of birth. Crowds disturbed the boundaries of individual and collective responsibility, not only by showing how one person's will could be put in thrall to unknown others but also by suggesting that this form of influence liberated the ghosts of man's uncivilized past and put them on display. To be taken up by the mood of the crowd was to reveal the existence of an 'invisible world' which was as much inside as outside our minds.

That keen investigator into the hidden causes of things, Sherlock Holmes, casts a beady but sympathetic eye on one version of this debate, when he describes the 'unsightly eccentricity' which some humans, like some trees, suddenly develop when they reach a certain height:

I have a theory that the individual represents in his development the whole procession of his ancestors, and that such a sudden turn to good or evil stands for some strong influence which came into the line of his pedigree. The person becomes, as it were, the epitome of the history of his own family.[198]

Watson meets this with 'It is surely rather fanciful!'—a reply so redolent of bluff English common sense that we are perhaps supposed to imagine Holmes allowing himself a little smile of triumph at Watson's obliging but unwitting revelation of his own intellectual family tree. The sceptical tone of Watson's reply would have cheered many of his contemporaries, for whom the idea that our behaviour had origins earlier than our own birth complicated the countervailing stress on 'self-reverence, self-knowledge, self-control'. But the word he chooses to express his doubt, 'fanciful', also suggests how scientific ideas of development and miscegenation could be translated into the less factbound worlds of plot, narrative, and metaphor.

*

In 1860, F. W. Farrar compared the reaches of the air with those of the page:

… in the fluid air, which he articulates into human utterance, man has preserved for ever the main facts of his past history, and the main processes of his inmost soul. The sonorous wave, indeed, which transmits to our ears the

---

[198] Daniel Pick discusses this example in *Faces of Degeneration*, 155.

uttered thought, reaches but a little distance, and then vanishes like the tremulous ripple on the surface of the sea; but, conscious of his destiny, man invented writing to give it perpetuity from age to age. Its short reach, its brief continuance, are the defects of the spoken word, but when graven on the stone or painted on the vellum it passes from one end of the earth to the other for all time; it conquers at once eternity and space.[199]

There are a number of weaknesses in Farrar's simple and confident association of writing and eternity. The idea that writing 'passes from one end of the earth to the other for all time' conveniently forgets the competition and fluctuating demands of the marketplace, as it does the fact that most books are more perishable than rocks. (Charles Tennyson Turner, drawing upon the same set of ideas, remarks in one sonnet that if nature does indeed possess a 'sin-recording force', then 'Each nobler act and utterance takes its course | Through the same air, and is immortal too'; the poem which limps to this conclusion has largely been left to rest in peace.)[200] Even the brief history of writing which is contained in Farrar's 'graven on the stone or painted on the vellum' seems curiously truncated, as if Farrar worried that his faith in 'the main processes of the human soul' would be abraded by any attempt to describe the developments in printing technology and trade which allowed a nineteenth-century writer to disseminate his or her words across the globe with a speed and range rather better than, say, inviting the neighbours round to admire a new cave-painting.[201] As Leigh Hunt had earlier pointed out, in a review of Shelley which gushes with an equal and opposite enthusiasm for the changes which print has seen, 'although the art of printing is not new, yet the Press in any great and true sense of the word is a modern engine ... *Books* did what was done before; they now have a million times the range and power'.[202] Yet for all the local limitations of his approach to the variable conditions of print, Farrar's loyal adherence to its 'main processes' answers well to a feature of writing which is recoverable from any historical period.

The double life of the printed page, as a fixing of evanescent speech and as an invitation to fresh speech, will make of it a key resource for all writers who are interested in 'influence' as something which is

---

[199] *An Essay on the Origin of Language*, 6.

[200] 'The Air Register', *Collected Sonnets Old and New* (1880), 39.

[201] See Allan C. Dooley, *Author and Printer in Victorian England* (1992).

[202] Review of *The Revolt of Islam*, repr. in *Shelley: The Critical Heritage*, ed. James E. Barcus (1975), 114.

both an event and a process, what happens to us and what we make of its effects. For example, one way of measuring the range of influences at work upon a poet, from the compound effects of trad- ition and habit to the more immediate expectations of his or her audience, is to observe how easily a particular poem settles into a recognizable shape, because it is in the nature of literary form to provide the sound of established patterns and temporary needs adjusting to one another. The dramatic monologue provides a clear example of a literary form which answered to this far-reaching Victorian interest in the multiple influences which are exercised on and by any act of speech, because the monologue's managed confron- tation of speaker and listener is always an encounter between more than two people. The voice which we hear is directed towards, and so in part by, another voice, which we hear only in its effects upon the speaker's choice and patterning of expression. We are then invited to judge the speaker's and interlocutor's impact upon one another, as their reactions (or lack of reaction) to particular verbal events produce sudden metrical judders, strains in the syntax of individual lines, and so on, and as these local moments of verbal contact combine into a narrative account of their developing relationship. But their shared poem can also absorb other voices into itself, from the audible after- shocks of the speaker's past actions, which continue to reverberate in present-tense speech, to the cumulative and self-questioning history of address which is written into the poet's chosen literary form. In this way, the dramatic monologue emerges as one finely wrought expression of the widespread Victorian desire to understand 'influ- ence' as both the momentary impact of individuals upon one another, and the lasting consequences which might emerge from these en- counters. But it is not the only literary form in which writers of the period attempted to come to terms with a double image of ourselves, diversely reflected in descriptions of 'influence', as creatures who are subject to irrevocable losses, but whose words and deeds stubbornly refuse to die.

When Hardy writes of 'a particular kiss' that 'in a trice [it] took wing', he is alert to the impacted senses of 'particular' as 'private', 'distinctive', and 'composed of particles':

> That kiss is gone where none can tell—
> Not even those who felt its spell:
> It cannot have died; that know we well.

> Somewhere it pursues its flight,
> One of a long procession of sounds
>   Travelling aethereal rounds
>   Far from earth's bounds
>   In the infinite.[203]

Tyndall had emphasized that the motion of a sound-wave should not be confused with the motion of the particles which at any moment form the wave.[204] Hardy's poem crosses such clean-cut distinctions, because its 'procession of sounds' emerges from a reader's mouth as a sequence of lapsing breaths, but each sound then falls into place within the poem's metrical and syntactic patterns of accumulation and delay, its spatial organization of sense. The last four lines are especially attentive to that creative tension between print and speech which can be stimulated by rival notions of utterance as fulfilling local and temporary needs or as making secure our perceptions of the world. As the knock-on effects of rhyme mime the after-shocks of the sound of the kiss (the absence of punctuation approaches the condition of an invisible 'ether' to transmit the energy of reading across the white spaces of the page),[205] so they are tugged against by the inexorable whittling down of major stresses from four to three, to two, and finally to one. One pleasure in reading these lines aloud, then, arises from our mournful knowledge that the sounds of our own mouths will pass as irretrievably from us as the smack of the kiss which, heard through the sudden linguistic zooming-out of Hardy's archaic 'aethereal', is made to sound already a relic from a bygone age. A further pleasure arises from our ability to reread Hardy's lines, and so to repeat the irreversible dissipation of energy which is reproduced in their failing rhythms. Indeed, once we know what to expect from these rhythms, we can do better with their own decline.

The fate of Hardy's poem will be shared by other forms of litera-ture, whether or not loss is their explicit subject, because although writing is forever threatening to lag behind speech, which travels at the speed of sound, the very endurance of its printed form can be used to reveal the effects of influence which would otherwise remain lost in the air. That is, because acts of reading take time, they can restore

---

[203] 'The Kiss' (pub. 1917), *HP*, II. 205.   [204] *Sound*, 3.
[205] Compare J. J. Sylvester, *The Laws of Verse* (1869) on 'phonetic syzygy', or the principle of 'respiratory and sonorific continuity in verse': the 'curvilinear threads of connexion (or say lines of force)' by which a poem makes a 'continuous or solid impression on the mind or organs of the listener', 45–6.

something of the timeliness of human experience, ready impression-ability, to the fixed impressions of print. Equally, because the page holds in abeyance what we have already read, we can use the trails and residues of our earlier reading to retrieve and check what was earlier passed over. The organization of a sentence, for example, might dramatize the workings of influence in a number of ways: the distance between cause and effect that can be covered in a single phrase; the felt impact of an event that can be measured in the relative weight of each phrase; the delayed after-shocks that can be realized in sprawling grammatical connections or an unexpected syntactic snarl. On a larger scale, the struts of plot or style which arch across a mass of surface detail will encourage a reader to scan for clues as to what is still at issue in a narrative, whether by drawing out those patterns of human relations which are reflected in the writer's patterning of his or her prose, or by redirecting the reader's attention back to the speeches of characters whose effects have outlasted their original utterance.

It is not only in Victorian writing that literary form offers a richly detailed medium for demonstrating influence in action, but writers of this period were especially well attuned to this task, because Victorian theories of 'influence' are frequently attracted to oppositions which are also central to literature's own workings. Like any literary work, influence reflects intentions and felicities; it can be described as a complete action, and as an unfinished one; its effects are explicable and unpredictable. A novelist who is brought to recognize in the development of his or her plot that to remove difference (what distinguishes one novel, or one part of a novel, from another) is to remove the narratable, is therefore likely to set about organizing his or her description of events so as to confirm our expectations in unexpected ways, creating narrative shapes which refuse the consola-tions of sameness, and so keep the unknown surprising. Thus, when we read *Great Expectations*, our passage through Pip's narrative re-hearses his preoccupation with 'the old strong influences' of the past 'which had so wrought upon me' (ch. 29), but also his developing sense of his place within a social world which always appears to be adapting itself one step ahead of his experience. In this sense, the popularity of those Victorian novels which, like *Great Expectations*, return obsessively to the domestic world as an ideal under threat, answers to a fundamental need of their readers, because although it is in literature that our image of the world is made hospitable to our most urgent interests, a good novel rarely encourages us to feel altogether at home in its pages. Like any form of desire, even the desire to know what happens next, reading thrives upon difficulty and the threat of disappointment. In *Middlemarch*, for example, when Dorothea mourns those 'epochs in our experience when some dear expectation dies, or some new motive is born',[206] her remark alerts us to the fact that this twin tugging upon the voice of foresight and hindsight represents more than the common human tendency to think of 'what if?' as an invitation to dwell upon those selections in a life which were not made, as well as upon those which might yet be made. It is also one of the conditions of reading.

Lyric verse is an especially attractive medium for these concerns, because here recurrence and return are not only produced by the accidents of reading, but also form the structural principles which first moved the poet, in the skeletons of rhythm, rhyme, and cadence which articulate the body of each stanza. However, the same learning process would be to some extent true of any piece of writing, including prose, which mimics in its internal designs the author's explicit interest in temporal and spatial relations. And where this narrative harking back is established in a Babbagean context of remorse, learning to listen 'better' to verbal patterns will be more than an aesthetic pleasure. It will also be a moral action.

*

Writing of the ambiguous tone of *Great Expectations*, at once innocent and knowing, G. K. Chesterton remarks that 'a saint after repentance will forgive himself for a sin'.[207] Pip's story is doubly one 'after repentance'. Take his description of Smithfield Market:

> When I told the clerk that I would take a turn in the air while I waited, he advised me to go round the corner and I should come into Smithfield. So, I came into Smithfield; and the shameful place, being all asmear with filth and fat and blood and foam, seemed to stick to me. So, I rubbed it off with all possible speed by turning into a street where I saw the great black dome of Saint Paul's bulging at me from behind a grim stone building which a bystander said was Newgate Prison.   (ch. 20)

It is in prison that Magwitch will die at the end of the novel, so with hindsight (the use of 'so' in this passage is especially marked by Pip's sense of hindsight) 'Newgate Prison' seems to be not the destination of this final sentence but its destiny, an ending which then casts guilty shadows back across Pip's recollection of the 'shameful place'. To young (experiencing) Pip, the market is shameful because it seems beastly, morally backward; but to old (narrating) Pip, any place that he describes now would seem shameful, because it would be filled with echoes of his own shame. Leaving Newgate Prison several chapters later, Pip recalls how he 'consumed the whole time in thinking how strange it was that I should be encompassed by all this taint of prison and crime':

> ... that, in my childhood out on our lonely marshes on a winter evening I should have first encountered it; that, it should have appeared on two occasions, starting out like a stain that was faded but not gone; that it should ... pervade my fortune and advancement ... I beat the prison dust off my feet as I sauntered to and fro, and I shook it out of my dress, and I exhaled it from my lungs. So contaminated did I feel ... (ch. 32)

As Pip exhales the prison dust from his lungs, he again expresses the lingering worry that any attempt to narrate scenes of vice and decay will unavoidably implicate the speaker in the dirty world he describes. Nor is he alone in wondering how far this dirtiness has affected his 'advancement', because for the reader too Pip's progress is largely structured by the sudden reappearance of events which '[start] out like a stain that was faded but not gone'. Repeatedly, the novel encourages its readers to perform sympathetic double-takes on earlier narrative and interpretative decisions, as chance events are discovered to be part of a meaningful pattern; physical movements are invested with moral significance; the casual is retrospectively revealed as the causal. Just as the individual phrases which describe Pip's 'turn in the air' and 'turning into the street' find their place within each sentence's toils of self-justification and self-reproach, so even this apparently superfluous detail of Pip beating the dust off his feet, once it is filtered through our later knowledge of Magwitch's death and decay, provides a faint and troubling echo of the convict's progress across the graveyard on the marshes: 'picking his way among the nettles, and among the brambles ... as if he were eluding the hands of the dead people, stretching up cautiously out of their graves, to get a twist upon his ankle and pull him in' (ch. 1).

It is not only in *Great Expectations* that Dickens explores this worry that dead bodies seem permanently reluctant to stay put. In *Bleak*

House, Jo recalls how the gravedigger who buried Hawdon's body 'was obliged to stamp upon it to git it in', and when Lady Dedlock goes to the churchyard to visit Hawdon's grave, she stands in the archway 'with its deadly stains contaminating her dress' (ch. 16). As John Carey points out, 'The suggestion that the corpses are a soluble deposit smeared on the very railings of the place, like the black fat which smears the neighbourhood where Krook blows up, stirs the reader's imagination.'[208] Plainly it also stirred the imagination of Dickens, for whom dead bodies often seem intent on continuing the shifty and leaky operations of their living selves. As a young man, Dickens once left a calling-card which announced himself as 'CHARLES DICKENS, RESURRECTIONIST, *In search of a subject*',[209] but his descriptions of the way that corpses in overcrowded graveyards rise to the surface, as if in a parody of resurrection,[210] are not the only evidence of his continued interest in the unpredictable excesses and spillages of the body as a human and narrative subject. Indeed, Silas Wegg, who regularly stumps into Mr Venus's shop in *Our Mutual Friend* to visit his own amputated leg, and laments being 'what I may call dispersed, a part of me here, and a part of me there' (ch. 7), merely makes explicit a predicament which is shared to a greater or lesser degree by most of Dickens's characters. Whether they are leaving characteristic smells trailing behind them, or staining their clothes with sweat and blood, or removing wigs and false teeth, so often do Dickens's bodies refuse to keep themselves to themselves that they come to represent in a concentrated form the excesses of his own narrative style—the threat that it will produce more material than it can organize into a coherent whole. And yet, Wegg's great hope, that he will one day 'collect myself like a genteel person', speaks of a competing and complementary feature of Dickens's style: a reliance upon metaphors of dispersal which are returned to so regularly that their contingent sprawl can be restrained; the creation of a form of narrative waste which the novelist can redeem through his own imaginative economy.

One of the glummest jokes of *Great Expectations* emerges in the way that Pip's dreams of social mobility are repeatedly thwarted by the

---

208 *The Violent Effigy*, 123.

209 J. C. Hotten, *Charles Dickens: The Story of his Life* (1870), 37. Dickens's joke is discussed in Andrew Sanders, *Charles Dickens, Resurrectionist* (1982), ix.

210 *Bleak House* describes how 'they lower our dear brother down a foot or two, sow him in corruption, to be raised in corruption', in a parodic echo of the burial service's 'it is sown in corruption; it is raised in incorruption' (ch. 16).

more obstinate nature of the human body, which seems unable to move from one place to another without leaving some tell-tale trace of itself behind. In London, he notices that his cab driver has a 'greasy great-coat', and the wall in Jaggers's office is 'greasy with shoulders' which 'seemed to have been shuffling up and down the staircase for years' (chs. 20, 24), while one of Jaggers's clients has a hat with 'a greasy and fatty surface like cold broth' (ch. 32). The confusion over whether this greasy surface has come from inside the man, as a form of sweaty secretion, or from outside him, as a soup stain, is fully characteristic of Pip's regular confusion of responsibility and chance, or the loitering impact and cumulative effects of his encounters with other people. When Magwitch determines to swear Herbert Pocket to secrecy, he pulls out of his own pocket 'a greasy little clasped black Testament' (ch. 40), and again it is unclear whether this book is greasy because it has been handled so often, or because it has been involved in an accident with the butter-dish, like the 'smeary newspaper' which Pip reads on the morning coach to Miss Havisham, 'which had nothing half so legible in its local news, as the foreign matter of coffee, pickles, fish sauces, gravy, melted butter, and wine, with which it was sprinkled all over, as if it had taken the measles in a highly irregular form' (ch. 43). Taken together, these narrative details suggest Pip's growing sensitivity to what has been removed from its proper place, and his willingness to find a metaphorical home for this anxiety in the idea that stains suggest the presence of the contaminated or defiled only because they are, to borrow Mary Douglas's celebrated definition of dirt, 'matter out of place'.[211] In this sense, the cameo appearance of the waiter who has 'wandering habits of putting the covers on the floor (where he fell over them), the melted butter in the arm-chair, the bread on the bookshelves, the cheese in the coal-scuttle, and the boiled fowl into my bed in the next room' (ch. 22), represents Pip's most concentrated self-image, because 'wandering habits' are also central to the shifts in his own narrative voice between the material and moral implications of being 'out of place'. The way Dickens passes over other incidental details, without comment or retrospective irony, shows his interest in the idea that although individuals are formed largely by their environment, they are also capable of resisting its pressures; obligations are not compulsions. At the same time, the way he singles out and links these moments of self-diagnosis into significant patterns encourages us to realize in our reading of this narrative what Pip realizes in its telling: only by placing isolated episodes within a broader moral economy of means and ends is it possible to discover at what point contact became influence, or a single error became an habitual one.

Lionel Trilling has described well how the autobiographical novel's 'influence on the moral sensibility' comes about 'by its hinting that we may not judge a man by any single moment in his life without taking into account the determining past and the expiating and fulfilling future'.[212] R. H. Hutton suggests one way in which *Great Expectations* approaches this sort of ethical perspective, when he describes how Dickens's novels reveal 'a keen eye on the stretch':

... all the veins and muscles in Dickens' nature were always on the stretch towards some eager end ... the singleness of his eager and strenuous search, as he follows up every cross-thread of association that his enormous power of observation had given him ... No man was ever able to stretch one or two lines of conception so tightly, and to exclude so completely all disturbing influences from the field of his vision.[213]

As with so much Victorian writing, this conjunction of 'exclusion' and 'influence' in Hutton's account is tellingly at odds with Bloom's notion of the writer as a triumphant solipsist. The foundations for Bloom's theories were laid by Walter Jackson Bate's claim that the 'rich and intimidating legacy of the past' leads to a 'remorseless deepening of self-consciousness':[214] the disturbing worry that everything has already been said, and the equally disturbing ease with which this can become a self-fulfilling prophecy. But, as *Great Expectations* demonstrates, legacies which attempt to mould future lives are just as likely to lead to a remorse*ful* deepening of self-consciousness, even a self-conscious deepening of remorse. A significant example of Dickens's fondness for structural 'cross-threads of association' can be seen in the 'fat sweltering one-pound notes' Pip receives from Magwitch, which 'seemed to have been on terms of the warmest intimacy with all the cattle markets in the country' (ch. 10), because although the detail of 'fat' again carries the idea of greasy handling, it gains a

212 *The Liberal Imagination* (1951), 37.
213 Review of Forster's *Life of Dickens*, in the *Spectator* (16 November 1872), repr. in Robert Tener and Malcolm Woodfield (ed.), *A Victorian Spectator: Uncollected Writings of R. H. Hutton* (1989), 192–4.
214 *The Burden of the Past and the English Poet*, 4.

further retrospective charge from Pip's subsequent description of the cattle market at Smithfield, 'all asmear with filth and fat and blood and foam', as if the idea that money touched by Magwitch would be fatty is a natural metaphoric extension of Pip's later knowledge that it has been in contact with a hand which, 'for anything I knew, ... might be stained with blood' (ch. 29). As a model of Dickens's return to certain keynotes of plot and style, then, Hutton's account cannot be faulted. However, as the passage of money across *Great Expectations* suggests, these 'cross-threads of association' could not result from the narrator's exclusion of 'all disturbing influences from the field of his vision', because one central question which organizes the novel's structure and tone is the point at which human associations become textual ones: influences which are not simply 'excluded' from Pip's voice, but instead form part of its composed drama of recognition and resistance.

*

One 'mem.' for *Our Mutual Friend* has simply '*Lizzie to work an influence on Bella's character at its wavering point.*'[215] Mary Dickens recalls her father's interest in 'the curious influence exercised by one personality over another':

One illustration I remember his using was, that meeting someone in the busy London streets, he was on the point of turning back to accost the supposed friend, when finding out his mistake in time he walked on again until he actually met the real friend, whose shadow, as it were, but a moment ago had come across his path.[216]

Great Expectations plots out this *déjà vu* in the 'nameless shadow' Pip notices passing across Estella's carriage-window, which provides a cognitive hover between young Pip's spooky premonition of the true relations of people and things which will 'start out like a stain', and old Pip's knowledge that these relations cast shadows across his narrative which are not only physical (ch. 32). These shadows lengthen from both directions: Estella's mother is a woman with a past, but there are shades of that past to be traced in the face of her daughter, a woman with a future. Pip's last action in the revised ending then shows how he situates his mistake in a context of 'the

---

[215] Harry Stone (ed.), *Dickens' Working Notes for His Novels* (1987), 359.
[216] Quoted in Fred Kaplan, *Dickens and Mesmerism* (1975), 108.

determining past and the expiating and fulfilling future', because his decision to take Estella by the hand in part atones for the cruel way that Jaggers had earlier taken her mother by the hand (ch. 59). This does nothing to remove the sense of artificiality which lingers around the ending; indeed, it heightens it by reminding us, immediately before we leave the ordered world of fiction for our own more recalcitrant world, that Dickens's novels provide a set of investigations into the effects of influence which can be restrained only within the controlled conditions of literary form. It is, then, entirely appropriate that the culminating tense of this ending ('I saw the shadow of no parting from her') should be so ambiguously suspended between factual record and imaginative possibility, because this is the tense which has operated throughout *Great Expectations*, a novel in which even grammar appears to have a conscience.

Victorian novels often use the timing of their narrative syntax to draw out the 'cross-threads' of influence over time, woundingly so in the case of *Bleak House*, as Esther's social and historical 'connexions' are progressively discovered in the novel's own connections, its points of contact with itself. Indeed, so common is the pattern that Dickens was occasionally sidetracked into vigilant and knowing parodies of its tempting excesses, as when Eugene and Lightwood, in *Our Mutual Friend*, are seen drinking at a riverside pub:

> Lightwood helped him to some more of the stuff, but it had been cooling, and didn't answer now.
>
> 'Pooh,' said Eugene, spitting it out among the ashes. 'Tastes like the wash of the river.'
>
> 'Are you so familiar with the flavour of the wash of the river?'
>
> 'I seem to be to-night. I feel as if I had been half-drowned, and swallowing a gallon of it.'
>
> 'Influence of locality,' suggested Lightwood.
>
> 'You are mighty learned to-night, you and your influences,' returned Eugene. (ch. 13)

When, a few pages later, we are shown the drowned body of Gaffer Hexam, the mocking banter is revealed as a sly structural joke; as so often in his novels, Dickens tests the flexibility and range of his narrative concerns by briefly stooging what he has carefully set up as their central seriousness. Some of his contemporaries are more single-minded, and correspondingly more open to the accusation of being one-eyed, in the way they turn ideas of social influence into a feature of their own style. Two years before he published *An Essay on the Origin of Language*, for example, F. W. Farrar had exploited its distinction between the 'perpetuity' of print, and the soundwave 'which vanishes like the tremendous ripple on the surface of the sea', in his popular morality tale *Eric, or, Little by Little* (1858). 'Little by little' is how Farrar sees boys going bad, but it also characterizes how he unfolds the plot of their undoing. One chapter, 'Ripples', begins with an epigraph from Tennyson: 'Our echoes roll from soul to soul, | And live for ever and for ever'. The prophetically named Brigson has been expelled after using his 'pernicious influence' to lure Eric into vice, but,

[']his works do follow him. Look there!' He took a large stone and threw it into the silver burn stream; there was a great splash, and then ever-widening circles of blue ripple broke the surface of the water, dying away one by one in the sedges on the bank. 'There,' he said, 'see how long these ripples last, and how numerous they are ... '

Proof of 'the contagion of Brigson's baseness' comes when some boys are seen drinking brandy ('One of the ripples, you see, of Brigson's influence'), but it is the ripple itself which later breaks the surface of the narrative. For while Eric is drifting along in a boat (' " 'The curse is come upon me, cried The Lady of Shalott'—those words keep ringing in my ears", murmured Eric'), his attempts at correcting his behaviour come too late to prevent his impressionable younger brother from falling off a cliff:

... and the little ripples fell over him wonderingly, with the low music of their musical laughter, and blurred and dimmed the vivid splashes and crimson streaks upon the white stone on which his head had fallen.[217]

Farrar's ripple is a refrain which invests the physical world with the enduring effects of an absent body, material with moral influence, and its regular reappearance means that the lines of his novel spin a moral web which is designed to cling to the reader as another form of refrain: the solemn injunction, 'no more'.

Great Expectations, similarly, uses narrative refrains to investigate the worry that, where our deepest convictions are first other people's, a slip of the pen into the invisible ruts and depressions of a shared palimpsest of human behaviour will mark the beginning of a long fall from grace. When Pip grows feverish after his arrest for debt, he fancies himself 'little Pip again. For, the tenderness of Joe was so

[217] pp. 196, 159, 196–7, 252, 239.

beautifully proportioned to my need, that I was like a child in his hands' (ch. 57). In describing the illiterate Joe, Pip could be describing his ideal reader, as we measure our expectations of him against his knowledge of where, ultimately, his expectations have led him: backwards. Joe's care repeats and revises an earlier scene when Pip was truly a child in someone's hands:

> That I had a fever and was avoided, that I suffered greatly, that I often lost my reason, that the time seemed interminable, that I confounded impossible existences with my own identity; that I was a brick in the house wall ...   (ch.57)

> My first most vivid and broad impression of the identity of things, seems to me to have been gained on a memorable raw afternoon towards evening. At such a time I found out for certain, that this bleak place overgrown with nettles was the churchyard; and that Philip Pirrip, late of this parish, and also Georgiana wife of the above, were dead and buried ... and that the distant savage lair from which the wind was rushing, was the sea; and that the small bundle of shivers growing afraid of it all and beginning to cry, was Pip ...   (ch. 1)

With Joe soothing him as an adult bundle of shivers, Pip returns to the 'impression' of a child's vision of his mother, presented with 'all kinds of extraordinary transformations of the human face', all 'much dilated in size', as his adult self persists in blowing up the most expressive features of his transformed life in the search for points of contact with his earlier self: an attempt to recover that grace of integrity which Lionel Trilling has called 'the own self'.[218] One 'dilation' of an impression in time can be heard in the narrative chain which joins these two moments, as the adult's 'that... that... that' reaches back to the child's 'and that... and that... and that': listing syntactical returns which allow us to hear the influence on Pip's adult voice of the child 'entreating to be released from the giddy place' where Magwitch has set him, as the wide-eyed gabble of the child is filtered through the weary compulsion of the adult. Pip's 'beginning to cry' is then drawn out through his story like the shaming sound of release rendered by the file: 'I stopped in the mist to listen, and the file was still going' (ch. 3).

The drawn-out rasp of the file in Pip's ears corresponds with Dickens's other writings on the lasting sensitivity of a child's senses. A year before Magwitch's birth, Dickens writes in *The Uncommercial Traveller* of being 'dragged by invisible force' into the Paris Morgue 'to see a large dark man whose disfigurement by water was in a frightful

---

[218] *Sincerity and Authenticity* (1972), 10.

manner comic'. The disturbing 'invisible force' of this dead mouth on the living is later deepened when Dickens is enjoying a communal bath and is suddenly 'seized with an unreasonable idea that the large dark body was floating straight at me'. This body is a swollen version of the smaller floating bodies which epidemiology was to discover and chart: 'In the shock I had taken some water into my mouth, and it turned me sick, for I fancied that the contamination of the creature was in it.' But the significant claims are that this stomach-turning 'possession' might equally have been 'the image of a living aversion', and that these dark shadows are especially fond of trailing children:

It would be difficult to overstate the intensity and accuracy of an intelligent child's observation. At that impressible time of life, it must sometimes produce a fixed impression. If the fixed impression be of an object terrible to the child, it will be (for want of reasoning upon) inseparable from great fear... (ch. 12)

As young Pip 'move[s] the table, like a Medium of the present day, by the vigour of my unseen hold upon it' (ch. 4), the narrator provides a neat parable for the 'fixed impression' of that first scene on the marshes, and its possession of the narrative. Like an Invisible Man, Magwitch is often present in the novel before his reappearance, but detectable only by his 'unseen hold' upon the world around him. So, Pip describes how the gun which Wemmick fires every evening from his fortress across waste ground 'went off with a bang that shook the crazy little box of a cottage as if it must fall to pieces' (ch. 25). From one point of view, this perceived threat to domestic security is itself a repercussion of the shots fired across the marshes to warn of the escaped convicts, and anticipates Pip going to pieces when he realizes that he cannot cut off 'lines of communication' as easily as pulling up a drawbridge, or be as snugly oblivious of people's returns as the deaf Aged P. From another point of view, though, these vibrations radiate from young Pip (the *un*aged P.) in the first scene: a 'small bundle of shivers' which is still sending out shockwaves.

When David Copperfield returns to Agnes, he relives the mood in which he had once considered other wanderers:

The feeling with which I used to watch the tramps, as they came into the town on those wet evenings... came freshly back to me; fraught, as then, with the smell of damp earth, and wet leaves and briar, and the sensation of the very airs that blew upon me. (ch. 60)

Earlier, David Copperfield's thought of his father rising from the dead had 'seemed to strike me like an unwholesome wind' (ch. 3), and we hear in this later description of returning men how the stresses of his childhood have given an involuntary inflection to the narrator's voice, swelling present-tense speech with echoes which are ambiguously situated between conscious and repressed knowledge. By using these narrative cross-currents to keep the ears of his readers on the stretch, Dickens provides in the timing of his narrative a sympathetic aural shape for some of the private cloggings and backtrackings which are involved in the human experience of time. In addition, we hear how some thoughts which the narrator hangs on to, and so hang on in his voice, circulate with a force which is as unpredictable and anonymous as the weather. Pip's storm breaks at the end of the second volume:

> If the wind and the rain had driven away the intervening years, had scattered all the intervening objects, had swept us to the church-yard where we first stood face to face on such different levels, I could not have known my convict more distinctly than I knew him now ... Throughout, I had seemed to myself to attend more to the wind and the rain than to him; even now, I could not separate his voice from those voices, though those were loud and his was silent.   (ch. 39)

The refrain of the wind and the rain casts 'young Telemachus' Pip back to the marshes, where it had first carried the voices of a man-hunt: 'For, there had reached us, on the wings of the wind and the rain, a long shout. It was repeated' (ch. 5). He cannot later separate the voice of Magwitch from the voices of the wind and rain, because that 'long shout' is a line of force which reaches through his narrative as a 'fixed impression', infesting the sensation of air with criminality, like the 'Low breathings' which pursue the young Wordsworth as he tries in vain to escape from the looming presence of the natural world in which he hears what else he cannot escape: the movements of his own body.[219] The pursuers' 'long shout' silently bubbles to the surface again with the breathing of a second convict, as he tries to make Pip 'a screen against the wind':

> It is impossible to express with what acuteness I felt the convict's breathing, not only on the back of my head, but all along my spine.... He seemed to have more breathing business to do than another man, and to make more

---

[219] *The Prelude* (1850), I. 323.

noise in doing it; and I was conscious of growing high-shouldered on one side, in my shrinking endeavours to fend him off.   (ch. 28)

The implication is that the convict is suffering from ethical halitosis: bad men have bad breath. Like the corpse in *The Uncommercial Traveller*, this is 'in a frightful manner comic', is indeed an affrighted comedy of manners, which relies on the reader's uneasy swerves between pleasure and discomfort—taking pleasure in Pip's squirming, and shrinking at this pleasure. But the convict's breaths are deeper than he could know, because Pip's resistance to them is a guilty echo of Magwitch's later chest injury, 'which rendered his breathing extremely painful', so that it seems as if he too has more breathing to do than another when, as a condemned man, he has rather less (ch. 56).

The tone of both passages suggests how adult Pip ruefully recognizes two foster-parents other than Joe (running after Magwitch on 'a Winder') or Miss Havisham (the spiked greeting 'And what wind … blows you here, Pip?' when he runs away from Magwitch). The first is Shakespeare's Feste. Pip is a Malvolio who believes that 'some are born great, some achieve greatness, and some have greatness thrust upon them', and is brought to understand that 'the whirligig of time brings in his revenges':

> When that I was and a little tiny boy,
>   With hey-ho, the wind and the rain;
> A foolish thing was but a toy,
>   For the rain it raineth every day.[220]

The second literary parent is Lear's Fool, in an allusion which brings together Pip's belated acknowledgement of himself as a thankless child, and his rueful knowledge that Magwitch is another poor fool who is hanged; like Cordelia, Magwitch returns to England out of love for one who ever but slenderly knew himself, and so will come no more. Shakespeare's return to the same refrain in separate plays had already signalled a loss of innocence between the song's occasions, as Feste's lyrical wind and rain take on a deafening life of their own to mock Lear's fall into second childhood, just as his repetition of the song had further developed the way that its alternating refrains seem to reflect upon their own workings as layered memory or reparative cycle, figurative rainfall. His example suggests that we need not take

---

[220] *Twelfth Night*, II. v. 140–2; V. i. 374, 386–9.

John Hollander quite at his word when he claims that 'refrains are, and have, memories—of their prior strophes or stretches of text, of their own preoccurrences, and of their own genealogies in earlier texts as well',[221] because a refrain can be invested with a past without being said to remember anything, as a child's genealogy will be revealed in its growth. Narrative provides a natural home for refrains which concentrate the reader's attention upon questions of development and reversion, because it allows more time for the conservation and release of a speaker's memories, and so for judgement of what has been summoned up. Refrain 'times' a narrative, as the writer thinks over his memories and rethinks them, and so discloses in the extended rhythms of his voice something like 'the autobiography of writing'.[222]

In this way Dickens's double allusion to Shakespeare concentrates the ambiguous effect of Pip's repetitions, which work to keep individual memories in proportion even as they are being strained towards breaking point, and so reveal the speaker to be in two minds and voices about a story which is both comically and tragically foolish. The allusion also reaches back to Dickens's own past. In 1851, he co-authored an article on 'The Wind and the Rain' for *Household Words*:

The clown in 'Twelfth Night' might have been a good geologist when he sang—

> 'A great while ago the world began,
> With hey, ho, the wind and the rain!'

for the wind and the rain have written illustrated books for this generation, from which it may learn how showers fell, tides ebbed and flowed, and great animals, long extinct, walked up the craggy sides of cliffs, in remote ages. The more we know of Nature, in any of her aspects, the more profound is the interest she offers to us ... [223]

In its etymological excavations of words like 'aspects' and 'profound', this looks forward to the narrative refrains of *Great Expectations* as a 'burden', by showing how the weight of the past, instead of crushing memories, might preserve them as an unwelcome inheritance, fossils of shame. (It also warns us that there are some ages, such as one's own childhood, which generate the most profound interest in an observer

[221] *Melodious Guile* (1988), 138.
[222] See Philip Davis, *Memory and Writing from Wordsworth to Lawrence* (1983), xl.
[223] Harry Stone (ed.), *Charles Dickens' Uncollected Writings from 'Household Words', 1850–1859* (2 vols., 1968), I. 286.

only when they appear to be safely remote.) In particular, the upward movement of Dickens's 'great animals, long extinct' is repeated in a human key in *Great Expectations*' trial scene as, for a moment, the wind and the rain are stilled into raindrops on the windows of the airless courtroom, and Pip's description of Magwitch is filtered simultaneously through recollection of his own mistakes and anticipation of 'the greater Judgment that knoweth all things and cannot err'. 'Rising for a moment, a distinct speck of face in this way of light': as a 'speck', Magwitch's body is subjected to a narrative withdrawal, an erosion of imaginative space, which acknowledges that characteristic mixture of distance and self-pity usually reserved for the young or the dead. As a 'rising' speck, though, he embodies great expectations for a future event which is wholly beyond his control: resurrection.

'... HOPE IN DUST ...'

Pacing through the tangled streets of London in 1854, as if attempting to escape from the gathering momentum of other routines, such as growing old, Dickens suddenly became aware that he was surrounded by 'motes of new books in the dirty air'.[224] What he meant by 'motes of new books' is not entirely clear. It may be that the dusty air reminded him of the flecks of dirt which he had introduced into earlier novels in order to concentrate his readers' attention upon the physical facts of their environment (as an alarmed polemic in *Dombey and Son* against public toleration of the slums describes 'the thick and sullen air where Vice and Fever propagate together'), and their unreliable perception of these facts (as the same passage goes on to express the hope that social reformers will be 'delayed no more by stumbling-blocks of their own making, which are but specks of dust upon the road between them and eternity', ch. 47). Maybe the circumambient nature of Dickens's 'motes' alerted him to the frequency with which he returned, in successive 'new books', to the same metaphors of dust, and so to the way that some of the ideas which dust carries around with it, of loss and endurance, what passes away and what remains, could also be used to reflect upon his own processes of composition.

The 'distinct speck' of *Great Expectations*' reformed criminal, for example, is a literary mote which provided Dickens with one germ

---

[224] Quoted in Peter Ackroyd, *Dickens* (1990), 696.

of his most sustained examination of dirt and redemption: *Our Mutual Friend*. (An alternative title which Dickens considered for this novel was *Dust*.) Published at a time (1864–5) when, as Owen Chadwick points out, 'the anthropologists confronted religious man with a new kind of conflict—the fall of man versus the rise of man',[225] *Our Mutual Friend* demonstrates the difficulty we would have in assuming, from the description of Magwitch as a speck 'rising' for judgement, that Christian resurrection was the only future for human dust which was anticipated in the period. Chadwick's summary of this conflict as 'the fall of man versus the rise of man' is so compact that it raises almost as many questions as it describes (it is not clear whether 'fall' refers primarily to lineal descent or to the lingering taint of original sin; 'rise' seems to aspire to development beyond earth as well as on it), but his overlap of religious and secular vocabularies is perfectly true to the Victorian habit of using shared grammatical and literary structures to judge between alternative models of the afterlife. As Dickens's novel responds to old and new anxieties about 'the fall of man versus the rise of man' by compressing them into a densely allusive symbolic language of mud and aspiration, the suspended value of money and people, so these rival models too dwell on and in one another's patterns of argument and vocabulary.

An especially contested example of this process is provided by Frederic Harrison's essay 'The Soul and Future Life', which appeared in the first issue of *The Nineteenth Century* and generated a symposium of responses. For Harrison, as for Comte, no act ends with itself, but 'meets with suitable intellects and characters into whose action it is incorporated'. Even if such actions are invisible at the time, 'Every life more or less forms another life, and lives in another life' (p. 837). Thus, according to Harrison, we can separate Newton's writings from his body, but not from any body, because the passage of influence, which requires the co-ordination of man's moral and material life, means that any 'posthumous activity' of the soul which we could recognize as such must be as embodied as the brain-activity through which we can think about our selves or other selves at all. In this way, Harrison reasons, the fact that we still owe to Newton an understanding of certain physical laws provides evidence that he, too, was subject to their operation. His writing hand formed a cause whose effects do not require his actual presence to make themselves felt:

[225] *The Victorian Church* (2 vols., 1966–70), II. 33.

At last the man Newton dies—that is, the body is dispersed into gas and dust.... His activity continues the same ... If he had discovered some means of prolonging a torpid existence till this hour, he might be living now, and it would not signify to us in the slightest degree whether his body breathed in the walls of his lodging or mouldered in the vaults of the Abbey.   (pp. 836–7)

It might have signified a great deal to Newton, of course, as it might to anyone else who worried that Harrison's enthusiasm for a form of posthumous 'activity' divorced from intention would not greatly distinguish human beings from any other living creatures. (Darwin was impressed with the 'collaborative generosity' of worms, whose bodies weave randomly through the soil in an unpredictable rhythm of conservation and renewal, but although they are the cause of some remarkable effects, worms could not be said to have planned for these effects, any more than the 'collaborative' nature of their work could be attributed to a sense of civic duty.[226]) However, Harrison can breezily dismiss the fate of individual bodies and their intentions for themselves, because his idea of 'incorporation' is driven not by traditional puzzles over how the dispersal and absorption of a body's gas and dust will affect belief in individual resurrection,[227] but instead by 'the doctrine of the social future'. Whereas some religious believers brood over their bodies as living proof of that continuity of personality which alone could make comprehensible *an* afterlife as *their* afterlife, a Positivist believer like Harrison contemplates the dissolution of his flesh with the serenity born of trusting to 'an eternity of spiritual influence':

I am ready to pass into the spiritual community of human souls, and when this man's flesh wastes away from me, may I be found worthy to become part of the influence of humanity itself, and so

> Join the choir invisible
> Whose music is the gladness of the world ...   (p. 840)

On this occasion, what Harrison intends by George Eliot's lines goes some way to fulfilling the future which Eliot anticipates for them. He practises what she preaches, by making the unattributed incorporation of these lines into his argument a visible contribution to the development of social harmony both writers envisage, a staggered

---

[226] See Adam Phillips's discussion of Darwin's *Formation of Vegetable Mould Through the Action of Worms, with Observations on their Habits* (1881), in *Darwin's Worms* (1999), 35–63.

[227] I draw here on Caroline Walker Bynum, *The Resurrection of the Body in Western Christianity, 200–1336* (1995).

chorus of assent. However, it does not follow from Eliot's 'choir invisible' that individuals who are equally concerned with the future of the human soul will all sing the same song about it, any more than it follows from the publication of Harrison's essay for an anticipated readership greater than that of the *Nineteenth Century*, or even of the nineteenth century, that all his readers conceded that the only possible future life would be one of dispersed consciousness. As R. H. Hutton sensibly pointed out, Harrison's indiscriminate enthusiasm for 'posthumous activity' ignored the fact that 'a considerable proportion of these posthumous activities of ours, even when we can justify the original activity as all that it ought to have been, are unfortunate'. After all, Hutton reports, Harrison's papers 'have already exerted a very vivid and very repulsive effect upon my mind', and the prospect of being incorporated into the same future as Harrison will therefore produce very little satisfaction, 'except so far, perhaps, as my "posthumous activity" may retard the acceptance of Mr. Harrison's glorious anticipations for the human race'. As the future will be produced by our current strivings and inertia, it should then perhaps be viewed in much the same way as the present: 'the whole constitutes a *mélange* to which, as far as I am concerned, I look with exceedingly mixed feelings' (pp. 323–3). This is sharp-eared criticism, because even Harrison's prose sometimes admits into itself the sort of 'mixed feelings' which his argument tends not to admit out loud:

Death is the one inevitable law of Life. The business of religion is to show us what are its compensations. The spiritualist orthodoxy, like every other creed, is willing to allow that death robs us of a great deal, that very much of us does die; nay, it teaches that this dies utterly, for ever, leaving no trace but dust....We, on the contrary, would seek to show that much of us, and that the best of us, does not die, or at least does not end.   (p. 840)

There is something odd in this belief, that our best thoughts will live on as models for future conduct, being expressed in a symposium whose participants largely dedicated themselves to alternative creeds by dwelling on their logical frailties, or quibbling with one another's intentions, or parodically stretching isolated sentences out of shape. A suitably equivocal response to the unpredictable progress of human thought is already built into the narrower development of Harrison's own syntax. 'We, on the contrary, would seek to show that much of us, and that the best of us, does not die' stutters over alternative versions of the future, because it is not clear whether Harrison means by this 'a large proportion of what we share, in addition to our finest qualities, does not die' ('the best of us' as a supplement to the many other parts of us which might be transmitted to posterity), or 'a large proportion of each one of us—which amounts to our finest qualities—does not die' ('the best of us' as a mysterious essence which lurks within us, like a transmissible soul, waiting to be released into the world by our death).

As a number of Harrison's adversaries pointed out, similar 'mixed feelings' may need to be reckoned with in any written attempt to come to terms with death, particularly where the author recognizes that his work will participate in the sort of posthumous activity which the work itself qualifies or rejects. 'Mr. Harrison does not adequately distinguish between the nature of the fiddle and the nature of a tune', complained Lord Blachford, 'and would contend (if consistent) that a violin which had been burnt to ashes would, notwithstanding, continue to exist, at least as long as a tune which had been played upon it survived in the memory of any one who had heard it' (p. 348). 'I never said the tune would exist', countered Harrison: 'he thinks the tune will go on playing when the fiddle is broken up and burned ... *I* say, you can't have a tune without a fiddle, nor a fiddle without wood' (pp. 528–9). Even as Harrison's '*I* say' attempts to trump his opponent, the heckle again implicitly concedes the interference to which the passage of influence could be subject, particularly where a later voice carries an earlier tune beyond its author's control by finding a new setting for its old words, or new words for its old setting. If this is the case with Dickens's resetting of Shakespeare's 'The Wind and the Rain' to new and remorseful harmonies, it is even more so with those Victorian poets who dramatize overlapping demands of literary, Positivist, and theological afterlives in their verse. Prose, similarly, can stage this drama of textual and human afterlives, as the example of Dickens proves, but printed verse will offer special resources for an author who believes (with Blachford) that his 'tune' crystallizes his uniqueness or (with Harrison) that it illustrates the successive embodiment of a developing soul, because the same poetic form can carry diverse, and possibly divergent, lines of thought. It is certainly true, as Harrison's use of Eliot demonstrates, that a shared literary form can provide individuals with a means of participating in something larger than themselves, at once amplifying their own voice and extending other people's voices. But it is also true, as the wary insistence of

Harrison's '*I* say' concedes, that writing which asserts the influence of specific writers will need to acknowledge how readily a shared form, like an echo-chamber, can obscure the dimensions of a specific voice. Indeed, as the remaining chapters of this study will show, often it is by their inflections of common literary forms that Victorian poets discover how best to respond to shared cultural preoccupations with the afterlife, such as whether an individual's death should be seen as a preparation for the resurrection of the body, or as the end of its temporary existence as a social transmitter, or as the end of the matter altogether.

Frederic Harrison's more single-minded view of 'influence' means that he is quickly and suspiciously drawn to poetry. As early as the first page of his essay, Harrison rejects 'dithyrambic hypotheses' as a way of approaching his ideal future:

Let us reason together in sober and precise prose. Why should this great end, staring at all of us along the vista of each human life, be for ever a matter for dithyrambic hypotheses and evasive tropes? What in the language of clear sense does any one of us hope for after death: what precise kind of life, and on what grounds? It is too great a thing to be trusted to poetic ejaculations ... (p. 623)

Harrison's assumption that 'sober and precise prose' can be neatly separated from 'poetic ejaculations' is not true to the skill with which his contemporaries confused these categories. Dickens's tendency to drift into lofty blank verse, when composing scenes which were particularly troublesome to write and to read, such as the deathbeds of Jo in *Bleak House* or Little Nell in *The Old Curiosity Shop*,[228] demonstrates how readily prose could follow Wordsworth's advice that 'more pathetic situations and sentiments, that is, those which have a greater proportion of pain connected with them, may be endured in metrical composition',[229] and how the rhythms of his descriptions could then be used to retrieve from this private suffering a lasting public significance. Dickens recognizes, in these moments of emotional and metrical stress, that death might indeed be too 'great' a thing, too massively and elusively demanding of our attentions, to be trusted to the sort of precision which Harrison values so highly.

---

[228] R. H. Horne, *A New Spirit of the Age* (1849, repr. 1907), 45, describes the 'curious circumstance' of Dickens's lapses into blank verse; compare George Gissing, *Charles Dickens: A Critical Study* (1903), 222, on Dickens's 'habit of writing metrically'.

[229] Preface to *Lyrical Ballads* (1850 text), repr. in *Owen & Smyser*, I. 147.

At least one poet was also brought to recognize that Harrison's celebration of rational social development could be challenged by some of the more erratic and senseless aspects of human experience. Early on the morning of 14 September 1877, Browning discovered the body of his old friend Anne Egerton Smith in the chalet, 'La Saisiaz', where they had been staying. Faced with a situation which painfully brought to mind the central and defining question of whether the 'great end' of death is better thought of as a *telos*, the fulfilment of our designs, or merely as a *finis*, the sudden curtailment of our designs, Browning was moved to reply to the *Nineteenth Century* symposium 'The Soul and Future Life'. In the intellectual tussles of this symposium, Browning discovered a model for the competing tugs of faith and doubt which he now felt upon his own mind and voice. It was an argument with himself which was subsequently organized into his poem's restless intellectual rummaging:

> If I dared no self-deception when, a week since, I and you
> Walked and talked along the grass-path, passing lightly in review
> What seemed hits and what seemed misses in a certain fence-play—strife
> Sundry minds of mark engaged in 'On the Soul and Future Life',—
> If I ventured estimating what was come of parried thrust,
> Subtle stroke, and, rightly, wrongly, estimating could be just
> —Just, though life seemed so abundant in the form that moved by mine,
> I might well have played at feigning, fooling,—laughed 'What need opine
> Pleasure must succeed to pleasure, else past pleasure turns to pain,
> And this first life claims a second, else I count its good no gain?'—
> Much less have I heart to palter when the matter to decide
> Now becomes 'Was ending ending once and always, when you died?'[230]

In a subsequent letter to J. D. Williams, Browning explained that 'I could not tell the incidents of that memorable week more faithfully in prose and as an accurate account of what happened: and they impressed me so much that I could proceed to nothing else till I had in some way put it all on paper.'[231] One way in which his poem responds to these incidents is by making it clear that they are continuing to happen, as we hear in the shifting tenses of his lines, which circle warily around the idea that events happen only once, and the competing idea that even single events are multiplied in our heads by the restless operations of memory and hope. The reading process then mimics these operations, by suggesting the sequence of their conversation, and

---

[230] 'La Saisiaz', *RBP*, II. 511.   [231] Quoted in *RBP*, II. 1057.

at the same time reminding us that not all the problems they discussed were capable of being solved by this sort of human encounter. For example, to estimate the success of these 'sundry minds' in justifying, 'rightly, wrongly', arguments for and against various forms of afterlife, will ask us to recognize that individual minds can be as 'sundry' as any group of minds, given how often an argument is variously right and wrong rather than wholly right or wrong. What most brings the doubts and perplexities of this conversation to life is the ambiguous situation of the silent interlocutor, since it is left searchingly unclear how we are to understand 'the form which moved by mine'. This could be simply a description of the body which walked beside him but can do so no longer, thereby adding a sudden sting of loss to the past tense in 'moved'. It could be testing out the idea that his friend has outstripped him by her death, in which case the vagueness of 'form' helpfully leaves open the question as to whether a dead person has any form other than a corpse. It could equally suggest that, just as they once walked and talked in sympathy with the movements of one another's bodies and voices, so Browning now questions whether a similar reciprocity is still at work in his verse. By accommodating such a generous set of glosses on 'the form which moved by mine', fully in keeping with one possible origin of 'saisiaz' as a fissure or cleft, 'La Saisiaz' then approaches from a number of angles the central and unresolved question which is raised by its own form: is this poem a dramatic monologue? If so, it is not clear whether we are supposed to imagine the speaker's interlocutor as present in memory, or spirit, or any of the other possible forms of afterlife which are debated in the *Nineteenth Century* symposium. This is not only a question for poets, of course, but it is raised with especial force by a poet like Browning, for whom the idea that human beings might want more than one kind of afterlife is not worked out of his voice, as it might need to be worked out of a defence of one philosophical position or another, but is instead worked into it, as he uses the ambiguities of his verse to adjudicate between rival models of immortality, and so between the competing demands upon his readers of rational agreement and instinctive assent.

Take, as an example, the rhyme of 'strife' with 'Life', which occupies a privileged position in this account, as it so often does in Browning's verse,[232] because 'life' only appears at the end of a line on

---

[232] Daniel Karlin describes how Browning's returns to this rhyme outline the shape of his belief that 'conflict is a universal law, struggle is the condition of existence, all progress is dependent on a perpetual warfare between opposed forces', in *Browning's Hatreds* (1993), 20–1.

three other occasions in 'La Saisiaz', and on two of these it rhymes with 'strife'. By drawing together words which appear to be so irreconcilably at odds, Browning's rhymes work to concentrate the pivotal argument of his poem. The rhyme of 'life' and 'strife', like the more predictable futures provided by his metre (borrowed from Tennyson's 'Locksley Hall', with a cautious nod to its earlier, equally cautious, enquiry into the future), asks us to entertain, within the ordered world of print, fantasies of control over conflicts which are likely to be less easily resolved in real life. But the fact that these words are united in a rhyme also asks us to acknowledge that such fantasies are founded upon nothing more substantial than the contingencies of language. What I mean by this is that a chime like 'strife' and 'life' is merely a coincidental overlap of two words, a brief linguistic squabble. Yet although 'strife' and 'life' have nothing to do with each other in fact, they have everything to do with each other in the folk wisdom which understands that we may never be able perfectly to reconcile ourselves to one another, or to the form of life we share, any more than two rhyme words can ever become one. Rhyme often functions in this way, as the repository of hard-earned lessons which are enshrined in a poem as clues to some of the most basic ways in which a culture has come to think about itself. Newman describes the importance of these ways of thinking in our daily lives when he writes about 'credences' in his *Essay in Aid of a Grammar of Assent*:

They give us in great measure our morality, our politics, our social code, our art of life. They supply the elements of public opinion, the watchwords of patriotism, the standards of thought and action; they are our mutual understandings, our channels of sympathy, our means of co-operation, and the bond of our civil union. They become our moral language; they distinguish us from foreigners; they are in each of us, not indeed personal, but national characteristics.[233]

A rhyming dictionary provides one such 'grammar of assent' in its revelation of the channels of sympathy—the social agreements—which have been gradually carved out in a language by the pressures of repeated use, so that in English verse 'breath' invariably ends with 'death', 'womb' leads to 'tomb', and so on. Individually, then, rhymes emerge only in the time of reading, as we anticipate what will happen to 'love', and have our prejudices confirmed when it is grasped by

---

[233] *An Essay in Aid of a Grammar of Assent* (1870), 52.

'glove'; together, the rhyme-words of a language emerge over a far longer time, as the audible residue of cultural development, the 'mutual understandings' which can be heard joining speakers across divisions of space and time.

Dickens plays on this idea in *Dombey and Son*, by hinting that the resounding fall of the House of Dombey has already been plotted out by the language which will describe it:

The Counting House soon got to be dirty and neglected. The principal slipper and dogs' collar seller, at the corner of the court, would have doubted the propriety of throwing up his forefinger to the brim of his hat, any more, if Mr. Dombey had appeared there now; and the ticket porter, with his hands under his white apron, moralised good sound morality about ambition, which (he observed) was not, in his opinion, made to rhyme with perdition, for nothing.   (ch. 58)

The rhyme 'ambition—perdition' has an 'I told you so' quality to it which is confirmed with the smug nod of 'opinion', making Mr Dombey's failure into just one more confirmation of this oracular truth. Rhyme can carry this stamp of certainty because its meetings are inescapably written into the language, so that the connection between 'ambition' and 'perdition' allows sophisticated modern thinkers briefly to entertain more primitive fantasies that everything in the world is controlled by fate, by the already-written. At the same time, it reminds us that linking 'ambition' and 'perdition' is not 'sound morality' at all, but merely sounds masquerading as morality, a chance encounter in language. As a set of connections which are both inevitable and surprising, rhyme can therefore convey some of a culture's most cherished disagreements over those ideas, such as those concerning the afterlife, which have come to be central to the way it thinks about itself. Because rhyme reiterates established trains of thought, it elevates perceptions to the status of principles; individual utterances are invested with the weight of common proverbs; relative truths sound like universal and permanent ones. Equally, because rhymes look back, they can seem backward, the surviving relics of a more ancient linguistic past. Either of these attitudes might be true of a poet's use of rhyme, and for some users both will be true, as a pleasure in the ease with which new ideas drop into the established channels of a language is met in a speaker's voice by an irritation at the equal ease with which the same ideas can get stuck in a rut. Indeed, where Victorian poets reflect self-consciously upon the influences which work through their lines, even Harrison's impatience with the idea that the afterlife 'is too great a thing to be trusted to poetic ejaculations' is likely to be given a sympathetic hearing.

The way in which different poets approach a shared rhyme on 'dust', for example, can express the variable strength of their confidence in God's ability to distinguish between their dust and everybody else's dust on the day of general resurrection. Compare the turn which *In Memoriam* and *Rubáiyát of Omar Khayyám* each gives to the rhyme of 'dust' and 'trust'.[234] First Tennyson:

> Yet if some voice that man could trust
> Should murmur from the narrow house,
> 'The cheeks drop in; the body bows;
> Man dies: nor is there hope in dust:'[235]

If we concede that human constancy cannot outlast inconstant human flesh, then the commonplace rhyme will reflect glumly upon our inevitable letdowns of one another and our selves by forever keeping 'dust' within earshot of 'trust',[236] and playing off a reader's confidence in the fulfilments of rhyme against the unfulfilled promises which they describe. However, for Tennyson 'dust' cannot be the end of the story so long as he maintains his faith in the resurrection of the individual body, and where human ends are imagined as being extended, even the resolutions of terminal rhyme will be instinct with fresh life. H. M. Butler recalled Tennyson's 'peculiar manner of reading', with 'a sudden lift of the voice as if into the air, at the end of a sentence or a clause'.[237] But *In Memoriam*'s rhymes speak of raising more than the voice:

> Thou wilt not leave us in the dust:
> Thou madest man, he knows not why,
> He thinks he was not made to die;
> And thou hast made him: thou art just.[238]

---

[234] Hereafter I abbreviate *Rubáiyát of Omar Khayyám* to *Rubáiyát* in the main text, and *ROK* in notes.

[235] *IM*, XXXV, *TP*, II. 353.

[236] Compare Francis Bacon, 'Who then to frail mortality shall trust, | But limns the water, or but writes in dust' ('The World'), Walter Scott, 'Woman's faith, and woman's trust— | Write the characters in dust' (*The Betrothed*), and Robert Southey, 'leaving here a name, I trust, | That will not perish in the dust' ('My Days Among the Dead are Past').

[237] Repr. in *Page*, 43.

[238] Prologue, *TP*, II. 316.

Not 'dust to dust', then, but 'dust' to 'just'. The quatrain begins by investing its trust in the hope that human life will come to be justified by resurrection, and then folds together this faith and the delay which tests it into a measured timespan of printed verse; it achieves what Arthur Hallam described as rhyme's 'constant appeal to Memory and to Hope' by revealing that 'just' had been implicitly present in 'dust' all along.[239]

The eschatological arguments of Tennyson's verse, and the questions of human development which they raise, are often designed to be echoed in the processes of reading, as our eyes and ears trace out its syntactic patterns of promise and fulfilment, patience and revelation. 'Dust—trust' or 'dust—just' provide concentrated examples of these designs, because they are rhymes about resurrection which also represent rhyme as resurrection. Echoing through *In Memoriam*, Tennyson's rhymes therefore confidently articulate what he does not always dare speak out loud, namely the continuity of his body and voice between this life and the afterlife: a body and voice which continue to exist just like his rhyming quatrains, single in all their self-divisions. However, for such hopes to be constant across larger stretches of the imagination than a rhyme will require the perpetuation of individual and social memories in ways which are at once more willed and haphazard than a writer like Harrison supposes. Both *In Memoriam* and *Rubáiyát* show how the partial incorporation of earlier writings leads the writer to consider the partialities of memory—the slips of forgetfulness and concentrations of thought—which would make for an afterlife less fully harmonious than many Positivists assumed. *In Memoriam* contrasts our 'hope in dust', which includes the suspended hope of that dust, with the appalled image of a primal scene in which such hopes had never been:

> Mere fellowship of sluggish moods,
>   Or in his coarsest Satyr-shape
>   Had bruised the herb and crushed the grape,
> And basked and battened in the woods.[240]

When FitzGerald comes to reshape this section, the 'fellowship' to which his translation aspires is—like most valued friendships—in part founded on good-humoured quarrelling, as he sets out to show how misguided Tennyson is in certain of his premises, by redirecting

---

239 'The Influence of Italian upon English Literature', *Motter*, 222.
240 *IM*, XXXV, *TP*, II. 353.

them through the shapes of satire. The crushed grape is relished, the bruised herb is redeemed as the sensitive plantlife of 'this delightful Herb',[241] and the key rhyme 'dust—trust' is mockingly thrown back, like a drunk spoiling for a fight:

> I must abjure the Balm of Life, I must,
> Scared by some After-reckoning ta'en on trust,
>   Or lured with Hope of some Diviner Drink,
> When the frail Cup is crumbled into Dust!   (2nd edn., LXIV)

Unlike the grudges which are revealed and avenged in a Bloomian *clinamen*, this swerve of attention speaks of frictions which are expressed in literature, but which are not only literary. It also focuses attention upon the cultural pressures which are built up behind individual words, such as 'dust', during Tennyson's and FitzGerald's writing careers. These words form crossing-points for some of the currents of Victorian thought described in this chapter: the ways in which one person is understood to influence another physically and morally; the overlapping interest of Positivists and theologians in what of the individual changes over time, and what remains; the resources of print which allow a writer like Dickens to investigate and dramatize the influence on his work of others, and of his own earlier self. As the second half of this study will show, the 'ethos' which links these currents forms the intellectual atmosphere in which Tennyson and FitzGerald moved. It is the air their poetry breathes.

[241] *ROK* 1st edn., XIX.

3 Tennyson's Sympathy

'THE PASSION OF THE PAST'

'The most pathetic utterance in history', Tennyson told his son, 'is that of Christ on the Cross, "It is finished."' [1] Tennyson was seldom finished. After months or years without a meeting, Jane Brookfield recalled, he 'took up the thread of former days, and even sometimes of former conversations, exactly as if we had continued to see each other without any break at all', [2] while William Allingham remembered the 'sonorous manner' in which Tennyson recited his own verse: 'lingering with solemn sweetness on every vowel sound,—a peculiar incomplete cadence at the end'. [3] This sense of incomplete achievement, or achieved incompleteness, was drawn out further through Tennyson's protracted attachment to individual poems. Hearing him read *Maud*, some sixty years after the 'germ' of the poem had sprouted, his son was given the impression

> that he had just written the poem, and that the emotion which created it was fresh in him. This had an extraordinary influence on the listener, who felt that the reader had been *present* at the scenes described, and that he still felt their bliss or agony. [4]

In his methods of composition, as in his ways of speaking, Tennyson was reluctant to settle for his own conclusions. He prided himself that 'very often what is published as the latest edition has been the original version in his first manuscript', [5] qualifying his horror at physical reversion by proving that such lines could be adapted without being superseded—not dead, but waiting to be settled in a context which would release their restive energies:

> He said that 'The passion of the past, the abiding in the transient, was expressed in "Tears, idle tears," which was written in the yellowing autumn-tide at Tintern Abbey, full for me of its bygone memories.' [6]

---

[1] *Memoir*, I. 326.   [2] *Temple Bar*, 101 (1894), 203, repr. in *Page*, 8.
[3] *Allingham* (25 August 1867), 158.
[4] *Memoir*, II. 409 (Hallam Tennyson's emphasis).
[5] *Memoir*, I. 118.   [6] *Memoir*, I. 253.

Arthur Hallam was therefore uncharacteristically off-key when he wrote to Tennyson with a shy pride in the 'community of feeling between us', and attempted to clinch this fellow-feeling by declaring that he was 'not without some knowledge and experience of your passion for the past', because Tennyson's claim was for a passion *of* the past, disclosed in the creative resurrections and reanimations by which he echoed his 'extraordinary influence on the listener' in the practised skill with which he listened in on himself.[7] 'So sad, so strange, the days that are no more': it is central to Tennyson's creative self-identity that lines on the irrevocable should not themselves be irrevocable, so testing on a local scale an idea which also spans his writing career, that no poem is finished only once. As 'Tears, idle tears' survives its translation into *The Princess*, and 'no more' stubbornly persists with the thought of the early lyric 'No More', so the phrase 'passion of the past' is later turned to fresh account in 'The Ancient Sage'. In each case, the abiding in the transient is not only what Tennyson describes but also what he achieves.

So often are individual lines of Tennyson haunted by the ghosts of poems past, and the ghosts of those to come, that his development within and between these poems can be thought of as a literary version of Newman's 'living idea':

It is indeed sometimes said that the stream is clearest near the spring. Whatever use may fairly be made of this image, it does not apply to the history of a philosophy or belief, which on the contrary is more equable, and purer, and stronger when its bed has become deep, and broad, and full. It necessarily rises out of an existing state of things, and for a time savours of the soil. Its vital element needs disengaging from what is foreign and temporary, and is employed in efforts after freedom which become more vigorous and hopeful as its years increase. Its beginnings are no measure of its capabilities, nor of its scope. At first no one knows what it is, or what it is worth. It remains perhaps for a time quiescent; it tries, as it were, its limbs, and proves the ground under it, and feels its way. From time to time it makes essays which fail, and are in consequence abandoned. It seems in suspense which way to go; it wavers, and at length strikes out in one definite direction. In time it enters upon strange territory; points of controversy alter their bearings; parties rise and fall around it; dangers and hopes appear in new relations; and old principles reappear under new forms. It changes with them in order to remain the same.[8]

---

[7] *Kolb*, 446.
[8] John Henry Newman, *An Essay on the Development of Christian Doctrine* (1845), 63.

This could have been written as a commentary upon Tennyson's poetic career. Take Newman's description of an idea's meandering advance: 'From time to time it makes essays which fail, and are in consequence abandoned.' Many of Tennyson's poems attempt to find lyric shapes for the variety of ways in which a voice on the page might falter, from choked misery to speechless wonder.[9] When Tennyson read his own works aloud, some of his listeners became aware of the repeated temptation to trail off into silence which seemed to be offered by the subject-matter of his verse, and by the stuttering advance of its lines down the page:

Nor can I forget how, at the intervals or ends of a phrase such as 'And sorrow darkens the hamlet and hall', the whole voice which had been mourning forth the impassioned lament suddenly seemed to fail for very grief, to collapse, to drop and die away into silence, but so abruptly that the effect upon one was—'He has come to a full stop; he will not read another line.'[10]

His working manuscripts, similarly, show how frequently Tennyson was tempted to abandon his poems, and how stubbornly he refused to take his own uncertainty as the last word on even the most permanently troubled and incomplete of them. *In Memoriam*, according to T. S. Eliot, was 'a diary of which we have to read every word'.[11] The poem's drafts, though, show that Tennyson was not clear that he wanted anyone other than himself to read every word (several sections are retained in the protective arms of brackets), and that on occasion he could not even write every word:

> So draw him home to [those that mourn]
> In vain. A favourab[le speed]
> Ruffle t[12]

Here the draft breaks off into the wordless sketch of a face creased with sorrow, as if tacitly admitting that even the composed mourning of an elegy could be in vain when confronted with the sheer fact of grief. Yet one measure of Tennyson's literary integrity is his unflinching willingness to absorb what he most feared from his poetic development into the poems themselves, as when his Guinevere realizes that some human losses cannot be restored:

---

[9] See Eric Griffiths, *The Printed Voice of Victorian Poetry*, 97–170, to which this chapter is indebted throughout.

[10] H. D. Rawnsley, *Memories of the Tennysons* (1900), repr. in *Page*, 63.

[11] 'In Memoriam', repr. in *Selected Prose of T. S. Eliot*, 243.

[12] *TA*, III. 26.

Then she stretched out her arms and cried aloud
'Oh Arthur!' there her voice brake suddenly,
Then—as a stream that spouting from a cliff
Fails in mid-air, but gathering at the base
Re-makes itself, and flashes down the vale—
Went on in passionate utterance:
                              'Gone—my lord!'[13]

As Guinevere's voice breaks, but then remakes itself to go on in 'passionate utterance', so Tennyson, too, retrieves lasting spans of thought from individual lines of verse. For although Guinevere's Arthur is gone from her forever, the way he chooses to describe her unhappiness shows how another Arthur remains present to his own ways of thinking and speaking. From the early, unfinished paper on 'Ghosts' (which explained that the 'minister and expounder of human sympathies ... who has the power of speaking of the spiritual world' would have a voice 'like a mountain stream on a still night'),[14] through to 'In the Valley of Cauteretz' (in which Tennyson confirms that his dead friend remains as present to his mind and voice as the current of the 'stream that flashest white' does to the landscape which it continues to pulse across and seep through),[15] the comparison of a stream 'flash[ing] down the vale' to the shifting sameness of a human personality is sunk into his imagination like a watermark. In the resolute transformations of his poetry, as in the impassioned yearning of his religious faith, 'the dead are not dead but alive'.[16]

*

  Hallam's ear was usually better attuned to the details of Tennyson's verse than his remark on the 'passion for the past' suggests, but he was not the last critic to fail to hear how these details establish their edge and direction on the page only in relation to the full historical range of the voice from which they emerge. In his influential essay 'Tennyson and the Histories of Criticism', Jerome McGann has attempted to restore what he describes as the 'sympathetic contact' of Tennyson's poetry with its time: 'The study of Tennyson's poetry must

---

[13] 'Guinevere' (1859), *TP*, III. 545.
[14] Prologue to Tennyson's unfinished paper on 'Ghosts', *Memoir*, I. 498.
[15] *TP*, II. 618.
[16] 'Vastness', *TP*, III. 137.

begin and conclude in a field of historical particulars.'[17] This 'contact' is also a contract, because as the self-doubting spokesman for a self-divided readership, Tennyson is said to work according to an 'aesthetic of reconciliations' or 'ideology of accommodations' (p. 179). By anticipating and retaining multiple interpretations within the same lines of verse, his poems 'cross class lines'; in their style, as in their arguments, they admit difference (p. 193). This is a challenging claim, and one which would be hard to prove while retaining an unbroken respect for all the 'salient and specific matters of time, place and circumstance' which may affect a writer (p. 183). Perhaps this is why McGann's rhetoric is sometimes stronger than his evidence. It is not clear, for instance, what he means by 'a specifically Victorianized form of thought which operates in Tennyson's work in a specifically Victorian way', nor how we could recognize 'a Victorian set of attitudes which are peculiarly [Tennyson's] own' (p. 181). Many of McGann's conclusions arise from his reading of 'Tears, idle tears', but the attempt to abstract an argument for Tennyson's 'peculiar mid-Victorian qualities' from this poem is complicated by the fact that, though published in 1847, it was written in 1833, four years before Victoria's accession (p. 201). Indeed, a case could be made for thinking that, by 1837, Tennyson had already settled on the subjects and styles which would come to be considered peculiarly his own, and that he was to devote the textual revisions and imaginative recastings of the next fifty years primarily to investigation of what these qualities were, and might yet be.

To some extent, these local wrinkles in McGann's argument reflect the inevitable problems involved in any attempt to define the exact limits of a writer's shifting and contested 'sympathetic contact' with his or her time. By drawing attention to these problems, however, McGann successfully alerts us to an intersection of the aesthetic and moral vocabularies through which Tennyson's contemporaries too questioned how far poetry could, or should, exercise a Wordsworthian 'habitual and direct sympathy connecting us with our fellowbeings'.[18] McGann's explanation of the way Tennyson channelled 'national sympathies' into his verse, for example, or his repeated appeals that we should now read this verse with 'sympathy and

---

[17] 'Tennyson and the Histories of Criticism', repr. in *BI*, 173–203: 175, 183. Further page references to this essay are given in the main text.

[18] Preface to *Lyrical Ballads* (1850), repr. in *Owen & Smyser*, 141.

judgement', or 'sympathy and understanding', or 'critical sympathy', echo standard claims and complaints of Tennyson's reviewers (pp. 193, 181, 190, 202). Critical reaction to *In Memoriam* shows how readily 'sympathy' could be expanded or contracted:

… but the widest sympathy has been given to those who have shown a power to endure and surmount, as well as a sensibility to feel and express, their trials and sorrows.[19]

… bereavement has never found before so many touching symbols, so many answering relationships in the common experience of life, as are here presented, peopling the neighbourhood of sadness with unlooked-for sympathies.[20]

… the varied experiences of his fellow-men lie open to his gaze, and his sympathies flow out to all truth, be it to the prayer of the little child, to the earnest enquiry of the sceptic, or to the choiring of angels.[21]

Evidently Arthur Hallam was justified in his observation that 'the word sympathy … has a fluctuating import', flexing to accommodate individual nuance in a way that makes the word's own generous reach a good example of what it describes.[22] It might be thought that such irregular fluctuations would make 'sympathy' unwelcome in any critical account that aimed to measure an author's changing relationship with his or her readership, without the critic's vocabulary suffering from the same vicissitudes which it describes. But the vagueness of a word like 'sympathy' could itself be a useful resource for a critic who wished to pass over the rifts of understanding which threaten to open up in this relationship as it is stretched across unpredictable gaps of space and time. For example, when Hallam Tennyson concluded his introduction to the *Memoir* by praising his father's 'open-hearted and helpful sympathy' as the key to his 'special influence over the world',[23] his remark carefully sidestepped the knowledge, gleaned from many dutiful years of snipping out reviews and answering his father's correspondence, that not all readers found Tennyson's sympathies helpful:

---

[19] *Inquirer*, 22 (June 1850), 389.

[20] *British Quarterly Review*, 12 (August 1850), 292.

[21] *Westminster Review*, 54 (October 1850), 93.

[22] *Motter*, 133. On the wide range of meanings which 'sympathy' has attracted to itself, see Philip Mercer, *Sympathy and Ethics* (1972), 3.

[23] *Memoir*, I. xvii.

... it is one thing to trust in this separateness of our natures, and another to aim at producing evidences of it. The poet's true object should rather be to excite sympathy in spite of it, to strike upon those chords which prove the whole world kin.[24]

This echoes Tennyson's approval of the other human lives which are involved in the developing life of a poem: 'some event which comes to the poet's knowledge, some hint flashed from another mind ... may strike a chord from which a poem evolves its life'.[25] However, it seems to be in two minds about the poet 'producing evidences' of them, as if implicitly acknowledging that the separateness of our natures could be one of the conditions of literary enquiry, as well as one of its objects.

As Isobel Armstrong has shown, Tennyson's early critics regularly make competing, and often contradictory, claims about what a 'sympathetic poem' should be and do: whether the poet should distinguish between popular and representative utterances; whether his verse should set itself to resolve social and intellectual differences, or address only a culture's most familiar concerns; whether a poetic language which seeks to embody not just the time of its first publication, but the broader life of its times, should purge itself of those accidental events and expressions which arise from 'the fashion of the moment or the sentiment of the hour';[26] even whether, if the poet speaks with the voice of a society which no longer has much in common with its own past, Wordsworth's 'habitual' and 'direct' sympathy will differ in type as well as in degree.[27] McGann's understanding of Tennyson's 'sympathy' appears to be less troubled by these concerns:

In such verse the reader finds himself encouraged to read in many different ways, for many different meanings. 'Every reader must find his own interpretation according to his ability'; which is to say that the poetry believes itself able to anticipate those multifarious readings and readers. (p. 180)

This is less discriminating than the sentence from the *Memoir* which it trims ('Every reader must find his own interpretation according to his

---

[24] *Christian Remembrancer*, n.s., 21 (April 1851), 347.

[25] *Memoir*, II. 330.

[26] Aubrey de Vere, distinguishing between 'Ideal' and 'National' poetry, in *Edinburgh Review*, 60 (October 1849), 418.

[27] *Victorian Scrutinies* (1972). My discussion of 'sympathy' draws upon Armstrong's introduction.

ability, and according to his sympathy with the poet'),[28] and so goes some way to justifying Tennyson's suspicion that even writers who encourage their readers in certain interpretative directions will often be disappointed by what these readers go on to make of their work. Tennyson was unconvinced that any reader's abilities could match his own:

One of his neverended stories was about an anonymous letter running thus (received since *Maud* came out)—'Sir, I used to worship you, but now I hate you. I loathe and detest you. You beast! So you've taken to imitating Longfellow. Yours in aversion,—' and no name, says Alfred, scoring the table with an indignant thumb, and glaring round with suspended pipe, while his auditors look as sympathising as their view of the matter permits.[29]

Rossetti's story rings true with other reports which describe the disconcerting ease with which Tennyson's sensitivity to the criticism of strangers could be translated into a prickly distrust of even his closest supporters. 'He is the shyest person I ever knew', Benjamin Jowett observed, 'feeling sympathy and needing it to a degree quite painful.'[30] The ambiguity tactfully hints that Tennyson's search for sympathy sometimes pained other people too. But as the even-handed, or poker-faced, tone of Rossetti's account suggests, even with the glaring Tennyson present to squash dissenting views, it is unlikely that all of his listeners would have been equally sympathetic in 'their view of the matter', any more than Tennyson could have told simply by looking at their expressions whether they sympathized more with the reader's aversion or his own.

Given the potential in lyric address for the ideal existence of a poet's projected 'I' to be fractured against the everyday actualities of his or her readers, Tennyson's poems are equally circumspect about the whole soul of man being brought into their activity. *In Memoriam* was, Tennyson told Knowles, 'rather the cry of the whole human race than mine',[31] but the verse which sustains this cry is also conscious that if, as he also claimed, 'the whole truth is that assurance and doubt must alternate in the moral world in which we at present live',[32] then the 'wholeness' of any poem will speak not only of the stresses and strains of a divided readership, but also of each reader's

[28] *Memoir*, II. 127.

[29] D. G. Rossetti, letter of 8 January 1856, repr. in *Letters of D. G. Rossetti*, ed. O. Doughty and J. R. Wahl (2 vols., 1965), I. 282–3.

[30] Quoted in Ann Thwaite, *Emily Tennyson: The Poet's Wife* (1996), 355.

[31] *Nineteenth Century*, 33 (1893), 182.   [32] *Memoir*, I. 304.

divided soul. Tennyson's 'at present' touches upon a further difficulty for a theory, such as McGann's, which emphasizes the poet's 'concern to reach as large an audience as possible', but does not point out that this concern might best be met by a poet who has decided to write for an audience beyond the immediate moment of publication (p. 177). McGann's explanation of the critical tact required to read Tennyson assumes an Arnoldian faith in the reader's ability to recover each poem 'as in itself it really is' (p. 176). Yet Arnold was clear that the modern writer was defined not by his hair-trigger responsiveness to the present moment but by his patience: 'the growth of a tolerant spirit; that spirit which is the offspring of an enlarged knowledge; a spirit patient of the diversities of habits and opinions'.[33] Many of Tennyson's readers, similarly, urged him not to be 'rapt in the spirit of this age', but to write in a manner which would 'command the next', while others, like R. H. Hutton, pointed out the need 'to set ourselves free from the exclusive domination of temporary influences' in judging him, even as they recognized the charm which many of these influences would exercise on nostalgic future ages.[34] This was a matter of concern for Tennyson as well as for his readers, because although the 'sympathy' of humans for one another, whether alive or dead, forms one of his central poetic subjects, investigation into what constitutes 'sympathy' also lies at the heart of his poetic development, or lack of it. For the 'field of historical particulars' to which Tennyson devotes his most scrupulous and perplexed attention is not the set of ideological ventures and restraints to which McGann is committed, but the more private histories of composition and revision. His poems call for 'critical sympathy', but they also evince it, as they emerge from the scattered patchwork of his notebook drafts in a process of creative self-interpretation which depends as much upon Tennyson's reading of himself as it does upon the reactions he expected from the literary marketplace. To borrow his thoughtful change to a note made on 'Genius', before these poems are interpreted in their published states, they should first be read as:

~~public~~ ^combin^ations[35].

*

[33] 'On the Modern Element in Literature', repr. in *Super*, I. 23.
[34] Edward Bulwer-Lytton, *New Monthly Magazine*, 37 (January 1833), 74; 'Weighing Tennyson', repr. in *R. H. Hutton: A Victorian Spectator*, 162.   [35] *TA*, I. 164.

McGann selects 'The Charge of the Light Brigade' as a test-case to prove the material rootedness of Tennyson's poetry. Tennyson's view of the Crimean War, he suggests, is drawn from reports and leaders in *The Times*: 'his poem in fact follows this narrative in a number of details, and even uses some of its exact phrasing'—an important touchstone for a critical method which prides itself upon 'accurate transmission of facts' (pp. 194, 173). As this suggestive joining of 'in fact' and 'narrative' reminds us, the historical and literary contexts of 'The Charge of the Light Brigade' cannot readily be separated. For instance, it is possible that Tennyson's 'Flashed all their sabres bare, | Flashed as they turned in air' was influenced by Russell's Crimean War reports in *The Times*;[36] it is equally possible that Russell remembered Bedivere's hurling of Excalibur in 'Morte d'Arthur', 'flashing round and round, and whirled in an arch', when he lit upon his image of the Light Brigade's 'halo of flashing steel above their heads', choosing a turn of phrase already coloured by heroic failure and a return of arms.[37] McGann does not consider that some facts of a poem (such as details of idiom or style) will be as significant to its writer as the facts contained in that poem (such as references to historical events). Many poems are touched by public events without being deflected by them, but 'The Charge of the Light Brigade' is especially alive to the idea that the news it reports should be of a more lasting significance than occasional verse usually provides, as Tennyson abandoned in his revisions not only the specific individual 'Nolan' to whom McGann attaches so much significance, but a further hundred of the Light Brigade, once his duty to report precise casualty figures had been checked by the requirements of his own 'numbers', his metre: 'Six is much better than seven hundred (as I think) metrically so keep it.'[38]

A better model for Tennyson's poem is offered by McGann's valuable suggestion that 'poetry's subject is human experience in time' (p. 182), because human experience in time is not only the subject of 'The Charge of the Light Brigade', but the very air it breathes. As the poem's surface patterns submit to the pulse of a

---

[36] *The Times* reports of 13 and 14 November 1854 often return to 'the flashes which gleamed from the masses of armed men': 'As lightning flashes through a cloud, the Grays and Enniskillens pierced through the dark masses of Russians ... They swept proudly past, glittering in the morning sun ... Through the clouds of smoke we could see their sabres flashing as they rode up to the guns and dashed between them ... a light play of sword blades in the air.'

[37] *TP*, II. 12.

[38] *TL*, II. 101.

reader's voice, so this voice is in turn pulled back by regularities of style to which the poet's own fluctuating sympathies are subject:

> Half a league, half a league,
> Half a league onward,
> All in the valley of Death
> Rode the six hundred.[39]

'The historical fact', as Edgar Shannon and Christopher Ricks point out, 'in the words of *The Times* (leader, 13 November), is that "the whole brigade advanced at a trot for more than a mile." But "half a league" is more than a poetical (albeit accurate) way of saying "more than a mile", since it allows the poem to set before us from the very start the sense of "Half", just as the Charge forward was only half the story.'[40] This is sharply put, because the events of the poem are at once *faits accomplis* and history in the making. The subject of 'The Charge of the Light Brigade' is a particular set of events passing in time, in addition to their place in past time, as the charge takes place both 'in the valley of Death' and 'Into the valley of Death'. We hear how Tennyson's lines take their time in momentary double-takes ('do and die' mourning the schoolboy bravado of 'do or die'; 'Some one had blundered' interrupting the anticipated 'Someone had blundered' with a visible pause for the thought that a single decision could have so many human consequences), and in the way they preserve their own orderly shape, even as the opening lines of the poem, like the lines of cavalry which they describe, are returning in distressed and mangled forms. The Light Brigade's mistake was that at no point did they understand their orders to mean that they should turn and attack the Russian gun placements on the adjacent hillside. This forms part of a 'field of historical particulars' which is 'exact', but also exacting; facts which 'The Charge of the Light Brigade' starts from, but then undergoes. For what moves Tennyson's lines is not fact alone, but what Ricks has described in another context as 'the sense of fact'.[41] As his verse repeatedly, scrupulously, refuses to turn away from the consequences of the cavalry's error, so each line-break simultaneously offers and rejects a change of direction, before the next line proceeds with the same relentless tread: 'Half a league, half

---

[39] *TP*, II. 511.

[40] Edgar F. Shannon and Christopher Ricks, '"The Charge of the Light Brigade": The Creation of a Poem', *Studies in Bibliography*, 38 (1985), 19.

[41] See Christopher Ricks, *Essays in Appreciation*, 283.

a league, | Half a league onward'. The 'force of this poem', then, answers better to that 'force of poetry' heard by Johnson, 'which embodies sentiment, and animates matter',[42] because matters of fact must first rely upon the facts of matter, and two of the most vital statistics of a doomed body are that it will take time to arrive at its death, and that any reader must take time to recover this journey in the smaller movements of his or her own body, from the rhythms of breathing to the steady advance of eyes across the page.

In this way, the 'human drama' of 'The Charge of the Light Brigade' works by playing two forms of determination against each other: the oblivious resolve of the riders ('Only another half a league'), and the knowledge of their helpless witnesses ('*Another* half a league?'). It is this twin tugging of possibility and inevitability upon the reader's voice that makes the natural home of 'The Charge of the Light Brigade' not heroic painting (as McGann suggests), but the cultural form which had more thoroughly exercised eighteenth- and nineteenth-century discussions of that mingled pity and indifference which human miseries often encounter once they are reproduced for the public gaze: tragedy. As Ruskin wrote to Tennyson, 'I am very sorry you put the "some one had blundered" out of the "Light Brigade." It was precisely the most tragical line in the poem. It is as true to its history as essential to its tragedy.'[43] This sense of dramatic plot, of wilful preparation for fatalities, is echoed in Russell's account of how the watching officers and men 'shouted with delight, and thus keeping up the scenic character of their position, they clapped their hands again and again', as it is in *The Times* leader of 14 November: 'As nature itself, the poets tell us, prepares for a storm, the events of that day seemed gradually to work up to the closing catastrophe.' Such a blurring of military and dramatic vocabularies is not unusual in itself: the figurative sense of 'theatre', used to describe the scene of a battle, dates from at least the early eighteenth century.[44] It also seems to have been popular, at the time Russell and Tennyson were writing, as a way of imposing the order and completeness of fiction onto the unfinished mess of the Crimean campaign, even if the tragic frame of this fiction confronted the public with the limitations of their response to human suffering: that unbridgeable divide between the scream of somebody in pain and the

[42] *The Rambler*, No. 168 (26 October 1751).
[43] *Memoir*, I. 411.
[44] *OED*, 'theatre', 6b (the first example given, from 1720, predates the phrase 'theatre of war' by more than 200 years).

open-mouthed horror of a spectator which Browning described, with brilliant economy, as 'the gaping impotence of sympathy'.[45] While Russell watched a real battle in a 'vast amphitheatre' and felt he was watching a play, his readers were being persuaded that they could watch a play and feel they were watching a real battle: above *The Times* leader for both 13 and 14 November is an advertisement for Astley's Royal Amphitheatre and its performance of 'The Battle of Alma', which promises a cast of 400 auxiliaries performing 'charges of cavalry' with 'attack and repulse' amid 'the roaring of cannon', so 'forming a coup d'oeil unparalleled, and inducing the beholder to believe he is actually witnessing the fearful reality. It will be repeated EVERY EVENING.' The leader of 13 November had anxiously noted of the Light Brigade: 'Such a spectacle was never seen before, and we trust will never be repeated.' But 'The Charge of the Light Brigade', like 'The Battle of Alma', is a military review which is both unparalleled and repeatable: an accurately uncertain response to any tragic play, given how often the tussle between design and chance which structures the plot of a tragedy is then drawn out and echoed in the rehearsed actions and improvisations of stage performance.

The Light Brigade goes on; it goes back; and it is through his compositional returns that Tennyson discovers an imaginative correlative for the time-lag which was observed between the first warnings of danger and their fulfilment. Shannon and Ricks note that 'The Charge of the Light Brigade' is 'Tennyson's most familiar poem',[46] and this is also central to Tennyson's methods of composition. Familiarity bred content. The 'Cannon volleyed and thundered' because an earlier elegy upon a military subject had rehearsed this satisfying blend of sound-effects in a line which described how 'the volleying cannon thunder his loss' ('Ode on the Death of the Duke of Wellington'); the Light Brigade charge into 'the jaws of Death' of medieval iconographic tradition, but more recently of 'The Lover's Tale' ('The Jaws of Death'); even the valley half-remembers the 'valleys, half in light' of *The Princess*.[47] And so on, and so back, as fragments of earlier poems drift into place to become a literary context with the force of historical circumstance.[48] The poem's drive towards the inescapable is

---

[45] *The Ring and the Book*, IX. 1001.
[46] Shannon and Ricks, 'The Charge of the Light Brigade', 1.
[47] *TP*, II. 484; I. 369; II. 294.
[48] On Tennyson's 'poetry of aftermath' as 'a coming to terms with the inevitable', see Herbert F. Tucker, *Tennyson and the Doom of Romanticism* (1988), 14.

compounded by its own creative evolution, as Tennyson's borrowings here and in subsequent poems (each of the later 'half a league's of 'The Ancient Sage', 'Gareth and Lynette', 'The Holy Grail', and 'The Last Tournament', finds its place in a narrative pulled on by the gravity of death) discover imaginative trajectories for those questions of premonition and hindsight which the charge itself had raised.[49]

These 'sympathetic contacts' of Tennyson's poems often begin in the pages of his working notebooks. Indeed, although McGann claims that 'the character of [a poem's] uniqueness is always socially and historically embedded' in publication (p. 187), many of the details of Tennyson's poems emerge from the more immediate textual surroundings in which they were first composed. Reading through Tennyson's notebooks, then, is often an exercise in reading between the lines, because between the scribbled lines of one embryonic poem may be lines which eventually form quite another poem, or something quite other than a poem. Text and context blur and merge, as Tennyson's methods of composition proceed like the lines he cut from 'Edwin Morris':

> He left his episode and on he went
> Like one that cuts an eight upon the ice
> Returning on himself.[50]

Just as the same lines of verse can stretch to accommodate different historical circumstances, so the same circumstances can be stretched to accommodate different lines. Turning the pages of Harvard Notebook 16:[51]

fol.19ʳ–19ᵛ: *In Memoriam* ix: 'Fair ship ... '
fol.20ʳ: quotation from Malory marked 'M.d'A.'
fol.20ᵛ–21ᵛ: 'Notes on Arthurian legend'
fol.23ʳ–23ᵛ: 'Hark! the dogs howl!'

Reading backwards, we see how Tennyson may have reacted poetically to the loss of Arthur Hallam in 1833. His son explained that Tennyson 'had already noted down in his scrap-book some fragmentary lines ["Hark! the dogs howl! the sleetwinds blow"], which proved to be the germ of *In Memoriam*.'[52] The Heath and Yale MSS of 'Fair

---

[49] *TP*, III. 139, 298, 480, 521.
[50] *TP*, II. 144n.; the lines were themselves returned to in 'The Epic'.
[51] *TA*, III. 16–20.
[52] *Memoir*, I. 107.

ship' are dated '6 Oct. 1833' (the news of Hallam's death reached Tennyson on 1 October), and are later than Harvard Notebook 16, but the imaginative overlaps and frictions of this notebook's pages reveal how difficult it might be to determine the way in which Tennyson composed *In Memoriam* by fixing upon a single fragment as its 'germ'—as difficult as it might be to determine the processes of mourning by chronological sequence alone, given the rhythms of grief which could come to pattern a life, and so the collapse of any particular loss into a more general sense of loss. A poem written under these circumstances does more than cross class lines; like a letter written in 'sympathetic ink', it also crosses its own lines, as the version of events which is described out loud touches upon alternative versions of the same events which are held in abeyance, under its breath. Connections which cannot yet be argued out can be approached through fragmentary hints and glances, as 'Hark! The dogs howl!'s' voice-wasting 'sleet*winds*' and the frustrated desire to '*wind* my arms for one embrace' are reconciled into the airy embrace of 'Fair ship's' 'gentle *winds*': a movement from choked eloquence to lyrical withdrawal which would take a further seventeen years, and 132 sections, to be fully worked out through *In Memoriam*'s compositional and narrative development.

Valéry once pointed out that, in poetry, there is much which flowers in the spaces between the words: those places where the trailing edges of writing are transformed into otherwise unspoken attachments between people and ideas. In Tennyson's notebook sketches we see these spaces being charged with potential, but even in book form his poems resist their own confines on the page and reach out to test, unsettle, quarrel with one another. The first periodical publication of 'The Charge of the Light Brigade' in the *Examiner* of 9 December 1854, McGann claims, 'focuses the poem's choice of a certain ideological point of view' (p. 191). However, the poem's first volume publication, in *Maud, and other poems* (1855), makes it less than certain in its point of view. Aubrey de Vere explained the 'singular' way in which Tennyson assembled *Maud*: beginning with 'O that 'twere possible', 'the whole work was written, as it were, backwards'.[53] A fuller understanding of *Maud*'s singular backwardness would need to take account of Tennyson's composition and placing of 'The Charge of the Light Brigade' as the final poem in the 1855

---

[53] *Memoir*, I. 379.

volume. Final, but not conclusive, because while its last lines—'Long shall the tale be told | ... How they rode onward!'—anticipate successful tellings of the charge beyond the limits of this printed edition, the length of the tale is also to be measured by the way it stretches back to the first poem, *Maud*. Read in this way, the extremes of the volume answer to the extreme positions open to a 'sympathetic' poet, expected to offer his readership models of conduct (private self-obsession or public duty; 'the dialogue of the mind with itself' or physical action),[54] both in his choice of subjects and his poetic treatment of them. In the extended compositional histories of 'The Charge of the Light Brigade' and *Maud*, these extremes meet.

The earliest autograph manuscript of 'The Charge of the Light Brigade' (48 lines in 5 stanzas, untitled) is in a notebook, written back to front on pages 26 and 25, after nineteen pages of *Maud*.[55] This notebook includes most of Part III, 'Written when the cannon was heard booming from the battleships in the Solent before the Crimean War.'[56] Parliament declared war against Russia on 22 March 1854, eleven days after the Baltic fleet had set sail from Spithead on 11 March. Its guns had been thoroughly tested: Emily's journal for 20 February noted that 'in the kitchen garden facing the down ... we heard the sound of the cannon practising for the Crimea. Their booming sounded somewhat knell-like.'[57] Rehearsals for the Crimean War were popular in the Tennyson household. In September, Emily was vowing that the first songs she would teach her children were stirring military ones, and their son Hallam's favourite game was to roll around on the floor, saying 'This is the way the Russians fall when they are killed'.[58] But although *Maud*'s speaker celebrates the fact that 'the cobweb woven across the cannon's throat | Shall shake its threaded tears in the wind no more' (III. vi. 27–8), and ends by prophesying 'the sudden making of splendid names', his poem does not only look forward to war. It also looks back.

Between August 1854 and February 1855—the period in which 'The Charge of the Light Brigade' was written and polished—Tennyson revised *Maud* by adding sections in separate notebooks, later in the poem's compositional history, but earlier in its narrative, which

---

54 Matthew Arnold, Preface to the 1853 *Poems*, repr. in *Super*, I. 1.
55 Harvard MS. Eng 952 * 54M–203 [30], repr. in *TA*, IV.
56 *TP*, II. 582.
57 Quoted in Susan Shatto (ed.), *Tennyson's Maud: A Definitive Edition* (1986), 9.
58 See Robert Bernard Martin, *Tennyson: The Unquiet Heart* (1980), 381.

also rehearse the Light Brigade's self-destructive 'half a league'. Section I. ix was written in 1854, after Section III:

> I was walking a mile,
> More than a mile from the shore,
> The sun look'd out with a smile
> Betwixt the sun and the moor,
> And riding at set of day
> Over the dark moor land,
> Rapidly riding far away,
> She waved to me with her hand.
> There were two at her side,
> Something flash'd in the sun,
> Down by the hill I saw them ride,
> In a moment they were gone:
> Like a sudden spark
> Struck vainly in the night,
> Then returns the dark
> With no more hope of light.[59]

The riders do not turn to the spectator, who thereby wins nothing more than this flash in the sun before the return of darkness. But on rereading *Maud*'s sections in their narrative sequence, the reversal of direction in this image between I. ix and III ('Tho' many a light shall darken ... many a darkness into the light shall leap') also points to a revision of the poem's ending. Tennyson had already described Maud's gestures towards the Crimea's 'deathful-grinning mouths' (III. 52). The Light Brigade itself later charged into, and out from, 'the jaws of Death', which became the jaws of death only with the cry 'Forward, the Light Brigade! | Charge for the guns!' (the only instance of direct speech in the poem). Given the slaughter which followed this cry, the incorporation of I. ix into the revised *Maud* modifies the trustworthiness of Maud as a military leader, and fixes a suspicious eye upon the heroic rhetoric of 'The Charge of the Light Brigade'. It also shows Tennyson readjusting his voice to a sound of retreating steps which both poems share:

> / x x   / x x
> Half a league, half a league,
> / x x   / x
> Half a league onward

59 *TP*, II. 539.

```
x  x   /  x  x   /
I was walking a mile,
    /   x  x /   x   x   /
More than a mile from the shore
```

With these little dactylic dabs, the valley of death creates echoes of a falling rhythm, a measured poetry of departures, as both poems move in and out of step with one another, and so in and out of step with one of the even pulses of Tennyson's career.

As models of expectation and fulfilment, Tennyson's metrical shapes carry his lyric continuities: the steady, and steadying sound of a voice that can register individual moments of shock and chance, but without being unduly deflected by them from its own regular course through time. They also confirm the human 'tendency towards unity of form' which Arthur Hallam had detected in the workings of sympathy.[60]

'THE RETURN OF THE MIND UPON ITSELF'

Hallam's essay 'On Sympathy' adapts the mechanisms of Hartleyan psychology to question how two souls could 'associate' together in a sympathetic union, given that 'I' and 'You' are not fixed in themselves any more than they are fixed in relation to one another. Hazlitt had valued actors as models of sympathetic behaviour, because 'The height of their ambition is to be beside themselves'.[61] Hallam suggests that whether or not being beside one's self is the stuff of human ambition, it is an inevitable consequence of what it means to be human. We are never at one with our selves, he argues, because although personal identity is inextricably bound up with personal history, we cannot again be what we have been. The human soul is disintegrating, 'piece-meal', in the flux of time; cut into it by the operations of memory, and you can count the rings:

> To know a thing as past, and to know it as similar to something present, is a source of mingled emotions. There is pleasure, in so far as it is a revelation of self; but there is pain, in so far that it is a divided self, a being at once our own and not our own, a portion cut away from what we feel, nevertheless, to be single and indivisible. (p. 138)

[60] 'On Sympathy', *Motter*, 137; further page references to this essay are given in the main text.

[61] *Howe*, IV. 153.

Like other attempts to explain the origin of our affections, such as Aristophanes' story of the original double-human in Plato's *Symposium*, Hallam's account of our search to reunite our selves has the attractiveness of a myth: the pleasures of explanation freed from the responsibilities of proof. However, his model of sympathy is more grippingly inevitable than some other versions of separation-anxiety, such as Freud's theories of birth-trauma and its psychological residues, or John Bowlby's studies of childhood attachment and loss, because it envisages mourning for our selves as the primary condition of our fondness for other people: ' ... were it conceivable that the soul in one state should coexist with the soul in another, how impetuous would be that desire of reunion, which even the awful laws of time cannot entirely forbid' (p. 138). Tennyson would have approved of this serious use of 'awful',[62] emerging from 'laws', as the movements of Hallam's prose echo the impossible 'desire of reunion' which it describes. A yearning for sympathetic accord is sunk more clearly into the phrase 'coexist with the soul in another', which does not distinguish clearly between another state of the same soul, othered by time, and the parallel state of an other soul altogether. But if Hallam's argument is accepted, this ambiguity is one we would experience in all human encounters, not only the act of reading. We sympathize with a beloved because our 'desire of reunion' between our separated selves drives us to look into this other face as early enthusiasts of photography looked at the daguerreotype, as 'a mirror with a memory':

The soul ... contemplates a separate being as a separate state of itself, the only being it can conceive. But the two exist simultaneously. Therefore that impetuous desire arises. Therefore, in her anxiety to break down all obstacles, and to amalgamate two portions of her divided substance, she will hasten to blend emotions and desires with those apparent in the kindred spirit. (p. 138)

Hallam's 'sympathy' makes itself felt as an anxiety for influence, and the word's 'fluctuating import' then echoes the larger fluctuations of human personality, which prepare us for 'this expectation of sameness, so perpetually answered' in others: 'The order of nature is uniform under the sway of invariable laws, the same phenomena perpetually recur. And there is a pre-established harmony in mind by which it anticipates this uniformity' (pp. 137–8).

---

[62] See *Memoir*, II. 384, on Tennyson's irritation with ' "the people of to-day who will say 'awfully jolly' ", etc.'

Anticipation is central to the workings of sympathy, because although the contemplation of another being 'as a separate part of self, a state of [the self's] own consciousness existing apart from the present' could result from memories which are rooted in the past, Hallam notes that this sense of a split self could equally result from regarding other people 'as imagined states [which] exist in the future' (p. 137). As reflections of our past, friends engage our sympathy because they meet our expectations of what we once were; as images of our future, the same friends engage our sympathy because in them we see hints and glimpses of what we might yet become.

*

George Eliot would have been stern with how little Hallam seemed to ask of these 'imagined states', particularly after her understanding of sympathy (the means by which the constraining bonds of egoism are replaced by the loving ties of altruism) broadens 'state' to mean not just the condition of the individual human soul but also the developing nation-state which we should live for as well as live in. Eliot's call for 'the extension and intensification of our sympathetic nature' itself enlarges upon eighteenth-century attempts to discover a means of social integration which would outlast individual lives,[63] and forms an important focus for those nineteenth-century debates about the spread of influence which I described in the previous chapter. This conjunction of sympathy and influence ranges from the ties of duty which Samuel Smiles sees joining familial loving-kindness and philanthropic works to Eliot's own stress, notably in *Daniel Deronda*, upon the personal and social inheritances which an individual should fulfil and pass on, once she or he has grasped that individual futures cannot readily be separated from the fate of the nation.[64] These reciprocal dealings of personal sympathy and national prosperity had been identified early in Tennyson's career. For example, William Johnson Fox's assessment of *Poems, Chiefly Lyrical* (1830) in the *Westminster Review*—the first discussion of Tennyson to appear in a major quarterly—worries away at the possibilities for dramatic lyric, in a

[63] George Eliot, 'Worldliness and other-Worldliness: The Poet Young' (1859), quoted in Bernard Semmel, *George Eliot and the Politics of National Inheritance* (1994), 13.

[64] *Duty* (1880), ch. 10: 'Sympathy'; compare Leslie Stephen's chapter on 'Altruism' (which includes a section on sympathy) in *The Science of Ethics* (1882).

period still coming to terms with the insights into shared laws of mental operations which empirical psychologists claimed could be abstracted from 'the analysis of particular states of mind'.[65] Thus, when Fox claims that 'Our author has the secret of the transmigration of the soul. He can cast his own spirit into any living thing, real or imaginary' (p. 27), his enthusiasm for Tennyson's skill in dissolving some of the otherness of other beings, by grasping the 'mutual relations and influences' of each inner world, is directed by a combination of associationist psychology and Adam Smith's notion of dramatic sympathy (p. 27).[66] Towards the end of his essay, Fox senses some of the more worrying ethical implications for poems which investigate 'particular states' of mind, such as the danger that even the strangest utterances will not remain peculiar to the poet once published: 'A genuine poet has deep responsibilities to his country and the world.... [Poets] can influence the associations of unnumbered minds; they can command the sympathies of unnumbered hearts' (p. 33). Fox's essay anticipates many of the arguments which were to surround Tennyson's later dramatic monologues, notably the accusations, often linked to ill-defined yearnings for some Great British national poem, that the monologue replaced healthy social sympathies with morbid self-absorption.[67] In particular, the uneasy swerves in this essay, between individual states of mind and the state of the nation, alert us to a widespread critical preoccupation with Tennyson's verse, which also comes to be a central focus of that verse: the association of sympathy and futurity.

'The human soul', wrote Spedding of Tennyson's 1842 *Poems*, 'in its infinite variety of moods and trials, is his favourite haunt; nor can he dwell long upon any subject, however apparently remote from scenes and objects of modern sympathy, without touching some strings

---

[65] January 1831, 14, 210–24, repr. in *TCH*, 21–33 (further page references to Fox's essay are given in the main text). The terms of Fox's discussion draw heavily on James Stuart Mill's *Analysis of the Phenomena of the Human Mind* (2 vols., 1829).

[66] Smith's *Theory of Moral Sentiments* (1759) argues for the substitution of 'sympathy' in place of 'moral sense' as man's internal monitor; see Walter Jackson Bate, 'The Sympathetic Imagination in Eighteenth-Century English Criticism', *English Literary History*, 12: 1 (March 1945), 144–64; and Stephen D. Cox, '*The Stranger Within Thee': Concepts of the Self in Late-Eighteenth-Century Literature* (1980), 27–33.

[67] See, e.g., *Hogg's Weekly Instructor*, 6 (25 December 1847), which praises Tennyson's dramatic projections of self ('He loses himself in his subject, and thus ... gains admission to the heart and sympathy of his sympathetic auditor'), but complains that such private extensions of the imagination are also withdrawals from shared experience: 'he does not speak to us in the language of sympathy, and hope' (283).

which brings it within the range of our common life.'[68] Bulwer-
Lytton was unsure what this 'common life' would look or sound
like: 'common sense should be the staple of fine verse', he claims,
but Tennyson fails to tap 'the common springs of emotion'.[69] *Maud, a
Monodrama* especially taxed those readers who proposed simultaneously that the poet should exercise shared forms of knowledge or
feeling, and that the form of poetry which best enlarged his or her
readers' sympathies was the dramatic.[70] As Tennyson read *Maud*
aloud, his son thought that 'You were at once put into sympathy
with the hero.'[71] Other readers were more disturbed by the prospect
of sympathizing with the outpourings of a mind which seemed
incapable of responding in kind. When Browning remarks of Shelley
that 'sympathy with his kind was evidently developed in him to an
extraordinary and even morbid degree',[72] the linking of 'sympathy'
and 'morbid' through 'developed' is typical of much Victorian criticism in attending to the potential unhealthiness of a sensibility which
could slip so easily from the finely tuned to the highly strung. Many of
the disapproving noises made about Tennyson's lapses into morbidity
go further, to suggest the potential of his poems to spread unhealthiness, by liberating the latent insanity which was popularly supposed
to lurk behind even the most poised social performer. Put another
way, although Arthur Hallam had described Tennyson's 'habit of
seeking relief in idiosyncrasy rather than community of interest',
some later critics seemed more worried by the possibility of a community *of* idiosyncrasy. Like sympathy, madness could be catching.[73]

Matthew Arnold was impatient with situations from which, he
claimed, 'no poetical enjoyment can be derived':

They are those in which the suffering finds no vent in action; in which a
continuous state of mental distress is prolonged, unrelieved by incident,

---

[68] *Edinburgh Review*, 77 (April 1843), 382.

[69] *New Monthly Magazine*, 37 (January 1833), 69, 73.

[70] See especially E. S. Dallas, *Poetics* (1852), although the link between sympathy and
drama had been commonplace since Hume's *Enquiry Concerning the Principles of Morals* (1751).

[71] *Memoir*, I. 396.

[72] 'Introductory Essay' (1852) to *Letters of Percy Bysshe Shelley*; see Griffiths, *The Printed Voice
of Victorian Poetry*, 153.

[73] Alexander Gerard's conjunction of sympathy and pathology in his 1759 *Essay on Taste*
('the force of sympathy' which prepares the observer 'for readily catching, as by infection,
any passion') is typical of a popular eighteenth-century distinction between two forms
of sympathy—pleasurable 'sharing' and disruptive 'contagion'—which lingered in
nineteenth-century medical discourse; see Bate, 'The Sympathetic Imagination', 153.

hope, or resistance; in which there is everything to be endured, nothing to be done.[74]

Although Arnold's 'continuous state' appears gloomily resigned to private brooding, physiological writings of the period often draw attention to the possible extension of mental distress between individuals as well as within them. John Conolly observes in *An Inquiry Concerning the Indications of Insanity* (1830) that 'Every man is interested in this subject; for no man can confidently reckon on the continuance of his perfect reason.'[75] Like many doctors, he had good cause to be interested in this question, and to hedge his bets over a possible answer, because for much of the nineteenth century medical opinion was divided over how far the continuance of reason was a matter of biological necessity or self-control. While John Reid warns of the 'floating atoms or minute embryos of insanity', which the individual might nurse unsuspectingly in his body for years as the seeds of a strange new self,[76] Conolly is more reluctant to absolve the mad of their responsibilities: 'it is only when ... passion impairs one or more faculties of the mind ... that the reason is overturned; ... He is mad only while this state continues.'[77] As Sally Shuttleworth has recently shown, the 'continuous state of mental distress' which most disturbed these and other writers, besides a prolonged depression of the individual psyche, was the prospect of the entire country sinking into morbid habits: a distressed nation-state.[78] Early in the century, Thomas Trotter cautioned that if the 'convulsions' of revolutionary Europe were not to be caught by the English, they should take steps to 'check the increasing prevalence of nervous disorders; which, if not restrained soon, must inevitably sap our physical strength of constitution'.[79] 'Check' and 'restrained' suggest measures usually reserved for individual asylum dwellers, which Trotter would like to introduce as a general principle of social hygiene, as if the nation would recover its wits if only a large enough straitjacket could be found to keep its self-destructive tendencies under control. However, even when medical treatment was based more on the alienist's 'sympathizing distress at moral pain' than stern policing of the patient's body, the rhetoric of

---

[74] Preface to 1853 *Poems*, repr. in *Super*, I. 2–3.
[75] (Repr. 1964), 8.
[76] *Essays on Hypochondriasis* (1821), 314.
[77] Ibid., 227.
[78] *Charlotte Brontë and Victorian Psychology* (1996).
[79] *A View of the Nervous Temperament* (1807), xi.

mental disease continued to gesture warily towards an examination of the nation, linking the healthy growth of its political and psychological 'constitution' through shared images of circulation, whether of money through the social body, or electrical impulses through individual bodies: vigorous or sluggish; regulated or unchecked; self-contained or spreading.[80]

Tennyson was stirred by these problems of defining and regulating madness, because they were also his problems. There was the inherited 'black blood', which he worried about as a shared dark past and a personal dark future. There was the long tradition of associating eloquence and disease, in and against which he worked. (Henry Maudesley identifies zeugma, punning, and ambiguity as key indications of mental disturbance, the audible distress flares which a speaker sends out into the world.[81]) There was the separation of the individual from his kind (as *Maud*'s speaker promises sadly to 'bury myself in myself'),[82] which was widely argued to be a symptom of 'moral insanity', but which also allowed the writer to forge 'sympathetic contact' through the authorial remove of the printed page (as Tennyson explained that he needed 'quiet, and myself to myself' in order to write).[83] Finally, of central and immediate concern to a poet so self-conscious about his habits of composition, there was the ease with which certain key aspects of lyric address, such as its skilful patterning of speech, could turn between a composed pleasure in verbal dexterity and a symptom of morbid self-indulgence.

The possibility that poems influenced the behaviour of their readers works against the grain of the idea, frequently articulated in Victorian literary criticism, that poetry was somehow set apart from the world of public action—a world that included the political and economic pressures which continued to be exerted upon, and by, the practical business of publication. J. S. Mill's argument that 'Poetry is feeling, confessing itself to itself in moments of solitude ... Eloquence is feeling pouring itself out to other minds, courting their sympathy, or endeavouring to influence their belief, or move them to passion or to action', was itself an eloquent expression of this widespread desire

---

[80] J. C. Bucknill and D. H. Tuke, *A Manual of Psychological Medicine* (1874), 672.

[81] *The Physiology and Pathology of Mind* (1867), 257; see also William Newnham, *Essay on the Disorders Inherent to Literary Men* (1836).

[82] See, e.g., J. E. D. Esquirol, *Des malades mentales* (1838), trans. by E. K. Hunt as *Mental Maladies: A Treatise on Insanity* (1845), discussed in Sally Shuttleworth, *George Eliot and Nineteenth-Century Science* (1984), ch. 1.

[83] *Memoir*, I. 173.

to separate the private brooding of 'poetry' from the public declarations of 'eloquence', and so the accidental influence of a writer who
is 'overheard' from the intentional influence of one who sets out to be
'heard'.[84] But as Mill would have known from reading the work of his
contemporaries, in the dramatic monologue a number of poets had
already discovered a form which could work simultaneously within
and between these distinctions, because the reader of a dramatic
monologue encounters an utterance which is 'overheard' (it is addressed to ears other than our own), and at the same time is shaped
by the speaker's desire to be 'heard' (the consciousness of a listener,
towards whom he or she establishes the overall stance and local
movement of his or her speech). The monologue then offers itself as
a staged encounter between lyrical confession and critical diagnosis,
the sound of somebody thinking and a settled assessment of those
thoughts. But it is because the speaker's voice seems simultaneously to
entertain passing fancies (the immediate influence of the interlocutor)
and engrained habits (the character-traits which are revealed in
particular speech-tics) that the reader of this speech frequently discovers particular turns of phrase to have been shaped by points of
contact with the interlocutor which are imagined by the speaker
rather than actually achieved by him or her. A reader who was
guided into rehearsing disturbed thought processes, without maintaining a critical distance from them, could then discover that in his
or her voice and mind they found a natural and permanent home.
Even the most 'self-involved' speakers (to borrow Tennyson's coinage)
might not be altogether removed from the world of public speech.[85]

One set of literary responses to these ideas is provided by Tennyson's varied ways with 'strange'. In 'The Sisters', this word produces a
quick self-rebuke when the speaker recalls how his lover packed her
bags and left:

> Selfish, strange!
> What dwarfs are men! my strangled vanity
> Uttered a stifled cry—to have vext myself
> And all in vain for her—cold heart or none—
> No bride for me.[86]

---

[84] 'Thoughts on Poetry and its Varieties' (1833), repr. in *Dissertations and Discussions,
Political, Philosophical and Historical* (4 vols., 1859), I. 71.

[85] 'The Day-Dream' (1842), *TP*, II. 58.

[86] 'The Sisters' [They have left the door ajar], *TP*, III. 83.

Held between 'strange' and 'stifled', 'strangled' is a catch in the voice which is provoked by remembering an earlier moment of despair, and despairing now at how tiny was its cause. (Tennyson seems to be remembering Shakespeare's Sonnet 89, where a similar vocal slither expresses more murderous intent: 'I will acquaintance strangle, and look strange.') The independence of other people's hearts often produces this kind of verbal awkwardness in Tennyson's dramatic speakers, as a voice which fails to share in what E. M. Forster described as the lover's 'exaltation of relevance' takes its revenge by clinging onto its own words. 'The return of the mind upon itself',[87] which Arthur Hallam identified in Tennyson's early verse, then makes itself heard in the sound of a voice turning on itself, caught on the page in the throes of harking back as a form of therapy or torture. Compare the case of another abandoned lover, Mariana:

> *Mariana in the moated grange*
> *(Measure for Measure)*
>
> With blackest moss the flower-plots
>   Were thickly crusted, one and all:
> The rusted nails fell from the knots
>   That held the pear to the gable-wall.
> The broken sheds looked sad and strange:
>   Unlifted was the clinking latch;
>   Weeded and worn the ancient thatch
> Upon the lonely moated grange.
>   She only said, 'My life is dreary,
>   He cometh not,' she said;
>   She said, 'I am aweary, aweary,
>   I would that I were dead!'[88]

To begin with, Tennyson's epigraph, 'Mariana in the moated grange', remembers Shakespeare's *Measure for Measure* (III. i), where we learn that Angelo 'Left her in her tears, and dried not one of them with his comfort... What a merit were it in death to take this poor maid from the world. There, at the moated grange, resides this dejected Mariana'. Tennyson's lines, as he said, 'rose to the music of Shakespeare's words',[89] and did so by rising to the challenge of depicting Mariana's situation *in* rather than *at* the moated grange, because as described in his poem the grange represents not only a place but a state of mind. Her own name is a reproach to her: no-one

---

[87] *Motter*, 190.   [88] *TP*, I. 206–7.   [89] *TP*, I. 205.

will marry Mariana. This is one of many sides of the story which are not expressed by Shakespeare's words, but are heard shaping them from within, as the public declarations of affection which help to structure his play also draw attention to the unspoken worlds of private experience which refuse to be reconciled to the needs of a shared plot, and so are left lurking in its cracks or hanging over its edges. The rhyme of 'grange' with 'strange' then provides a central pivot of uncertainty and despair around which Tennyson's poem slowly revolves, as it approaches its own words with the caution of a speaker for whom no longer can anything be taken for granted. In the absence of Mariana's lover, everything is filled with unpredictable promise. Take a word like 'unlifted'. As the eye reaches this word, it stumbles and rights itself: not *up*lifted, but *un*lifted, as Mariana's hopes are raised and dashed. Similarly, *weeded* (so near to and yet so far from being 'wedded') is not spruce and houseproud, but choked. Even flower-*plots* appear to scheme. Each stanza focuses upon objects which are suddenly made strange to the reader, as if entertaining the possibility of a change of heart, a shadow-plot of fulfilment being cast across the poem, before the stanza reasserts the sameness of its refrain: 'She said, I am aweary, aweary, | I would that I were dead.' 'Grange' and 'strange' refuse to precipitate 'change'.

When J. S. Mill listened to Mariana's refrain, he heard how the regular return of these rhymes, unaffected by the time and place of their utterance, seem audibly to mourn the absence of the interlocutor whose presence would turn this poem into a dramatic monologue:

Words surely never excited a more vivid feeling of physical and spiritual dreariness: and not dreariness alone—for that might be felt under many other circumstances of solitude—but the dreariness which speaks not merely of being far from human converse and sympathy, but of being *deserted* by it.[90]

Rhyme will be an especially helpful device in staging Mariana's disappointment, because it is in the nature of rhymes to propose meetings which they cannot make. Yet Mariana is not altogether removed from human sympathy. It is because a reader can see and hear more on the page at any moment than he or she can read—such as the hazy promise of a clinching rhyme-word which is caught out of the corner of the eye or ear—that our reading process comes to mime Mariana's thought processes, as each moment of perception is thickened with hints of the future and residues of the past. But then

[90] *London Review* (July 1835), repr. in *TCH*, 87.

Mariana's repeated chime of 'dreary' and 'aweary' is equally suggestive of her ability to find a comfort in the very unchangingness of her grief. When she expresses her unhappiness in this way, it always comes at the same moment in the stanza: it is predictable, controllable, a measured response to her unchanging situation. Unlike her lover, these words will come back; unlike him, they are constant.

The ease with which Mariana's story can be pieced together through her rhymes offers some support to the idea that, although the world is repeatedly strange to her eyes, her own story of abandonment is rather more familiar. As Wittgenstein puts it:

Many people have, at some period, serious trouble in their lives—so serious as to lead to thoughts of suicide. This is likely to appear to one as something nasty, as a situation which is too foul to be a subject of a tragedy. And it may then be an immense relief if it can be shown that one's life has the pattern rather of a tragedy ... [91]

So many tragedies are plays of aftermath, belatedness, troubling personal and cultural remains, that we should not be surprised at the frequency with which tragic figures themselves seem conscious that their stories echo deeper narrative patterns, sunk into human history like a seal in wax. 'Can there be misery loftier than mine?' asks Hamm in Beckett's *Endgame*, bringing together the anguish that no-one suffers as much as him, and the pride that no-one suffers quite like him, not with his stamina and eloquence. The history of tragedy could be summed up as a history of the question 'Can there be misery loftier than mine?', as it repeatedly splits into the tragic speaker's twin anxieties: afraid that his or her suffering is unique, and equally afraid that it might not be unique. So too with Tennyson's dramatic speakers, each of whose voices delivers a set of variations upon the worry that their strange way of looking at the world separates them from the lives which surround and influence their own, and the competing worry that it does not.

When George Brimley read *Maud*, he complained that 'to strong men the world is not made bitter by a father's ruin and suicide, by the prevalence of meanness and cruelty, by contemporary neglect, and general absence of sympathy'.[92] Clearly, Brimley was made of strong stuff ('general absence of sympathy' in particular seems to meet his

[91] *Lectures and Conversations on Aesthetics, Psychology and Religious Belief*, ed. Cyril Barrett (1983), 51.

[92] 'Tennyson's Poems', *Essays*, ed. W. G. Clark (1858, repr. 1882), 79.

approval), but of the many features of *Maud* which he seems deaf to, one is the way that the poem's speaker too sets out to investigate the limits of human sympathy with the cool eye of a critic, and then works this argument with himself into the grain of his voice. He remembers catching sight of his unintended:

> She came to the village church,
> And sat by a pillar alone;
> An angel watching an urn
> Wept over her, carved in stone;
> And once, but once, she lifted her eyes,
> And suddenly, sweetly, strangely blush'd
> To find they were met by my own;
> And suddenly, sweetly, my heart beat stronger
> And thicker ... [93]

'He begins with universal hatred of all things', Tennyson claimed of his speaker, '& gets more human by the influence of Maud.'[94] His comment echoes the pioneering therapeutic regime instigated by Matthew Allen, who recommended that alienists use a 'healing influence' upon patients in their care, in order to check their nervous susceptibility to those other 'unobserved and secret influences' ('Lunar Influence', 'Influence of the Seasons', 'Atmospheric Influence', and so on) which were understood to make the mad such sensitive barometers of environmental effects. Even in medicine, 'There is no influence so powerful as the sphere of a moral influence ... Whatever influences prevail externally, they must in all cases, sane and insane, be counteracted and modified by internal influences.'[95] Good examples boost the patient's moral immune system, not by regulating his behaviour from the outside but by encouraging his powers of self-control. We hear how *Maud*'s speaker gets more human as he describes his heart beating 'stronger | And thicker', becoming more aware of his own body by observing Maud's body, and yearning for her heart to join with his. We also hear how Maud gets less human

---

[93] *TP*, II. 538–9.

[94] *TP*, II. 550.

[95] Matthew Allen, *Cases of Insanity* (1831), vii–viii, 109, 134; *Essay on the Classification of the Insane* (n.d.), 68, 130. Compare Charles Bucknill's presidential address on 5 July 1860 to the Association of Medical Officers of Asylums and Hospitals for the Insane: 'No one can understand the insane, or exercise guiding and health-giving moral influence upon them, who cannot and does not, so to say, throw his mind into theirs, and sympathize with their state so far as to make it, at least during brief periods, almost subjectively his own.' (Quoted in R. Hunter and I. Macalpine, *Three Hundred Years of Psychiatry 1535–1860* (1963), 1067–8.)

in the speaker's description of her, because in revision Tennyson added a comma to 'Wept over her carved in stone' between 'her' and 'carved'. Not for the first time in this poem, Tennyson's revision gives a new turn of thought to his speaker's self-portrait of self-doubt, because it allows him to hesitate over the thought that Maud is as unattainable a beauty as the carved angel, and the alternative thought that a 'heart of stone' like his own ('Courage, poor heart of stone' is his appeal to himself not to be heartbroken as easily as his parents were) could not conceive of any lover whose heart is not equally hard and chilly. This is a disturbing choice for the speaker; it is an equally disturbing choice for a reader who attempts to discriminate between the speaker's view of events and the events themselves (the 'extraordinary or false appearance of things to us', in Ruskin's formulation of the 'pathetic fallacy', 'when we are under the influence of emotion or contemplative fancy'),[96] because the poem never gives us reliable grounds for distinguishing between the false appearances which its speaker projects onto the world, and those he correctly deduces from the world. Here, for instance, he could be speaking 'under the influence of emotion or contemplative fancy' because he is suffering from delusions (he thinks Maud is turning into a statue), or because he has accurately registered, and absorbed into his speech, her stony indifference towards his loving looks. Caught between these equally unhappy possibilities, the revision also glances anxiously at medical warnings that, where the 'associations of sympathy' are imagined by the patient, rather than freely offered, other bodies could merely stimulate further morbid fixation, as Mrs Allen's 'almost exhaustless fund of sympathy failed' with one patient, who then 'conceived herself condemned to eternal punishment'.[97]

Tennyson claimed that *Maud* provided 'the history of a morbid, poetic soul, under the blighting influence of a recklessly speculative age'.[98] 'Morbid, poetic': it is, as Ricks notes, 'an equivocal comma',[99] the catch on a Pandora's box of social ills which, in the eyes of some readers, poems like *Maud* were threatening to release. A further equivocation comes in Tennyson's association of finance and disease, which echoes common metaphors joining the state of the nation to

[96] 'Of The Pathetic Fallacy', *Modern Painters*, III (1856), repr. in *The Victorian Poet: Poetics and Persona*, ed. Joseph Bristow (1987), 86.

[97] *Cases of Insanity*, 52; *Essay on the Classification of the Insane*, 38–40.

[98] *TP*, II. 517.

[99] 'Tennyson Inheriting the Earth', in *Studies in Tennyson*, ed. Hallam Tennyson (1981), 91.

the nervous economy of the body: Matthew Allen, for example, worries that it is by disrupting 'the binding and sweet influence of faithful dealings in trade' that 'all our sympathies [are] poisoned and deranged'.[100] But however true 'recklessly speculative' is of the period which produced *Maud*, it is not true of the poem itself, because whenever Tennyson's speaker speculates, it is far more cautiously reckoned: 'If I be dear. | If I be dear to some one else'; 'There is none like her, none'; 'Let all be well, be well'. Repeatedly, his speech invests in the future and then has its desires visibly and audibly crushed, as Maud's airy 'tread'—its oddly disembodied nature already hinting that she will *not* come into the garden—confirms and bruises the speaker's earlier 'tender dread'.[101] In the passage quoted above, for example, a reluctance to abandon the hopes even of the most recent past speaks in 'And once, but once', as for the first time in this section the verse registers its speaker's quickening pulse by shifting from three to four major beats in the line, and 'once', uttered twice, brings together the voice of regret (she turned only once) and the voice of pride (at least she turned once). At the same time, it forms a sample of the way his voice might 'stammer and trip' not only as a private speech defect, but as one symptom of a shared grammar of madness:[102]

Altogether, the use of words and the faculty of speech is much troubled in a majority of the insane. They often seem to employ words which they do not mean to employ.... Some alter the terminations of words, or have a pleasure in talking with a foreign accent, or in speaking like little children learning to talk.[103]

What Conolly does not point out is the difficulty we could have in determining whether individuals are speaking 'like little children learning to talk' because they have recovered the unselfconscious innocence of a child, or because they have come to recognize that using a child's register provides something like an alibi for the adult who is speaking, a way of coming to terms with his or her self-estrangement. Indeed, one of the saddest features of *Maud* is the frequency with which the speaker falls into the lilting rhythms of

[100] *Essay on the Classification of the Insane*, 20–1; see Janet Oppenheim, *Shattered Nerves* (1991), 84.

[101] *Maud*, I. 917, I. 550, *TP*, II. 565, 551.

[102] *Maud*, I. 272, *TP*, II. 537.

[103] John Conolly, *On Some of the Forms of Insanity* (1849), 12; compare William B. Neville, *On Insanity* (1837) on 'misapplied' words (34).

nursery rhymes and lullabies, because it is never made clear whether this is an unwitting compulsion, returning his voice to the happier days which he imagines existed at the time Maud had been promised to him as an infant, or a deliberate attempt to help him adjust his voice to the demands of his loneliness, by rehearsing forms of song that do not expect much more from their listener than a silently loving response. T. S. Clouston also draws attention to the problems which insane speakers often have in coming to terms with change, whether by slipping into childish uncertainties of register and syntax, or by suffering the muscular tremors of lips and tongue which make a sentence like 'Now, you take that' shudder to a halt: 'Now, you ter, ter, ter.'[104] Stuttering speech-patterns depict breakdowns of mental connections: popular mechanistic models of the brain stressed that if 'associations of sympathy' are not successfully stimulated by social contact, 'the mind will be thrown upon itself, and feed on its notions.'[105] Once intermittent acts have been transformed into involuntary tendencies, the speaker's isolation will be heard in an atrophied parody of the poet's own creative integrity, as the established grooves of thought determine what a voice can say, and how it can be said. Shattered nerves produce dislocated speech.

The speaker of *Maud* talks of this ('I will bury myself in myself'), and he talks through it, as his speech repeatedly reaches out and recoils, limed in its own words. Yet even these peculiar ways of speaking are not sufficient to mark him out on the page, or limit the tendency of his lines to extend themselves beyond the bounds of their own poem—as if seeking sympathetic attachments with other lonely speakers—given how often Tennyson's verse falls into similar patterns of delay and brooding.

*

From the early lyrics—many of them ending with question-marks which are tense with a struggle between continuity and closure—to 'Crossing the Bar', Tennyson's narratives and designs combine to

---

[104] *Disorders of Speech in Insanity* (1876), 14.

[105] *Essay on the Classification of the Insane*, 103. Allen records the case of one patient who 'so shook and overwhelmed my nervous system' that it was necessary 'to dissever my sympathies from this overwhelming influence', ibid., 38–9. On the self-influence ('nervous sympathy') of the body, see William Newnham, *Essay on Superstition* (1830), 52, and *The Reciprocal Influence of Body and Mind Considered* (1842), ch. 2.

turn speculation in different directions, from delighted anticipation, to rapt craving, to grim forbearance. 'Tennyson lingers', John Bayley remarks, 'indeed it is his genius to linger in a situation in which nothing appears to be done—nothing else, it appears, can be done—but to hang around.'[106] 'Hanging around' sounds less fraught than Tennyson's usual way of going about imagining situations in which everything has yet to happen; his sleeping Kraken will never fulfil its destiny by rising to the surface and dying, but neither the poet nor his subject could accurately be described as 'hanging around', like a couple of bored teenagers lolling about at the local swimming-pool. But the critic is fully in accord with his author in the word he chooses to soften Arnold's 1853 strictures on that class of situations in which there is 'nothing to be done' ('nothing *appears* to be done'), because a central preoccupation of Tennyson's career is to discover shapes of enquiry for what else, other than the writer, pursues its course while hidden away from human eyes, from the pressures and collapses of geological formation, to the evolutionary ascent of the dead.

For example, Tennyson explained the 'stepping-stones' of *In Memoriam*, I, with the remark that 'Among [Goethe's] last words were … "from changes to higher changes".' The most recent editors of *In Memoriam* note that 'These words have not been found among all the reported "last words" of Goethe.'[107] It is more likely that their significance to Tennyson lay in the suggestion of lasting things, rather than last things, because 'from changes to higher changes' echoes his persistent recourse to phrases which fall into the pattern 'from X to X' or 'X by X', and which then provide a literary model of the 'living idea' described by Newman, which develops by creating 'anticipation of its future'.[108] The intellectual shape which can be abstracted from a phrase such as 'from X to X' is not intrinsic to its grammatical shape, of course, as becomes clear if we compare Arnold's use of the same locution to speak not of gradualist progress but rather of the unhappy frequency with which people are separated from one another by stretches of time, space, or understanding: the 'echoing straits between us thrown' across which the poet throws his voice, like the nightingale's 'lovely notes, from shore to shore'.[109] In Tennyson's hands, by contrast, a line's intellectual directions can be played

---

[106] 'Tennyson and the Idea of Decadence', in *Studies in Tennyson*, 193.
[107] *In Memoriam*, ed. Susan Shatto and Marion Shaw (1982), 162.
[108] *Essay on the Development of Christian Doctrine*, 197.
[109] 'To Marguerite—continued' (1852); I quote from Kenneth Allott's edition (1954), 136.

against the drag of its form, to show—in the ease with which this line falls into a patterned shape—that slow and massive change is no less susceptible of design than the smaller spans of time in which it can be retained. Form embodies reform.

Even where Tennyson describes the impossibility of progress, he does more than 'hang around'. More often, his verse stages the desire for change as it encounters a resistance to change, by encouraging the reader's voice to proceed across the interruptions and delays which are written into the poem's own form. The strains of his bird of paradise are typically far-reaching:

> ... a weary bird on wing
> Cursed never to alight, no resting place,
> No stay—no shrouding of the weary head
> Beneath the weary plume but onward still
> Sustaining with no pleasant balm of thought
> That inner fire which eats into the heart ... [110]

Tennyson's lines give a perfect illustration of the 'poised and stationary' style which Henry James heard in 'Tithonus':

... like a bird whose wings have borne him high, but the beauty of whose movements is less in great ethereal sweeps and circles than in the way he hangs motionless in the blue air, with only a vague tremor of his pinions ... When he wishes to represent movement, the phrase always seems to me to pause and slowly pivot upon itself, or at most to move backward.[111]

Like the a–b–b–a movement of the *In Memoriam* stanza, Tennyson's blank verse lines 'circle moaning in the air', forever doomed to ask ' "Is this the end? Is this the end?" ',[112] of themselves as well as of their subject, as if recognizing that blank verse always threatens to sound incomplete until it is linked into a more extended stretch of narrative thought. In one sense, these lines are similarly cursed to have 'no stay', unfulfilled alike in their manuscript state and their movement, as they repeatedly settle upon the sinking cadence of 'weary' without

---

[110] 'The Lover's Tale', MS, *TP*, III. 579, recalling the torments of Dante's lovers in *Inferno* V. 40–5: 'As in the cold season their wings bear the starlings along in a broad, dense flock, so does that blast the wicked spirits. Hither, thither, downward, upward, it drives them; no hope ever comforts them, not to say of rest, but of less pain', trans. John D. Sinclair (1939, repr. 1961), 75.

[111] 'Tennyson's Drama', in *Views and Reviews* (1908), 171.

[112] *IM*, XII, *TP*, II. 331.

ever discovering the resting-place of a full-stop. But in another sense, with their treble insistence on 'no resting place, | No stay—no shrouding' drawing out even further the exemplary stamina of their source in Dante, they are nothing but staying—a literary achievement of delay.

Hallam Tennyson recalled how, looking upon the periodic movements of nature which Arthur Hallam had compared to the sympathetic imagination's 'tendency towards unity of form', his father 'felt a rest in her steadfastness, patient progress and hopefulness'.[113] Walter Bagehot captures one way in which Tennyson's methods of composition and verbal surfaces come together to tap these values of 'patient progress', when he draws a distinction between dialogue (which 'requires a very changing imagination') and 'prolonged soliloquy' ('steadily accumulating'): 'His genius gives the notion of a slow depositing instinct; day by day, as the hours pass, the delicate sand falls into beautiful forms—in stillness, in peace, in brooding.'[114] The patterned reflections of Tennyson's verse formed one standard by which his sympathies with a world of more conspicuous material progress were occasionally tested and found wanting: the dramatic situations which were accused of 'still life';[115] the textual alterations which led to appeals that he should not 'stand still and alter, but by all means go on and improve';[116] the uneasy reactions to monologues such as 'St Simeon Stylites', which exercises the dramatic self-consciousness of a speaker who is standing still *and* altering. However, of itself this poetic lingering—whether in his habitual borrowings and revisions, or in the characteristic weave of his lines—would not be enough to define the unique signature of Tennyson's style. Indeed, for a theorist like Valéry, the possibility that 'human things returning on themselves | Move onward' could not refer only to Tennysonian things,[117] because such linguistic tenacity forms one backbone of any body's thought: 'the sound, I might even say the physique, of [a] little phrase returns inside me, repeats itself inside me ... I enjoy

---

[113] *Memoir*, I. 312.

[114] *National Review* (October 1859), repr. in *TCH*, 230.

[115] Alfred Austin, 'The Poetry of the Period' (1870), repr. in *The Victorian Poet*, 124: 'Turn to Mr Tennyson, and what do we see? Still life—almost uniform still life'; R. H. Hutton, 'Tennyson' (1888), repr. in *TCH*, 365: 'There is nothing like "still" life to be found in his poems.'

[116] [Fanny Kemble Butler], 'Tennyson's Poems', in *United States Magazine and Democratic Review*, 14 (January 1844), 63–4.

[117] 'The Golden Year' ll. 25–6, *TP*, II. 150.

hearing my lips form it again and again.'[118] Valéry's enthusiasm is engaging, but when Whitman read Tennyson, he recognized what, other than a serene aesthetic pleasure, could lie beneath later performances of these compositional returns:

There is such a latent charm in mere words, cunning collocutions, and in the voice ringing them, which he has caught and brought out, beyond all others—as in the line, 'And hollow, hollow, hollow, all delight,' in 'The Passing of Arthur'.[119]

Tennyson worked hard for these hollows, creating through his repetitions a set of echo-chambers for his speakers to listen in on themselves, so that a reader might bring out the 'latent charm' of their words, and at the same time exercise a suspicion of being charmed by words hollow of anything other than delight. F. T. Palgrave described how Tennyson once brooded over a memory of Clough reading aloud from the unfinished fragments of *Mari Magno*: ' "When he read them his voice faltered at times: like every poet, *he was moved by his own pathos.*" '[120] But Tennyson was not always satisfied with what seemed to hang on in his speech, conscious that a mournful pleasure in the sound of one's own voice could seem in other ears morbidly self-absorbed rather than vigilantly self-possessed. Guinevere hears Arthur's denunciation of her shame (words that sound 'Monotonous and hollow' in her ears) by reflecting that to renounce Lancelot fully would mean letting go of more than his body:

> [']For what is true repentance but in thought—
> Not even in inmost thought to think again
> The sins that made the past so pleasant to us:
> And I have sworn never to see him more,
> To see him more.'
>   And even in saying this,
> Her memory from old habit of the mind
> Went slipping back upon the golden days
> In which she saw him first … [121]

Like the charged repetitions of 'in', which spread out from 'sins', like a stain, to suggest Guinevere's slide from the deliberation of 'in

---

[118] 'Poetry and Abstract Thought', in *The Art of Poetry*, 77. Eric Griffiths discusses some of the implications of Valéry's remark for Victorian poetry in 'The Disappointment of Christina G. Rossetti', *Essays in Criticism*, 47 (April 1997), 107–42.

[119] Quoted in Christopher Ricks, *Tennyson*, 312.

[120] *Memoir*, II. 502 (Palgrave's emphasis).

[121] 'Guinevere' ll. 370–8, *TP*, III. 539–40.

thought … in inmost thought' to the flightiness of 'in saying this … In which she saw him first', the narrator's delicately poised 'slipping' is at once sympathetic and knowing, and so asks for retrospective stress to be laid on Guinevere's 'never to see him more, | To see him more.' At first blush, this is an unwitting echo as her voice fades out, an involuntary memory of Lancelot; but it is also left open to us to decide that she forswears only in order to call him up at the start of a new line: the behaviour of the addict who refuses to give up even her thoughts of what has been given up. The lines express Tennyson's broad suspicion of speakers 'who may be almost termed callous to all the kindlier sympathies, however they may cloak their deficiencies with the vesture of *form*',[122] as they do his parallel suspicion of his own poems as forms of speech which were, in his view, all too frequently interpreted as models of ethical conduct.

I have already outlined some widespread anxieties in the period that the dramatic monologue was a literary form which threatened to take over the voices and minds of its readers in more permanent and antisocial ways than they might have wished. A parallel threat was carried by lyric verse, because its lulling patterns of rhythm and rhyme always risk disciplining and seducing a reader into accepting other forms of repeated behaviour. To dwell upon 'commonplace things', for example, as urged by George Eliot and others as the quickest means of stimulating social feelings,[123] might 'exercise' a reader's sympathy so successfully as to wear it out, by atrophying a ready suppleness of response into nothing more than a series of moral speech tics. Arthur Hallam suggests one example of this worry, when he confesses to Emily Tennyson how he used to stage domestic tragedies:[124]

But if I run on thus in prose & rhyme, I shall have you fancy I wish you unhappy, that I may have the luxury of sympathising with you, and support-ing you. I remember indeed, when a child I used to entrap flies into water for the pleasure of taking them out again—a process, seldom so satisfactorily completed, but two or three of them perished by the way.[125]

'As flies to wanton boys are we to the gods, | They kill us for their sport': Hallam's 'by the way' ('in the process', or an apologetic

[122] *TL*, I. 89.

[123] See *Adam Bede*, ch. 17.

[124] It is a frequent complaint of eighteenth-century writers on sympathy that dramatic representations of suffering can foster indifference to its real counterpart; see David Marshall, *The Surprising Effects of Sympathy* (1988).

[125] *Kolb*, 434.

cough?) leaves open-ended whether he now feels remorse for the little deaths which came about as a result of his choreographed displays of tenderness, and so whether Emily might be justly cautious of a lover who has rehearsed the lethal potential of his finer feelings so success- fully that he can now move on to larger prey. Tennyson too worried about what he had 'satisfactorily completed' in his poems, and about the more unpredictable satisfactions which these poems could pro- duce in a reader. Such concerns are not limited to verse, as Hallam's letter proves by 'running on in prose' rather than in rhyme, but they are especially concentrated in verse, because it is built upon recur- rence, so that by encouraging the reader to luxuriate over his or her success in anticipating the small-scale outcomes of metre and rhyme, a poet's lines can invite an unmerited over-familiarity with larger and less predictable objects of the reader's attentions.

These problems of sympathy are sharpened where Tennyson's speakers are overheard composing themselves for death, because such poems must retrieve imaginative life from utterances which are all and only for dying, sufficient for a reader seriously to entertain these desires without seriously intending them. Simeon Stylites stands on his pillar, eagerly awaiting the end which he hopes will make him into the title of his poem, '*St* Simeon Stylites':

> Now I am feeble grown; my end draws nigh;
> I hope my end draws nigh: half deaf I am,
> So that I scarce can hear the people hum
> About the column's base, and almost blind,
> And scarce can recognise the fields I know;
> And both my thighs are rotted with the dew;
> Yet cease I not to clamour and to cry,
> While my stiff spine can hold my weary head,
> Till all my limbs drop piecemeal from the stone,
> Have mercy, mercy: take away my sin.[126]

There are not many sins you can commit up a pillar. One exception is pride, as we hear in Simeon's pauses, as if his commas and semi- colons were really disguised appeals: 'Haven't I suffered enough?' Near the end of *King Lear*, Kent asks: 'Is this the promised end?', and Edgar adds, 'Or image of that horror?'[127] In the hands of a writer like Tennyson, so often drawn to the ongoing struggle between human ends (desires) and their inevitable ending (death), punctuation—or, as

---

[126] *TP*, I. 596–7.   [127] V. iii. 237–8.

it used to be known, 'stopping'—often provides tiny but concentrated images of that horror, ghostly promises of an end of speech and life which open up in the stories of his speakers like old wounds. Tennyson is not alone in this way of thinking and working: Beckett, too, uses the writer's control over the timing of printed speech to measure the growing pressure of that impending silence which his speakers both fear and yearn for. But poets can do this sort of thing more easily, because, as T. S. Eliot noted, 'Verse, whatever else it may or may not be, is itself a system of punctuation',[128] not least in the suspense and fulfilment of its line-endings.

Line-endings often work as a counterpoint to punctuation in this way, because they create units of syntax which may or may not turn out to be units of sense, and so can reinvest some of the unexpectedness of the future into the fixed conclusions of print. The ethical drama of Simeon's monologue, for example, is largely plotted out according to the co-ordinates of his line-endings, as we listen to the rising cadences of his voice striving in the same direction as his soul, and then become aware that he is granted a full-stop only when he reaches the word 'sin'. But this is not an elegy, yet, so with each interrupted pause Simeon is forced to carry on, making more and more of less and less, as if rehearsing for the time when his rotten flesh will have been wholly replaced by a shapely eloquence, the unpredictable passage of his human existence crystallized into the orderly narrative of a saint's life. Yet Simeon is living on the edge in more senses than one, because although his words point towards the future which he imagines for himself, the punctuation we see tells a rather different story from the one we hear, creating the dot-to-dot picture of a speaker who is audibly caught in the coils of self-obsession. Indeed, Simeon's relentless search for a full-stop should remind us of what he seems to have forgotten, which is that never to be granted rest, like Tennyson's inaptly named bird of paradise, is traditionally a distinguishing feature of the torments of the damned. In this way, the appeal 'Have mercy, mercy' which Simeon makes to his imagined divine interlocutor (the poem leaves open the question as to whether this interlocutor is silent because He is choked with compassion, or indifferent, or absent) parallels the appeal which the poem makes to its readers. For it is impossible to feel merciful towards Simeon, and to

---

[128] *The Times Literary Supplement* (27 September 1928), quoted by Christopher Ricks in *The Force of Poetry* (1984), 89.

exercise this mercy, without either ignoring or silencing his wish for muteness, his prayer to be done with prayer. Simeon is being whittled away by time, but he also takes up our time, so that to enjoy Simeon's preening eloquence, as he witnesses his body's slow collapse, is also to risk suffering from a similar self-importance at our skill in reassembling his personality from these scattered clues on the page.

The ethical balance of 'St Simeon Stylites' concentrates many of the period's unsettled questions about the nature and limits of sympathy, because the dramatic monologue occupies a form which perfectly succeeds in calibrating the fine distinctions of sympathetic response against the general impulse to sympathetic conduct. It allows us to measure our knowledge that the speaker's faults are already written into the poem, against our knowledge that the process of reading allows us to exercise our finer feelings upon a victim of our own making; it brings to our attention the danger of immersing ourselves in the travails of a single speaker (and so seeming to care for too little), and the corresponding danger of refusing to immerse ourselves in them (and so seeming to care for too much). This practical scrutiny of sympathy makes 'St Simeon Stylites' a consistently surprising poem, but it is not unusual in entertaining speculation about the afterlife which works against the poet's own deepest beliefs:

He held undoubtingly the doctrine of a personal immortality, and was by no means content to accept our present existence as a mere preparation for the life of more perfect beings. He had once asked John Sterling whether he would be content with such an arrangement, and Sterling had replied that he would. 'I would *not*,' added Tennyson emphatically; 'I should consider that a liberty had been taken with me if I were made simply a means of ushering in something higher than myself.'[129]

The emphasis announces Tennyson's firmly embodied view that a Positivist afterlife in which 'no sympathies shall thrill along our nerves' would betray the irreplaceable self in which these sympathies were now felt.[130] Indeed, where Frederic Harrison promotes 'a patience and a happiness equal to that of any martyr of theology',[131] Tennyson shows, in Simeon's over-zealous anticipation of being 'Example, pattern' to his followers, that a 'conviction of posthumous

---

129 *Memoir*, II. 274.
130 Frederic Harrison, 'The Soul and Future Life', 839.
131 Ibid., 838.

activity' could be as precipitate and self-centred as the 'future hope of personal beatitude' which it sought to replace. 'Well if I were a Comtist', Tennyson told Harrison at the Metaphysical Society, 'No God—no soul—no future—*no right and wrong*!! I should not care to live.'[132] Tennyson was not alone in thinking Comte's ideas unhelpful. He agreed with R. H. Hutton that the Positivist distinction between an egoistic and altruistic afterlife was curiously lop-sided in imagining as selfish 'the perpetual ministry of one soul to another',[133] and self-contradictory in professing an abstract belief in Man without being able to find any room for the beliefs of individual human beings. Similarly, his distrust of a system which appeared to prefer unpredictable posthumous influence to impulses good in themselves was shared by Comte's translator, Mill, who pointed out that the compulsory altruism at the heart of Comtean Positivism 'absolutely demanded that all other people should model themselves after M. Comte'.[134] But as reported by Harrison, with those insistent accents so characteristic of Tennyson's awkward public persona, the comment upholds his confidence in the existence of a soul which often made its yearnings for an independent future life distinctly felt and heard in his living social relations:

After dinner we talk of dreams. T. said, 'In my boyhood I had *intuitions* of Immortality—inexpressible! I have never been able to express them. I shall try some day.'

I say that I too have felt something of the kind; whereat T. (being in one of his less amiable moods) growls, 'I don't believe you have. You say so out of rivalry.'[135]

There are eighteenth-century commentators for whom even Tennyson's uncompromising growl would have provided evidence of 'sympathy'. In David Hartley's *Observations on Man* of 1749, for instance, John Mullan has shown how 'sympathy is invoked to explain what appears to be a type of incompatibility—such as "envy"—as the

---

[132] Harrison, quoted in T. R. Wright, *The Religion of Humanity*, 238. Compare Elizabeth Rachel Chapman's dramatic dialogue, *A Comtist Lover* (1886), which enlists *In Memoriam* in its conclusion that 'If we are indeed, each one of us, not merely under sentence of death, but under sentence of everlasting nothingness, I, at least, will have none of a life so conditioned' (95). Tennyson wrote to the author: 'I really could almost fancy that p. 95 was written by myself. I have been saying the same thing for years in all but the same words' (*Memoir*, II. 332).

[133] *Memoir*, II. 421; for Hutton's objection, see *Nineteenth Century* (September 1877), 330.

[134] J. S. Mill, *Auguste Comte and Positivism* (1865, repr. 1968), 142.

[135] *Allingham* (22 July 1866), 137.

sub-category of a more general principle of compatibility: even rivalry depends upon a bond, a sympathetic appreciation of another's pleasure or privilege.'[136] Yet even the generous conceptual reach of Hartley's 'sympathy' assumes that the education of individuals into the pleasures and benefits of sociability is based upon something they already share: 'their common relation to God as their creator, governor, and father; their common concern in a future life'. Sympathy is underwritten by 'Theopathy'.[137] As Mullan points out, 'Hartley's reliance on the theses of educability and religious perception lead him away from an encounter with the problem of contradictory desires and interests.'[138] It is not until the nineteenth century that the encounter which Hartley shied away from becomes a defining feature of similar discussions on the limits of sympathy, as writers come to recognize that a 'common concern in a future life' is not the same thing as a concern in a common future life, and weave their knowledge of these 'contradictory desires and interests' into the texture of their work.

Compare what Harrison and Tennyson each heard in 'John Brown's Body':

The great must always feel with Kepler,—'It is enough as yet if I have a hearer now and then in a century.' John Brown's body lies a-mouldering in the grave, but his soul is marching along.[139]

After dinner Tennyson called on Hallam [Tennyson] to sing 'John Brown,' which he accordingly began in a strong bass voice, T. joining in ... and sometimes thumping with his fists on the table—

> John Brown's body lies mouldering in the grave,
> But his soul is marching on!

He urged Hallam to go on, saying, 'I like it, I like it,' but Hallam thought the noise too great, and drew off. The soul marching on delighted Tennyson.[140]

It also worried him. If dead men like Arthur Hallam continued to rise on stepping-stones of their dead selves to higher things, he might never catch up, his loyalty to the thought of change increasingly at odds with the facts of change. This is 'An awful thought, a life removed': awful that Hallam's life has been removed, and still more

---

[136] John Mullan, *Sentiment and Sociability: The Language of Feeling in the Eighteenth Century* (1988), 31.

[137] David Hartley, *Observations on Man* (1749, repr. 1791), 286.

[138] *Sentiment and Sociability*, 31.   [139] Harrison, 'The Soul and Future Life', 837.

[140] *Allingham* (21 October 1880), 304.

awful that the mourner's loss could continue beyond his own death, their lives forever at one remove from one another.[141]

Tennyson's worry touches on a major area of debate, particularly for unbelievers in Positivism, during the period in which *In Memoriam* was written and revised: how to reconcile an anthropocentric heaven suited to 'the Soul's continuous progress in the after-life' with claims that this setting would witness the joyful recognition and restoration of earthly relationships.[142] Kant's emphasis on 'moral improvement' had led him to think of a state, emerging in 'the course of things to come', where 'the creature who has remained true to his nature and who has made himself worthy of happiness through morality will actually participate in this happiness.'[143] For many Victorian commentators, the course of Darwinian/physical and Goethian/moral evolution should encourage a view of human nature as being like other forms of nature, the earthly analogy of a heaven of continued development. The afterlife would then prove what Isaac Taylor called the 'correspondence between the present and the future employment of the active principle of human nature'.[144] However, the same commentators who stress these continuities are less forthcoming about how the individual soul could both 'participate' in a social afterlife and remain true to his or her individual nature:

T.—'Wallace says the system he believes in is a far finer one than Christianity: it is Eternal Progress—I have always felt that there must be somewhere *Some one who knows*—that is, *God*. But I am in hopes that I shall find something human in Him too.'[145]

Frederic Harrison might have enjoyed Tennyson's hope, clearly held but dimly articulated in Allingham's account, that he would find 'something human' in God:

In a religious discussion years ago we once asked one of the Broad Church, a disciple of one of its eminent founders, what he understood by the third Person of the Trinity; and he said doubtfully 'that he fancied there was a sort of a something.' Since those days the process of disintegration and vaporisation of belief has gone on rapidly; and now very religious minds, and men

[141] *IM*, XIII, *TP*, II. 332.

[142] On the waning popularity of static and theocentric models of heaven, see Colleen McDannell and Bernard Lang, *Heaven: A History* (1988), 204; on heaven as a place of reunion, see, e.g., [Robert Bickersteth] *et al.*, *The Recognition of Friends in Heaven* (1866).

[143] *Lectures on Philosophical Theology*, trans. Allen W. Wood and Gertrude M. Clark (1978), 110.

[144] *The Physical Theory of Another Life* (1836), 181–2.

[145] *Allingham* (5 December 1884), 339.

who think themselves to be religious, are ready to apply this 'sort of a something' to all the verities in turn. They half hope that there is a 'sort of a something' fluttering about, or inside, their human frames, that there may turn out to be a 'something' somewhere after Death, and that there must be a sort of a somebody or ... a sort of a something controlling and comprehending human life.[146]

As the possessor of a religious mind which was periodically troubled by the possibility that it merely thought itself to be religious, it is not clear what Tennyson hoped this 'something' would be, nor how he would recognize it if he found it. Even leaving aside philosophical puzzles about the practical difficulties involved in the resurrection of individual bodies, his contemporaries were equally uncertain as to which of the defining characteristics of being 'human' would survive the transformation from life to afterlife. It was, then, hard to say what the dead would find even in one another, given the difficulties in conceiving of continued identity without those imperfections through which they had understood, when still alive, what it meant to be human. Lord Blachford, responding to Harrison, anticipated 'the thrill of pleasure at a sympathetic interchange of look, or word, or touch with a fellow-creature kind and noble and brilliant, and engaged in the exhibition of those qualities of heart and intellect which make him what he is'.[147] But, as Bernard Williams has suggested, of the many enduring problems which we have in thinking about the afterlife, one of the most awkward is that, if there are recognizable continuities between earthly and heavenly ways of thinking, immortality may well be unliveable by the person who contemplates it while he or she is alive. If I am so easily bored by this life, which I know is end-stopped, how could I not be infinitely more bored by the prospect of an afterlife which has no such constraints?[148]

Isaac Taylor's description of heaven includes a chapter on 'The Survivance of Individual Character, and of the Moral Consciousness', which sets out the reciprocal dependence of the individual's consciousness and body, and anticipates that 'A short season, probably, will be enough to impart to us an easy familiarity with our new home, a ready use of our corporeal instruments, and a facility in joining in with the economy around us.'[149] Taylor's 'corporeal

---

[146] 'The Soul and Future Life', 833.
[147] Ibid., 347.
[148] See Bernard Williams, *Problems of the Self: Philosophical Papers 1956–1972* (1973), 95–6.
[149] *The Physical Theory of Another Life*, 170.

instruments' is suitably cautious as a description of how we shall get around our new home (the phrase could refer to wheels or telescopic crutches as easily as to legs), but other writers are less self-assured, or self-reassuring, about how an immortal 'instrument' could sustain mortal relationships which have developed alongside, and in some cases inside, our changing bodies. Arthur Hallam described 'that mood between contentment and despair' in Cicero's writings which 'is within the range of most men's feeling', in which 'suffering appears so associated with existence that we would willingly give up one with the other, and look forward with a sort of hope to that silent void where, if there are no smiles, there are at least no tears, and since the heart cannot beat, it will not ever be broken'.[150] But as his grudging 'sort of' concedes, to be forever free of heartbreak would free the dead from the ability to feel for the living hearts they have broken: 'Canst thou feel for me | Some painless sympathy with pain?' is the line on which Tennyson ceases his questioning of Arthur Hallam's spirit in *In Memoriam*, LXXXV, the moment his voice breaks.[151] Furthermore, any later reconciliation would require bringing together individuals whose different stages of development would make it difficult to line up their souls, like the patterns on wallpaper, without seeing the joins.

It is by tracing the particular vocal contours of each of his dramatic speakers (in Proust's terms, the discovery of their unique 'accent')[152] that Tennyson rehearses the sound of a sympathetic imagination which he hoped would persist between this life and the afterlife. Internal rhyme, in particular, responds to calls for the poet 'to strike upon those chords which prove the whole world kin', because it can speak of the fractured bonds of a self by striking broken chords in language.[153] Take Tithonus's reluctant exploration of an immortal state which not only retains a mortal body, but will not let it go, and so is painfully conscious that Hallam's 'silent void' will not necessarily be tearless:

---

[150] 'Essay on the Philosophical Writings of Cicero', *Motter*, 176.

[151] *TP,* II. 398.

[152] Proust's remarks on 'accent' are scattered throughout *A la recherche du temps perdu*; John Sturrock discusses Proust's interest in 'the work of *transformation* that writers do, whereby their experience of things is raised by the shaping power of thought, temperament and a unique "voice" into literature', in his introduction to *Against Sainte-Beuve and Other Essays* (1988), xxv.

[153] Compare Smiles's suggestion that individual acts of sympathy will 'make the world kin', *Duty* (1880), 263.

Lo! ever thus thou growest beautiful
In silence, then before thine answer given
Departest, and thy tears are on my cheek.[154]

J. W. Marston had suggested in 1838 that human relationships consolidated natural laws: human bodies are drawn together as, 'in the external world, one drop of water *sympathises* with another, and the two *unite*'.[155] Tennyson's lines provide for these physical unions a grammatical form which is equally responsive to human separation and loss. The tears belong to Aurora (they represent the morning dew), and are left on Tithonus's cheek, but it is possible that his cheek is wetted with tears cried for her as well as by her. 'In silence', similarly, depicts Aurora's helpless witnessing of his plight as at once a cause of and response to his own impotence. In each case, the equivocal syntax intimates a blameless tragedy, as if realizing that the precise boundaries of 'thy' and 'my' can be confused for lovers in private recollection, as well as in the shared meetings of their bodies.

Tithonus is an opposite of Mariana, for while her lover will never come, his will never stop coming, and then going again; in his eyes, the future is as predictable as the past. But like Mariana, Tithonus's experience of an overly prolonged life is made especially hurtful by what he cannot shake out of his voice: his memory. Max Müller recalled Tennyson explaining that 'the only excuse for rhyme is that it helps the memory'.[156] Tithonus's voice, however, suggests that memory will not always wish to be helped in this way, as the internal rhymes of his blank verse counterpoint the sounds of remembered and felt desire, the wish to live forever and the wish not to. In Walker's *Rhyming Dictionary* (one source of the lists of rhyme-words which Tennyson compiled in notebooks), the 'Preface to the Index of Perfect and Allowable Rhymes' allows that although this is a 'dictionary of terminations', 'there seems to be sometimes a beauty in departing from a perfect exactness of rhyme, as it agreeably breaks that sameness of returning sounds on the expecting ears'.[157] No body knows more than Tithonus's does about the sameness of returning sounds

[154] 'Tithonus', *TP*, II. 610.
[155] *Poetry as an Universal Nature*, 6.
[156] Foreword by Robert Lewins to *The Complete Poetical Works of Constance Naden* (1894), 8.
[157] John Walker, *A Rhyming Dictionary* (1775), xlvii, 669. Tennyson owned the 1800 edition; references here are to the 1865 edition revised and enlarged by J. Longmuir, which is studded with examples from Tennyson (see, e.g., xviii, xix, xx, xxviii, xli). For Tennyson's personal lists of rhyme-words, see *TA*, V. 162, VIII. 218, XII. 324, XV. 233

upon expecting ears, and this frays the returns of rhyme into something appropriately less than full, as his regular appeals for death
revolve mournfully around the competing promises held out by the
prefixes 'de-' ('decay' and 'Departest') and 're-' ('recall', 'Release',
'restore', 'renew', and 'returning'). In this way, the elegiac self-echo-
ing of his voice makes a poetic virtue of the 'weary sameness in the
rhymes' which Tennyson described in 'The Miller's Daughter',[158]
because this aubade is always the same old song, and its mourning of
the lovers' daily separation under the pressure of daylight is all the
crueller in that Aurora *is* the daylight.

    An earlier lyric, 'Ode to Memory', had also shackled together
'dewy dawn' and 'memory' through the bonds of rhyme. There, the
connection is straightforward: the speaker draws strength from 'the
fountains of the past', and the poem concludes with lines addressed to
Arthur Hallam on the prospect of settling down together in a country
cottage, 'in after life retired ... With youthful fancy re-inspired.'[159]
Tithonus's 'after life' is grimmer, because there are signs that the
'clear memory' which underpins the workings of sympathy is not
dwindling along with his body. Although the self who cried 'Give me
immortality' is no longer recognizable to the self who now remembers
this cry (the 'ever-silent spaces of the East' hint at an enfeebled voice
and faded hearing), Tithonus's memory, in a form of historical
ventriloquism, continues to throw the voice of his past body into
present tense speech; even 'Me only cruel immortality consumes'
shows 'immortality' consuming 'me'. One of the things which
Tithonus must remember is that 'The Gods themselves cannot recall
their gifts', and as Ricks observes, '*recall* superbly suggests not only
"call back" but "recollect", an infinite divine forgetfulness of old
age.'[160] For Tithonus, though, such obliviousness remains a consum-
mation devoutly to be wished, as his voice directs through the living
currents of memory a yearning for what Henry James's Isabel
enjoyed, 'the liberty to forget':[161]

> Release me, and restore me to the ground;
> Thou seest all things, thou wilt see my grave:
> Thou wilt renew thy beauty morn by morn;
> I earth in earth forget these empty courts,
> And thee returning on thy silver wheels.

---

[158] *TP*, I. 410.   [159] *TP*, I. 235.   [160] *Tennyson*, 131.
[161] *The Portrait of a Lady*, ch. 43.

A. C. Bradley commented finely upon *In Memoriam*'s use of the word
'dawn': 'The word is repeated throughout the poem almost as if it
were a term of reproach.'[162] In its end, as in its beginning (a setting of
the 'woods decaying, never to be decayed', from Wordsworth's great
poem of recovered memory, to new and accusing harmonies: 'The
woods decay, the woods decay and fall'),[163] Tithonus's voice establishes literary timescales for his 'terms of reproach', as he enviously
settles the immeasurable period of his life into the fixed lines and
sinking cadences of his verse, repeatedly denied the completion of a
full-stop until the poem's own 'quiet limit' is reached with 'wheels'—
itself poised ominously on the turn of a line. For the first time in the
poem, a future is glimpsed with future tenses; but even in announcing
his wish to forget, Tithonus cannot forget, because 'earth in earth'
recalls Dante's encounter with that other sunny figure, St John:

> Qual è colui ch'adocchia e s'argomenta
> di vedere eclissar lo sole un poco,
> che, per veder, non vedente diventa;
> tal mi fec' io a quell'ultimo foco
> mentre che detto fu: Perchè t'abbagli
> per veder cosa che qui non ha loco?
> In terra terra è'l mio corpo, e saràgli
> tanto con li altri, che'l numero nostro
> con l'etterno proposito s'agguagli.

[As one that strains his eyes, trying to see the sun in partial eclipse, and by
seeing becomes sightless, such I became before that last fire, while it spoke:
Why dost thou dazzle thyself to see that which has no place here? My body is
earth in the earth, and it will be there with the rest until our number tallies
with the eternal purpose.][164]

Tithonus answers Aurora's daily renewals with a renewal of his own,
as the return of his sun is momentarily eclipsed by Dante's vision of an
immortality freed of the corruptible body which, 'In terra terra',
awaits its resurrection. Yet 'earth in earth' cannot quite eclipse
'I ... forget', as Tithonus's voice schools him in what Dante too
must learn: such a body has no place here.

*

[162] *A Commentary on 'In Memoriam'* (3rd edn., 1910), 164.
[163] *The Prelude*, VI. 624–5 (published in 1845), quoted in *TP*, II. 607n.
[164] *Paradiso*, XXV. 118–26 (trans. John D. Sinclair). In his copy of John Churton Collins's
'A New Study of Tennyson' in *The Cornhill Magazine*, CCXCI (January 1880), Tennyson
annotated 'I earth in earth forget these empty courts' with 'terra in terra (Dante)' (43).

Although Tithonus may be living outside time, 'Tithonus' is not. For Tennyson's is not the only nineteenth-century voice troubled by the thought that memory could be central to our grasp of the future, as well as the past, if the sympathies of this life are to last into the next.

George Eliot prided herself on her ability 'to recall beloved faces and accents with great clearness', claiming that 'in this way my friends are continually with me'.[165] Other writers in this period were to miss her pitch of high confidence: Pater, for example, who refers both to 'our intensely realised memory' of the dead and, less firmly, to our 'sympathy with a body of persons outlived but perhaps vaguely present to our minds'.[166] His doubts parallel a series of psychological experiments which had shown how a conviction of 'clear memory' could be misplaced, or itself displaced, given that memory is less often a transparent window onto the past than one which is variously scratched and smeared by the mind's day-to-day operations.[167] When 'J. S.' explains in 1880 that recollection is 'a resurrection of the buried past' by which we 'recover a part of our seemingly "dead selves"', his partial echo of *In Memoriam* raises a further difficulty for memories which record past selves other than one's own. Individuals will not always be remembered as they would wish; our self-image will rarely be identical to our reputation.[168] (Of the many anxieties which plague Pip in *Great Expectations*, the most far-reaching is 'the dread of being misremembered after death'.[169]) Similarly, Tennyson's elegy on an other 'J. S.' checks its confidence that 'His memory long will live alone | In all our hearts' by recognizing that individual memories cannot endure in splendid isolation, in the way that some Victorians preserved their photographs under glass. Memory occupies a position which is intimate with both fact and imagination, but committed to neither, so that even surviving fragments of the past could be subject

---

[165] *George Eliot's Letters*, ed. G. S. Haight (9 vols., 1954–78), I. 80–1.

[166] *Marius the Epicurean* (1885, 2 vols., 1910), I. 20; MS note cited in T. R. Wright, *The Religion of Humanity*, 137.

[167] See, especially, Théodule Ribot, *Les maladies de la mémoire* (1881); Francis Galton, *Inquiries into Human Faculty and its Development* (1883); Hermann Ebbinghaus, *Über das Gedächtnis* (1885). I discuss the period's attention to memory in more detail in Ch. 4.

[168] 'The Illusions of Memory', *Cornhill Magazine*, 41 (January–June 1880), 416.

[169] Ch. 53. The relations between memory and death in Dickens's work are helpfully set out in Alexander Welsh, *The City of Dickens* (1971).

to shrinking, fading, and mutual interference: 'Memory standing near | Cast down her eyes, and in her throat | Her voice seemed distant.'[170]

A related and persistent concern for Victorian writings on personal identity is whether these downcast eyes and distanced voices will belong not only to those remembering the dead but also to the dead themselves. F. D. Maurice explained in 1857 that he could not read about the raising of Lazarus, 'without feeling that, among those things in heaven and earth that are so to be restored, the sympathies and affections of the family are some of the chief'.[171] But, as H. L. Mansell had already pointed out in 1854, recognition of these restored sympathies implies a firm sense of self-identity between life and afterlife.[172] Any future state which could be experienced as such would require present forms of understanding to be extended beyond death. Thus, if Locke was correct in thinking that the integrity of the self resided less in bodily continuity than in 'extended consciousness',[173] and if one of the conditions of a self-aware personality is memory, it would follow that 'the use of memory must go with the soul as ... one of the conditions of a consciousness of immortality'.[174] But how could the 'acutely time-conscious' Victorian self described by T. S. Eliot recognizably endure other than in time?[175] And how could an afterlife which is set beyond the world of change be accurately described in the measured sequences of a piece of writing? *In Memoriam*, XLV, in part answers these objections with the suggestion that our 'blood and breath' may act as a model for whichever form of body, new or renewed, emerges from this 'second Birth'. Tennyson's note on the previous section goes even further:

The dead after this life may have no remembrance of life, like the living babe who forgets the time before the sutures of the skull are closed, yet the living

---

[170] 'To J. S.', *TP*, I. 506.

[171] *The Gospel of St John: A Series of Discourses* (1857), 318; compare Lord Blachford's avowal of a heavenly 'interchange of sympathy [which] is warm and perpetual', in 'The Soul and Future Life', 347.

[172] *Man's Conception of Eternity* (1854), 22–3, discussed in Geoffrey Rowell, *Hell and the Victorians* (1974), 86.

[173] See Mary Warnock, *Memory* (1987), 58.

[174] 'E. F.', 'Memory and Conscience in the Future State', in *Universalist and Quarterly Review*, 5 (April 1848), 224.

[175] See Roden Noel, 'Memory and Personal Identity', in *The Modern Review*, 4 (1888), 180–7.

babe grows in knowledge, and though the remembrance of his earliest days has vanished, yet with his increasing knowledge there comes a dreamy vision of what has been.[176]

In immortal as in mortal life, it may be that 'Our birth is but a sleep and a forgetting',[177] as a heaven of endless growth stretches the sympathies of the dead by giving them ever more to reflect upon, and so forever more to overlook. And in this context, there is more than one way in which an elegy such as *In Memoriam* will need to reflect upon the loss of the living, and the mourning of the dead.

'THE GROWTH OF SONG'

When George Eliot sought to explain the beliefs which lay behind 'The Spanish Gypsy', she pointed out that our submission to the demands of an 'inherited organisation' (socio-political or corporeal) was seldom achieved by 'rational reflection' alone. 'Happily', she concluded, 'we are not left to that':

Love, pity, constituting sympathy, and generous joy with regard to the lot of our fellowmen ... has been growing since the beginning—enormously enhanced by wider vision of results—by an imagination actively interested in the lot of mankind generally.[178]

Eliot's principled distrust of thought is bracing, but the replacement of 'rational reflection' by 'the all-sufficiency of the soul's passions in determining sympathetic action' risks being so eager to embrace 'the lot of mankind generally' as to be an insufficient measure of the passions of individual human souls, many of whom are likely to be more actively interested in particular others than in one another 'generally'.[179] As stated, Eliot's evolutionary principles appear unable to discriminate between the moral obligations exacted by the past and its immoral prejudices, and unwilling to countenance evolution's wastefulness and dead ends. Given that the future too can exert its

---

[176] *TP*, II. 361–2.

[177] Wordsworth, 'Ode: Intimations of Immortality from Recollections of Early Childhood', *WP*, I. 525.

[178] Note on 'The Spanish Gypsy', repr. in J. W. Cross, *George Eliot's Life* (3 vols., 1885), III. 38–9.

[179] Ibid., 34.

pressures on present convictions, a further danger smoothed over by Eliot's account is that this 'constituting sympathy' will raise as many suspicions as those political theories which, another Eliot drily pointed out, inculcate 'a belief in a future inflexibly determined and at the same time in a future which we are wholly free to shape as we like'.[180] Nietzsche, who was alert to a penitential streak running through Eliot's beliefs ('In England', he notes, 'one must rehabilitate oneself after every little emancipation from theology by showing in a veritably awe-inspiring manner what a moral fanatic one is'),[181] offers a less generous view of cultural development, as he describes the need to protect against the injuries of time which are inflicted by an 'historical sense':

To fix this degree and the limits to the memory of the past, if it is not to become the gravedigger of the present, we must see clearly how great is the 'plastic power' of a man or a community or a culture; I mean the power of specifically growing out of one's self, of making the past and the strange one body with the near and the present, of healing wounds, replacing what is lost, repairing broken moulds.[182]

As with George Eliot's resolute faith in the 'growth of song' which reveals man's 'larger soul',[183] Nietzsche's view of this 'plastic power' is perhaps too optimistic about its potential always to grow out of, and never to outgrow, itself. There are grounds for thinking that fracture and discontinuity are among the enabling conditions of any historical writing which aims to encounter the past on other than its own terms, and that the gaps and elisions of this writing will bear witness not only to the historian's selective hearing of the past but also to those events which slip silently between the cracks of the historical record. Similarly, a 'growth of song' could proceed by substitution as well as by assimilation, willed forgetting as well as remembering, if a writer recognizes in the uneven development of his or her literary culture, or of his or her own writing, the need to reject those parts which come to seem stale or backward.

The idea that a past could be outgrown rather than grown out of is central to Tennyson's poetic development, and to the non-literary

[180] T. S. Eliot, *Notes towards the Definition of Culture*, 88–9.

[181] *Twilight of the Gods*, repr. in *The Portable Nietzsche*, ed. Walter Kaufmann (1971), 515.

[182] 'On the Use and Abuse of History' (1874), repr. in *Thoughts out of Season*, trans. Adrian Collins (1909), 9.

[183] 'The Legend of Jubal', *Works of George Eliot* (24 vols., 1878–85), X. 41, 29.

sympathies which it cautiously sustains. In this section, I examine how far these questions of continuity and change are concentrated into, and structured by, two aspects of literary form—parody and rhyme—which Tennyson also considers in relation to the development of his own form: his body.

*

In 1855, Lewis Carroll was impressed by the care which Tennyson took over individual revisions, but irritated by his imaginative thrift:

> Aug:14. (Tu)... He has improved the 'Ode to the Duke' and the 'Balaclava Charge' very much; the 'some one had blundered' has disappeared, but the sabres are still 'sabring'. The idyll of 'The Brook' is pretty, but is rather too like repetition in one who wrote
>
>> 'Love may come and love may go',
>
> and
>
>> 'But not by thee my steps shall be
>> For ever and for ever.'
>
> which reappear reunited in 'The Brook'
>
>> 'For men may come and men may go,
>> But I go on for ever.'[184]

One danger which Tennyson regularly confronted in his career was the possibility that individual poems can similarly over-extend themselves, whether by going on too long in their compositional development, or by giving disproportionate space to concerns which were unduly confessional and idiosyncratic for their public forms. For E. S. Dallas, no writer 'is better employed than he ... who widens the range of our sympathies and teaches us not less to care for the narrow aims of small people than for the vast schemes of the great and mighty.'[185] However, as Carroll gleefully demonstrates in the *Alice* books, if the writer has a duty to respect small people, he or she has a corresponding duty to be disrespectful towards writing which has stretched sympathy out of all scale to the objects of its attention:

---

[184] *The Diaries of Lewis Carroll*, ed. Roger Lancelyn Green (2 vols., 1953), I. 59.
[185] *The Gay Science* (1866), II. 287.

the twin duty which is fulfilled by the literary double-vision of the parodist.[186] For example, William Empson's brilliant suggestion that *Maud*'s 'improper freedom was parodied by the flowers at the beginning of the *Looking-Glass*' is carried further by his note that the ominous rumble of the Red Queen's approach is especially funny 'if you compare [the flowers] to their indestructible originals': ' "She's coming!" cried the Larkspur. "I hear her footstep, thump, thump, along the gravel-walk!" ' performs a panicked double-take on *Maud*'s fairy footsteps: 'She is coming, my life, my fate; | The red rose cries, "She is near, she is near".'[187] One requirement of good parody is that it upholds a similar trust in the indestructibility of its originals. It is because *Maud*'s self-involved speaker appears so reluctant to countenance the less rapt ways in which his expectations might be answered, that the lofty 'She is near, she is near' can be brought down to earth with 'thump, thump'. But although this offers a comic turn on *Maud*'s shifting attachments to and detachments from the world (coolly observing living people as things; jerking inanimate objects into momentary life), Carroll's rewriting cannot be altogether unkind, because the parodist too is in the peculiar position of both deadening and enlivening the objects of his or her enquiry. The root 'para' can be translated to mean either 'nearness' or 'opposition', and so captures within itself the parodist's necessary ambivalence, as he or she tests the limits of his sympathy for an original whose absurdities his or her version finds both appealing and appalling. As Susan Sontag reminds us, 'To name a sensibility, to draw its contours and to recount its history, requires a deep sympathy modified by revulsion.'[188] Whether it represents social credences hardening into dogma, or the over-familiar speech tic of an individual literary style, the parodist fixes on this sensibility and renovates it in his or her own image. It is for this reason that, although parody is conventionally referred to as a literary genre, it might better be seen as literature's defence against genre, a means of defining and defamiliarizing those settled shapes of expression which Tennyson's critics identified as one unwelcome consequence of 'sympathetic' writing.

'When Mr. Tennyson is reached', the author of 'The Poetry of Parody' noted in 1881, 'we become somewhat embarrassed by the

---

[186] See, e.g., Carroll's 'The Three Voices', a parody of Tennyson's 'The Two Voices', repr. in J. Postma, *Tennyson As Seen By His Parodists* (1926), 145–53.

[187] *Some Versions of Pastoral* (1938), 285–6.

[188] 'Notes on "Camp" ' (1964), repr. in *A Susan Sontag Reader* (1982), 105.

riches in the way of parody which have accumulated around certain of his poems.' He goes on to link this accumulation to parody's own limiting ambitions:[189]

It should be the aim of the parodist to create his effects in the smallest possible space; the smaller the space in which he performs the feat, the more worthy is that feat of commendation.[190]

However, it is not always the case that the parodist will seek to reduce esteem for his or her original by physically cutting it down to size. He or she might equally decide to draw out its uneven features in a form of verbal caricature: humbling the lowly; puffing up the inflated; encouraging the prolix to sprawl. Tennyson was especially vulnerable to parody's outgrowths and puckerings because across his career he searched for forms of verse which could negotiate between size and significance, between subjects and styles which were suited to a large and diverse readership, and those which answered his desire to project an eloquence unrepeatably his own. Like the bells which he described in *In Memoriam*, Tennyson's poems often 'swell out and fail',[191] growing from draft to draft without either accomplishing their stories or offering a fixed position from which to view such un- or under-achievement. Within individual poems, similarly, the range of approaches which he takes to his own vocabulary succeeds in translating this compositional habit into a characteristic feature of style. Even a modest word, such as 'little', shifts its meaning from tender solicitude ('Little bosom, not yet cold'), to destructive relish ('Dash the brains of the little one out'), and often spans both at once ('We men are a little breed').[192] Tennyson described his longest dramatic monologue, *Maud*, as 'a little *Hamlet*', and it is as important that its speaker is a *little* Hamlet as it is that his poem is a little *Hamlet*, as he cautiously explores the capacities of 'little' to suggest concentrated potential or shrunken lack, seed or relic: 'the little wood', 'little space', 'little hearts', 'the little living will', and more.[193]

[189] 'The Poetry of Parody', in *The Gentleman's Magazine* (September 1881), 323. In Walter Hamilton's multivolume collection published at the end of the century, Tennyson is represented by more than 350 parodies (Shakespeare: 216; Byron: 138; Scott: 125). There were notable defences of Tennyson against the parasitical nature of parody in the *Westminster Review* (July 1854) and *Notes & Queries* (26 June 1880).

[190] 'The Poetry of Parody', 305.

[191] *IM*, XXVIII, *TP*, II. 346. See Ricks, *Tennyson*, 49.

[192] 'Little bosom not yet cold' l. 1, 'Boädicea' l. 68, *Maud*, l. 131, *TP*, II. 465, 617, 530.

[193] *Memoir*, I. 396.

Tennyson was annoyed by literary imitations (he complained on his death-bed that 'Burlesque, the true enemy of humour, the thin bastard sister of poetical caricature, would, I verily believe, from her utter want of human feeling, in a revolution be the first to dabble her hands in blood'),[194] and was especially sensitive to comic versions of his own work. This can partly be explained by the insinuating ease with which his parodists crossed the line which separated literary creation from literary criticism, and so had to be included in any assessment of the readers for whom Tennyson wrote with such generous and grudging care. When he reported that an obscure critic was dismissing his claims to being a great poet, Meredith asked him 'Why should you mind what such a man says?', and Tennyson replied 'I mind what *everybody* says.'[195] Yet a writer who minded what *everybody* said might also need to take account of the possibility that he had a better sense of humour than many of the writers who sought to turn him into a figure of fun. On one occasion, Tennyson remarked that the first pipe after breakfast was the best of the day, and Sir William Harcourt waggishly punned: 'Ah, the earliest pipe of half-awakened bards'.[196] Tennyson did not seem amused. What is not recorded is whether he objected to a joke being made at his expense, or whether the joke was so weak that the kindest response would have been to allow it to die on Harcourt's lips. But it is because Tennyson was so self-consciously alert to the ease with which his own utterances could be stripped down and hollowed out, once released into the capricious world of public speech, that he was not only 'embarrassed by the riches in the way of parody' which accumulate around certain of his poems. Like most good writers, his literary opinions do not run through his literary practice, but run alongside it, and the best of his work emerges from those places in his career where their lines of thought touch. In 1855, he was in Oxford to receive an honorary degree, and several students came up to ask him: 'Did they call you early, Mr. Tennyson?' Charles Tennyson records that his grandfather met the question 'with a grim smile'.[197] His choice of phrase is apt, recalling as it does how 'the world-worn Dante grasped his song' in 'The Palace of Art', 'And somewhat grimly smiled', because this is how Tennyson sought to grasp his own song: with that 'Strength,

[194] *Memoir*, II. 423.
[195] Reported by T. H. Warren, in *Page*, 157.
[196] Sir Charles Tennyson, *Alfred Tennyson* (1949), 469.
[197] Ibid., 285.

greatness, and grasp unmistakable' which Sir Charles Stanford noticed in Tennyson's hands, and in the controlled spans of the verse they produced.[198] Nobody could parody Tennyson quite like Tennyson. 'I mind what *everybody* says': it is Tennyson's skill to 'mind' (take heed of and tend) what could be made of his poems, not only by revising them in the light of hostile reviews but also by anticipating the shades of a critical future as they are cast onto and into present writing. His poems absorb both the ghosts of time past and the ghosts of time to come.[199] And as we shall see, this is another form of literary afterlife which Tennyson used to enquire into something he worried was not 'unmistakable', but about which he was confident he was not mistaken: personal immortality.

*

Tennyson often delivered critical post-mortems on his creative self, whether by writing answers to poems which had become questionable since their first publication ('Locksley Hall', 'Locksley Hall Sixty Years After'), or by incorporating swerves of attention into individual poems to show how the confined sequences of reading might similarly reveal a series of truths, if not the whole truth, about the writer. Love poems concentrate these concerns, because it is in the nature of the lover's utterances to make greater claims for the speaker than he or she can fulfil, as a swollen heart produces the inflated rhetoric of this room as an everywhere, this time a forever. Wilfred Ward remembered that when Tennyson read 'Vastness' to him, it had 'two distinct voices—the last line being placed in the mouth of a separate speaker who answers the rest of the poem':[200]

> Peace, let it be! for I loved him, and love him for ever:
> the dead are not dead but alive.

The line pivots on 'let it be!', which turns between a refusal to quibble with the past and a yearning for the future: the conclusion (announced with confidence, but beset with the doubts of the rest of the poem) that what was loved once is loved still. But, as Browning recognized, when he wrote the second of his poems on 'Earth's

---

[198] *TP*, I. 447; Sir Charles Villiers Stanford, *Studies and Memories* (1908), repr. in *Page*, 130.

[199] See John Bayley's suggestive essay, 'Tennyson and the Idea of Decadence', on Tennyson's reticence as 'a source of buried humour', in *Studies in Tennyson*, 202.

[200] *New Review*, 15 (1896), quoted in *TP*, III. 137.

Immortalities', it is one of the conditions of living speech that time might not let it be:

> So, the year's done with!
> *(Love me for ever!)*
> All March begun with,
>   April's endeavour;
> May-wreaths that bound me
>   June must needs sever;
> Now snow falls round me,
>   Quenching June's fever—
>   *(Love me for ever!)*[201]

Browning's sly repetition of '*(Love me for ever!)*', at once hopeful and conscience-stricken, mocks the naïvety that would seek to make each 'for ever' last forever, just as the gloating of *Maud*'s speaker at the thought of Maud being 'For ever and ever, mine' is then retuned and mourned by a later attempt at permanence, the longing to be buried 'Deeper, ever so little deeper'.[202]

However, this worry that what has been done is not yet 'done with' is also the writer's hope. Before, and after, Positivism turned it into a fashionable ethical doctrine, the writer announces his wish to live forever, to compose for himself and his beloved an extended life in eyes and lungs to come, as Arthur Hallam celebrated the fact that Cicero was 'living among us all, by his thoughts perpetuated in writing' which is 'present without difficulty to several points of place and time'.[203] Yet living writers too are present to several points of place and time, not only in the 'piece-meal' life of their memory but also in the sheer persistence of their writing. Once achieved in print, and so capable of comparison, it is always possible that a poet's appeals to integrity will be undermined by their own instabilities of conviction and form. It is equally possible that the same utterances will reveal the consistency of the poet's approaches to these very questions of impermanence, as the climactic dying fall of *In Memoriam*, XCV—'"The dawn, the dawn", and died away'— is drawn out further by the conclusion to a poem which was composed at the same time as, and often in the same notebooks as, *In Memoriam*:

---

[201] *RBP*, I. 447.   [202] *TP*, II. 564, 581.
[203] 'Essay on the Philosophical Writings of Cicero', *Motter*, 142–3.

> Long stood Sir Bedivere
> Revolving many memories, till the hull
> Looked one black dot against the verge of dawn,
> And on the mere the wailing died away.

Like King Arthur, the 'Morte d'Arthur' cannot die, as Tennyson's methods of composition here anticipate the last moments of his St Telemachus: 'And preachers lingered o'er his dying words, | Which would not die, but echoed on … '.[204] Such self-confrontations in print are not 'without difficulty', however, being subject both to the poet's waning allegiances, and to fickle public sympathies which will perhaps never be fully in tune with his own. 'One believes in a poet', Allingham suggested, 'whose lines are perpetually coming into one's mind. Yours do with me.' Tennyson's response showed how suspicious he could be even of his most trusted readers' beliefs: 'Repeat a line.'[205] Elegy concentrates these problems, because expressions of mourning often imagine outlasting their moment of utterance, whether by wishing to countenance no future on earth which does not include the dead beloved, or by seeking consolation in a future state which is set beyond a world of loss and change. But as the impulse which prompts these expressions passes on and away from the poet, so their very lastingness can come to seem a parody of the constancy they continue to proclaim. In order to avoid this fate, even utterances which respond to the most solemn and absolute of events, such as a bereavement, will therefore need to show evidence of the sort of imaginative suppleness which T. S. Eliot identified in his definition of 'wit': 'It involves, probably, a recognition, implicit in the expression of every experience, of other kinds of experience which are possible.'[206]

When E. M. Forster read Marianne Thornton's memoir of her parents, he recognized how quickly an unstinting grief will appear unsatisfactory to others if it seems, in its single-minded drive, unaware of other kinds of experience which are possible:

On goes her sad narrative, gently, relentlessly, as if the spirit of the age, which adored death beds, was speaking through her lips. Nothing is insincere, nothing strained or in bad taste, but on it goes, on.[207]

---

[204] *TP*, III. 227.
[205] *Allingham* (27 July 1884), 327.
[206] 'Andrew Marvell' (1921), repr. in *Selected Prose of T. S. Eliot*, 170.
[207] Quoted in Pat Jalland, *Death in the Victorian Family* (1996), 11.

Forster's tone sharply collides two possible reactions to sustained grief: admiration at its stamina, and irritation that 'she does go on', as if Marianne Thornton, like Tennyson's Mariana, had got stuck in the perpetual present tense of mourning, and so had lost that sense of perspective which is built into the grammar of ordinary speech. *In Memoriam* answers this sort of objection by concentrating several different long times into itself: the time it took to write, the time it takes to read, and the time it strives to span in and between individual lines. All lyric verse offers an audible restructuring of time, whether in the measured returns of metre and rhyme or in lines which allude to earlier poems, and so turn themselves into palpable vessels of time. But for all the exemplary patience of its form, not all of the times which *In Memoriam* imagines are subject to the poet's or reader's control. For example, one of the most stubborn lines of questioning over the afterlife which runs through *In Memoriam* concerns the length of its own future, such as whether Hallam's memory could survive his elegy being forgotten, or whether if, as Beckett pointed out, 'habit is a great deadener',[208] then a grief which is repeatedly articulated may be not only monotonous, but murderous, elegy killing what it purports most to love. *In Memoriam*, XXIX, is more worried by the possibility that deadening one's self to grief could be an unavoidable consequence of speech, rather than an articulated choice, as it wonders how Christmas can be celebrated when even 'the birth of Christ' seems more like a deathday than a birthday:

> With such compelling cause to grieve
> As daily vexes household peace,
> And chains regret to his decease,
> How dare we keep our Christmas-eve ... [209]

Each day, Hallam's death is so regretted that the speaker feels remorse for continuing with the everyday activities which they would otherwise be enjoying together. As so often in the poem, a present tense is haunted simultaneously by an unrepeatable past and an unknowable future. This grieving process then 'chains regret to his decease', because every kind of sorrow now experienced by the speaker seems to have its source in this one death: an event which has come to form the vanishing-point of all subsequent experience.

[208] Vladimir, in *Waiting for Godot* (1956), 91.   [209] *TP*, II. 346.

The phrase further suggests how the bereaved sometimes come to mourn the compulsions of grief along with the dead beloved, and so anticipates the outcome which is suggested by a later section, 'O last regret, regret can die!', and is then confirmed in the 'Conclusion': 'No longer caring to embalm | In dying songs a dead regret.'[210] Animated with the animosity of 'vexes', one suspicion is that this second death is not altogether to be regretted. Another is that elegy's limited lifespan could be affected less by the endurance of individual grief and its speaker, and more by the growth of the language in which expressions of 'regret' and 'love' are both sustained. Reading *In Memoriam*, LXXXVI, to Allingham, Tennyson took pride in his ability to bring together the 'air' it describes with the breath he needed to keep it going: ' "It all goes together," said he.'[211] Other sections of *In Memoriam*, however, are aware that the poem as a whole might not go together. Instead, once subject to the drifting and fracturing of the social memory which supports the fullness of individual utterance, it might 'go', disappear, piece by piece.

For Comte, all linguistic expressions were by their nature expressions of community: 'The man who dares to think himself independent of others, either in feelings, thoughts, or actions, cannot even put the blasphemous conception into words without immediate self-contradiction, since the very language he uses is not his own.'[212] Central to Comte's ethical system is a confidence in the semantic stability which would allow this solidarity to be extended in time as well as in space. As a thinker 'portentously devoid of a sense of humour',[213] though, Comte lacked the sense of proportion by which he might have recognized less appealing forms of long-lasting utterance, such as the preening *longeurs* which characterize so many stretches of his own writing. Tennyson is more likely to have sided with Pater: 'A kind of humour is one of the conditions of the true mental attitude in the criticism of past stages of thought':[214]

---

[210] *TP*, II. 392, 452.

[211] *Allingham* (27 July 1884), 328.

[212] *System of Positive Polity*, trans. J. H. Bridges, *et al.* (4 vols., 1875–7), I. 177.

[213] Henry Sidgwick (1906), quoted in Wright, *The Religion of Humanity*, 148; compare J. S. Mill's conclusion that 'There is nothing in [Comte's] writings from which it could be inferred that he knew of the existence of such things as wit and humour', *Auguste Comte and Positivism*, 153–4.

[214] Quoted in Wright, *The Religion of Humanity*, 136.

I dare not tell how high I rate humour, which is generally most fruitful in the highest and most solemn human spirits. Dante is full of it, Shakespeare, Cervantes, and almost all the greatest have been pregnant with this glorious power. You will find it even in the Gospel of Christ.[215]

Tennyson was not above extracting humour even from the Old Testament, as when 'he asked Thomas Hardy to name the first person mentioned in the Bible, to which the required answer was Chap. I.'[216] Even so, the claim made for the Gospels is surprising, given that Christ is reported to have wept three times, but never laughed. (Whether an omnipotent being can be imagined as incapable of laughing is less often considered.) It may be that Tennyson had in mind Christ's attempt to identify Peter as a rock of faith by punning on 'petrus', which would accord with his sense of humour's 'fruitful' and 'pregnant' power. But as *In Memoriam*, LXXVII, makes clear, the changing face of literature's readership and language means that the potential of serious utterances to disclose a latent humour will not always be artful or welcome:

> What hope is here for modern rhyme
> To him, who turns a musing eye
> On songs, and deeds, and lives, that lie
> Foreshortened in the tract of time?
>
> These mortal lullabies of pain
> May bind a book, may line a box,
> May serve to curl a maiden's locks;
> Or when a thousand moons shall wane
>
> A man upon a stall may find,
> And, passing, turn the page that tells
> A grief, then changed to something else,
> Sung by a long-forgotten mind.[217]

Compare this with Tennyson's own reading of *Maud*:

When I came down to drawing-room found A.T. with a book in his hand; ... He accosted me, 'Allingham, would it disgust you if I read "Maud"? Would you expire?'

---

[215] *Memoir*, I. 167.

[216] Michael Millgate, *Testamentary Acts*, 55, paraphrasing Edward Clodd's diary entry for 15 December 1892.

[217] *IM*, LXXVII, *TP*, II. 390.

I gave a satisfactory reply and he accordingly read 'Maud' all through, with some additions recently made. His interpolated comments very amusing.

'This is what was called namby-pamby!'—'That's wonderfully fine!'—'That was very hard to read; could you have read it? I don't think so.'[218]

'His interpolated comments very amusing', but the poker-face of *In Memoriam*'s printed page holds out the possibility that, where the poet's voice is not on hand to direct his published forms, this page too could be 'turned', made strange to itself. Note the chime of 'rhyme' with 'time': for a reader less capable of fleshing out what has become 'Foreshortened in the tract of time', 'a musing' eye cast briskly over the poem might so quicken the pace of the grief it describes as to render it 'amusing' ('comedy', as Norman Holland remarked brightly, 'is tragedy speeded up'),[219] as 'lie' holds over the line-break the worry that poems frequently make claims for their endurance which they do not stay around long enough to put to the test.

There is no reason to assume that this sort of anxiety will be limited to the elegist. As I have already suggested, a love poet may also wonder whether any form of expression can be adequate to the experience which prompted his or her poem, and at the same time be true to the way its contours are likely to be redrawn in the future, whether by the poet's own changes of heart, or by the variable assumptions of a developing readership. Any piece of writing might confront similar problems once it is released into the unpredictable economy of literary fame. Proust incorporates one such warning into *A la recherche*, as he describes how the fictional novelist Bergotte dies into an afterlife which will be no more than the temporary satisfaction of market forces:

They buried him, but all through that night of mourning, in the lighted shop-windows, his books, arranged three by three, kept vigil like angels with outspread wings and seemed, for him who was no more, the symbol of his resurrection.[220]

An elegy is likely to concentrate fears which surround the author's loss of control over his or her work's 'resurrection', because once a poem is delivered into the public world of print, it is not only the poet whose

---

[218] *Allingham* (25 June 1865), 118.

[219] *Laughing: A Psychology of Humor* (1982), 47.

[220] *A la recherche du temps perdu*, trans. C. K. Scott Moncrieff *et al.* (3 vols., 1981), III. 186. The passage is superbly discussed by Malcolm Bowie in *Proust Among the Stars* (1998), 69.

literary afterlife will be compromised by the wandering eyes of posterity. The elegy's subject, too, is threatened with a lingering second demise, this time at the hands of its readers, whose decision to 'bury' or 'resurrect' any literary work will reflect the central human dilemma that death is not only a natural law but also a process which our minds selectively exercise upon one another.

In Memoriam occasionally describes this process, in sections (such as LXXVII) which wonder aloud what will become of themselves, and so ask us to consider how far the relationship between poet and reader, like other kinds of human relationship, encourages us to retrieve pleasure from our knowledge of its impermanence. More often, though, the poem absorbs this knowledge of the limited afterlife of elegy into its own form, as Tennyson's suspicion that looking at the world *sub specie aeternitatis* will reveal 'the indifference to be' (XXVI), the threat of a change of heart which is forever lurking in the crevices of love, adapts an earlier elegy by twisting it free of its subject: Wordsworth's lament that Lucy is in her grave, 'and, oh, | The difference to me'.[221] In this way, although the long development of *In Memoriam* supported Tennyson's sense of how much remained to be said about its subject, his delays in finishing the poem suggest a related anxiety over what would remain of it once it had been said. Given the reader's ability to 'change the bearing of a word' ('bearing' supports ideas both of the word's direction and its intellectual freight), there is always the residual fear that *In Memoriam* will come to mourn those parts of itself that are dead or dying, as if realizing the sinister promise of its title-page, which shifts from the unspoken (a dead language) to the unspeakable (the numerals which visibly linger over Hallam's death): 'Obit MDCCCXXXIII.'[222]

Several of the poem's sections investigate the importance to elegy of its own 'matter-moulded forms of speech', where 'moulded' compacts their ready corruptibility and their capacities for refreshing themselves with new and renewed life.[223] This emerges most clearly in Tennyson's etymological investigations. 'Infant', for instance, is an important choice for *In Memoriam*, LIV, which trusts 'that somehow good | Will be the final goal of ill', because the description of 'An infant ... with no language but a cry' restores 'infans' to its Latin roots

---

[221] 'She dwelt among the untrodden ways', *WP*, I. 366.

[222] *IM*, CXXVIII, *TP*, II. 449.

[223] *IM*, XCV, *TP*, II. 413.

('unable to speak'), and so embodies hope of future resurrection in a speaker who gives voice to what else is not dead but only resting: the survival of Latin in English.[224] However, the potential obsolescence of words less eager to be reborn than 'infans' suggest an additional difficulty for Victorian models of that other place of potential growth and development: heaven. Arthur Hallam echoes Tennyson's characteristic resistance to one such model when he urges, 'O tell me not, ye sages, that our end | Shall merge us in the godhead; I am made | To seek with kindred souls my soul to blend.'[225] What he does not explain is how he could continue to argue with these sages if all were to retain their full individuality in the afterlife, given the likelihood that although Chaucer and Jeanette Winterson, say, might have much to talk about in heaven, they might not have much in common to talk with, given the changes undergone by the language since 'The Legend of Good Women'.

Not everyone recognized this as a problem. Like many spiritualists, Victor Hugo's enthusiasm for conversing with the dead seems to have stemmed largely from his assumption that all the great minds of the past would speak more or less like Victor Hugo. As his most recent biographer recounts, the complete guest-list at the seances which he conducted during the 1850s, with his friend and literary executor Auguste Vacquerie,

eventually included Cain, Jacob, Moses, Isaiah, Sappho, Socrates, Jesus, Judas, Mohammed, Joan of Arc, Luther, Galileo, Molière, the Marquis de Sade (whose comments have not survived), Mozart, Walter Scott, some angels, Androcles' Lion, Balaam's Ass, a comet, and an inhabitant of Jupiter called Tyatafia ... The language was mid-nineteenth-century French, though Walter Scott tapped out a little poem in English (when an Englishman was present), Hannibal spoke in Latin, and Androcles' Lion imparted a few words of lion language.[226]

Occasionally, Hugo worried that his spirits sounded so alike, and tested the more ancient among them by seeing if they could supply a cure for rabies, or the secret of steering balloons. However, his suspicions were largely soothed by the healthy respect they seemed to share for the literary opinions of the man who had summoned them from the shadows:

---

[224] *TP*, II. 370.
[225] 'To One Early Loved, Now in India', *Motter*, 80.
[226] Graham Robb, *Victor Hugo*, 334.

VACQUERIE: Do you acknowledge that Shakespeare is a tree and that you are a stone?

RACINE: Yes.

VACQUERIE: Do you acknowledge that you were wrong to write constricted plays?

RACINE: I am embarrassed.

VACQUERIE: Do you now feel remorse because your reputation is superior to your talent?

RACINE: My wig is singed.[227]

'Having always insisted that his poems were simply an echo of Nature's voice', Graham Robb points out, 'Hugo was quite ready to believe that the after-life expressed itself in a manner very similar to his own':

Hugo's dead audience could be used to construct a recipe for his style, a universal Esperanto based on grand, simple concepts that could be understood at any age and in any civilisation, terrestrial or not; powerful, repetitive phrases with the volume and solidity of ships setting out on long journeys through time and space.[228]

Other writers were less confident in the idea that the voices of the dead would slot together with such assured and stately calm. Christina G. Rossetti returns to the theocentric heaven of everlasting worship, as she imagines joyfully 'tak[ing] up my part' in song:

> Swelling those Hallejulahs full of rest,
> One, tenfold, hundredfold, with heavenly art,
>   Fulfilling north and south and east and west,
> Thousand, ten thousandfold, innumerable,
>   All blent in one yet each one manifest ... [229]

Doubts about the prospect of singing parts 'All blent in one yet each one manifest' were not entirely assuaged by the traditional answer that the saved would immediately enter into the pre-Babelian perfection of 'heaven's language'. Robert Pollok's earlier solution has the Bard of Earth explain that, although in heaven all languages are instantly translated, the perfected strains of this speech do not entirely muffle traces of earlier dialects:

---

[227] Quoted by Robb, ibid., 335.

[228] Ibid., 334.

[229] 'After this the Judgment' (1856), *The Complete Poems of Christina Rossetti*, ed. R. W. Crump (3 vols., 1979–90), I. 185.

> ... for each in heaven a relish holds
> Of former speech, that points to whence he came.
> But whether I of person speak, or place
>   ... the meaning still,
> With easy apprehension, thou shalt take.[230]

However, a heaven of advance rather than one 'full of rest' will ask
difficult questions of such 'easy apprehension', because where this
community depends upon the endurance of the embodied memories
which would allow us to recognize our friends, by 'tone of voice, or a
quick lighting up of the face with an old familiar smile',[231] it could
follow that the death which put Tennyson and Hallam 'so far
apart | We cannot hear each other speak' would continue to separate
them, even after Tennyson's own death, if he could no longer understand or reply in Hallam's finer tone.[232]

What Tennyson fears above and below all else is expressed in *In
Memoriam*, XLI:

> But thou art turned to something strange,
>   And I have lost the links that bound
>   Thy changes; here upon the ground,
> No more partaker of thy change.[233]

It is not only the dead selves of other people which could raise these
concerns for a writer. When Elizabeth Barrett listened to Tennyson's
blank verse, she reported that she heard 'A "linked music ... " in
which there are no links ... ! ... & I have wondered curiously again &
again how there could be so much union & no fastening.'[234] She
seems to have had in mind, and in earshot, the blank verse of poems
such as 'Tithonus', which achieves a form of 'linked music' through
its rich chains of internal rhyme:

> Ay me! ay me! with what another heart
> In days far-off, and with what other eyes
> I used to watch—if I be he that watched—
> The lucid outline forming round thee ...[235]

As I have already suggested, it is Tennyson's skill in this poem to
retrieve the hidden 'links' of personality from the seams of memory,
and then to unpick them in present-tense speech—as with the uneasy

---

[230] Robert Pollok, *The Course of Time: A Poem* (1827, repr. 1857), 29.
[231] *The Recognition of Friends in Heaven*, 210.   [232] *IM*, LXXXII, *TP*, II. 394.
[233] *TP*, II. 358–9.   [234] Letter to Robert Browning (13 June 1845), *Kintner*, 93.
[235] 'Tithonus', *TP*, II. 611.

encounters here of 'Ay me', 'eyes' and 'I', or 'be' and 'he'. These lines, added when Tennyson expanded 'Tithon' into 'Tithonus', extend the speaker's doubts even further, by filtering them through the self-questioning responses of the revising poet. For a writer, Barrett's 'wonder'—exactly held between astonishment and doubt—is likely to be the very medium in which she or he works, because the experience of confronting an old poem might confirm that it too has turned to something strange, as Henry James, attempting to extend his creative evolution for the New York Edition, sadly reported coming across 'Intervals of thought and a desolation of missing links'.[236] Even where the writer continues to see eye to eye with his or her previous self, the poem which they share may still threaten to estrange itself from a speaker's full understanding, not only through the unpredictable changes of the language in which it is embedded but also through the formal features, such as rhyme, which threaten to blur the individual edges of the expressions which this poem is attempting to carve out of common speech. (Compare *In Memoriam*'s use of 'strange—change' with the same rhyme as it is applied in Tennyson's Sleeping Beauty fantasy, 'The Day-Dream', and his early elegy 'To J. S.'[237]) I pointed out in my second chapter, when comparing the use to which Tennyson and FitzGerald each puts 'dust' and 'trust', that because rhyme joins words together, it has a habit of making an argument seem already clinched, as if the rhyming dictionary which brings together 'breath' and 'death', or 'womb' and 'tomb', was also the repository of hard-earned wisdom, transforming the chance encounters of a language into matters of settled principle. But although the appearance of a rhyme like 'dust—trust' can work like an ethical tuning-fork, allowing the poet to check the acoustics of his or her lines against tried and tested ways of thinking and speaking, the way he or she approaches this expected chime can equally stage a range of possible attitudes towards what the words themselves seem to take for granted, from dutiful acceptance, to ironic smirking, to reminiscing over traditional ways of thinking which now seem arch or quaint, like someone humming a tune they cannot quite get back. As Joseph Brodsky points out in his discussion of Martina Tsvetaeva, 'A poet is someone for whom every word is not the end but the beginning of a thought; someone who, having uttered *rai* ('paradise') or *tot*

---

[236] *Henry James's Literary Criticism*, ed. Leon Edel and Mark Wilson (2 vols., 1984), II. 1284.
[237] *TP*, II. 57, I. 507.

svet ('next world'), must mentally take the next step of finding a rhyme for it.'[238] Any published conviction concerning the afterlife may need to incorporate a similarly wary approach towards its subject, given that its printed form assumes a constancy of view which will not always be upheld by the development of ideas, or of the language in which it is expressed. It is precisely these effects of self-confirmation and self-surprise which Tennyson achieves with his return to particular rhymes, because by calling upon the same meetings of sound in recognizably altered circumstances (textual and personal), his verse suggests, in Pater's words, 'Not the truth of eternal outlines effected once for all, but a world of fine gradations and subtly linked conditions, shifting intricately as we ourselves change.'[239]

'Did he ever use a rhyming dictionary? He had tried it in earlier days, but found it of little use: "There was no natural congruity between the rhymes thus alphabetically grouped together." '[240] This very lack of congruity can become a creative resource for a poet writing of the skewing and jarring of relations over time. A poem about delayed satisfaction, for example, might summon up the ghost of a rhyme, but not the rhyme itself, as one of the lists of rhyming-words in Tennyson's notebooks begins with 'awaken' and ends with 'Kraken', a lurking connection which is not realized in 'The Kraken' as published: a poem of unresolved expectation which works by thwarting the smaller expectations of its own form.[241] Rhyme casts the ear back, and so can seem backward, as an adult might recall the nursery rhymes which he enjoyed as a child, but which now seem like 'echoes out of weaker times'.[242] Rhyme also looks forward, and so can seem premature, as 'The Lady of Shalott' precipitates the doomed meeting of 'Shalott' (originally 'Shalot') with 'Camelot' and 'Lancelot' in rhymes which appear to be scheming against their subject, at once soliciting agreement and signalling constraint. Most significantly, rhyme compasses change, emerging as the coincidence of sounds over time, so that the cumulative sense it carries is often completed only over time. It is for this reason that, not only within poems (the implicit 'therefore' which Wimsatt detected joining the

---

[238] *Less Than One*, 265.

[239] Walter Pater, *Essays on Literature and Art*, ed. Jenny Uglow (1973), 1–2.

[240] *Memoir*, II. 496.   [241] *TA*, X. 5ʳ.

[242] *IM*, 'Conclusion', once more linking 'time' and 'rhyme': 'half but idle brawling rhymes'; *TP*, II. 453. Tennyson assembled around forty traditional nursery-rhymes in one of his working notebooks; see *TA*, I.

rhyme-words of couplets)[243] but also between them, a shared rhyme can heal the divisions opened up between a poet's utterances with its own distinctive grammar of assent. Faced with the vicissitudes of public debate, and the intermittencies of his own beliefs, Tennyson's rhymes form a fixed centre of gravity around which individual lines of verse revolve. Like the connections which Tithonus tentatively forges in his speech, they are the links that bind his changes.

*

Not all of Tennyson's critics thought he was capable of this sort of constancy. When Browning became aware of the revisions made for the 1842 *Poems*, he was in no doubt that Tennyson's second thoughts were mostly second-rate versions of his first thoughts, corrupted by a very un-Browning-like desire to please the critics: 'Tennyson reads the "Quarterly" and does as they bid him, with the most solemn face in the world—out goes this, in goes that, all is changed and ranged ... Oh me!'[244] It is unfortunate that Browning's ear was not as sharp as his tongue in offering this criticism, because although the image of Tennyson cravenly agreeing with the critics is not an accurate one, his account unwittingly succeeds in putting its finger upon a more private form of reception anxiety which Tennyson did address in his verse. His son recorded that, 'as a boy he would reel off hundreds of lines such as these:

> The quick-wing'd gnat doth make a boat
> Of his old husk wherewith to float
> To a new life! all low things range
> To higher! but I cannot change.'[245]

Because rhyme exists between words, rhyme-words are frequently in-between words, the points of transition for a voice to conduct internal enquiries over ideas of loss and recovery, promise and compromise, thoughts which are affirmed or have their precise edges smudged by echo. *In Memoriam* often rhymes 'change' with 'range':

> Could I have said while he was here,
>   'My love shall now no further range;

[243] 'One Relation of Rhyme to Reason: Alexander Pope', *Modern Language Quarterly*, 5 (1944), 323–38.
[244] Letter to EBB (11 February 1845), *Kintner*, 19.
[245] *Memoir*, I. 18.

> There cannot come a mellower change,
> For now is love mature in ear.'[246]

Adapting 'Beyond a mellower growth mature in ear' from an early draft of *The Gardener's Daughter*, Tennyson's speech has matured in his own ear, and because this manuscript line was not incorporated into the published version of the poem, his borrowing privately listens in on the sound of realized potential, together with the promise of this change being no more conclusive than the stanza form in which it is momentarily clinched:

> Our voices took a higher range;
>   Once more we sang: 'They do not die
>   Nor lose their mortal sympathy,
> Nor change to us, although they change ... '[247]

'Range' and 'change' are now put further apart by 'die' and 'sympathy', as the child's boast 'I cannot change' is subjected to the growing pains of ageing and bereavement. Yet this hope, that sympathetic bonds will survive changes of form, itself stubbornly sings out in Tennyson's rhymes, creating the sound of a mind raising its past, and itself on that past: rhymes as stepping-stones.

Rhyme-words sound out their agreements through the accidents of language, and can dramatize a range of attitudes towards the established patterns of a life, from fated inevitability to obdurate custom. Equally, because its returns of sound arch across boundaries of sense, it is possible for rhyme to construct a scaffolding of faith that evades the demands of rational thought. As Seamus Heaney remarks of Herbert:

An unconstrained, undebilitated mind measured itself against impositions and expectations which were both fundamental and contingent to it. Its disciplines, however, proved equal to its challenges, so that ... a rhyme of 'child' with 'wild' could put the distress of his personal predicament into a divinely ordained perspective.[248]

Running through his reflections upon the transformations already wrought in his poetic and physical forms, and the transformations both could suffer after his death, Tennyson's rhymes form a central discipline by which he measures 'personal predicament' against

---

[246] *IM*, LXXXI, *TP*, II. 393 and n.
[247] *IM*, XXX, *TP*, II. 348.
[248] *The Government of the Tongue* (1988), 96.

'ordained perspective'. In particular, as they span and structure his poetic voice, rhymes such as 'range' and 'change' operate as sounding-boards for that 'pre-established harmony of mind' which Arthur Hallam saw moving the soul to sympathy, and which he also thought would be seen by God when he examined this soul after death: 'For in the Eternal Idea of God a created spirit is perhaps not seen as a series of successive states ... but as one indivisible object of these almost infinitely divisible modes.'[249] *In Memoriam*, XLV, develops Hallam's concern by paraphrasing a section of 'On Sympathy' which describes the baby's growing sense of separateness from its mother:

> So rounds he to a separate mind
>   From whence clear memory may begin,
>   As through the frame that binds him in
> His isolation grows defined.
>
> This use may lie in blood and breath,
>   Which else were fruitless of their due,
>   Had man to learn himself anew
> Beyond the second birth of Death.[250]

A sudden accession of self-consciousness is realized across the line-break of 'the frame that binds him in | His isolation', miming the baby's dawning knowledge that the frame which embraces him most closely is not his mother's arms, but his own flesh. This association of bodily and stanzaic 'frames' also sustains Tennyson's faith in the coherence of the self 'Beyond the second birth of Death':

> I hope to see my Pilot face to face
>   When I have crost the bar.[251]

One part of this hope is carried by the fleeting recollection of 1 Corinthians 13 ('For we know in part, and we prophesy in part ... For now we see through a glass, darkly; but then face to face'), as the fragment of the text which is still recognizable—'face to face'—looks forward to retaining the self which had put away its childish things, such as rhyme, not as a renunciation, but for safe keeping. At the same time, as the separate mind rounds back to where it began, hope is carried across the visible barrier of Tennyson's line-break which

---

[249] 'Theodiciaea Novissima', *Motter*, 210.
[250] *TP*, II. 362–3.
[251] 'Crossing the Bar', *TP*, III. 254.

divides the first 'I' from the second, self-identical, 'I', like a soul yearning to cross the great divide.

*

Tennyson's attempts to discover a poetic shape for his faith in the human individual as 'one indivisible subject' extend beyond the local splitting and recombination of single lines of verse, and into the narrative and compositional development of *In Memoriam*.

George Eliot writes with tact of the difficulty in returning to 'our old selves' once it is recognized that grief, like the dead, can be outlived: 'Let us rather be thankful that our sorrow lives in us as an indestructible force, only changing its form, as forces do, and passing from pain into sympathy.'[252] The textual history of *In Memoriam* shows how the passage from pain to sympathy will not only be forward-looking, as it enacts Tennyson's belief that evolving poetic forms do not abandon their pasts any more than he could slip his own ancestors, given that 'every human being is a vanful of human beings, of those who have gone before him, and of those who form part of his life'.[253] If Tennyson had attempted to follow the guidance of modern bereavement counsellor Beverley Raphael, for example, he might have warmed to her advice that 'the bereaved reviews, piece by piece, memories, thoughts, and feelings associated with the image of the dead partner': compare his re-reading of Arthur Hallam's letters in *In Memoriam*, XCV: 'So word by word, and line by line, | The dead man touched me from the past.' However, he is unlikely to have been impressed with her brisk conclusion that these 'aspects of the lost relationship' should be worked through, 'in order that the bonds binding the bereaved to the dead partner may gradually be relinquished, freeing the emotional investment for ongoing life and further relationships': compare 'And I have lost the links that bound thy changes.'[254] The bereaved frequently refuse to countenance change, unhappy that life will go on without one life in particular, but Tennyson would not have understood why 'ongoing life' requires us to shuffle off this outgoing life; nor how a process which is 'inevitably painful, yet must progress' could do so without wondering whether the dead too will suffer loss, as their contact with the living is weakened or broken in the light of *their* ongoing life and further relationships.

---

252 *Adam Bede*, ch. 50.   253 *Memoir*, I. 323.
254 *The Anatomy of Bereavement* (1984), 186–9.

Psychological models of mourning cannot successfully be applied to the published form of *In Memoriam*, because the poem's creative evolution does not map neatly onto its finished narrative: the saddest sections were not written first; the most resigned not written last. Instead, the composed, poetic time of *In Memoriam* replaces the crude narratives imposed by clocks and calendars with the more unpredictable coincidences of heart and history which Tennyson experienced during the years of reflection that followed Arthur Hallam's death. Through *In Memoriam*'s extended development, there emerges a structure of anniversaries and domestic routines, modelled on the rhythms of the natural world (the 'fixed and perpetual necessity' of seasonal pause and resurgence which Hallam detected underpinning Tennyson's lyrical periodicities),[255] which educates a reader in the patterns of grief which outlast any particular sorrow, and recur, with different variations, in the weave of a life. As Wittgenstein remarks, 'If a man's bodily expression of sorrow and of joy alternated, say with the ticking of a clock, here we should not have the characteristic formation of the pattern of sorrow or of the pattern of joy.'[256] The trained recurrences of *In Memoriam* preserve both strands, plaited into the reader's voice, to suggest how their 'formation' is, like a rock formation, both a fixed mass and a process still underway.

Sir Charles Stanford noticed the 'many little customs' which ordered Tennyson's life at Aldworth into 'one of the most wholesome regularity':

> The daily walk from 11 to 1 and the shorter stroll in the afternoon were timed to the moment. Sometimes on returning from his morning walk he would find that he had taken five minutes less than his fixed two hours, and would insist upon finishing the allotted period by pacing up and down in front of the door.[257]

A writer's pacings, real or imagined, can have important repercussions on the pacing of his or her writing, as Valéry claimed he could hear a poem emerge in the steady rhythm of his walk,[258] or as Henry James delighted that the measured gait of his prose had not so altered with age that it prevented him from revisiting his words, black print on white page, as the footprints in snow into which his feet still snugly

[255] *Motter*, 195.
[256] *Philosophical Investigations*, 174.
[257] *Studies and Memories* (1908), repr. in *Page*, 128.
[258] See his essay 'Poetry and Abstract Thought', repr. in *The Art of Poetry*, 61–2.

fitted.[259] 'We read fine things', Keats writes to Reynolds, 'but never feel them to the full until we have gone the same steps as the Author.'[260] Steps can plot out shared stairways, in addition to an individual's tread, and so provide a useful metaphor to account for the contribution to social development which is made by the course of a single life. For example, when Arthur Hallam advised Tennyson's readers to 'perceive the proper dependence of every step on that which preceded' if he was to 'sympathize with his state', he was especially following in the footsteps of Tennyson's earlier response to the 1832 Reform Bill:[261]

> I trust the leaders of the land
>   May well surmount the coming shock
> By climbing steps their fathers carved
>   Within the living rock.[262]

This Whig view of the march of history, following and extending earlier human paths, is itself reformed in the way *In Memoriam* comes to terms with the shock of bereavement by finding its feet, poetically, in its living past. The section of 'On Sympathy' which *In Memoriam*, XLV, paraphrases had argued that, 'wherever [the child] perceives indications of pain, he is grieved. ... A great step is thus gained in the soul's progress.'[263] Similarly, Tennyson had considered calling *In Memoriam* 'The Way of the Soul', a title which pointedly equivocates between the ways of the deceased and those of his mourner, the passing of Arthur Hallam's life and the manner in which Tennyson passes his time describing it. It is by bringing together their respective progress in its own 'steps' that *In Memoriam* then links its evolution to the object of its enquiry, as the poem's steady growth enlarges the poet's sympathy with the living, while laying itself open to the prospect of Hallam becoming one of those 'Larger than human' heavenly creatures, the 'colossal Presences of the Past, *majores humano*',[264] which Tennyson associated with the evolutionary ascent of the dead.

Tennyson claimed that his 'general way' of writing *In Memoriam* was that 'if there were a blank space I would put in a poem'.[265] He also left blank spaces in his poem. The earliest surviving draft of *In Memoriam*, CXXXI, reads:

---

[259] See Philip Horne, *Henry James and Revision* (1990), 93–6.   [260] *KL*, I. 279.
[261] *Motter*, 188.   [262] 'I loving Freedom for herself', *TP*, II. 44.   [263] *Motter*, 134.
[264] 'Prologue' of Tennyson's unfinished paper on 'Ghosts', *Memoir*, I. 498.
[265] To James Knowles, *Nineteenth Century*, 33 (1893), 182.

O living will that shalt endure
When mountains shock
Rise in the spiritual rock
Flow thro' our deeds & make them pure

That we may speak from out the dust
As unto one that hears & see
Some little of the vast to be
                    trust[266]

Ezra Pound looked back in his Canto XIII to a time when authors 'left blanks in their writings, | I mean for the things they didn't know.'[267] Tennyson's draft shows that some blanks might need more than knowledge to fill; rather, such leaps of faith as were required by the gaps which he continued to preserve visibly between the stanzas and sections of his completed poem, and which concentrate attention upon the vaster reaches of space and time that *In Memoriam* repeatedly invokes, and repeatedly acknowledges that it cannot explain. Here, poetic, political, and geological change are compacted into the rhymes 'shock' and 'rock', which become footholds for the poet to surmount his past without surpassing it, their presence in the draft allowing Tennyson to generate seismic upheavals of thought (from tectonic shifts to the dusty collapse of the dead) which their very obduracy then settles into organized patterns of belief. Charles Kingsley recognized how the *In Memoriam* stanza could imagine changes which it could not encompass: 'while the major rhyme in the second and third lines of each stanza gives the solidity and self-restraint required for such deep themes, the mournful minor rhyme of each first and fourth line always leads the ear to expect something beyond'.[268] We would expect an elegist to be sensitive to line-endings, but a sustained faith in the 'something beyond' of a personal afterlife can also be seen in the gap before 'trust', itself a 'little of the vast to be', which flickers with that 'passionate earnestness' with which Tennyson's son records him holding onto 'the Reality of the Unseen'.[269] In this way, the blank spaces of *In Memoriam* provided Tennyson with opportunities to investigate vacancies which were larger and more permanent than his textual lacunae, as he learned to accommodate his voice on the page to the enduring emptiness of his surroundings:

---

[266] *TA*, III. 49.   [267] *The Cantos of Ezra Pound* (1975), 60.
[268] Unsigned review, *Fraser's Magazine*, 42 (September 1850), repr. in *TCH*, 183.
[269] *Memoir*, II. 90.

> This truth came borne with bier & pall
> I felt it when I sorrowed most
> Tis better to have loved & lost
> Than never to have loved at all.
>
> And so my passion hath not swerved
> To works of weakness but I find
> An image comforting my mind
> And in my grief a strength reserved.[270]

These consecutive stanzas in Tennyson's draft might have been the first eight lines of *In Memoriam*, LXXXV. In fact, they correspond in the published version to lines 1–4 and 49–52: 'And so' was used to justify the speaker's 'strength reserved' through the addition of eleven further stanzas. Unchanged through change, 'a strength reserved' becomes a living proof of what it describes, a composed image comforting the mind, as Tennyson's self-postponement discovers a patience in his writing like that which he would also need in his life, if he were to prove that even if he had lost Arthur Hallam, this loss too could be restored.

*

Reading Tennyson's early poems, Hallam had been struck by the modern creative temper as one which lost its social influence to the extent that it suffered the 'fresh productive spirit' of Shakespeare's time to retreat from its 'unreservedness of communion, and reciprocity of vigor between different orders of intelligence'.[271] The last section of this chapter sets out to show that the 'strength reserved' of *In Memoriam* restores this reciprocity in a way which is far removed from Harold Bloom's notion of poetry as a form of antithetical struggle. Indeed, as Tennyson searches in the textual evolution of his poem for what continues to be most wanted from its completed state—the sound of a voice that is 'influence-rich to soothe and save'—the poem's textual history is better understood as a form of sympathetic completion.[272] I have already described the problems Tennyson faced in producing dramatic monologues whose speakers are so audibly 'self-involved'. *In Memoriam* is Tennyson's longest and most reluctant dramatic monologue, as he shapes his poem in response to a silent interlocutor, Arthur Hallam, but thereby discovers Hallam's

---

[270] *TA*, XI. 265.   [271] *Motter*, 189.   [272] *IM*, LXXX, *TP*, II. 393.

voice to be sunk so deeply into his own that the twined afterlives of their writing rehearse a hope which the poem often struggles to articulate out loud: that Tennyson will continue to be 'involved in thee' even after his own death.[273] By incorporating such recollections of Arthur Hallam's own writings as allow simultaneously the mourning of a literary friendship of 'equal-poised control', and anticipation of 'some strong bond which is to be',[274] *In Memoriam* therefore evinces a more than Bloomian 'strength'. Rather, the influence upon Tennyson of Hallam, and of his own earlier self, provides a worked example of the Victorian ideal of 'strong' influence which I outlined in the second chapter of this book. Formally and ethically, the compositional history of *In Memoriam* offers an intricately worked example of a simple pairing of qualities: what Hallam Tennyson, whose own name kept alive a friendship which death seemed to have split apart, described as his father's 'union of strength with refinement'.[275]

'A VITAL SYMPATHY'

While working on his translation of Omar Khayyám, FitzGerald remarked upon the gaps in his Persian sources:

I always think it touching when in these MSS one comes upon a half finisht line as sometimes happens; I suppose sometimes the Scribe could not decypher his original, and left a space which he meant to fill in one day— which never came! ... MSS have a vital Sympathy with us which our printed books cannot have ... [276]

FitzGerald's comment also comes in a handwritten manuscript: a letter to Edward Cowell, which forms one fragment of the wide-ranging correspondence through which he attempted to create a comparable 'vital Sympathy' on the page. A private letter is 'vital' and 'touching' because it is directed by and towards a living hand, like a handshake at one remove. However tightly ordered its structure, or polished its expressions, this sort of letter is only ever 'half finisht' on the page because, like Arthur Hallam's sonnet 'To I. M. G. II', its sentiments are 'half fulfilled' by their

---

[273] See *IM*, XVI, LXXXIV, *TP*, II. 334, 396.   [274] *IM*, CXVI, *TP*, II. 437.

[275] *Memoir*, I. 35; compare T. H. Warren on Tennyson's 'union of strength and sensitiveness', *Page*, 155.

[276] *EFGL*, II. 253.

transference into writing, but also 'half wait the future day' on which they will be read by the person whose responses they anticipate and invite.[277] The momentary delay which interrupts FitzGerald's own letter ('which he meant to fill in one day—which never came!') is, then, not simply a local interval in his text, but—to borrow Tennyson's coinage—a concentrated proof of its 'intervital' status,[278] creating a visible confession of incompletion which is also an appeal. In the final section of this chapter, I shall be showing how the textual development of *In Memoriam A. H. H.* investigates and extends this principle of 'intervital' writing, by thickening the voice which Tennyson projects through his elegy with the voice of its subject. The *A. H. H.* of his title is both a sigh and a signature.

*

Hallam Tennyson described how, on one of the 'sad winter days' which followed news of Arthur Hallam's death, his father 'noted down in his scrap-book some fragmentary lines, which proved to be the germ of "In Memoriam":

> Where is the voice that I have loved? ah where
> Is that dear hand that I would press?'[279]

One answer to 'ah where' was to be provided by the entranced climax of *In Memoriam*, XCV, in which Arthur Hallam's voice is, at last, conjured out of letters which have 'kept their green', until, at once, 'The living soul was flashed on mine.'[280] An earlier answer was provided by Tennyson's revision of 'Mariana in the South'. In 1842, lines 9–12 changed the object of Mariana's devotions from 'Madonna' to the more narcissistic 'Mary':

> But 'Ave Mary,' made she moan,
>   And 'Ave Mary,' night and morn,
> And 'Ah,' she sang, 'to be all alone,
>   To live forgotten, and love forlorn.'[281]

Abandoned by her lover, but unable to leave off talking about him, her rejected flesh dissolves into a sigh, from Mariana to '*Ah*'. She also

---

[277] *Motter*, 74.   [278] *IM*, XLIII, *TP*, II. 360 (the first recorded use in *OED*).
[279] *Memoir*, I. 107.   [280] *TP*, II. 413.   [281] *TP*, I. 397.

turns to A. H. H. As published in 1832, 'Mariana in the South' had borne witness to Tennyson's tour of the Pyrenees with Hallam in 1830. Hallam approved of the change of style between 'Mariana' and 'Mariana in the South':

> You will, I think, agree with me that the essential & distinguishing character of the conception requires in the Southern Mariana a greater lingering on the outward circumstances, and a less palpable transition of the poet into Mariana's feelings, than was the case in the former poem.[282]

Revising the poem for his 1842 volume, Tennyson lingered further, by adding twenty-three lines which follow Mariana's dream that her lover 'was and was not there'. Like the speaker left 'all alone' in *In Memoriam*, XCV, she takes from her breast 'old letters', but on this occasion they summon another speaker, who completes an *In Memoriam* stanza in his or her own words:

> An image seemed to pass the door,
>   To look at her with slight, and say
>   'But now thy beauty flows away,
> So be alone for evermore.'   (ll. 65–8)

Allusion provides a particularly rich creative resource for staging a speaker's feeling that the focus of her attention both is and is not there, as it measures thoughts of human abandonment against its own poetic retrievals. Here, for example, we notice how Tennyson's addition of an *In Memoriam* stanza to this earlier investigation of loss produces an imaginative parallel between Mariana's situation and his own: allusion as an expression of solidarity. At the same time, the echo of *In Memoriam* provides a way of distinguishing between a speaker who is coming to accept that she will be 'alone for evermore', and one who understands that his loneliness represents the lingering trace of a mutual dependence which will eventually be restored: allusion as the discovery of difference. So many of *In Memoriam*'s literary echoes emerge from contexts of loss (the splintered remains of earlier elegies that rise unpredictably to the surface of Tennyson's verse, like the debris of shipwrecks), that the very process of allusion can sound like a form of mourning. Yet those allusions which seek points of contact between one context of loss and another, as Tennyson's allusions to Hallam's own writings frequently do, also come to speak of what has

---

[282] *Kolb*, 401.

survived the changes which both writers have experienced: a friendship that developed through the physical contact of their hands with
one another, but also through their developing intimacy on paper,
hand in hand even when they were joined only by their writing. This
may explain why, as Mariana reads letters 'breathing of her worth'
(compare 'love's dumb cry defying change | To test his worth' in *In
Memoriam*, XCV), the phrase is squeezed so tightly against 'from her
bosom' that the breath which animates it cannot readily distinguish
between the feelings of sender and receiver. It is a syntactic embrace
which echoes the sympathetic ambition of *In Memoriam*, XVIII:

> Ah yet, even yet, if this might be,
>   I, falling on his faithful heart,
>   Would breathing through his lips impart
> The life that almost dies in me ... [283]

Again, 'breathing through his lips' does not discriminate between
normal breathing and artificial respiration, because by giving Hallam
breath, a kiss of life, the poet himself may be inspired.

  This could easily drift into a less productive form of sympathy with
the dead, as the survivor proclaims his desire to exchange his life for
the return of the person who has died, and so uses his voice to reach
what Joseph Brodsky has acutely described as 'a certain emotional
limit that spares the imagination further responsibility'.[284] Tennyson
recognized in himself the temptation for the bereaved to collapse into
a sentimental eloquence that spares them the additional pain of
thinking about their loss, but he also recognized that only the living
are afforded the luxury of entertaining this sort of alternative life for
themselves. The original publication of 'To J. S.' in 1832, for example,
attempted to comfort James Spedding on the loss of his brother with
the claim that, 'to calm you I would take | The place of him that
sleeps in peace'. FitzGerald, whose eye for the overwritten and
underthought phrase was usually sharper when reading his friend's
poems than his own, was not fooled: 'I used to ask if this was not *un peu
trop fort* ... It is all rather affected.' By 1842, Tennyson would have
agreed: the revised version reads, 'myself could almost take | The
place of him that sleeps in peace'.[285] Almost, but not quite. *In
Memoriam* expresses a similar ambivalence over the need to abandon

---

[283] *TP*, II. 337.   [284] *Less Than One*, 219.
[285] *TP*, I. 506; FitzGerald's note is in his copy of the 1842 *Poems*.

speech for death, and the need not to, because it is only by allowing his friend's words to take the place of his own on the page that Tennyson can measure what they once had in common, and might continue to have in common if this shared textual afterlife proved to be an accurate model for the human afterlife which it describes. For this reason, it is especially significant that Hallam had quoted the earlier version of 'Mariana in the South' complete in a letter to a mutual friend.[286] When Tennyson came to republish this poem in 1842, he could therefore respond to *In Memoriam*'s haunted question (written in 1841): 'Do we indeed desire the dead | Should still be near us at our side?', by showing in his revisions, so often sensitive to absent bodies and to those which must live on, that he continued to hear Hallam's voice at his side.[287]

Hallam had introduced his discussion of Tennyson's *Poems, Chiefly Lyrical* with the warning that they were 'preludes of a loftier strain'.[288] Several of these early poems are echoed in *In Memoriam*, as Tennyson reaches back to lines which Hallam knew and extends their imaginative scope. Certain of these echoes confirm the analogies which, I have suggested, existed for Tennyson between the continuity of life and afterlife, and his own creative coherences. Consider, for example, the 'still garden' of 'The Lover's Tale', in which young lovers grow up together in 'earthly-heavenliest harmony', or the 'still garden' of 'The Gardener's Daughter', which witnesses 'How passion rose through circumstantial grades | Beyond all grades developed'. *In Memoriam*, XLIII, revisits both gardens in 'that still garden of the souls', and so suggests that even this timeless setting has seen some changes in its time.[289] Or we might pause over some lines which Tennyson added to 'The Lotos-Eaters' in 1842:

> ... but all hath suffered change:
> ... Our sons inherit us: our looks are strange:
> And we should come like ghosts to trouble joy.[290]

In Memoriam reflects upon the same danger in the same terms: in both poems, the return of the dead, or missing-presumed-dead, to their old houses is described as an event which makes 'confusion worse than death'.[291] However, it does not follow from this that Tennyson's poetic inheritance provides a worked example of *apophrades*, Bloom's

---

[286] *Kolb*, 401–4.   [287] *IM*, LI, *TP*, II. 367.   [288] *Motter*, 191.
[289] *TP*, I. 338, 565; II. 361.   [290] *TP*, I. 473.
[291] 'The Lotos-Eaters', l.128, *IM*, XC, *TP*, I. 473, II. 408.

strongest revisionary ratio, because where these rhymes are recovered, with the imagined return of Hallam from a sea-voyage, it
is not to trouble joy, but to confirm it:

> [If] I perceived no touch of change,
>   No hint of death in all his frame,
>   But found him all in all the same,
> I should not feel it to be strange.[292]

Hallam's father, whose memoir of his son's life praised his 'great
and lofty expectations',[293] understood that an inevitable part of
mourning one who died so young would involve wondering how he
would have changed, had he survived, and how 'strange' these
changes would have made his later writing. Even the accomplished
essays which Hallam produced towards the end of his life were
regularly discussed, by the friends who survived him, as 'preludes of
a loftier strain': halting early drafts of the work he did not live to let his
readers see.[294] But then Hallam was always a promising writer, as full
of promises as he was of promise. Several of his essays end with an
expectant fade:

… But these considerations I must leave to some other and more favourable
opportunity.[295]

… who knows whether even we might not disappoint [the malice of the
Englishman's Magazine] by a cheerful adaptation of our theory to 'existing
circumstances'?[296]

… which further reflection may bring to light.[297]

If he had continued to develop at the same rate, his father suggested,
'the very highest rank among the Poets of thought and philosophy
would have been at his command'—but only as a critic.[298] This
reference to 'Poets', more evaluative than descriptive, does not tell
us much about Hallam's skill in writing verse. Tennyson's assessment
was more discriminating: 'He would have been known, if he had lived,

---

[292] *IM*, XIV, answering Ariel's song from *The Tempest*: 'Nothing of him that doth
fade, | But doth suffer a sea-change | Into something rich and strange' (I. ii. 398–404),
TP, II. 333.

[293] *Remains in Verse and Prose of Arthur Henry Hallam*, ed. Henry Hallam (1863), xxxiii.

[294] Ibid.

[295] 'On Sympathy', *Motter*, 142.

[296] 'On Some of the Characteristics … ', repr. in *Motter*, 198.

[297] 'Theodiciae Novissima', *Motter*, 212.

[298] *Remains in Verse and Prose of Arthur Henry Hallam*, xxxiii.

as a great man but not as a great poet.'[299] The idea that Hallam would
not have developed into a great poet is probably just (his surviving
poems are better at striking attitudes than they are at controlling his
emotional or technical resources), but it was a troubling one for
Tennyson to contemplate, given that he had once trusted in the
sympathy of their writing enough to have seriously considered plans
for a joint publication. *In Memoriam* provides touching evidence that
Tennyson never fully abandoned this plan, as he adopts fragments of
his friend's writings, and so dramatizes his poem's developing enquiry
into how Hallam's restricted literary development (he died before his
potential as a writer could be fulfilled) could be reconciled with
Tennyson's own restricted human development (his promise as a
person cannot be fulfilled until he has died). Take *In Memoriam*, VIII,
which expresses how 'all is dark where thou art not', by recalling
anxieties which Hallam had earlier directed towards Emily Tennyson:

> Thou hearest not, alas! thou art afar,
> And I am lone as ever, sick and lone
> Roaming the weary desert of my doom
> Where thou art not, altho' all speaks of thee.[300]

Now that Hallam's poem survives where he has not, Tennyson
discovers in it words to describe his own anticipated reunion with a
beloved, as he replies in kind to the need for sympathy which his
friend had earlier claimed. He can mourn for Hallam because Hallam too could once mourn.

T. S. Eliot famously observed of *In Memoriam*: 'It is a long poem
made by putting together lyrics, which have only the unity and
continuity of a diary, the concentrated diary of a man confessing
himself.'[301] But like all confessions, a diary will also bear the traces
of other speakers: all the friends, enemies, and indifferent observers
whose imagined voices form the background against which the writer
projects his expressions of self-accusation and self-justification. It is by
bringing together speculations about Hallam's 'Unused example' with
the scraps he has salvaged from his friend's writing that Tennyson
can fulfil their promise without compromising his own literary development ('Unused example' is itself a self-borrowing).[302] The new

[299] *Memoir*, I. 38; compare II. 70.   [300] 'To Two Sisters' [II], *Motter*, 90.
[301] 'In Memoriam', repr. in *Selected Prose of T. S. Eliot*, 243.
[302] *IM*, LXXX, *TP*, II. 393 and n. Ricks (*Tennyson*, 220) notes Tennyson's habit of
incorporating into *In Memoriam* 'details of Hallam's life and writings'.

directions he silently turns these lines in, with that 'graceful tact' he praised Hallam for possessing,[303] then confirm Tennyson to have been the better poet, and getting better, even as he wonders aloud how much better than a poet Hallam might now be. 'Tennyson', complained Verlaine, 'when he should have been broken-hearted, had many reminiscences.'[304] 'The interesting question', for A. C. Bradley, 'is whether most of the "borrowings" in Tennyson's poetry are to be regarded as coincidences or as reminiscences.'[305] Many of his borrowings from Hallam are both, a coincidence of reminiscence: broken off from their source, and heartbroken in their incompleteness, they return to the forward-looking stance of Hallam's writings and retune them into 'broken lights' of his own future state:[306]

> We ranging down this lower track,
>   The path we came by, thorn and flower,
>   Is shadowed by the growing hour,
> Lest life should fail in looking back.

Tennyson commented: 'If there was a perfect memory of all sorrows & sins we should not be able to bear it.'[307] However, his own lines are shadowed by a poem which uses the growing hour to look forward, not back:

> My own dear sister, thy career
> Is all before thee, thorn and flower:
> Scarce hast thou known by joy or fear
> The still heart-pride of Friendship's hour.[308]

Once again, Tennyson's allusion reflects on the past, but is then redirected by it towards the future: an afterlife which will reveal 'The eternal landscape of the past', of which this 'thorn and flower' is but a momentary glance.

As expressions of faith, these echoes of Hallam in Tennyson's lines suggest the shared spiritual trajectory of their lives. As poetry, the same lines supplement their mourning for Hallam with an intermittent regret for one of the sources of their own creative power. *In Memoriam*,

---

303 *IM*, CX, *TP*, II. 432.
304 Verlaine, reported by Yeats, 'Verlaine in 1894', *The Savoy*, 2 (April 1896), 118.
305 *A Commentary on 'In Memoriam'*, 72.
306 *IM*, Prologue: 'Our little systems ... are but broken lights of thee' (*TP*, II. 316); Hallam: 'On Free Submission to God's Will': 'The broken light of a sunned waterfall', which the speaker begins 'to moralise ... Into quaint semblances of higher things' (*Motter*, 67–8).
307 To Knowles; see *TP*, II. 363n.
308 'On My Sister's Birthday', *Motter*, 60.

CXII, praises Hallam's 'novel power' ('For what wert thou? some novel power | Sprang up for ever at a touch'), by shading the public compliment with a private nod to the self-astonishment of an early poem: 'What novel power is mine that makes me bold?'[309] Tennyson's borrowing fulfils one duty of poetic allusion: to answer the question which his original has come to represent; it goes further by retaining the questioning presence behind Hallam's line, and so recognizes that even the answer provided by this line will invite revision, given how easily our memories of the dead can be reshaped to fit the needs of the living. The form of *In Memoriam* supports this vigilant, provisional stance of the speaker towards Hallam, because a 'novel power' is also what it builds into the echoes which keep Tennyson's elegy audibly in contact with its subject. Even where its troubled questions about the place and status of Hallam are largely replaced by confident descriptions of him as the 'herald of a higher race',[310] the poem retains its earlier ability to be surprised by the fissures of argument and expression into which Hallam's voice has seeped, so that the question 'what wert thou?' can open itself out through the poem as the shadowy twin of the other question which *In Memoriam* continues to put to Hallam, and to itself: 'what art thou?'

Hallam had argued that Tennyson's mind could not be judged by fragments because it 'conceives nothing isolated, nothing abrupt, but every part with reference to some other part, and in subservience to the idea of the whole'.[311] R. H. Hutton, replying to Bagehot's criticism of Tennyson's 'ornate' poetry, agreed: 'We should object to ornate poetry simply because it does *not* individualize, because it fails to connect the many touches into a living whole.'[312] *In Memoriam*, LV, sets out Tennyson's belief that this is not only a literary problem:

> The wish, that of the living whole
> No life may fail beyond the grave,
> Derives it not from what we have
> The likest God within the soul?[313]

---

[309] Untitled sonnet, repr. in *Victorian Poetry*, 3 (December 1965), 9.

[310] *IM*, CIII, *TP*, II 425.

[311] *Motter*, 42–3. Compare R. H. Horne (ed.), *A New Spirit of the Age*, 164: 'there is nothing broken or incomplete in his two full volumes. His few "fragments" are entire in themselves, and suggest the remainder.'

[312] *A Victorian Spectator*, 85.

[313] *TP*, II. 370.

Tennyson claimed that *In Memoriam* expressed the view: 'We are parts of the infinite whole.'[314] Together, his allusions to Hallam's writings reflect his hope that, even after death, 'we' shall remain distinct within this whole, simultaneously a part of and set apart from one another, like the sections of his poem. Compare:

> Friend of old times, and places faint in mind,
> Th'innumerable waves divide us now ... [315]

and:

> If thou wert with me, and the grave
>   Divide us not, be with me now,
>   And enter in at breast and brow
> Till all my blood, a fuller wave,
>
> Be quickened with a livelier breath ... [316]

Hallam's 'divide us now' is itself divided and rejoined in Tennyson's yearning for his blood to pump more thickly in his friend's living presence—'Divide us [not, be with me] now'—and this 'fuller wave' too stirs the rhythmic and expressive surfaces of his verse. Notice the faint irruption of dactyls into 'livelier breath' to 'quicken' the hope of which it speaks, as Tennyson adjusts his voice to the 'deep pulsations of the world' in which Hallam can now be heard.[317] Notice, too, in the lingering monosyllables of his line-endings, evidence of what T. S. Eliot described as Tennyson's fine 'ear for vowel sounds'.[318] Many of Tennyson's listeners remarked upon the way he intoned his vowels. When H. D. Rawnsley heard Tennnyson read 'Ode on the Death of the Duke of Wellington' in 1884, he observed 'how he lengthened out the vowel *a* in the words 'great' and 'lamentation' till the words seemed as if they had been spelt 'greaat' and 'lamentaation', and how he rolled out and lengthened the open oes in the words 'To the nooise of the moourning of a mighty naation'.[319] FitzGerald heard something similar, and drew upon Tennyson's fictional account of a recitation of the 'Morte d'Arthur' to express what he heard: 'Mouthing out his hollow oes and aes, deep-chested music,

---

[314] Reported by William Knight, 'A Reminiscence of Tennyson'(1897), repr. in *Page*, 183.
[315] Arthur Hallam, 'To One Early Loved, Now in India', *Motter*, 78.
[316] *IM*, CXXII, *TP*, II. 442.
[317] *IM*, XCV, *TP*, II. 413.
[318] 'In Memoriam', repr. in *Selected Prose of T. S. Eliot*, 246.
[319] *Page*, 63.

this is something as A. T. reads....His voice, very deep and deep-chested ... like the sound of a far sea.'[320]

T. S. Eliot was alert to the way Tennyson's verse sounds out more than first meets the ear:

The surface of Tennyson stirred about with his time; and he had nothing to which to hold fast except his unique and unerring feeling for the sounds of words.... Tennyson's surface, his technical accomplishment, is intimate with his depths.[321]

Tennyson's verse in *In Memoriam* is stirred as much by the timeless as it is by the contingent pressures of his time, because it is by concentrating Hallam's 'waves' into his own 'fuller wave' that he generates verbal surfaces which are intimate with the immortal deeps towards which he imagines himself journeying; his oes and aes are long, but they are also longing. Put another way, the full 'circumstances' of these lines (*OED*: 'That which stands around or surrounds materially, morally, or logically') encourage the voice of their reader to submit to the pressures of more than the material world; rather, what Tennyson once described as 'A great ocean pressing round us on every side, and only leaking in by a few chinks.'[322] Or, as he also put it, with a characteristic mixture of modesty and pride, 'I can sympathize with God in my poor little way.'[323]

---

[320] *Memoir*, I. 162. Donald S. Hair, *Tennyson's Language* (1991), compares Augustus and Julius Hare, *Guesses at Truth* (1827), read by Arthur Hallam in 1828, which argues that 'the proportion between the vowels and consonants in a language will shew the relative influence of the feelings and of the understanding over the people who speak it... the interjections in which our bursting emotions find vent, consist chiefly of vowels, repeated sometimes over and over again' (62).

[321] 'In Memoriam', repr. in *Selected Prose of T. S. Eliot*, 246.

[322] *Allingham* (6 November 1884), 333; Tennyson is drawing upon commonplaces of spiritualist vocabulary; compare William James, 'Our "normal" consciousness is circumscribed for adaptation to our external earthly environment, but the fence is weak in spots, and fitful influences from beyond leak in' ('Final Impressions of a Psychical Researcher' (1909), repr. in F. O. Matthiessen (ed.), *The James Family* (1948), 589); and 'The Manners of Posthumous Man', *Cornhill Magazine*, n.s., 1 (July–December 1883), which explains how ghosts 'can flow in through chinks' (223).

[323] *Memoir*, I. 320.

4 Edward FitzGerald: Under the Influence

Reading through Tennyson's 1842 *Poems*, FitzGerald recalled an earlier occasion on which 'Morte d'Arthur' had been brought to life:

Resting on our oars one calm day on Windemere ... at the end of May 1835,—resting on our oars, and looking into the lake quite unruffled and clear, [Tennyson] quoted from the lines he had lately read us from the MS of 'Morte d'Arthur' about the lonely Lady of the Lake and Excalibur.

> Nine days she wrought it, sitting all alone
> Upon the hidden bases of the Hills.

'Not bad that, Fitz, is it?'[1]

The story is not bad either, the way FitzGerald tells it, as the internal echoes of 'looking into the lake ... lonely Lady of the Lake' sympathetically bring to the surface of his account a point of imaginative contact between the poet and his subject, both silently observed in the throes of creation, and 'quite unruffled and clear' discovers a reflection of Tennyson's composed delivery in the undisturbed surface of the lake. However, Tennyson might not have remained unruffled if he had known that FitzGerald's account would misquote the lines which he claimed to have heard so clearly:

> Nine years she wrought it, sitting in the deeps
> Upon the hidden bases of the hills.[2]

'Sitting all alone' is an understandable substitution for 'sitting in the deeps', because the lines immediately preceding these describe 'King Arthur's sword, Excalibur, | Wrought by the lonely maiden of the Lake', which suggests that here FitzGerald's memory has merged two

---

[1] 'Some Recollections of Tennyson's Talk from 1835 to 1853', in Hallam Tennyson (ed.), *Tennyson and his Friends* (1911), 142.
[2] *TP*, II. 10–11.

lines of verse in much the same way that 'quite unruffled and clear' had earlier merged two lines of thought. But 'Nine days' is strangely removed from 'Nine years', because the Lady of the Lake fashions Excalibur according to Horace's advice in the *Ars Poetica* ('nonumque prematur in annum, | membranis intus positis'),[3] and since these lines were printed in 1842, but have their foundations in 1833 (the 'bases of the hills' were quarried from *The Lover's Tale*, and remained hidden once this poem was withdrawn from publication),[4] it is an additional felicity of 'Nine years she wrought it' that Tennyson's verse embodies the Horatian reserve which it describes: the patience, demanded of any writer who expects his work to last, which in these lines is a presence as well as a theme.

FitzGerald set great store by his powers of recall, referring to himself in one letter as 'the venerable Remembrancer',[5] even if the growing frequency with which his letters misquote other writers suggests a still more time-honoured connection, between the advancing age of his mind and the increasingly ambitious clogging and wandering of his memories.[6] FitzGerald is not alone in having a bad memory. Borges tells a sharp fable about the man who remembered everything, and 'knew by heart the forms of the southern clouds at dawn on 30 April 1882, and could compare them in his memory with the mottled streaks on a book in Spanish binding he had only seen once and with the outlines of the foam raised by an oar in the Rio Negro the night before the Quebracho uprising'; but as the spectator of a world only ever seen in intolerably precise detail, like an infinitely extended Pre-Raphaelite painting, he is almost incapable of thought: 'To think is to forget differences, generalize, make abstractions ... His own face in the mirror, his own hands, surprised him every time he saw them.'[7] Nor is FitzGerald alone in being compassionately interested in the shared problem of human loneliness, even if 'The lonely Lady of the Lake' who, in his version of Tennyson's lines, is 'sitting all alone', implies a distinction between being lonely and merely being alone to which somebody who lives on their own, as FitzGerald did

---

[3] 'Put your parchment in the closet and keep it back until the ninth year', *Ars Poetica*, ll. 388–9; I quote from the parallel-text edition of H. Rushdon Fairclough (1926), 482–3.

[4] See *TP*, II. 11n.; the earlier volume was in fact published at the end of 1832, but was dated 1833.

[5] *EFGL*, IV. 343. Further references appear in the main text.

[6] See, e.g., *EFGL*, I. 302, 337, 432, 444; II. 78, 219, 374, 413, 487; III. 131, 224, 365, 391, 434, 447, 491, 516, 543, 550, 625, 632.

[7] 'Funes the Memorious', trans. James E. Irby, repr. in *Labyrinths* (1964, repr. 1970), 92–4.

during the many years which bracketed his brief attempt at marriage, might be especially sensitive. Arnold spoke for much of his dispersed and divided readership, as well as for himself, when he pointed out that it is not only immortal individuals, like the Lady of the Lake, who are 'all alone'. We are all alone:

> YES! in the sea of life enisled,
> With echoing straits between us thrown,
> Dotting the shoreless watery wild,
> We mortal millions live *alone*.[8]

That sudden emphasis on '*alone*' sharply focuses a widespread and growing anxiety of the period, that our natural loneliness is being multiplied by time, which also forms one imaginative centre of FitzGerald's literary career.

The range and variety of FitzGerald's references to his solitary existence, self-consciously removed from his fellow human beings by echoing straits of space and understanding, invite comparisons with T. S. Eliot's assessment of Tennyson:

It happens now and then that a poet by some strange accident expresses the mood of his generation, at the same time that he is expressing a mood of his own which is quite remote from that of his generation.[9]

Much of FitzGerald's correspondence investigates the accidents of character and circumstance which led to him being 'quite remote' from his contemporaries; the flexible meaning of 'quite' in Eliot's description—equally open to 'extremely' and 'slightly'—further suggests a distinctive hinge of thought and tone on which individual letters turn:

I am sitting as of old in my accustomed Bedroom, looking out on a Landscape which your Eyes would drink. It is said there has not been such a Flush of Verdure for years: and they are making hay on the Lawn before the house, so one wakes to the tune of the Mower's Scythe-whetting, and with the old Perfume blowing in at open windows.[10]

The idea that the air brings back familiar smells or carries old tunes is a mid-Victorian commonplace, as I argued in Chapter 2, but the way FitzGerald chooses to describe this revival is peculiarly his own, as he

---

[8] 'To Marguerite—continued' (1852); I quote from Kenneth Allott's edition of the poems (1954, repr. 1985), 136.

[9] 'In Memoriam', repr. in *Selected Prose of T. S. Eliot*, 243.

[10] Letter to Edward Cowell, quoted in A. C. Benson, *Edward FitzGerald* (1905), 191.

adopts the slightly archaic 'Flush of Verdure' and brings it back to life in the warm glow of his prose ('making hay' hints that it is not only in the grass that sap is rising). FitzGerald's choice of phrase is fully characteristic of the stereoscopic imagination which allowed him to be in two places or times at once. Its place in this account is equally characteristic of his haunted understanding that it is only human beings for whom this sort of scene would provide a source of regret. For although nature has its renewals, it has no memory, and so could be forever at odds with someone whose thinking was mostly done in the past tense: 'Only after we have to part with a thing do we feel its value—unless indeed *after* we have parted with it.'[11] For FitzGerald, human beings, too, were best appreciated after they had been parted with, because although many people discover that their most abiding affections are tested by memory, FitzGerald's were largely created by it. Some of this may be connected to the erotic-sentimental friendships with younger men which he enjoyed, or endured, because his attraction to their youth was by definition short-lived, forever poised on the brink of nostalgia. But even his oldest friends might have been worried by FitzGerald's tendency to use his writing not only to come to terms with his settled social isolation but also actively to prepare for fresh losses. Many of his letters read like a set of footnotes to the longing, expressed by the hero of Henry James's short story 'The Altar of the Dead', to speed up the steady drift of the living into a less independent posthumous existence:

There were hours at which he almost caught himself wishing that certain of his friends would die, that he might establish with them in this manner a connexion more charming than, as it happened, it was possible to enjoy with them in life. In regard to those from whom one was separated by the long curves of the globe such a connexion could only be an improvement; it brought them instantly within reach.[12]

FitzGerald, similarly, preferred social 'connexions' once they had been organized into the private constellations of memory. In 1852, Thackeray wrote an affectionate letter to his 'best and oldest friend', in which he explained that he was to spend the next six months lecturing in America.[13] The regret expressed in FitzGerald's reply does not limit itself to Thackeray's departure:

[11] Preface to *Polonius, A Collection of Wise Saws and Modern Instances* (1852), repr. in *EFGW*, V. 204.
[12] 'The Altar of the Dead' (1895), repr. in *Ten Short Stories of Henry James* (1948), 219.
[13] *EFGL*, II. 71.

I had your note—I dare scarce read it as it lies in my desk. It affects me partly as those old foolscap letters did, of which I told you I burned so many this spring: and why: I was really ashamed of their kindness! If ever we get to another world, you will perhaps know why all this is so. I must not talk any more of what I have so often tried to explain to you. Meanwhile, I truly believe there is no Man alive loves you (in his own way of love) more than I do. Now you are gone out [of] England, I can feel something of what I should feel for you if you were dead ... were you back again, I should see no more of you than before. But this is not from want of love on my part: it is because we live in different worlds: and it is almost painful to me to tease anybody with my seedy dullness, which is just bearable by myself. Life every day seems a more total failure and mess to me: but it is yet bearable: and I am become a sad Epicurean ...   (*EFGL*, II. 75)

However painful this was to write, it is now wincingly painful to read, as FitzGerald's 'seedy dullness' causes his prose to twitch into life with 'but it is yet bearable': a meeting of endurance and despair which the rest of the letter moves towards like a vice. It is difficult to know how Thackeray was expected to respond to the news that FitzGerald could now 'feel something of what I should feel for you if you were dead', as if the only opportunity to enjoy a friendship free of the mutual shame and social awkwardness which now separated their 'different worlds' would be provided by their reunion in 'another world' altogether. But Thackeray would have recognized the importance of the letter itself as a way of articulating these feelings, because it was through the letters which he sent and received that FitzGerald could simultaneously bridge 'different worlds' and keep them at a respectful distance from one another.

In 1842, FitzGerald explained to Frederick Tennyson why he preferred to see Italy through somebody else's eyes. Experienced at first hand, the country would be refracted through a set of impressions already gleaned from its existence in the parallel world of art, 'with the additional annoyance of being bitten with fleas perhaps'. By travelling the world at one remove, however, as his eyes roamed across the letters he received from abroad, his view of the foreign could be framed by the reassuring familiarity of his correspondent's ways: 'Like the Lady of Shalott I should be dished if I turned to gaze at the truth' (*EFGL*, I. 332). His literary translations show a similar desire to gaze at foreign subjects through a mirror which worked in time as well as space. *Rubáiyát*, in particular, provided FitzGerald with an impeccable scholarly justification for his most intimate obsessions, because it allowed him to inspect the world through several pairs of eyes other than his own, including those of the friend who had first introduced him to the study of Persian, Edward Cowell.

By writing to Cowell in India, and enclosing his translations of Omar Khayyám, FitzGerald extended their friendship on paper in directions which largely followed the lines of the poet they had once translated together in person. Cast into 'monkish Latin', the first quatrains of *Rubáiyát* which FitzGerald sent to Cowell begin with renewal: 'Tempus est quo Orientis Aura mundis renovatur' ('This is the season when the world is refreshed by the breeze of the East', *EFGL*, II. 273). Translated into English, these lines reappear unchanged in every edition of the poem:

> Now the New Year reviving old Desires,
> The thoughtful Soul to Solitude retires (1st edn., IV)

'The wonder is that no critic has observed that FitzGerald's lines make no sense: for why should anyone return to solitude because Spring has come?'[14] One answer is suggested by the illicit nature of the love to which FitzGerald's own fancies regularly and ruefully turned, which gives a reproachful sting to 'old Desires' (the ageing would-be lover who is conscious that this sort of same-sex attachment seemed more acceptable in Omar's time than in his own), and to 'thoughtful' ('oh, not *again*'). Another is FitzGerald's attraction to Spring as a time which invited expressions of shock over lost potential, but which could then be brooded over in a style that controlled these losses by making their surprises more predictable. This is why FitzGerald's 'Now' overlays a time of recollection and the time it conjures up, because he sends his translation '*almost* a Year since we last met at Rushmere: your MS of Omar was [finished] July 11, 1856 and I believe I left you that day or the next' (*EFGL*, II. 274).

When FitzGerald writes to Tennyson of Omar's appeal ('Drink— for the Moon will often come round to look for us in this Garden and find us not') the sudden, decisive transplantation of the Persian setting to a garden comes in a paragraph which returns to the 'us' who first read Omar's quatrains in the Cowells' garden (*EFGL*, II. 234). The published version whittles down 'us' to a solitary 'me':

> How oft hereafter rising shall she look
> Through this same Garden after me—in vain! (1st edn., LXXIV)

---

[14] Sir E. Denison Ross (ed.), Golden Cockerel Edition of *ROK* (1938), 100.

'He has gone and we too will all go' is the accusing flourish of Persian which opens FitzGerald's first letter to India, and the textual evolution of *Rubáiyát* is largely structured by these memorial allegiances, as FitzGerald translates and revises quatrains which describe the 'sort of *triste Plaisir*' of seeing everything pass away,[15] through the 'strange sort of Pleasure' of remembering a second writer in the East, Cowell, whose absence had moved him to secure their survival (*EFGL*, II. 224, 322):

> 'You know how little while we have to stay,
> And, once departed, may return no more.' (1st edn., III)

I passed through [your former home] a week ago; it looked so pretty ... that it made me sad remembering the Days that are no more.   (To Cowell, *EFGL*, III. 725)[16]

In this way, a line like 'Jesus-spiritusque Salutaris terram pervagatur' ('And the life-giving spirit of Jesus pervades the earth') still 'breathes a sort of Consolation' to FitzGerald, but one he cannot fully place, because it returns him to the time when he and Cowell worked side-by-side on the same transcript, but it is to his renewed solitude that he owes the 'remorseful delight' of its remembrance (*EFGL*, II. 4). As Cowell moved to and from the East while remaining, through his letters of scholarly advice, 'Thou | Beside me singing in the Wilderness' (the equivocal syntax emulates *Rubáiyát*'s shared authorship by encouraging 'singing' to mediate between 'Thou' and 'me'), so the movement of these letters makes of FitzGerald's translation both a 'carrying over' of Omar into England ('translatus' as the past participle of 'transferre'), and something he carries on with: 'transferre' includes the sense of endurance.

This chapter argues that FitzGerald's interest in questions of literary endurance reflects his private imaginative habits, but also more general principles of composition, because in the same way that his letters assert a sense of continuity and community with the individuals to whom his poem owes so much of its imaginative life, so the study of translation turns out to be an investigation into the way a culture renews itself through contact with the geographically and linguistically foreign, and with its own forebears estranged by time. As he waited for Tennyson's 1842 *Poems* to be published, FitzGerald offered

---

[15] Quoted in A. C. Benson, *Edward FitzGerald*, 114.

[16] Recalling Tennyson, 'So sad, so strange, the days that are no more', 'Tears, idle tears', *TP*, II. 233.

a critical judgement which has not yet been disproved: '... with all his faults, he will publish such a volume ... which, once published, will never be suffered to die. This is my prophecy: for I live before Posterity' (*EFGL*, I. 315). The generosity of this prophecy can be heard in the echo of 'Morte d'Arthur' which rises up in FitzGerald's voice: ' "Arthur is come again: he cannot die" ',[17] as his letter tests and confirms the idea that Tennyson's poem will meet the needs of posterity by being absorbed into the common life of print. FitzGerald was more confident than many of his contemporaries, including Tennyson, that posterity would know what was good for it, or that a prophet could clarify anything apart from his own prejudices. James Froude's declaration in 1868 that 'none can tell what will be after us',[18] for example, had reference to more than the sense of inexpressible possibility which thinking about the future invites. It also gestured warily towards the idea that what is 'after us' will be a more absolute affair than merely one generation of humans inheriting the successes and failures of another. With the laws of thermodynamics pointing towards a distant but inevitable death of the sun, even the Positivist future was end-stopped:

> Yon rising Moon that looks for us again—
> How oft hereafter will she wax and wane;
> How oft hereafter rising look for us
> Through this same Garden—and for *one* in vain!
>
> (5th edn., C)

Like most of *Rubáiyát*'s rhetorical questions, 'How oft hereafter' is not one that can yet be answered, because to know precisely when '*one* in vain' will stop referring to the deaths of individual humans, and will instead refer to the death of the species, would be to know the date on which recorded history itself will stop. But even within the more limited timespan already covered by literature, the moon might rightly confuse whether she is looking at 'us' or at 'one' when she lights upon the grave of a translator.

'We mortal millions live *alone*': Arnold's claim offers a sympathetic expansion of the dilemma confronted by Bloom's latecomer poet, who is unavoidably 'burdened by an imaginative solitude'.[19] Yet a poet need not find his or her solitude a burden in the sense which

---

[17] *TP*, II. 19.
[18] 'The Science of History', *Short Studies on Great Subjects* (1868), 35.
[19] *AI*, 15.

Bloom assumes. It is by speaking with a voice which sets out to bring together what time and circumstance have split apart that FitzGerald proves the truth of Hazlitt's alternative description of writers: 'they are never less alone than when alone'.[20]

'THE CONSTANT APPEAL OF TIME'

Early reviewers of FitzGerald's *Rubáiyát* were understandably uncertain about how to respond to a poem which urges its readers to seize the moment, but in lines which were by then already several centuries old. The *Atlantic Monthly* refers to its 'intensely modern spirit';[21] *Fraser's Magazine* praises FitzGerald for 'the infusion of a modern element', before grudgingly conceding that these 'deepest questions of human life are for all time';[22] the *Spectator* hedges its bets—'Oriental as he is, Omar is always modern'—with an equivocal 'as' which cannot decide whether these Orientals are up to date or quaintly dated.[23] Both claims would be tested in the years that followed, with the repeated use of FitzGerald's translation to launch ephemeral slogans and jingles, ranging from Kipling's 'Rupaiyat of Omar Kal'vin' (protesting against the introduction of a new income-tax in India), to the more private mirth of 'The Ruby Yacht of Henry Morgan', 'Whereamiat Away from Homer Khayyam', 'The Budgai'at of I'm A-Khrying', and others.[24]

These interpretative uncertainties had been anticipated, if not answered, by Edward Cowell's attempt in an early essay to explain why ancient Persian literature was present to English readers even if they could not read it. Indeed, Cowell suggested, it was present to them even if they could not read:

Persian literature has spread its roots deep into the nation's heart; and we have too high an opinion of our common nature to suppose that anything worthless could have twined round the human heart under any clime, as we find this has done.[25]

[20] *Howe*, XII. 278.

[21] No. 41 (April 1878), 426.

[22] May 1879, repr. in Nathan Haskell Dole's variorum edition of *ROK* (2 vols., 1898), I. lxxxiii.

[23] 11 March 1876, 336.

[24] See Vinnie-Marie D'Ambrosio, *Eliot Possessed: T. S. Eliot and FitzGerald's Rubáiyát* (1989), 82.

[25] 'Persian Poetry', *The Westminster and Foreign Quarterly Review*, 47: 2 (July 1847), 276.

Cowell's empire-building shift, from 'the nation's heart' to 'the human heart', further anticipates the difficulties in 'placing' *Rubáiyát* which were to be acted out beside, and in, FitzGerald's own grave. On Saturday, 7 October 1893, the *East Anglian Daily Times* reported that the Omar Khayyám Club had visited Boulge Churchyard, where Maurice D. Conway's graveside address gave 'heart' some further massaging: *Rubáiyát* is 'almost like the re-appearance of Omar Khayyám in an English heart'; its translator had 'a certain personality which wins the affection and touches the heart'; 'Here we are in large-hearted England ... symbolising in a small way that large-heartedness which is now ... the great and living breath of the world.'[26] Conway's appeal to translation as a form of cultural heart-transplant was weirdly supported by the Club's floral tribute to FitzGerald: 'Two small but healthy-looking rose bushes, about a foot in height, were then unpacked and carefully planted at the head of the tombstone.'[27] Planted, but also transplanted, because these bushes had been grown at Kew Gardens from hips originally snipped off the ancient roses tangled over Omar Khayyám's grave at Naishápúr. As their roots fed off his corpse, FitzGerald would then slowly accomplish the 'corporeal transmigration' which *Rubáiyát* had described,[28] as if anticipating Walter Benjamin's metaphor of the translator ('The spirit of the originals attains in [translation] its ever-renewed latest and most abundant flowering'), and bringing it creepily to life.[29]

This desire to discover and assert a 'common nature' is true of many literary relationships. (It is one of the organizing principles of Wordsworth and Coleridge's early verse, for example, which often supports its declarations in favour of 'common life' with mutual borrowings, so that even those poems which do not address themselves directly to a listener are, compositionally at least, conversation-poems.) However, it is likely to be an especially significant desire for the translator, who seeks to confirm his or her kinship with a foreign original, but must first confront the possibility that the language in which this search is made does not even possess a common nature of its own. Pasted onto the flyleaf of his marked-up copy of the Orientalist Selden's *Table-Talk* is a note in FitzGerald's hand:

---

[26] A. J. Arberry, *The Romance of the Rubáiyát* (1959), 33–4.
[27] *East Anglian Daily Times*, repr. ibid., 33.
[28] Edward Cowell, *Calcutta Review*, 30: 60 (June 1858), 155
[29] *Illuminations*, 72.

Every living language, like ye perspiring Bodies of living Creatures, is in perpetual motion & Alteration; some words go off, become obsolete; others are taken in, & by degrees grow into common use; or ye same word is inverted to a new sense & notion; which in tract of Time makes as observable a Change in ye living Features of a language as Age makes in ye lines & Mien of a Face.[30]

It is because a language is inherently transitory, part of the general drift of things it describes, that it will be especially pressed upon by transience, by the changes in its speakers which its own adjustments record. Thus, when Henry James remarks upon the extent to which the 'conservative interest' within a living language should predominate, he gauges its 'constant quality' against 'the constant appeal of time, perpetually demanding new tricks, new experiences, new amusements of it'.[31] For FitzGerald, however, the 'constant appeal of time' lay more in its ability to reveal other forms of constancy, such as the loyalty of his friendships, and his willingness to test this loyalty against the durability of writing: 'I wonder at your writing to me that I gave you his Journal so long as thirty years ago. I scarce knew that I was so constant in my Affections: and yet I think I do not change in literary cases' (*EFGL*, I. 55).

We hear this appeal of and to constancy in FitzGerald's correspondence, as the welcome stubbornnesses of his past emerge in the evolving attractions of individual words. When Benson writes that 'The old stories, the old days, had always a kind of gentle consecration for him',[32] for example, his repetition of 'old' is sympathetic to FitzGerald's own fond returns to the word as one small consecrated ground of memory: 'For I think, and I find, that as one grows old one returns to one's old haunts' (*EFGL*, III. 439). This is true to the nostalgic cast of FitzGerald's imagination, forever homesick for a past which existed only in the eyes of the unsatisfied present, but it is false to the unswerving path of his imagination through time, because FitzGerald did not need to grow old in order to appreciate the ways of the old. He began signing himself 'Old Fitz' while still a young man, and even when describing his first published poem (a

---

[30] 1777 edn., *Trinity*, Adv.d.11.15.

[31] *The Question of Our Speech* (1905), 46–7.

[32] *Edward FitzGerald*, 5. Compare *Trinity*, Add.MSa.10[2], FitzGerald's 'Nelly-ad', a rewriting of *The Old Curiosity Shop* for children, in which the word 'old' is dwelt on with relentless enthusiasm from beginning ('There lived in London an old man', 1) to end ('there she lay with a smile on her lips as she used to do when asleep in her little bedroom in the Old Curiosity Shop', 77).

poem which dwells upon the pleasure of 'Reading old things'), he
sighed, like Beckett's Winnie, that 'These verses are in the old style'.[33]
The tone of 'old' in these examples, at once reverent and indifferent,
goes to the divided heart of FitzGerald's literary personality: always
careful to appear careless; cherishing the affections which he most
neglected, in himself and others; like Tennyson, in Spedding's acute
description, using his writing to project the image of 'a man [who is]
always discontented with the Present until it has become the Past, and
then he yearns toward it and not only worships it, but is discontented
because it is past.'[34] The source of FitzGerald's creativity conditioned
its method, because a word like 'old' allowed simultaneously for a
restoration of the past, and a recognition of it as past. 'Old' friends
might be those we have kept ('old' as 'still'), or those we have lost and
left behind ('old' as 'former'), so the word's returns could speak of
what was taken for granted even as they brooded over these very
assumptions. Reading and writing to Tennyson, FitzGerald often
meditates upon 'the old style', where 'old' wistfully weighs up his
own age, Tennyson's age, the age in which they had grown old
together, the changes of Tennyson's writing, and the tenacity of his
own critical judgements. Repeatedly, his letters strike off in different
directions, but are drawn back to the same imaginative centre, as
'old' exerts its gravitational pull:

… Tennyson's *old* poems … fresh as when I first heard them nearly twenty
years ago: perhaps *fresher* from being remembered so long.   (*EFGL*, II. 28)[35]

… Oh the dear old 1842 Days and Editions!   (*EFGL*, III. 59)

… the old Poems—which are still quite young to me …   (*EFGL*, II. 31)

But I don't think of you so little, my dear old Alfred: but rejoice in the Old
Poems, and in yourself, young or old …   (*EFGL*, II. 441)

I mumble over your old Verses in my Memory … So you see I remain always
the same crotchety old Fitz.   (*EFGL*, III. 290)

After what was to be their final meeting in 1876, FitzGerald's account
took pleasure in playing off 'old' against 'same': 'the old Poet' had
written to ' "Dear old Fitz" ', and together they 'fell at once into the

---

[33] See Robert Bernard Martin, *With Friends Possessed: A Life of Edward FitzGerald* (1985), 71;
for Winnie's 'old style', see Samuel Beckett, *Happy Days* (1961), 13.

[34] Quoted in Frances Brookfield, *The Cambridge Apostles* (1906), 168.

[35] FitzGerald's memory is again refreshing one of these old poems: '[F]resh as when
I first heard them' recalls and answers 'So sad, so fresh, the days that are no more', 'Tears,
idle tears', *TP*, II. 233.

old Humour, ... went over the same old grounds of Debate, told some of the old Stories.' Looking at Tennyson's features, though now 'the old Poet' was truly old, 'He looked much the same', as if the lines of his friend's face had remained as fixed as the lines of his own letters (*EFGL*, III. 707).

Poetic translation compounds these pulls and pushes of an individual's settled idiom because, as Valéry observes, the poet is already 'a peculiar type of translator', whose 'inner labour consists less of seeking words for his ideas than of seeking ideas for his words and paramount rhythms':

At bottom there are always the same problems—that is, the same attitudes: the 'inner' ear alert for the possible, for what will murmur 'of itself' and, once murmured, will return to the condition of desire; the same suspense and the same verbal crystallisations; the same oriented sensitivity of the subjective vocabulary, as though all the words in the memory were watching their chance to try their luck in reaching the voice.[36]

Valéry's 'attitudes' are anticipated in FitzGerald's more cautious response to the stance which Tennyson's fey early poems seemed to have taken up towards the reading public: 'The affectation &c was not of *The Man*; but of the Time & Society he lived in, & from which he had not yet emerged to his proper & distinct attitude.'[37] The assumption held by a number of more recent critics, that writers inescapably mirror their 'Time & Society' (recall McGann's reference to 'a Victorian set of attitudes which are peculiarly [Tennyson's] own'),[38] sits uneasily with FitzGerald's apparent preference for one half of the dictionary definition of 'attitude' ('Settled behaviour or manner of acting ... ') over the other (' ... as representative of feeling or opinion', *OED* 3). However, both FitzGerald's 'attitude' and Valéry's 'attitudes' are likely to be too picky for the translator, who responds to the work that has called him by recognizing that, in Griffiths's description of this calling, he 'does not encounter his past originals as an isolated individual', like Bloom's anguished solipsist, 'but as the ambassador of his time and place, as an envoy from his contemporaries to the other country of the past'.[39]

---

[36] 'Variations on the Eclogues' (1953), trans. Denise Foliot, repr. in Rainer Schulte and John Biguenet (eds.), *Theories of Translation* (1992), 119.

[37] Written in FitzGerald's copy of the 1842 *Poems*, 19.

[38] See Ch. 3.

[39] Eric Griffiths, 'Dryden's Past', in *Proceedings of the British Academy*, 84 (1993), 147.

Umberto Eco has pointed out that 'the task of literature is to keep exercising language'.[40] Translations are especially good at showing up where a language is falling into sluggish habits, and where its literary forms remain trim and alert, because in seeking to project the voice of his or her foreign original through a shared tongue, often the writer discovers that the voice which speaks loudest in this translation is that of his or her contemporaries. As Wittgenstein remarks:

How does it come about that this arrow ⟶ *points?* Doesn't it seem to carry in it something besides itself?—'No, not the dead line on paper; only the psychical thing, the meaning, can do that.'—That is both true and false. The arrow points only in the application that a living being makes of it.

Translations too are not dead lines on paper, but evidence of the application that living beings have made of such lines.[41] It is for this reason that the translator who attempts to move words from a source-language into a target-language, with the precision of an arrow hitting a bullseye, may find his or her efforts compromised by the apparent reluctance of words to travel in certain directions, given how often the patterns of a language determine in advance what can be said in it. Some of these patterns run through all utterances which are possible in that language at all times, its grammatical DNA, as the accusation 'traduttore traditore' ('to translate is to betray') proves its point by making the two words seem doomed to involve one another, but only in Italian, which is inherently thick with rhyme. These grammatical patterns have a cognitive function, in that they shape our view of the world, as well as reflecting the shapes we retrieve from the world. Because there is no Eskimo word for 'sheep', for example, Bible translators are denied 'the lamb of God', and must make do with 'the seal pup of God', as translators into Arabic are spoilt for choice if they are asked to describe the fine distinctions between different types of camel behaviour. There are also certain premisses which a language may carry, but which are historically variable. For example, every translation of a poem, like all poems, will to some extent be an answer to the question 'What is a poem?', but because

---

[40] Quoted in *Beckett Translating / Translating Beckett*, ed. Alan Warren Friedman, Charles Rossman, and Dina Sherzer (1987), 49.

[41] *Philosophical Investigations*, 454; compare Eric Griffiths's remarks on editorial practice in 'Newman's Leading', *Presenting Poetry: Composition, Publication, Reception*, ed. Howard Erskine-Hill and Richard A. McCabe (1995), 195.

the answers to this question change over time, comparing two or more translations of the same foreign original is likely to uncover some of the cultural home truths which different writers have shared with their readers. Having resolved to write again what has already been resolved, the translator then redeems the cry 'traduttore traditore' by confirming, through a practised skill in following and extending the established orientations of his or her own language, that the root 'trad-' points to tradition as well as traducement.

Stephen Prickett summarizes the translator's difficulties:

Translation, especially from one period of time into another, is not just a matter of finding the nearest equivalents for words or syntactic structures. In addition it involves altering the fine network of unconscious or half-conscious presuppositions that underlie the actual words or phrases, and which differentiate so characteristically the climate of thought and feeling of one age from that of another.[42]

The Biblical translator faces an especially acute practical version of these questions, because so many of our most cherished cultural assumptions are derived from the Bible that the 'climate' in which he or she works is likely to be as inaccessible to impartial investigation as the air he or she breathes. As Coleridge observes:

I take up [the Bible] with the purpose to read it for the first time as I should any other work,—as far at least as I can or dare. For I neither can, nor dare, throw off a strong and awful prepossession in its favour—certain as I am that a large part of the light and life, in which and by which I see, love, and embrace the truths and strengths co-organised into a living body of faith and knowledge ... has been directly or indirectly derived to me from this sacred volume,—and unable to determine what I do not owe to its influences.[43]

The extent of this 'prepossession' is suggested by the self-involved syntax of 'the light ... by which I see', and 'life ... by which I ... love' because, as stated, 'light' and 'life' are at once the objects and conditions of perception. 'In the Bible', as Coleridge admits a few pages later, 'there is more that *finds* me than in all other books put together',[44] and his repetitions of 'in' carry a charge: to live in this time and place is already to live in the Bible, as it lives in us. The Biblical translator therefore

---

[42] *Words and The Word: Language, Poetics and Biblical Interpretation* (1986), 7.
[43] *Confessions of an Inquiring Spirit* (1840), ed. H. St J. Hart (1956), 9.
[44] Ibid., 13.

runs the double risk either of modernising or of archaising: to modernise is to ignore the culture gap of many centuries and to read the Bible as though it were contemporary literature; and to archaise is to exaggerate the culture gap and to ignore the similarities between the biblical world and our own.[45]

FitzGerald's writing and revision of *Rubáiyát* coincide with and focus a lively mid-Victorian debate over how familiar or foreign to the ear a translation should sound. Broadly speaking, the translator is advised to find words which will express cultural differences (sending the domestic reader abroad), or efface them (bringing the foreign author home), and is reminded that the extent to which a translation identifies itself as an alien discourse can be mapped out in the historical discontinuities and displacements of its vocabulary, as the writer attempts to 'make it new',[46] as Pound was to urge, or, as is more often the case with Pound's own practice, makes it old. Here, Arnold's 1853 praise for those readers who are at home with the classics, and so are 'more independent of the language current among those with whom they live' (classical scholarship providing a 'language current' like the current of Newman's stream, which 'needs disengaging from what is foreign and temporary'),[47] is met by Charles Kingsley's 1854 reply that Arnold should translate Homer into sturdy modern English, if he is to distinguish himself from those ivory-towered scholars who live too much 'under the influence of past facts, rather than present ones'.[48] By contrast, Francis Newman's translation of the *Iliad* (1856) stages a historical analogy between earlier forms of Greek and English, by rewriting Homer in a style 'similar to the old English ballad' in its prosody, syntax, and the reproduction antiques of its diction: 'callant', 'gride', 'bragly', 'gramsome', and more.[49]

FitzGerald's stance within this debate is suggested by a personal dictionary of words 'linked with Alliteration', from Abbies to Zealots, which he compiled in one of his commonplace books. It includes this entry:

After-born – after-gang – After-yule (January)
After-thought: after-cast: after-shot: after-feed: after-grass:
after-math: (gr. *Math*) After-ale, small-beer![50]

[45] G. B. Caird, *The Language and Imagery of the Bible* (1980), 2.
[46] See Lawrence Venuti, *The Translator's Invisibility* (1995), 18–28.
[47] See Ch. 3.
[48] *Super*, I. 13; *Frasers' Magazine*, 49 (February 1854), 149.
[49] Preface to *The Iliad of Homer* (1856), iv.
[50] *Trinity*, o.11.12., 5.

'After' attracted many linguistic followers during FitzGerald's writing career. 'Afterword' (first used in the sense of 'epilogue' in 1900) conveniently caps a century in which 'after-' had been further extended into medical 'after-care' (1854), 'after-death' (1899) as an alternative to 'afterlife', 'afterglow' (1873), 'after-image' (1874), 'after-shock' (1894), Wordsworth's 'after-years' (*The Excursion*, 1814), and Swinburne's 'after-birth' (late-born children, 1871). In each instance, the dash of 'after-' plugs into or locks onto its suffix, as if in response to Coleridge's call in the *Biographia Literaria* (1817) for the 'beneficial after-effects of verbal precision': 'after-effects' being the precise coinage here, in an argument for organic development which also brought forth 'aftergrowth'.[51] FitzGerald was adept at fixing upon unusual 'after-' compounds (*The Mighty Magician* has 'after-vengeance'), and giving a new slant to more familiar conceits (*Rubáiyát*'s 'After-reckoning' imagines God totting up sins on the day of judgement, like a pub landlord keeping a tab behind the bar), but so many of his chosen examples hark back to earlier authors (he cites Dryden on 'After-spring'), that he seems stubbornly at odds with those of his contemporaries who took 'after-' as an invitation to linguistic innovation rather than renewal. Yet although FitzGerald's translations routinely justify and extend this loyalty to old saws (the musty diction of *Rubáiyát* includes 'Lo', 'enow', 'sans', 'whither', 'make Carouse', 'prithee', 'peradventure', 'doth', 'jocund', 'Ayes and Noes', and more), part of his resourcefulness as a poet is to discover for archaic diction an unexpected contemporary relevance, as when the speaker of *Rubáiyát* complains 'Oh Thou, who didst with Pitfall and with Gin | Beset the Road I was to wander in', and so shades the old sense of 'gin' as 'trap' (not cited by the *OED* after 1879) with something else currently exerting its pressure on the behaviour and speech of his readers: the gin which was still being downed by some drinkers as a nerve-tonic, but which could then result in 'alcoholism' (first cited in 1852), or the 'alcoholic' (1892).

FitzGerald is less willing than Arnold to think that only scholars are in a position to judge a translation's lasting worth (FitzGerald's *Agamemnon* is 'not for Scholars, but for those who are ignorant of Greek'),[52] but he shares with Arnold the idea that a translation can best occupy more than one time and place at once if the idiom it uses has already acquired a recognizable patina of common use. Thus,

[51] All examples drawn from *OED*.   [52] *EFGW*, II. xiv.

when Arnold remarks that 'It is the spirit that quickeneth; and no one will so well render Homer's swift-flowing movement as he who has himself something of the swift-moving spirit of Homer', his punning on 'quick' as 'alive' and 'speedy' anticipates his later claim that the Bible 'is undoubtedly the grand mine of diction for the translator of Homer',[53] because 'the spirit that quickeneth' reworks the reasoning behind holy communion: 'It is the spirit that quickeneth; the flesh profiteth nothing: the words that I speak unto you, *they* are spirit, and *they* are life.'[54] Arnold's 'spirit' draws upon a tradition which views the possibility of translation as evidence of the Holy Spirit moving our speech, and so the fleeting hope that languages might one day give up their secret hiding-places by revealing the shared tongue that was shattered with the fall of Babel. FitzGerald's attitude towards the 'go' and 'spirit' of translation often draws upon more corporeal metaphors (he shares with Dryden, whose Prefaces he privately bound and edited, a pleasure in thinking of translation as a form of 'transfusion'),[55] but he too justifies them with Biblical analogies:

… very many beside myself, with as much fair Dramatic Spirit, knowledge of good English and English Verse, would do quite as well as you think I do, if they would not hamper themselves with Forms of Verse—and Thought— irreconcilable with English Ways of Thinking. I am persuaded that, to keep *Life* in the Work … the Translator (however inferior to his Original) must re-cast that original into his own Likeness, more or less: the less like his original, so much the worse: but still, the live Dog better than the dead Lion. (*EFGL*, I. 168)

To support 'English Ways', then, is to be supported by the ways of English, the routemap of expressions which has been created by linguistic wear and tear, and for FitzGerald the demands upon a translator to make the foreign sound familiar will be in large part fulfilled by using 'strong' words, 'which have proved their worth by general admission into the Language' (*EFGL*, I. 50). 'Drunk', for example, is an appropriately sturdy word for 're-casting' the Persian poets' 'strength of mind' in writing of strong liquor, and FitzGerald is scornful of the translators of 'Fiery Háfiz' who 'dilute' the idea with mealy-mouthed alternatives, such as 'Be not tipsy' or 'intoxicated', when 'not only Milton, Taylor, and even Cowper … use the word,

[53] *On Translating Homer*, repr. in *Super*, I. 142, 156.   [54] John 6: 63.
[55] See *EFGL*, II. 53, on the need for 'go' in poetry; I discuss 'transfusion' later in this chapter. FitzGerald's copy of Dryden's prefaces is located at *Trinity*, Adv.d.11.2.

but the Bible Translators too' (*EFGL*, II. 411, 137). These older poets had thicker blood running in their veins than modern milksops, fortunate to write in a 'vigorous' style 'before the Language got diluted as it now is': the spirit of the age in which he works being less significant to the translator than the concentrated spirit of the language through which he works (*EFGL*, II. 220–1). Unlike the self-begetting struggles of Bloom's 'strong' poet, FitzGerald's 'strong' words act like the muscles of the social body, gaining in strength the more they are exercised. Similarly, his understanding of the nation's linguistic vigour echoes the terms of literary debates which took place during the 1850s and 1860s (Francis Newman's decision to render Horace in unrhyming accentual metres, for example, was attacked for its failure to uphold 'the strength of our poetical language'), but also draws upon a series of metaphors which stretches from Hopkins's praise of Dryden ('his style and his rhythms lay the strongest stress of all our literature on the naked thew and sinew of the English language'), back to Rymer's explanation of English literary superiority over the French: 'The *French* wants sinews for great and heroick Subjects.'[56] As the surviving relics of an earlier and more powerful state of the language, 'strong' words will instantly beef up a new translation, as FitzGerald justifies his theory with an allusion to that book of the Bible which is so concerned with our living in time, Ecclesiastes: 'For to him that is joined to all the living there is hope: for a living dog is better than a dead lion.'[57]

The idea that his speech was joined to *all* the living occasionally troubled FitzGerald, who grumbles in a number of letters about the 'Drawing-room-European' which his countrymen persisted in speaking, and responds by urging that the translator should remove from his vocabulary any words which smack of its 'European Prejudices and Associations' (*EFGL*, II. 180, 192). At the same time, he recognized that so many living English words began as foreign loanwords, before their transplants 'took' in the King James Bible, that a 'knowledge of good English and English Verse' cannot be separated from a

---

[56] For Newman's remarks, see *London Quarterly Review* (1858), quoted in Venuti, *The Translator's Invisibility*, 127; for poetic 'sinews', see Griffiths, 'Dryden's Past', 115, and compare Edward Clodd's *Concerning a Pilgrimmage to the Grave of Edward FitzGerald* (1894), which argues that the original 'sluggard plant' reared at Kew was 'of too delicate a nature' to survive transplantation until 'grafted on a lusty English stock'—an emblem of 'the new life which FitzGerald gave to the *Rubáiyát* of Omar in translating them into vigorous English verse' and the 'virile English tongue', 12–18.

[57] Ecclesiastes 9: 4.

knowledge of this translation, as it directs 'English Ways of Thinking' through its 'Forms of Verse'. As early as 1855, FitzGerald claims it as '*the* rule never to be lost sight of' that translations of Oriental literature should be filtered through those earlier books from the East which we now know as the Bible:

> I always refer back to the Bible: which Selden says is translated so strangely as no Book then ever was, keeping so close to almost unintelligible idioms both of Country and Era. Well—it is done: and has succeeded: and, whether well or ill, *has prepared all Englishmen at least for the reception of other Oriental works under the same forms*: both of *words* and *grammar*. (*EFGL*, II. 164; FitzGerald's emphasis)

FitzGerald's letters can be more misty-eyed than this in describing the effects of the King James Bible upon contemporary speech patterns, as when he argues that its translators fixed England's 'standard of language', like a flag of conquest planted in the linguistic history of the nation (*EFGL*, II. 421). But his literary practice shows how fully he understood that, however intelligible its idioms were in 1611, as an old translation the King James Bible is now foreign as well as familiar to our understanding. For however persuasively the translators of Ecclesiastes might speak of considerations of the moment (a time for living, a time for dying, and so on), the changes undergone by their '*words* and *grammar*' also alert us to their influence on the later life of the English language. 'Joined to all the *living*' then acts as a warning as well as a promise, because where a reader detects fragments of the Bible's 'obscure' and 'almost unintelligible forms', even new poems could resemble echoes of a more primitive linguistic past, or disclose hitherto unsuspected weaknesses in those beliefs which are being sustained by an idiom audibly cracking under the pressures of contemporary usage.[58] In 1847, FitzGerald contemplates the Niagara Falls:

> ... one fancies that the Poet of today may as well fold his hands, or turn them to dig and delve, considering how soon the march of discovery will distance

---

[58] Advances in archaeology and prehistory confronted comparative philologists with the likelihood that this past was darker than the traditional myth of fluting shepherds. In 1860, F. W. Farrar could still dismiss 'the error of man's slow and toilsome development from an almost bestial condition', and call up the ancient defence of poetry as historically and aesthetically first among the arts by announcing that 'the dawn of language took place in the bright infancy, in the joyous boyhood of the world'; by 1865, his confidence in man's ancestors had been sapped: 'a miserable population ... forced to dispute their cave-dwellings with the hyena and the wolf'; see his *Essay on the Origin of Language* (1860), 140, and *Chapters on Language* (1865), 49.

his imaginations, dissolve the language in which they are uttered. Martial, as you say, lives now—after two thousand years—a space that seems long to us whose lives are so brief; but a moment—the twinkling of an eye—if compared (not to Eternity alone) but to the ages which it is now known the world must have existed, and (unless for some external violence) must continue to exist. (*EFGL*, I. 566)

When Cowell read Omar Khayyám, he discovered a world which was rather less changeable:

Omar lived in an age of poetical mysticism, but he is himself no mystic ... he plants his foot on the *terra firma* of to-day; and builds on it as if it were a rock, and not a quicksand.[59]

The excellence of this is that it succeeds in describing Omar's age in a manner which is so much of its own age, as Cowell expresses his trust in an unalterable bedrock of belief, but chooses a metaphor which implicitly acknowledges that not everyone shared a similar confidence in the idea that, as FitzGerald puts it in his preface to *Rubáiyát*, 'Time is slipping underneath our Feet', without causing any adjustment to the way time itself should be understood. 'If only the Geologists would leave me alone, I could do very well', Ruskin famously complained, 'but those dreadful Hammers. I hear the clink of them at the end of every cadence of the Bible verses.'[60] FitzGerald is more rueful: the geologists' 'vision of Time must wither the Poet's hope of immortality', by obliging him to recognize that 'we all live in a ridiculous parenthesis of Time on a shelf made by insects and planted by stray sea mews', our corpses destined to be preserved between rock strata like stray words coffined between brackets (*EFGL*, I. 566, 435). One example of this withering and splintering of hope over time can be heard in his letter on the Niagara Falls, as the small parenthesis of '—the twinkling of an eye—' chips away a Biblical cadence from its bedrock of faith, and raises it into his doubting Victorian air as a fossilized remembrance of earlier ways of thinking which now seem wide-eyed or blinkered.[61] Unlike Arnold's 1853 insistence that poetry should treat of 'those elementary feelings which subsist permanently in the race, and which are independent of time', this 'twinkling of an eye' speaks more of cultural subsidence than of cultural subsistence. Broken off from its source, the fragment thus works something like

---

[59] Cited in Dole's variorum edition of *ROK*, I. xxi.
[60] Letter of 24 May 1851 to Henry Acland, quoted in Buckley, *The Triumph of Time*, 28.
[61] For the Biblical text (St Paul on resurrection), see Ch. 2.

Lyell's own uniformitarianism, which argued that the deep changes hidden by dusty movements of erosion and sedimentation can be shown 'by reference to causes now in action', as FitzGerald shows in his retrieval of St Paul that even a verse which speaks of the everlasting may not remain unchanged forever.[62]

Compare FitzGerald's 'vision of Time' with Coleridge's glimpses of eternity:

> You say Time is subjective merely: but unless you call Action itself, and 'Before and After' subjective also, you must admit some objective succession of events and acts, which succession we call Time ... Therefore I think that Geology which has certainly discovered to us so much of the Past—and the Being of this Earth when *we were not*; is a more wonderful, grand, and awful, and therefore *Poetical*, idea than any we can find in our Poetry. (*EFGL*, I. 569)

> The sense of Before and After becomes both intelligible and intellectual when, and *only* when, we contemplate the succession in the relations of Cause and Effect, which ... give, as it were, a substratum of permanence, of identity, and therefore of reality, to the shadowy flux of Time. It is Eternity revealing itself in the phenomena of Time: and the perception and acknowledgement of the proportionality and appropriateness of the Present to the Past, prove to the afflicted Soul, that it has not yet been deprived of the sight of God.[63]

Translation is well placed to observe the 'shadowy flux of time' as it passes over a 'substratum of permanence' because, as Walter Benjamin explains:

> ... in its afterlife—which could not be called that if it were not a transformation and a renewal of something living—the original undergoes a change ... While a poet's words endure in his own language, even the greatest translation is destined to become part of the growth of its own language and destined to be absorbed by its renewal ... of all literary forms [translation] is the one charged with the special mission of watching over the maturing process of the original language and the birthpangs of its own.[64]

Even poems which urge their readers to live for today will be more or less opportune, as their warnings about the shifting sands of time become subject in turn to the historical movements of the language (deathpangs as well as birthpangs) they have helped to shape. For a number of Victorian writers, translation was central to the most

[62] *Super*, I. 4; *Principles of Geology* (3 vols., 1833), title page.
[63] J. Shawcross (ed.), *Biographia Literaria* (2 vols., 1907), II. 207.
[64] *Illuminations*, 73–4.

far-reaching implications of this way of thinking, as the historical method of the Higher Criticism led to claims that the Scriptures, far from providing a 'substratum of permanence', were no more permanent in their own forms than they were in human understanding of them. In particular, by 1840 Coleridge's comment that a 'sense of Before and After' could not be made intelligible merely by 'bringing together into logical dependency detached sentences from books composed at the distance of centuries ... from each other',[65] echoes widespread and growing doubts that a 'living idea', in Newman's terms,[66] could become many but remain one where it depended upon the vagaries of textual transmission.

One version of these doubts emerged in the controversy surrounding the decision to produce a Revised Version of the Bible. Although the Committee of Convocation for the Revised Version promised, on 25 May 1870, 'To introduce as few alterations as possible into the text of the Authorized Version, consistent with faithfulness', the Bishop of Lincoln, Christopher Wordsworth, was not alone in being loudly unconvinced that a more faithful translation would square with the beliefs which it was intended to uphold: 'Beware lest by altering the text of the authorized version of the Bible, you shake the faith of many.'[67] Critics like John William Burgon warned that this translation put faith on especially shaky ground by introducing new words, odd grammatical constructions, and changes to word-order, so threatening permanently to estrange traditional forms of belief from their accustomed forms of expression.[68] Other commentators were to bind together textual transmission with questions of a Christian afterlife. F. W. Farrar, for example, writing after the *Essays and Reviews* controversy, cites Coleridge in support of his view that the doctrine of eternal punishment was based partly upon mistranslation in the King James Bible, and partly upon the translation's own atomistic form, which had encouraged 'the wresting of texts', whereby a single shred is 'torn from its context' and applied 'mistakenly'. Printing the Revised Version in paragraphs rather than in verses, Farrar argued, would therefore draw attention to the nonsense of attempting a proof

---

[65] *Confessions of an Inquiring Spirit*, 64.

[66] I discuss Newman's 'living idea' in Ch. 3.

[67] See Owen Chadwick, *The Victorian Church* (2 vols., 1970), II. 44.

[68] *The Revision Revised* (1883). Burgon's examples include: assassin, apparition, boon, disparagement, divinity, fickleness, irksome, interpose, pitiable, sluggish, tranquil, self-control, and world-ruler (233).

of 'eternal torment' from Isaiah 23: 14, when 'even a moderate study of the context might have sufficed to show that the verse has not the most remote connexion with that terrific dogma'.[69] However, as writers like Pusey pointed out, one difficulty with the methods of the Higher Criticism was that the context of a Biblical verse cannot be limited to its immediate textual surroundings, so that arguing away the eternity of punishment merely on account of its moral repugnance would prepare the ground for other beliefs to suffer the same fate: 'For if the word "eternal" were taken out of its known historical meaning in the Church ... there would ... be an end of all teachings.'[70] Other readers continued to be impressed by the 'terrific dogma' of hell. Tennyson recalled the words of his Calvinist aunt: ' "Alfred, Alfred, when I look at you, I think of the words of Holy Scripture—'Depart from me, ye cursed, into everlasting fire' ".'[71] It is an odd way to greet your nephew, perhaps, but she was not unusual in assuming that one version of the afterlife would involve eternal hellfire; nor was Tennyson unusual in being disappointed that the translators of the Revised Version had not responded to the moral doubts which religious thinkers more liberal than his aunt, such as F. D. Maurice, had cast upon the doctrine of eternal punishment, by changing 'everlasting' into something like 'æonian'.[72]

Rubáiyát touches upon these restless debates both directly and more glancingly. A quatrain protesting at 'threats of Hell', for instance, produces a claim for self-reliance ('I Myself am Heav'n and Hell') which echoes the traditional view, recently revived by Maurice and others, that the real Hell would be the absence of God from the human soul. At the same time, working within and between these explicit arguments, the poem's wary rejections of 'some After-reckoning ta'en on trust' are conducted through the ethically charged semantic fields of individual words.[73] In his last year, Tennyson remembered a conversation with Carlyle and FitzGerald about the afterlife:

[69] *The Bible: Its Meaning and Supremacy* (1897), 191, 203–6; compare *Eternal Hope* (1878), 78–9.
[70] Letter to W. K. Hamilton, 22 June 1881 or 1882, discussed in Griffiths, *The Printed Voice of Victorian Poetry*, 113.
[71] *Memoir*, I. 15, quoting Matthew 25: 41.
[72] See Geoffrey Rowell, *Hell and the Victorians*, 116–40, and *Memoir*, I. 322; compare the lines which 'my father would quote as giving his own belief that "the after-life is one of progress" ': 'No sudden heaven, nor sudden hell, for man, | But ... Æonian Evolution', *Memoir*, II. 365.
[73] 5th edn., LXIII–LXVI; Maurice, *Theological Essays* (1853), 388; 5th edn., LXII.

He said that when he was stopping at a coffee-house in London, Carlyle had come to smoke a pipe with him in the evening and the talk turned upon the immortality of the soul; upon which Carlyle said: 'Eh! old Jewish rags: you must clear your mind of all that. Why should we expect a hereafter? Your traveller comes to an inn, and he takes his bed, it's only for one night, he leaves next day, and another man takes his place and sleeps in the bed that he has vacated.' My father continued: 'I answered, "Your traveller comes to his inn, and lies down in his bed, and leaves the inn in the morning, and goes on his way rejoicing, with the sure and certain hope and belief that he is going somewhere, where he will sleep the next night," and then Edward Fitzgerald [*sic*], who was present, said, "You have him there"'.[74]

Hallam's account neatly catches the personalities involved: Carlyle's spiky interruption, Tennyson smoothly rolling over it, and FitzGerald appearing quietly at the edges of the argument ('who was present') like Lewis Carroll's dormouse. In this context, Carlyle's 'Why should we expect a hereafter?' turns out to be an especially good question, because it raises other questions, such as whether all individuals will expect the same future state, or whether each will experience the one he or she looked forward to while alive. However, Carlyle's question is not the only feature of this account which resists being settled by a single answer. Much of an argument like this will be conducted through the directions and indirections of tone, the questionable attitude of a speaker which, like other forms of question, extends beyond the present tense in which all speech is situated, by anticipating and conditioning possible responses to itself. For example, as FitzGerald's listeners might have wondered about his 'You have him there'—a solemn umpiring decision? a wry poke at Carlyle? 'You *have* him *there*' or '*You* have *him* there'?—so Tennyson's listeners might have wondered how his 'sure and certain hope' was being offered, and how it was to be taken, if they picked up his allusion to the Burial of the Dead: ' ... earth to earth, ashes to ashes, dust to dust; in sure and certain hope of the Resurrection to eternal life, through our Lord Jesus Christ ... '. 'What a thing it would be if we could be sure, or even have a good hope, that we could, by striving, meet again' (*EFGL*, II. 76): FitzGerald's nervous self-qualifications are echoed in the sceptical counter-voice which Tennyson's 'sure and certain hope *and belief*' opens itself to and steels itself against, as it picks up Carlyle's present tense 'sleeps', and changes it into a future tense 'will sleep'. And in this, both Carlyle and Tennyson draw upon a common pattern in Victorian writings on the afterlife: the mediation of tone through tense as one way in which different speakers situate themselves in, and contemplate being removed from, time.

Michael Wheeler has shown how the imprecise nature of New Testament teaching on the future life allowed Victorian preachers considerable latitude when they came to interpret the 'sure and certain hope of the Resurrection'.[75] 'Hope', in particular, is a key word in debates over liturgical reform during the 1850s and 1860s. The young J. H. Newman had listed in his journal, among the reasons for accepting the damnatory clause of the Athanasian Creed ('and they that have done ... evil shall go into everlasting fire'), the opinion that it would not be uncharitable to hold that drunkards were in a state of perdition, since a person's choice of faith and lifestyle were intimately related.[76] By the time of Charles John Vaughan's explanation of the Burial Service, this relation has been weakened. Despite 'the contrast in certain cases between the words employed and the circumstances which contradict them', Vaughan points out, the minister can truthfully 'give thanks to God for the sure and certain hope of another world' even 'by the grave of the drunkard', because however uncertain the fate of this individual, the hope expressed is of '*the* (not *his* or *her*) resurrection to eternal life', so allowing even a definite article to avoid judging one way or the other.[77] Other writings further extend this sort of semantic wriggling to include the secularization of 'hope' from heavenly to earthly kingdoms (FitzGerald's first biographer, A. C. Benson, wrote 'Land of Hope and Glory'), and its weakening from expectant desire to wishful thinking (Tennyson's 'And faintly trust the larger hope' crosses these senses in 'faintly', as if wondering whether a time suspicious of full-throated praising would instead be damned with its faint hopes).[78] Several theological tracts of the period explicitly link complaints about the infiltration of doubt into 'hope' with a writer's use of tense. Edward Henry Bickersteth, like Vaughan, refers to 'the resurrection' as an important saving grace of the burial service, and meditates upon 'the language of holy hope' which should be heard in the text 'It is raised':

[75] Parts of this discussion draw on his *Heaven, Hell, and the Victorians* (1994).
[76] *Autobiographical Writings*, ed. H. Tristram (1956), 162.
[77] *Revision of the Liturgy: Five Discourses* (1860), 73–91.
[78] *IM*, LV, *TP*, II. 372.

It is raised. We are tempted to think we misread the words, and that they should run, It *shall be* raised. Nay, this is the triumphant present of anticipative faith. Faith overleaps the interval.[79]

This 'interval', between an individual death and the last judgement, echoes the intersection of the timeless with time which we hear in St Paul's 'and' in 'paradise now and not yet', implying no break between an order which is already established in heaven and immanent on earth, and that which is yet to be fulfilled.[80] Where these negotiations between past, present, and future inform Victorian religious poetry, the continuities between this life and the next are often glimpsed and bridged in the syntactic organization, the timed spans, of verse. Bickersteth's 'Seer' lies on his deathbed, 'intolerant of suspense', while his wife speaks to him:

> But softly laying
> Her hand upon my burning brow, she said,
> 'I know it all, beloved husband. God
> Hath spoken to me also, and hath given
> These brief hours to my wrestling prayers. Enough,
> Tomorrow and all after life for tears,
> To-day and all eternity for love.'[81]

By 'after life' she means 'my life without you', but as she imagines him crossing the bar of death, the movement of her voice across the line-break which follows 'tears' also points to a shift between two orders of existence, because this pause holds three kinds of present tense experience in loving suspense: the existential present of their overlapping lives, the locutionary present of her speech, and the 'eternity' of heaven.

FitzGerald's principled distrust of organized religion makes it unlikely that he would have had much sympathy with this sort of idea, but he might have appreciated the skill with which Bickersteth rehearses possible approaches to the future in the syntax of his verse. As early as 1840, FitzGerald remarks that 'Time goes on, and we get older; and whether my idleness comprehends the distinctions of the 1st and 2nd Aorist will not be noted much in the Book of Life, either on this or the other side of the leaf' (*EFGL*, I. 254). It is a glum joke: the implication is that although time will go on, he may not for much

---

[79] *The Shadowed Home, and the Light Beyond* (1875), 179, 123.
[80] See Andrew Lincoln, *Paradise Now and Not Yet* (1981).
[81] Edward Henry Bickersteth, *Yesterday, Today, and For Ever* (1866), 5.

longer, so that his entry in the 'Book of Life' should itself be made in a tense—the aorist—which locates an action in some unspecified past time without necessarily implying its continuance. As FitzGerald sketches out his Latin paraphrases for *Rubáiyát*, we see him beginning to adapt Christian verse to a secular voice which shrinks from using future tenses, not because 'Faith overleaps the interval', but because this voice has looked and decided not to leap:

> Quisquis est Interitum qui sempiternum reformidet,
> Illa longa mihi Nox quam Dies brevis plus arridet:
> Aliquantum mihi Vitam credidit Creator Deus:
> Cum solvendi Dies adsit, adsum Ego, Deus meus!
>
> (XVI)

> [There may be some who fear eternal death.
> That long night smiles on me more than the short day,
> God the Creator has lent me a portion of life:
> When the day of Settlement comes, I am ready, my God.][82]

As FitzGerald's Latin connects 'Dies' and 'Deus' through 'adsum ego', his commas switch the tense of 'adsum' between the present moment of utterance and an imagined future in God's presence, like the slide from life to afterlife which speaks in the dying word of Thackeray's Colonel Newcome:

At the usual evening hour the chapel bell began to toll, and Thomas Newcome's hands outside the bed feebly beat time. And just as the last bell struck, a peculiar sweet smile shone over his face, and he lifted up his head a little, and quickly said, 'Adsum!' and fell back. It was the word we used at school, when names were called; and lo, he, whose heart was as that of a little child, had answered to his name, and stood in the presence of The Master.[83]

Not all Victorian death-beds are composed with such assured calm. (One of Tennyson's mourners remembered how, towards the end, 'It was almost impossible to make out more than a word here and there of what he said owing greatly I think to his having no teeth in.'[84]) Even Newcome's death, at first hearing so unambiguously pious, is

---

[82] *Trinity*, Add.MSa.6.[1]; Persian translation by Sir E. Denison Ross in the Golden Cockerel Edition of *ROK*, 84.

[83] *The Newcomes* (1853–5), ch. 80.

[84] Audrey Tennyson, as reported in Robert Bernard Martin, *Tennyson: The Unquiet Heart*, 581.

organized on the page so as to dramatize the living contradictions which are contained in certain doctrines of personal immortality, because 'Adsum!' is at once an act of obedience and of self-assertion, the remembered cry of an individual's childhood and the cultural residua of a shared linguistic past. Like Thackeray's 'Adsum!', FitzGerald's 'Adsum Ego' takes a locution that has survived the death of Latin as a spoken language, and transforms it into a figure of the speaker's presence in the afterlife. In both cases, the present tense anticipates 'beating time' more lastingly than Newcome's hands.

Bickersteth's best-selling gloss on 'The Order for the Burial of the Dead' extends still further into the future, as it considers St Paul's own meditation on Isaiah 22: 13: 'what advantageth it me, if the dead rise not? let us eat and drink; for tomorrow we die.' For if we are to awake from the sleep of death, Bickersteth reasons, we must first wake up to moral life:

And then they would sleep away, dream away, aye, as under the influence of intoxicating wine, drink away their immortality. Let them awake in right earnest, awake as from the sleep of wine, so as to come to a true realisation of things as they are.[85]

Central to this sort of eschatological argument is the belief that continuities between earthly and heavenly life can be seen in the analogical language of the New Testament, which uses this-worldly experiences and expressions as figures of other-worldly states. Analogical metaphors draw heavily upon a book which FitzGerald admired, Joseph Butler's *The Analogy of Religion, to the Constitution and Course of Nature* (first published in 1736).[86] Butler's chapter 'Of a Future Life', for example, sees the 'new accommodations' of birds and insects emerging from their shells, and the 'continuance' of such processes in time, as analogous to 'the several changes we have undergone, and those which we know we may undergo without being destroyed'.[87] As Michael Wheeler has shown, graveyard contemplations traditionally conflate deathbeds with seedbeds, finding a natural analogy to resurrection in the flowers which spring up from

[85] *The Shadowed Home and the Light Beyond* (1875), 108.

[86] See *EFGL*, I. 653.

[87] W. E. Gladstone (ed.), *The Works of Joseph Butler* (1896), I. 19–24. The appeal of analogy to human thought processes is critically considered in James Buchanan, *Analogy, Considered as a Guide to Truth, and Applied as an Aid to Truth* (1864).

the slow changes of the wormy earth.[88] In this sense, Victorian consolatory writings on death are themselves part of a long process of metaphorical transformation, as Bickersteth's Pauline equation of sleep : waking and death : resurrection develops the traditional conflation of analogy's literal and figurative associations in order to suggest the passage between life and afterlife, but also allows the sentimental deathbed scene to smuggle in hints of spiritual transcendence under the cover of assurances that the death itself was painless. However, Bickersteth's 'things as they are' are not FitzGerald's things, any more than Bickersteth's time-travelling 'Today' is Fitz-Gerald's pumped-up 'TO-DAY':

> Ah, my Beloved, fill the Cup that clears
> TO-DAY of past Regrets and future Fears—
> *To-morrow?*—Why, To-morrow I may be
> Myself with Yesterday's Sev'n Thousand Years.
>
> (1st edn., XX)

Quatrains such as this are directed not only by contemplation of the future but also towards contemplation in the future, because they alert us to the fact that the first of the 'circumstances which contradict ... the words employed', which Vaughan uses to defend the drunkard's 'hope', will be the setting of these words into later voices. Consider the case of Molvik, the drunk theology student in Ibsen's *The Wild Duck*, who blurts out the standard formula 'The child is not dead, but sleepeth', and has his figurative uplift brought down to earth by Relling's brisk heckle: 'Nonsense';[89] or George Crabbe writing on 14 June 1883 that early in the morning he had heard FitzGerald shuffling around in his room, and discovered him soon afterwards, 'as if sleeping peacefully but quite dead' (*EFGL*, I. 597). In both instances, a sceptical inflection of consolatory language reminds us that a 'realization of things as they are' will forever need to be realized in junctures of thought and speech which do not rest in peace, whatever our own chances of doing so.

FitzGerald does not neutrally adopt this contemporary unease over the return of analogical language to its material roots, but combatively takes it on, by sinking key words into the transforming contexts of his verse. Repeatedly, teasing snippets of pious texts are planted in

---

88 See *Heaven , Hell , and the Victorians*, ch. 1.
89 Trans. Una Ellis-Fermor (1950), 258.

Rubáiyát, but are then diverted by it to new ends, as FitzGerald makes the idea of living with an unalterable past and an unpredictable future consonant with the reading process, by luring us into completing Biblical tags and then mocking us for getting ahead of ourselves. 'Wordly Hope' flourishes or founders, but soon 'is gone'; only 'one thing is certain', which is not everlasting life, but 'The Flower that once has blown for ever dies'; the 'Devout ... rose before us' when they 'awoke from Sleep' into life, but then 'to Sleep return'd', just as a drinking session will also be rounded with a little sleep; earthly sleep is not the end of the matter, but only because earthly matter rots, so 'Jesus from the ground suspires' not because his breath is hopeful of animating the dead but because, through the poem's grim punning on 'arose', his corpse is still fertilizing perfumed roses; 'AWAKE!' not to repentance and righteousness,[90] but to postpone a hangover with more wine:

Awake thou that sleepest, and arise from the dead ... And be not drunk with wine ... but be filled with the Spirit ...   (Ephesians 5: 14–18)

    Awake, awake: fling off the night!   (*Hymns Ancient and Modern*, 342)

AWAKE! for Morning in the Bowl of Night
Has flung the Stone that puts the Stars to Flight   (*Rubáiyát*, 1st edn., I)

In each case, the activity of reading tests and confirms the argument which FitzGerald's translation is putting forward. The small acts of suspense which structure each sentence, echoing the larger feelings of dread and longing which are built into each human life, remind us that the future we expect is not necessarily the one which will be provided for us.

    Although FitzGerald's translation alternately embraces and shrugs off the assumptions which are carried by its archaic idiom, it is not only consolatory religious writings which are subjected to this sort of close and unsentimental scrutiny. The difficulties involved in awaking to 'a realization of things as they are', where the 'influence' of wine has taken the place of divine inspiration, are expressed directly, but also more indirectly, as FitzGerald demonstrates what sort of poem would be produced by a translator who took seriously *Rubáiyát*'s appeals to drink and forgetfulness. Omar's 'spirit' produces poetic hangovers.

---

[90]   See, e.g., J. W. Cunningham's Evangelical appeal: 'Awake, awake, poor lost creature, to a sense of your miserable condition!', *Sermons* (2 vols., 1822–4), I. 242.

'A CERTAIN CONSCIOUSNESS'

In 1859, the year in which the first edition of *Rubáiyát* was published, George Eliot described Adam Bede's attempt to raise his voice in prayer:

But Adam's thoughts of Hetty did not deafen him to the service; they rather blended with all the other deep feelings for which the church service was a channel to him this afternoon, as a certain consciousness of our entire past and imagined future blends itself with all our moments of keen sensibility. And to Adam the church service was the best channel he could have found for his mingled regret, yearning, and resignation; its interchange of beseeching cries for help, with outbursts of faith and praise—its recurrent responses and the familiar rhythm of its collects, seemed to speak for him as no other form of worship could have done ... [91]

As Geoffrey Hill notes, '"recurrent responses" is a wide-ranging term'. It refers not only to the responses which are chanted within the limited timespan of this particular evensong, following the established patterns of the Anglican Prayer Book, but also to the recurrence of these responses over the weeks of the liturgical year, season by season, and so to "the continuity of human response in general to an ancient process of parochial and national life".'[92] In this way, both the subject and form of Eliot's description answer to her abiding interest in those 'deep' channels of transmission which are carved out by 'the coercive influence of tradition',[93] because her lines dwell on time, but they also dwell in time, as the patternings of her prose sink the individual stresses and slacks of Adam's thoughts into the balanced periods of congregational call and reply: 'beseeching cries for help, with outbursts of faith and praise ... recurrent responses ... familiar rhythms'. Here Wittgenstein provides some of the best criticism of George Eliot never written:

What is a *deep* feeling? Could someone have a feeling of ardent love or hope for the space of one second—*no matter what* preceded or followed this second?—What is happening now has significance—in these surroundings.[94]

---

[91] Ch.18. Eliot's language echoes the Positivist slant of two Journal entries: the main function of Church services is to make 'the past vividly present' (14 April 1858), and the individual 'feel part of one whole' (30 August 1865); see T. R. Wright, *The Religion of Humanity*, 186.

[92] *The Lords of Limit*, 88–9.

[93] T. Pinney (ed.), *The Essays of George Eliot* (1963), 409.

[94] *Philosophical Investigations*, 583.

As Adam Bede discovers, the surroundings of church worshippers include more than the physical fabric of pews and stained-glass windows, as the collective voice of worship rises inside and around them, and so sets each moment of prayer into the broader human perspective which Eliot describes as 'a certain consciousness of our entire past and imagined future'. Yet in taking for granted that the sentiments of individual worshippers are as firmly 'established' as the Church whose services they attend, this 'certain consciousness' risks sounding too sure of itself. Hardy, for instance, had less confident responses to Anglican worship, ruefully conscious that for him, as for many Victorian speakers, Eliot's 'channels' had been silted up by doubt:

We enter church, and we have to say, 'We have erred and strayed from thy ways like lost sheep', when what we want to say is, 'Why are we made to err and stray like lost sheep?' ...

Still, being present, we say the established words full of the historic sentiment only, mentally adding, 'How happy our ancestors were in repeating in all sincerity these articles of faith!' But we perceive that none of the congregation recognizes that we repeat the words from an antiquarian interest in them, and in a historic sense ... [95]

It is not only 'How happy ... ' which carries Hardy's accents of 'mingled regret, yearning and resignation' towards the believers whose words he now emptily echoed. His verse, too, repeatedly attempts to find shapes for his unsettled convictions over those 'established' forms of expression to which he was intellectually averse but sentimentally attached. For example, he remained fond of hymns long after he had decided that their ideas were quaint and backward, of antiquarian interest only, and his own use of traditional hymn measures often conveys this fear that a 'historic sense' is little more than 'historic sentiment', as the unpredictable pressures of everyday speech struggle to adjust themselves to the welcome and suspect 'familiar rhythm' of old stanzaic shapes. The tone of 'The Impercipient (At a Cathedral Service)' is typically torn between irritation and remorse:

> That with this bright believing band
> I have no claim to be,
> That faiths by which my comrades stand
> Seem fantasies to me,

> And mirage-mists their Shining Land,
>   Is a strange destiny.[96]

The first four lines of each stanza are in common metre, the most popular measure for church hymns, but Hardy's poem skews the sense of his words across their customary rhythms, and then draws out this stanza for an extra two lines, longingly and mockingly, as if wondering what a speaker who no longer believes in the afterlife could still have in common with the sentiments which this metre regularly carries. The growing distance between this 'bright believing band' and the speaker is then confirmed in a rhythmic estrangement, as the thoughtless sing-song of 'Is *a* strange *destiny*' is pulled up short with 'Is a *strange* destiny', as if 'The Impercipient' had suddenly recalled that the word 'stanza' literally means 'a room', and so recognized that the acoustics of the poetic space which he is using to amplify his voice have become damaged over time, like the bulging walls and collapsing roof of an abandoned church.

FitzGerald shared with Hardy a fondness for collecting and playing 'old Tunes which really are characteristic of the various Times and habits of Thought from which they arose' (*EFGL*, II. 58) and, like Hardy, the lingering within his verse of these hymns and folk-ballads can preserve and assert a world of values which the lines now carrying them appear to have abandoned. Take the 'alcoholic Sacrament' of communion hymns (*EFGL*, I. 322):

> Here would I feed upon the Bread of God;
>   Here drink with Thee the royal Wine of heaven;
> Here would I lay aside each earthly load;
>   Here taste afresh the calm of sin forgiven.[97]

Bonar's lines imagine the eucharist as both a direct encounter with the divine, and a foretaste of heaven, as 'Here drink with Thee' looks to the sacramental wine here and now, and to the anticipated heavenly communion of which this is only a type. Fitz-Gerald, similarly, imagines bread, wine, and verse being brought together in a context of human longing, and supports the different shape of his thinking with a suitably warped recollection of English hymnody:

---

[96] First published in *Wessex Poems* (1898), *HP*, I. 87.
[97] Horatius Bonar, 'Here, O my Lord, I see Thee face to face', *Hymns Ancient and Modern*, 274.

> Here with a Loaf of Bread beneath the Bough,
> A Flask of Wine, a Book of Verse—and Thou
>   Beside me singing in the Wilderness—
> And Wilderness is Paradise enow.

(1st edn., XI)

In this context, 'Thou' is not the prophet John, 'crying in the Wilderness' because 'the Kingdom of Heaven is at Hand',[98] but a singer who completes an earthly heaven at the speaker's fingertips, just as FitzGerald's translation returns 'Paradise' to its etymological roots in Old Persian as a nobleman's enclosure or park. Even if we cannot know the tune of this song, the archaic rhyme-words 'Thou' | 'enow' which carry it in FitzGerald's verse have a sentimental lilt to them, like the song of a drunk nostalgic for a time before drink and religious doubt combined to produce a queasily uncertain consciousness of his personal and cultural past. It is as if the singer's 'book of Verse' was *Hymns Ancient and Modern*, but the way he shakes its cadences free of their traditional convictions then questions whether a hymn can be ancient *and* modern without disclosing what FitzGerald described as 'the influence of time' upon the way it has come to be understood.[99]

FitzGerald's association of drink and song is not surprising. We would expect a writer to be self-conscious about the effects of drink upon speech, not only as a source of metaphors (as Coleridge compares the invigorating and companionable effects of metre to 'wine during animated conversation')[100] but also as a way of drawing attention to those questions of delayed consequences which all written texts come to embody, whether or not they describe them out loud. As one mid-Victorian temperance confession argues:

Poets may sing of the Circean cup—praise in glowing terms the garlands which wreathe it—wit may lend its brilliant aid to celebrate it, and even learning invest it with a charm; but when the poet's song shall have died, and the garlands have all withered; when wit shall have ceased to sparkle, and the lore of ages be an unremembered thing; the baneful effects of the intoxicating draught will be felt … [101]

This is perhaps too unambitious for the fate of writing, if the 'baneful effects' of drink are understood to be limited to a throbbing headache

---

[98] Matthew 3: 3.   [99] *Euphranor, A Dialogue on Youth* (1851), repr. in *EFGW*, I. 147.
[100] *Biographia Literaria*, II. 51.
[101] John B. Gough, *An Autobiography* (1845), repr. in John W. Crowley (ed.) *Drunkard's Progress: Narratives of Addiction, Despair and Recovery* (1999), 154.

and a parched tongue. But the gloomy relish with which the passage goes on to warn of 'the miserable doom of the drunkard' makes it clear that for this writer, as for many temperance campaigners, it is impossible to distinguish clearly between the individual misery of a hangover, and the cumulative misery to which it contributes. 'Be always drunken', Baudelaire urges, 'If you would not feel the horrible burden of Time weighing on your shoulders and crushing you to the earth, be drunken continually.'[102] For many of his contemporaries, however, to be under the influence of alcohol is already to be under the burden of time, either because drunkenness is seen as a degenerate condition to which certain individuals are predisposed by birth or environment, less a temptation than a compulsion,[103] or because alcohol's quickening of the pulse can be observed in overlapping timescales: the shiny red face of a single drinking bout, which is then fixed into the capillaried blush of the regular drinker, and is finally rooted in the diseased internal organs of the confirmed drunkard.

When FitzGerald announces that 'this evil comes upon us gradually, without our knowing how it grows', or that a man tumbled out of a cart is in mortal danger, 'the wound he got telling on a Body corrupted by Drink', he assumes the lofty voice of the temperance preacher for whom drink influences the body's hidden future more than we can know (*EFGL*, III. 5, 282).[104] This is not only because we cannot see our own livers. 'The burden of Omar's song', FitzGerald writes in the Preface to the second edition of *Rubáiyát*, 'if not "Let us eat"—is assuredly—"Let us drink, for Tomorrow we die"'. For a number of temperance campaigners, though, his allusion to Isaiah 22: 13 would have been too rapid to dismiss its own preface ('what advantageth it me, if the dead rise not?'), because a prematurely corrupt body, it is argued, will significantly reduce our chances of being raised incorruptible at the last.[105] The aptly named Reverend

---

[102] Trans. Arthur Symons, repr. in Simon Rae (ed.), *The Faber Book of Drink, Drinkers, and Drinking* (1991), 65.

[103] See Daniel Pick, *Faces of Degeneration*, 195.

[104] See, e.g., the Revd R. B. Grindrod, *A Physician's Thoughts on Scriptural Temperance* (1884), 26: 'Unseen, apparently harmless, because minute, influences are more destructive to the health of the soul than occasional and more glaring outrages'; FitzGerald's brother, John, gained some notoriety as a temperance preacher.

[105] See, e.g., the Revd W. R. Baker, *The Curse of Britain* (1838), 13, on 'the influence of [the drunkard's] habits on his eternal state': 'believing that "after death will come the judgment", and that our present character will determine the nature of our future

Furniss provides a bloodthirsty example of this way of thinking in the seventh volume of his series *Books for Children and Young Person: The House of Death*. For the price of one penny, the young person who opened its pages could observe the opening of a drunkard's coffin:

> The cheeks were so dreadfully swollen out, that they touched each side of the coffin. The mouth was partly open, and seemed to grin at them! The legs also were dreadfully swollen, so that the coffin could scarcely hold them. Oh, that the drunkard could see what he will come to when he is put in the coffin. Oh, that he could see his body as it will be after the resurrection, far more frightful than in the coffin. Oh, that he could see his soul, which will be ten million times more frightful than his body. Poor children, if you have drunken parents, say the Hail Mary for them every day lest they should take you to hell along with them.[106]

Redemption is not only the subject of Furniss's gloating prose, but also what it sets out to achieve, as his description lingers remorsefully over words like 'frightful' and 'dreadful', and so attempts to restore the meaning of expressions which are usually thinned out in everyday speech. 'Dreadfully', for instance, catches in our throats, because the bloated corpse is not 'dreadfully swollen', as someone might complain about a sprained ankle, but forms instead the moral centre of a tract which is a penny dreadful in more than name: it is full of, and intended to fill its readers with, dread. Victorian temperance tracts often insist upon the drunkard's hidden life, as healthy domestic influences are replaced by the dangerous influence of secret new drinking companions,[107] or as a secret cache of bottles progresses to violence behind closed doors, so they are especially haunted by the location and contents of the drunkard's grave, because it is here that

---

condition, we should not do justice to our subject, were we not to exhibit the doom, however awful, which awaits the drunkard in that world to which his intemperance is fast hastening his approach.'

[106] Revd J. Furniss, *The House of Death* (1860), 17.

[107] See, e.g., Baker, *The Curse of Britain*, 56: 'It is estimated that in Britain, alone, there are no less than *Six hundred thousand* drunkards! Let the reader remember that each of these sustains an intimate relationship to other human beings, and exerts some degree of influence upon them, and that such influence can be no otherwise than injurious; and he will then form some idea of what must be the aggregate of domestic infelicity, produced by the one, monstrous vice of intemperance.' The word 'influence' itself becomes a central crossing-point for lines of enquiry over what degree of responsibility the drunkard should hold for his fate; Brian Harrison quotes one temperance preacher testily pointing out that 'the physical influence of liquor cannot be neutralised by any spiritual influence', *Drink and the Victorians* (1971), 122.

the most intimate of secrets are buried or dug up.[108] Their warnings give a grim new turn to *in vino veritas*: the truth will out, like vomit.

FitzGerald's revisions for the second edition of *Rubáiyát* strengthened his references to the alcoholic properties of wine, in reaction to the assumption made in J. B. Nicolas's 1867 French version that Omar believed in the mystical Súfí scheme, in which wine represents love for God, drunkenness represents religious ardour, and so on.[109] His sense of *Rubáiyát* as a continuous narrative, which dramatizes 'the Idea of *Time passing* while the Poet talks, and while his Humour changes', was further increased by these additions, which 'gave Omar's thoughts room to turn in, as also the Day which the Poem occupies. He begins with Dawn pretty sober and contemplative: then as he thinks and drinks, grows savage, blasphemous, etc., and then again sobers down into melancholy at nightfall' (*EFGL*, II. 60; III. 339). One potential difficulty with this attempt to develop a narrative 'Idea of Time passing', and then draw it together with the thought processes of the poem's speaker, is the drunkard's limited sense of time's passage as a cumulative process. Endeavouring to argue against the afterlife, for example, will be problematic for someone who has an increasingly shaky understanding of cause and effect, or of decisions and their lingering after-effects, as temperance tracts wearily pointed out how difficult it was for the drunkard to keep a daily pledge to reform 'after to-day'.[110] The collision of 'thinks' and 'drinks' in FitzGerald's description, like a cheery clinking of tankards, hints at these problems; it also alerts us to the importance of alcohol in Victorian writings on the secular afterlife of memory. In *Edwin Drood*, Dickens remarks that, 'in some cases of drunkenness ... there are two states of consciousness which never clash, but each of which pursues its separate course as though it were continuous instead of broken (thus, if I hide my watch when I am drunk, I must be drunk again before I can remember where).'[111] Individuals turn to drink,

---

108 This also seeps into mainstream poems such as Tennyson's 'The Northern Cobbler' (1879), *TP*, III. 41–5.

109 *Les Quatrains de Khèyam*, the Persian text and a prose translation of 464 quatrains.

110 See, e.g., the American temperance confession 'After To-Day', in T. S. Arthur, *Six Nights with the Washingtonians* (1842): ' "You ain't going to drink any more after to-day, neither am I; and surely we ought to have one good time before we bid our old friend brandy good-bye" '; repr. in *Drunkard's Progress*, 50.

111 Ch. 3, recalling the plot of Wilkie Collins's *The Moonstone* (1868). Compare Robert Macnish, *The Anatomy of Drunkenness* (1832): 'Drunkenness has sometimes a curious effect upon the memory. Actions committed during intoxication may be forgotten on a recovery from this state, and remembered distinctly when the person becomes again intoxicated', 46.

but they are also turned by drink, demonstrating continuities of social conduct which are unfathomable to their sober selves.[112] Experimental psychologists were further to emphasize the possibility of states of consciousness situated somewhere between full 'remembering' and 'forgetting', such as that 'fringe of felt familiarity' or 'penumbra of recognition' which is experienced when 'the idea being intact or nearly so, a part of the signs which translate it are temporarily forgotten':[113] the not-quite-absent-mindedness which Proust describes as 'a sort of pharmacy, a sort of chemical laboratory, in which our groping hand may come to rest now on a sedative drug, now on a dangerous poison'.[114] As a drug and a poison, alcohol is central to many Victorian discussions of the physiology and pathology of memory, such as the hypothesis that a damaged 'motor memory' clouds the 'acoustic memory' of individual utterances.[115] For FitzGerald, as later for Joyce in *Finnegans Wake*,[116] these discussions have a practical literary application.

'There are poems and songs about drinking, of course', writes Kingsley Amis, 'but none to speak of about getting drunk, let alone having been drunk.'[117] *Rubáiyát* is that still rarer thing: a drunk poem. For although the poem's speaker drinks to forget, the effects of drink help him to remember, as he admits into his speech traces of a revived literary past which are caught out of the corner of his ear:

---

[112] See Ribot, *The Diseases of Memory*, trans. J. Fitzgerald (1883), 27, on this 'double consciousness'.

[113] William James, *The Principles of Psychology* (1890, repr. 1981), I. 634, 37; compare 'Lapses of Memory', in *The Spectator*, 3,571 (5 December 1896), 814–15; and R. Verdon, 'Forgetfulness', in *Mind*, 2: 8 (October 1877), 29–52, on 'the invisible leaf of memory' which can become 'temporarily fastened to another leaf' (29).

[114] For Proust's 'pharmacy', see *La Prisonnière*, trans. C. K. Scott Moncrieff, *Remembrance of Things Past* (3 vols., 1981), III. 397.

[115] See Ribot, *The Diseases of Memory*, 39: 'the memory of words is a double memory, first a memory of words as far as they constitute a group of acoustic phenomena, and second a memory of words as motor images'; compare C. M. O'Leary, 'Memory and its Diseases', *The Catholic World*, 36 (1883), 101–11; and E. Eich and I. M. Birnbaum, 'Repetition, Cuing, and State-dependent Memory', in *Memory and Cognition* 10 (1982), 103–14; 'Korsakov's Psychosis', the 'syndrome of confabulation and peripheral neuritis [memory loss] in alcoholics', was named after Sergei Korsakov in 1887.

[116] Beckett selects a passage from what was then Joyce's '*Work in Progress*', which describes how 'To stir up love's young fizz I tilt with this bridle's cup champagne', to support his claim that 'Here form *is* content, content *is* form ... The language is drunk. The very words are tilted and effervescent', 'Dante ... Bruno. Vico..Joyce', repr. in *Disjecta: Miscellaneous Writings and a Dramatic Fragment*, ed. Ruby Cohn (1983), 27.

[117] Quoted in Rae, *The Faber Book of Drink*, 414.

Ah, my Beloved, fill the Cup that clears
TO-DAY of past Regrets and future Fears—

These lines are not quite clear of their own past, because 'the Cup that clears' is a slurred recollection of Cowper's 'cups | That cheer but not inebriate', and so attempts to drag this earlier poet to the drink which his own lines resist. (Some unworldly disciples of temperance, keen to replace alcohol with tea, drew particular comfort from pointing to the Orient as a place where 'the clusters of the grape are gathered to be manufactured only into raisins.'[118]) Similarly, 'Whither resorting from the vernal Heat | Shall Old Acquaintance Old Acquaintance greet' (*Rubáiyát*, 2nd edn., XCIX) replies to Burns's 'Tam o'Shanter' ('When chapman billies leave the street, | And drouthy neebors neebors meet') and 'Auld Lang Syne' ('Should auld acquaintance be forgot'), by showing that an earlier drinker-poet has not yet been forgotten, even if the blurred edges of these snatches hint that the present speaker has already enjoyed a dram or two.

The 1850s had seen a new connection established between drink and social behaviour, as 'drunk and disorderly' entered the statute-book and popular slang.[119] What FitzGerald's poem stages, however, is less a drinker's disorder than his clutches at order. One way in which his speaker attempts to restore his bearings is by organizing his thoughts around narrative signposts such as 'before' and 'after': 'Before Life's Liquor', 'who stood before the Tavern', 'a Round or two before', 'Before we too into the Dust descend', 'repentance oft before'; 'after a TO-MORROW stare', 'Sultán after Sultán', 'after Rage', 'after Silence', 'hereafter'. These unpredictable recurrences reproduce both the persistence and changefulness which could be contained in 'an Idea of Time passing' (FitzGerald's phrase equivo-cates between 'an idea of time-passing' and 'an idea-of-time passing'), by showing how the speaker's moods swing and return as he boozily whiles away his time, not least because a word like 'after' can act less like a signpost than a pivot, as its sense turns between prospect and retrospect. Given additional 'room to turn in', the poem's small-scale repetitions then form charged moments around which revolves the idea that we can be in two or more minds about how to fix time's passage into models of development, inheritance, reversion, stasis, and so on. 'Gently, brother, gently', 'About it and about', 'By and by',

---

118 Thomas Guthrie, *A Plea on Behalf of Drunkards and Against Drunkenness* (1851), 7.
119 1855 (*OED*).

'Were't not a shame—were't not a shame', 'And then, and then', 'Another and another': turns of verse dramatize a spinning head. Even the creed of 'Ah! fill the Cup:—what boots it to repeat | How Time is slipping underneath our Feet' (the slide from 'boots' to 'feet' is typical of the muzzy felicities of drunken speech which *Rubáiyát* reproduces) is expressed in verse which repeatedly attempts to shore up these slippages:

> Ah, make the most of what we yet may spend,
> Before we too into the Dust descend;
>   Dust into Dust, and under Dust, to lie,
> Sans Wine, sans Song, sans Singer, and—sans End!
>
> (1st edn., XXIII)

FitzGerald's cadences echo the material decay and renewal to which they refer. We hear how the interring of one life fertilizes the eruption of later life in the way this line draws out Jaques's interruption of the feast in *As You Like It* ('Sans teeth, sans eyes, sans taste, sans everything'), and in the repetitions of 'dust', as they animate the bleeding syntax of 'too', 'into', and 'to', so that by the end of the quatrain, 'to lie' is clenched between terminal rhymes, like a freshly buried corpse. Down, but not yet out, because although FitzGerald claimed of his a–a–b–a quatrains that 'the third line seems to lift and suspend the Wave that falls over the last',[120] a line like 'Dust into Dust, and under Dust, to lie' has further to fall. It imagines an unknowable future, but then brings this speculation under control in its own extended life, as 'lie' duly sprouts in the word which takes its place in the next quatrain: 'A Muezzín from the Tower of Darkness cries.' 'Lie' gives way to 'cries', and a new life is born in the silent passage between quatrains: rhyme as metempsychosis.

As with Tennyson's use of rhyme in *In Memoriam*, FitzGerald's sense of these human and narrative connections is often concentrated into individual words. The most important connection is a conjunction: 'and'. The first edition has forty-four of its 300 lines beginning with 'and'; the fourth edition has 'and' beginning fifty-nine of its 404 lines. 'And' adapts itself particularly well to thinking about transitions in time, because it simultaneously joins and separates the words it bridges, and so can accommodate ideas both of continuity and of rupture. For William Empson, the word 'and' is 'perhaps the

---

[120] 1859 Preface, repr. in Christopher Decker (ed.), *Rubáiyát of Omar Khayyám: a Critical Edition* (1997), 8–9.

flattest, most general, and least coloured in the English language';[121]
but this flatness can be what a writer works for rather than works
against, an achieved blankness of connection. This is especially true
of a poem like Tennyson's *Maud*, whose central narrative concern is
the bewildering variety of ways in which people are divided from one
another and themselves:

> But the broad light glares and beats,
> And the shadow flits and fleets
> And will not let me be;
> And I loathe the squares and streets,
> And the faces that one meets,
> Hearts with no love for me:
> Always I long to creep
> Into some cavern deep,
> There to weep, and weep, and weep
> My whole soul out to thee.[122]

Within a narrative, 'and' usually implies a structure of ideas in time, as
well as in relation to one another. *Maud's* repeated 'ands', however,
speak of a mind reminiscing obsessively upon what is less a clean break
with the past than a compound fracture, so that each 'and' comes to
act as the buffer between memories which pain the speaker more than
he can altogether comprehend. As each line beginning with 'and'
opens up the possibility of development or atonement, and closes it
down again, so the repetitions of 'and' then become hypnotically
suggestive of the wraith which is hanging around the speaker and his
words: the audible residue of an attachment which, from the start of
his confession, has been most richly nourished by thoughts of separation. Not every use of 'and' will be this painful. The clauses 'so often
commencing with "and"', for example, are among the features of
Clare's *The Rural Muse* which his editor John Taylor thought disturb-
ingly childish, the literary equivalent of an adult still struggling with
joined-up handwriting, but here they represent an inherent part of the
wide-eyed inclusiveness of affection through which Clare caught 'the
inexorable one-thing-after-anotherness of the world', and sought to
recreate its irresistible momentum in his reader's mind.[123]

[121] *Seven Types of Ambiguity* (1930), 126.
[122] *TP*, II. 575–6; 'O that 'twere possible' had only 'I loathe the squares and streets'.
[123] See R. K. R. Thornton (ed.), *The Rural Muse* (1982), 19; and Seamus Heaney, 'John Clare: A Bi-centenary Lecture', in Haughton, Phillips, and Summerfield (eds.), *John Clare in Context* (1994), 137.

It is because 'and' so flatly collapses so many different kinds of connection—achronicity and sequence, accretion and causality, chance and intention—that it is so well placed to question assumptions about our grasp of past events and control over the future, such as whether we think of our actions as following one another in ordered progression, or as a sum of accidental encounters, or as being just one damned thing after another. Consider the grammar of predestination: is a life bound by divine will better expressed through a neutral 'and', or a directional 'and then'?

> Thou wilt not with Predestination round
> Enmesh me, and impute my Fall to Sin?
>
> (1st edn., LVII)
>
> Thou wilt not with Predestin'd Evil round
> Enmesh, and then impute my Fall to Sin!
>
> (3rd edn., LXXX)

The wary question-mark of the first edition, which turns between disbelief and plea-bargain, is more open to the question of free will than the third edition's exasperated laying down of the law, because like all questions it encourages the activities of expectation and prediction which evidence of a 'Predestined Evil' would render meaningless.[124] In this way, a flat 'and' can be more than a grammatical conjunction; it can also work as a junction for lines of thought, as FitzGerald's repetitions of 'and' concentrate the experiences which his poem describes: the uncertainty at each moment of what is known and unknown; the hope that drink will bind time into a history of predictable consequences; the worry that drinking will cause this history to collapse in ruins.

For George Saintsbury, the 'gnomic power' of FitzGerald's quatrains can be seen in their 'perfect disjuncture' from one another.[125] This judgement is itself oddly divorced from FitzGerald's methods of composition, because many of the transitions between 'TO-DAY' and 'TO-MORROW' which are mimed in FitzGerald's patterns of generation and descent between quatrains are themselves the result of changes made between editions. Revision is a further

---

[124] 'round | Enmesh' brings together a creed and a cadence of *Paradise Lost*: compare Satan's fallen state, 'within him Hell | He brings, and round about him' (IV. 20–1), with his movements: 'on all sides round | Environ'd wins his way' (II. 1015–16).

[125] *A History of English Prosody* (2nd edn., 3 vols., 1923), III. 273.

practical means by which his speaker's 'Idea of Time passing' emerges.

*

Writing to W. A. Wright, with whom he corresponded on problems of textual transmission in Shakespeare, FitzGerald was enthusiastic about Lamb's suggestion that if Wordsworth wanted to interest anyone else in his history of a poet's mind, he should have printed his poems in 'the order of Time in which they were written' (*EFGL*, III. 212). FitzGerald's own case was trickier, because the order of time in which he first translated Omar's quatrains could not be checked against the order in which they were first written. The copyist of the Calcutta manuscript had concluded his work with the colophon *tamán shud kár-i man nizám shud*: 'It has been completed, my work has now been set in order.'[126] The translation is awkward; as Foucault reminds us, 'Order is, at one and the same time, that which is given in things as their inner law, the hidden network that determines the way they confront one another, and also that which has no existence except in the grid created by a glance, an examination, a language.'[127] The 'order' of rubáiyát in Persian manuscripts bridges Foucault's definitions, because the scribes who gathered together these scattered quatrains arranged them into sequences based upon classes of sound. Each 'rubai' (quatrain) is fixed in position according to the last letter of the word which ends each 'misra' (line), so that, as FitzGerald explained in his 1859 Preface, 'the Rubáiyát follow one another according to Alphabetic Rhyme—a strange Farrago of Grave and Gay'.[128] FitzGerald's self-conscious attempts to echo this 'Farrago' (hinted at in the alphabetic links of his own sentence: 'Farrago', '*G*rave', '*G*ay') are detectable in his early translations, which deliberately 'dove-tailed' or 'mashed together' quatrains which contained the same key-word: words such as *lab-i kisht*, which signifies the margin or border between cultivation and dessication, and so 'just divides the desert from the sown', but also joins quatrains with one another.[129] (Against tetrastich 102 in the Calcutta transcript, for example, FitzGerald wrote 'Hooks on to 98', and the two

[126] Arberry, *The Romance of the Rubáiyát*, 134.
[127] *Les Mots et les choses* (1966) trans. as *The Order of Things* (1970), xx.
[128] *EFGW*, I. 15; the 'and' equivocates: grave, and gay? or grave-and-gay?
[129] See, e.g., *EFGL*, II. 318; III. 68.

reappeared together in the first edition as XVI and XVII.[130]) Later
editions replace 'Farrago' with 'Succession': a small change, but one
which reflects a far larger shift in understanding. Although 'a strange
Succession' of quatrains is more true of the translation than of its
original, FitzGerald's new self-description reflects his growing sense
of how far his translation had developed away from its source, and his
growing interest in the imaginative possibilities of mapping out the
passage of time through the more controlled passage of his words
across the page. In particular, it is by replacing a principle of alphabetic accumulation with one of narrative extension that FitzGerald
examines critically a 'genealogical view of time as descent and succession'.[131] I borrow the phrase from Gillian Beer, who has written
suggestively of the ways in which the transformations and redundan-
cies described by evolutionary theory were given an imaginative
shape in the developing plotlines of Victorian narrative. Textual
revision complicates this model, because often the tidy sequence of
a narrative paints over the cracks of its own production:

> For has not such a Story from of Old
> Down Man's successive generations roll'd
>   Of such a clod of saturated Earth
> Cast by the Maker into Human mould?
>
> (2nd edn., XLI)

Soon after the publication of the first edition, FitzGerald approvingly
quoted Johnson's estimate of Dryden's style: 'every word seems to
drop by chance, though it falls into its proper Place' (*EFGL*, II. 426).
This quatrain works according to a similar combination of contingency and design, as it organizes the workings of fate into the chances
of rhyme, and so asks us to consider whether the individual clues and
insights which are disclosed by our actions form significant patterns,
or whether the intellectual foundations which join, for instance,
'Old', 'generations roll'd', and 'Human mould' are instead as shifty
as the sound which links them. On a larger scale, the question falls
into place in the second edition as a response to the succession of
quatrains in the first edition, because this is a new quatrain added in
revision. The poem therefore achieves, in McGann's phrase, its
'unique order of unique appearances',[132] only by the appearance

---

[130] See Arberry, *The Romance of the Rubáiyát*, 23.
[131] *Darwin's Plots*, 184.　　[132] *BI*, 5.

and disappearance of quatrains between the lines of its earlier textual state.

When FitzGerald explained that he plugged the gaps in his stripped-down versions of Calderón with 'lines of after-narrative',[133] his phrase suggests how lines of type added as filler will alter the narrative thread which they interrupt and extend. There are concentrated examples of this narrative development in the descent of individual words through *Rubáiyát*; first through particular editions, and then sinking further through the poem's textual history, as their survival manifests itself in changes of situation and sense. Take 'credit'; the only use of the word in the first edition is in quatrain LXIX:

> Indeed the Idols I have loved so long
> Have done my Credit in Men's Eyes much wrong:
> Have drown'd my Honour in a shallow Cup,
> And sold my Reputation for a Song.

Here the general sense of credibility, personal influence based upon the confidence one inspires in others, is nudged by 'sold' towards a more specific financial sense: trusting to a buyer's ability and intention to repay at some later date. By the time of the third edition, we are alerted to this metaphor by an earlier quatrain:

> Some for the Glories of This World; and some
> Sigh for the Prophet's Paradise to come;
> Ah, take the Cash, and let the Credit go,
> Nor heed the rumble of a distant Drum!

(XIII)

The shamed return of 'credit', in 'Have done my Credit in Men's Eyes much wrong', dramatizes the speaker's reluctance to let it go unchallenged, so that with hindsight the word continues to tick away underneath the intervening financial images, like a moral timebomb. But the cry which 'credit' revises shows FitzGerald's reluctance to let this very remorse go, since the swagger of 'Ah, take the Cash and let the Credit go' is put earlier in the order of quatrains, but appears later in the order of publication.[134]

---

[133] *EFGW*, IV. 6.
[134] FitzGerald's 'credit' is up-to-date: the figurative sense 'To credit (something) *to* a person, or a person *with* something' dates from 1850 *(OED)*.

Such extensions put the past in order with a limited and practical application of 'the historical sense', as T. S. Eliot was to define it; a sense which compounds the translator's consciousness that he is striking new life into not what is dead, but what is already living:

> The existing order is complete before the new work arrives; for order to persist after the supervention of novelty, the whole exisiting order must be, if ever so slightly, altered; and so the relations, proportions, values of each work of art towards the whole are readjusted; and this is conformity between the old and the new.[135]

FitzGerald's repetition of 'credit' readjusts the relations and proportions of his poem, but the extended interest in 'credit' which *Rubáiyát* discovers also establishes the place of this translation within a wider literary order. Understandably, a word like 'credit' attracted attention to itself at a time when so many attempts were being made to distinguish between the moral worth which individuals should accumulate and transmit to posterity, and the more tangible goods they might choose to bequeath to their heirs. Dickens's Mr Dombey sums up the uneasy relations between these vocabularies of inheritance, as he imagines his son developing 'without waste of time'. It is a phrase that will hang guiltily over his own future, as he discovers that time is not only what we waste, but also what routinely lays waste to our attempts to control it: 'He will make what powerful friends he pleases in after-life, when he is actively maintaining—and extending, if that is possible—the dignity and credit of the Firm.'[136] Put so close to 'dignity', 'credit' does not distinguish between the financial and the moral, as 'will' flickers menacingly with the legal means of exerting influence after one's own life.[137] But as Dickens's description discloses, in the aftershocks which it continues to send through the rest of the novel, it is not only merchants or bankers who will be drawn to the language of finance when wondering what is at issue, and what is at stake, in planning for the future.

FitzGerald often associates translation with the transmission of property: 'In truth I take old Omar more as my property than yours: he and I are more akin, are we not?' (*EFGL*, II. 542). He returns to this association of property and kinship when explaining a revision to *Rubáiyát*'s 'the Caravan | Starts for the Dawn of Noth-

---

[135] 'Tradition and the Individual Talent', repr. in *Selected Prose of T. S. Eliot*, 38–9.
[136] *Dombey and Son*, ch. 5.
[137] See Jeff Nunokawa, *The Afterlife of Property* (1994), 64.

ing': '[I] altered the "Dawn of Nothing," etc., as A[lfred] T[ennyson] pointed out its likeness to his better Property' (*EFGL*, III. 389). Both examples use 'property' in a sense consistent with the ownership of copyright, which, in its 1842 formulation, 'shall be deemed Personal Property, and shall be deemed transmissible by Bequest'.[138] To this extent, Tennyson's earlier grumble that 'You stole a bit of [*Rubáiyát*] from the Gardener's Daughter' took FitzGerald's account of his own practice at its word,[139] because when a translation is introduced with 'taken from' (as *Agamemnon* was 'taken—I must not say translated— from Aeschylus', Quaritch's catalogue duly recording 'AGAMEM-NON, a tragedy taken from AESCHYLUS'), or 'of' (*Rubáiyát of Omar Khayyám*), it would not take an unnaturally suspicious reader to wonder how easily inheritance shades into theft.[140]

FitzGerald frequently slips into this sort of awkward tone, at once brazen and shifty, when attempting to justify his translation practice, like a burglar trying to explain away a bulging sack labelled 'swag'. A significant part of this uneasiness seems to have arisen from his knowledge that the discovery of likeness could be a matter of coincidence or private obsession, rather than genealogical descent. He was especially impressed by Carlyle's essay 'Signs of the Times' (1829):

It is no very good symptom either of nations or individuals, that they deal much in vaticination. Happy men are full of the present, for its bounty suffices them; and wise men also, for its duties engage them. Our grand business undoubtedly is, not to *see* what lies dimly at a distance, but to *do* what lies clearly at hand.

> Know'st thou *Yesterday*, its aim and reason;
> Work'st thou well *Today*, for worthy things?
> Calmly wait the *Morrow's* hidden season,
> Need'st not fear what hap soe'er it brings.

But man's 'large discourse of reason' *will* look 'before and after'; and, impatient of the 'ignorant present time', will indulge in anticipation far more than profits him.[141]

---

[138] *An Act to amend the Law of Copyright* (1 July 1842), Cap. XLV, 586.

[139] *EFGL*, III. 337. The lines Tennyson refers to are: 'The summer pilot of an empty heart | Unto the shores of nothing' (*TP*, I. 555).

[140] *EFGL*, III. 631, 723.

[141] *Critical and Miscellaneous Essays* (5 vols., 1899), II. 56; repr. with minor inaccuracies in *EFGW*, V. 252.

When FitzGerald adds this to *Polonius*, his published commonplace book, he responds to the general appeal of Carlyle's words, rather than to the urgency of their original demand, because his times are no longer 'the Times' for which Carlyle wrote. However, what also 'lies clearly at hand' in FitzGerald's method of composition is his ability to set this appeal into the 'before and after' of other snippets which have been cut loose from their historical moorings, and so to discover in this new textual environment connections which Carlyle could not have foreseen. A similar rage for order is detectable in FitzGerald's impressive scrapbook of murderers, sketched for popular journals just before execution, which he interleaves with pictures of another form of the living dead: waxworks.[142] Yet for all his genial interest in classifying criminals, like a naturalist poring over trays of zoological specimens, he was fully aware that persons and ideas which appear to be 'like' may reflect nothing more than the prejudices of the observer, as when he plays upon the contemporary fuss surrounding the Tich-borne Claimant by deciding that a portrait which might, or might not, be of C. J. Fox should be hung 'in order that others may judge of the *Likeness*' of his eyebrows and shoulders '*vide Claimant*' (*EFGL*, III. 459–60). Deciding upon 'likeness' is especially difficult when reading Persian rubáiyát, because problems of manuscript attribution mean that a number of texts going under Omar's name almost certainly take after him in appearance only. FitzGerald, who occasionally signed himself 'FitzOmar' ('bastard son of Omar'), might then be perpetuating the life of a pretender, one of the so-called 'wandering quatrains', which circulate under various names and hands like sophisticated limericks.

The complex compositional history of *Rubáiyát* raises questions about the relations between poetic borrowings and poetic coinci-dences which should make us cautious about accepting Bloom's account of the fragile basis upon which all poetic relations are founded. For Bloom, as occasionally for Tennyson and FitzGerald, 'Poetry is property',[143] and literary property is theft. And yet, for Tennyson and FitzGerald, as for many other Victorian writers, the

---

[142] *Ipswich*, Vol. V.

[143] *AI*, 78. On the extent to which modern conceptions of 'the author' are linked with developing ideas of intellectual property (including the emergence of copyright law), see Mark Rose, *Authors and Owners: The Invention of Copyright* (1993), Martha Woodmansee and Peter Jaszi (eds.), *The Construction of Authorship: Textual Appropriation in Law and Literature* (1994), and John O. Jordan and Robert L. Patten (eds.), *Literature in the Marketplace: British Publishing and Reading Practices* (1995).

literary economy of a poem cannot be explained by reference to its gains and losses, until it is understood that what a writer adapts or discards often provides a critical commentary upon connections which are human as well as textual. In writing, as in other areas of human activity, choice requires rejection. FitzGerald was well attuned to this task, having devoted much of his life to giving things up (the style of living expected of him by his ostentatiously wealthy mother; meat; the visits of friends), at the same time that he assembled the scrapbooks and letters in which he could meditate upon their loss. Even his letters to Tennyson, which routinely celebrate their long-lasting friendship, are usually more interested in preserving the old memories they shared than in creating the conditions for new ones—for example, by proposing that they meet in person, rather than through the detached intimacies of their correspondence. However, as the final section of this chapter will show, their literary relationship was tugged on by more than nostalgia, because among the ideas which they continued to share was a mutual suspicion over one another's hopes for the afterlife. What joins them is the past; what divides them is the future.

TOGETHER

A. J. Arberry translates quatrain 118 in FitzGerald's transcript of *Rubáiyát*'s Calcutta manuscript:

> I am a disobedient slave: where is Thy approval?
> My heart is dark: where is the light of Thy radiance?[144]

On a scribbled page of notes, FitzGerald responded to these rhetorical questions with one of his own: '*Very Good*—Who but Omar?'[145] This is partly directed at Cowell, whose *Calcutta Review* article had strained to accommodate *Rubáiyát* into a sober mainstream of Súfí thought, and whose faith-saving lines, added to the transcript he was sharing with FitzGerald, reflect a private struggle to align Omar's complaints with his own Christian forbearance:

> Thou hidden Love of God, whose height,
> Whose depth unfathomed no man knows,
> I see from far thy beauteous light,
> Inly I sigh for thy repose;

---

[144] Arberry, *The Romance of the Rubáiyát*, 136.   [145] *CUL*, Add.4510.E, loose sheet.

My soul is sick, nor can it be
At rest, till it find rest in Thee.

July 11 1856.[146]

FitzGerald's 1859 Preface is most disobedient towards the figure from whom he most sought approval, because it incorporates chunks of Cowell's *Calcutta Review* article into an argument for Omar's worldly hedonism which Cowell had explicitly attempted to refute, and so acknowledges *Rubáiyát* as a joint production which is also an achieved difference of opinion.

FitzGerald's literary disobedience was not limited to his relations with Cowell. He often described his translations as 'perversions', as if anticipating Bloom's 'history of fruitful poetic influence' as 'a history of... perverse, wilful revisionism'.[147] According to Bloom, this revisionism produces a literary genealogy of deviation and deformation, in which each strong poem is composed as 'a *mistranslation* of its precursors':[148]

I take the word [*Tessera*] from the ancient mystery cults, where it meant a token of recognition, the fragment say of a small pot which with the other fragments would re-constitute the vessel. A poet antithetically 'completes' his precursor, by so reading the parent-poem as to retain its terms but to mean them in another sense ... [149]

Bloom's 'mistranslation' assumes that accurate translations are possible, but his *Tessera* could not offer a complete account of what FitzGerald makes of his original:

Ah Love! could thou and I with Fate conspire
To grasp this sorry Scheme of Things entire,
    Would we not we shatter it to bits—and then
Re-mould it nearer to the Heart's Desire!

(1st edn., LXXIII)

FitzGerald was sharply aware of the disconcerting ease with which a writer's 'Scheme of Things' can be 're-moulded' once it is translated

---

[146] Ibid., p. 2 of transcript.

[147] See, e.g., *EFGL*, III. 107: 'What I now propose of Aeschylus is as much a *per*-version as in Calderon's case'; *EFGW*, II. 241: 'I do not like to put this version—or *per*-version—of Æschylus into the few friendly hands it is destined for, without some apology, to him as well as to them.'

[148] *AI*, 30, 71.

[149] Ibid., 14.

into a language, and so is forever having its shape threatened, whether by the bleeding edges of individual words, or by the unreliable skill of its readers. (Some of his later letters poke gentle fun at the 'strange work' of the boy who came to read to him: 'Last night he called a *harangue* in the French Assembly a "hangarue". I asked him if he knew what that was; he said he had heard of a *Kangaroo*—and I suppose there are worse things in the French Assembly.'[150]) He was equally aware that this process of remoulding will not always take place around a framework of 'the Heart's Desire', if only because our most heartfelt desires are likely to be the secrets we keep from ourselves. However, the most troubling word in FitzGerald's quatrain for Bloom's theory to accommodate is 'we': a word which refers not only to the fictional love whom his speaker is addressing but also to the earlier poet whose voice he is affectionately projecting through his own.

Consider Bloom's favourite metaphor for the belated poet's struggle for breath: 'the precursors flood us, and our imaginations can die by drowning in them'.[151] FitzGerald, whose interest in sailing was not limited to his fondness for sailors, was uneasily attracted to ideas of drowning. In particular, it is because we swallow drink, but can also be swallowed by it, that his verse often circles warily around the imaginative association of drowning one's sorrows and simply drowning. This is hinted at in two additions to *Rubáiyát*'s second edition: a quatrain which rhymes 'the Angel of the drink' with 'the river-brink' (XLVI), and two lines which compare 'Existence' to a 'Bowl' which 'has pour'd | Millions of Bubbles like us, and will pour' (XLVII). The notion that our lives are as empty and inconsequential as bubbles would be hard to reconcile with a conviction that we are substantially different from one another, particularly when we consider that the bursting of these bubbles will return our individual breaths to the shared air. But a description of drowning may also be the means of drawing together later lives, as a single body being pulled under water can create a whirlpool which sucks in others. Writing to Mrs Tennyson in 1862 about her husband's horse-like reluctance 'to be dragged to drink' (here meaning sources of inspiration), FitzGerald's letter turns smoothly to a memory of some earlier verses, pencilled into a Prayer Book, on the death at sea of his old coachman's son:

---

[150] *EFGL*, III. 284.   [151] *AI*, 154.

> A single Bubble bursting marks the Spot
> Where sleeps the Sailor in his Sailor's Grave.

Even if the image of a single bubble romanticizes drowning (Thackeray scoffed that a hundred bubbles would be more like it), as Tennyson 'took the pipe out of his old lips to remurmur' it (*EFGL*, II. 428), and FitzGerald polishes and reprints the poem in 1870,[152] the enduring life of 'A single Bubble bursting marks the Spot' becomes an imaginative redemption of the last sign of life it describes. Despite its heavy-handed attempt to reproduce the sound of this bursting bubble, with those finger-jabbing 'b's and hissing 's's, when FitzGerald writes of the poem that 'there is a Soul in it too', we also hear an echo of the metempsychosis between writers to which translation answers:

I doubt I have given but a very one-sided version of Omar: but what I do only comes up as a Bubble to the Surface, and breaks: whereas you, with exact Scholarship, might make a lasting impression of such an Author. (*EFGL*, II. 415)

This question of how far a translation reaches, within and between speech communities, will be significant in any attempt to assess how far it 're-moulds' its original. Even a 'perverse' translation unavoidably takes its place within a broader scheme of things, as Arnold criticized Newman's Homer for its 'powerful misdirection' of standard forms of speech: a deviation which is 'more likely to subjugate and pervert opinion than to be checked and corrected by it'.[153] A translation also takes its place between schemes of things. As Clifford Geertz has pointed out,[154] it is on its porous and contested edges that a culture tends to live most intensively and precariously, as some words, texts, or ideas are kept out (as with the French resistance to American imports like 'le snackbar' or 'le popstar', sometimes running parallel to suspicion over other kinds of immigration), and some seep in. Only in this limited sense is it ever helpful to describe a translation as 'definitive', because it is through its translations that a culture makes some of its most practical efforts to define and redefine itself, as the physical movement of a text across geographical and linguistic borders maps out each culture's ideological space or

---

[152] *East Anglian Notes and Queries*, repr. in *EFGW*, VI. 269.

[153] *On Translating Homer*, repr. in *Super*, I. 172.

[154] See his essay 'Blurred Genres', in *Local Knowledge: Further Essays in Interpretive Anthropology* (1983), 19–35.

imaginative reach. The 'aggression' which George Steiner has identified as one leading impulse behind the translator's linguistic border-
crossings, for example, crystallizes a long history of thinking about
translation as a literary echo of the patterns of conquest and trade
which have irrevocably shaped political relations between East and
West.[155] FitzGerald's claim that the translator should 're-cast the
original into his own Likeness' could then seem less benevolent if
set beside Disraeli gazing on Cairo in 1831: 'My eyes and mind yet
ache with a grandeur so little in unison with our own likeness' (*EFGL*,
I. 168).[156] However, when FitzGerald's 'thoughtful Soul to Solitude
retires', there are alternative models available to explain his attitude
towards the friends-as-authors (his correspondents) and authors-
as-friends (describing the qualities of Lucretius 'which make me like
him more than any of the Latin poets', FitzGerald's 'like him' hedges
happily and typically between liking him and being like him) who
are then invited into his writing (*EFGL*, I. 607).[157] One model is
provided by the Victorian discourse of influence outlined in earlier
chapters of this book, which is detectable in Samuel Smiles's confidence that 'human character is moulded by a thousand subtle
influences', or Frederic Harrison's assertion that 'all thoughtful
minds' recognize how 'our souls ... do marvellously influence and
mould each other'.[158] For although *Rubáiyát* is, as the title-page
promises, 'Translated into English Verse', it also has English verse
translated into it:

It is an amusement to me to take what Liberties I like with these Persians,
who (as I think) are *not* Poets enough to frighten one from such excursions,
and who really *do* want a little *Art* to shape them.   (*EFGL*, II. 261)

The displaced fragments of 'good English and English Verse' contained in *Rubáiyát* provide concentrated examples of the 'little Art'
which FitzGerald used to touch up his Persian sources, and which at
the same time assuaged his regular anxiety about 'talking big on a

---

[155] *After Babel* (1975), 313; compare Jacques Delille (1769): 'If you translate, you import the
riches contained in foreign languages into your own, by means of felicitous commerce'
(quoted in André Lefevere, *Translation, History, Culture* (1992), 37); Saint Jerome: 'he has
carried meaning over into his own language, just like prisoners, by right of conquest'
(quoted in Steiner, *After Babel*, 281).

[156] Quoted in Edward W. Said, *Orientalism* (1978), 102.

[157] Compare *AI*, 70: 'the precursor's ... poem says to its descendant poem: "Be like me
but unlike me."'

[158] *Self-Help*, 342; 'The Soul and Future Life', 839.

common matter' (*EFGL*, I. 559).[159] Certain of these fragments also provided for FitzGerald an opportunity to stage his disagreements with the poet to whom he most often complained regarding the dangers of 'talking big', and about whom he most often wrote concerning the gratitude and jealousy of being moulded by someone else: Tennyson.

*

When FitzGerald was writing the prose links for his *Readings in Crabbe*, he wondered 'does the present tense of my Narrative clash with the Past tense of the Original?' (*EFGL*, I. 206). In fact, FitzGerald's choice of tense is in full accord with his repeated judgement that poets continue to *live* only if they remain present to their readers:

> Had I published [Crabbe], I should have used your authority, though not your name, for advising the world to read a little of the old chap, now buried, but 'post tres dies' to rise again, if the critics and creators of two generations agone were not mistaken.   (To Tennyson, *EFGL*, IV. 221)

Crabbe is not the only poet getting a rise out of his readers here, as FitzGerald uses the secular afterlife of writing to twit Tennyson's deepest beliefs, while in 'a *little* of the old chap' we hear a sly nudge at Tennyson's drawn-out attempt to explore those beliefs in *In Memoriam*. During 1851, FitzGerald's correspondence with Mrs Cowell often broods over the way in which a poet's repetitions can aspire to constancy, but instead be read as flatly routine, particularly where a moment of unexpected loss is described in a style that itself becomes mechanically predictable:

> In these days there is no room but for the quintessence of one's poetry, at all events; and beside that, so many of [your] poems … are affectionate *remembrances*, that one must take care how one gets too many together too much alike. You know I think 'In Memoriam' tiresome and unwholesome partly on this account.   (*EFGL*, II. 20)

'Affectionate *remembrances*' hints at their own suspect fondness for one another's company, as well as Mrs Cowell's pleasure in their recollection. Yet FitzGerald's irritation with *In Memoriam* arose more from his recognition that Tennyson's elegiac impulses threatened to become a

---

[159] *ROK* 4th edn. was bound up with a revised edition of his *Salámán*, and pleased FitzGerald by being in a 'handy, pocketable, size', *EFGL*, IV. 166.

false memory driving poems other than his own, like a dog-eared card discarded by the relentless Jacquard loom of his 'poetical machine' (*EFGL*, I. 476).

Any writer might encounter similar anxieties when confronted with his or her work, given the tendency of publication to flatten out a written document's wrinkles of personality, and the disturbing ease with which the 'machineries' of poetry generalize individual utterances into types of speech, thus providing verse with the predictable shine of the production-line. FitzGerald is not always even-handed in the way he expresses these anxieties, as when he grumbles in one letter about the sonnet form, 'in which a man may mould very mechanically' (*EFGL*, I. 281), but does not stop to point out that all poems, even the most traditional and shapely among them, are exceptions to the rules they have helped to form. However, it is not any one complaint so much as their cumulative force, directed against himself as well as other poets, which best comes to express this nagging fear that a poem which carries a recognizable stamp, either of a shared form or a personal style, can all too quickly come to sound second-hand and second-rate:

[My poems] may possess sense, fancy etc.—but they always recall other and better poems. You see all *moulded* rather by Tennyson etc. than *growing* spontaneously from my own mind. No doubt there is original feeling, too; but it is not strong enough to grow up alone and whole of itself—it takes an alien form, and always gives evidence that it does so.   (*EFGL*, II. 14)

Even FitzGerald's worry that his writing lacked 'original feeling' was not uniquely his own. Hardy, similarly, was alive to the threat which was being posed to the work of art by an age of mechanical reproduction, as he describes what can happen when the writer tries to trim the shape of past events to fit the contours of memory: ' ... our imperfect memories insensibly formalize the fresh originality of living fact—from whose shapes they slowly depart, as machine-made castings depart by degrees from the sharp hand-work of the mould.'[160] Tennyson too worried that he was producing what one reviewer described as 'those curious mental manufactures which should rather come under the head of mechanism than anything else, [which] may indeed require the knife, the file, the

---

[160] Preface to the Wessex Edition (1912) of *Wessex Tales*, repr. in Harold Orel (ed.), *Thomas Hardy's Personal Writings*, 22.

turner's lathe',[161] as we read in his letters of 1841–2, which occasionally associate the mechanical reproduction of his poetry in 'the
press' with the 'pyroglyphs' which were (briefly) being produced
by 'the presses' of his Patent Decorative Carving and Sculpture
Company.

In Memoriam turns poetry's processes of sensible formalization
towards thoughts of being moulded by something other than a
poet:

> And out of darkness came the hands
> That reach through nature, moulding men.[162]

For all their differences of religious opinion—which in FitzGerald's
case often amounted to an indifference to religious opinion—Fitz-
Gerald, like Tennyson, accepted that the life of a poet cannot be
adequately reduced to, or explained by, the extended life of his or her
literary creations. He might then have been surprised by Harold
Bloom's assumption that the lives of all 'strong' poets, whatever
their sexual and literary preferences, can be satisfactorily explained
with reference to Freud's family romance.[163] The epitaph which he
requested for his gravestone, for example, also provided a mournful
summary of a life which was in large part spent explaining to itself
the instinctive feeling that it had been trapped in a form that was
alien to its own nature: 'IT IS HE THAT HATH MADE US, AND
NOT WE OURSELVES.'[164] Whether or not FitzGerald consciously
identified himself as a member of 'the third sex', or any of the several
other attempts which were made during the period to struggle towards a definition of what was not yet known as 'homosexuality',[165]
it is certainly the case that the 'Angel Shape' which he describes

---

[161] [Fanny Kemble Butler], 'Tennyson's Poems', *United States Magazine and Democratic Review*, 14 (January 1844), 64. Compare Croker's 1833 complaint: 'How curiously does an author mould and remould the plastic verse in order to fit in the favourite thought', repr. in *TCH*, 80.

[162] *IM*, CXXIV, *TP*, II. 444.

[163] Bloom's vocabulary has, however, been adopted in a number of recent critical attempts to recover a gay literary tradition, in much the same way that Sandra Gilbert and Susan Gubar adopted it for their earlier investigation into a female literary tradition, *The Madwoman in the Attic* (1979). Compare Alan Sinfield's comment that 'gay men seem doomed to wrestle with the canon', discussed in Gregory Woods, *A History of Gay Literature: The Male Tradition* (1998), 11.

[164] Psalms 100: 2.

[165] See especially Brian Reade (ed.), *Sexual Heretics: Male Homosexuality in English Literature from 1850–1900* (1970), Christopher Craft, *Another Kind of Love* (1994), and Linda Dowling, *Hellenism and Homosexuality in Victorian Oxford* (1994).

lurking in the dusk outside a tavern door (1st edn., XLII) is not the sort of figure whom many mid-century readers, more used to Coventry Patmore's homely goddess, would have felt comfortable in celebrating as an influence for good. Even so, FitzGerald would have been self-consciously aware that, for someone in his historical situation, this teasingly ambiguous shape was the closest he could approach to the alternative ideals celebrated by many of his contemporaries, given how fully his anguished pleasure in the company of young men eliminated him from a number of key Victorian models of the afterlife, from the marital reunions of a Christian heaven, to the extension of the family line through one's own children.

It is when faced with the threat of his poem taking on the 'alien form' of Tennyson's quatrains that FitzGerald comes closest to the form of antithetical completion described by Bloom, because his *Rubáiyát* does not shy away from encountering the massive and growing presence of *In Memoriam*. Instead, it domesticates the alien, and 'gives evidence that it does so', by filtering Tennyson's lines through a later speaker's befuddled voice until they have departed from their original shapes of enquiry. Tennyson's anguished section LVI on geological and evolutionary change ends by wondering whether man is destined to be 'No more?' than dust packed on the earlier dust of those who are already no more:

> O life as futile, then, as frail!
> O for thy voice to soothe and bless!
> What hope of answer, or redress?
> Behind the veil, behind the veil.[166]

'Behind the veil' offers the hope of an answer and, chant-like, answers to itself, with what could be read either as a firming of faith, or as nervous humming in the dark. Like many open-ended questions, although 'What hope of answer, or redress?' appeals for an answer, it mostly attracts repetition, as when Elizabeth Gaskell uses the last three lines of the stanza as an epigraph to her novel *Sylvia's Lovers* (1863). FitzGerald's answer to this question takes the form of transplanting 'Behind the veil' into alien contexts which redirect Tennyson's future hope (one day...) back to present pleasure (one day):

---

[166] *TP*, II. 374.

Then of the THEE IN ME who works behind
The Veil of Universe I cried to find
    A Lamp to guide me through the darkness; and
Something then said – 'An understanding blind.'

(XXXVII)

*

When You and I behind the Veil are past,
Oh but the long long while the World shall last,
    Which of our Coming and Departure heeds
As much as Ocean of a pebble-cast.

(XLVII)

These quatrains first appeared in the expanded second edition of *Rubáiyát*, which worked to narrow the individual's lifespan in relation to the overlapping timescales in which he lives. (The Latin paraphrases had already attempted this: the 'long night' and 'short day' quoted above are FitzGerald's invention.) The sultan who abides his 'Hour or two' in 1859 is reduced to 'His destin'd Hour' in 1868; 'How long, how long, in infinite Pursuit' (1859) becomes 'Waste not your Hour, nor in the vain pursuit' (1868); the fecundity of 'a thousand Blossoms with the Day | Woke—and a thousand scatter'd into Clay' (1859) is cut back in 1868: 'Morning a thousand Roses brings, you say: | Yes, but where leaves the Rose of yesterday.' Meanwhile, the individual's limited lifespan is placed in a series of timeframes which broaden out from the appointed hour, to the day, the seasons, the year, the 'Morning of Creation' and 'Last Dawn of Reckoning', and finally 'Eternity'.[167] FitzGerald's complaint about *In Memoriam* had been that Tennyson addicted himself to his loss by lingering over his writing, lovingly fingering his memories until 'one is aware all the time that the poet wilfully protracts what he complains of, magnifies it in the Imagination, puts it into all the shapes of Fancy' (*EFGL*, I. 486). But FitzGerald was too quick to blame Tennyson for being too slow. Recall his intention to dramatize 'the Idea of *Time passing*'. It takes time to read a poem, and how one line is approached will be influenced by the relative length of that approach. Thirty years after Tennyson had remarked that Marvell's 'But at my back

---

[167] Christopher Blair points this out in 'Tennyson and his Friends: Lives and Letters' (1993), 115.

I always hear | Time's winged Chariot hurrying near' is 'Sublime—I can hardly tell why', FitzGerald answered that 'this partly depends on its Place in the Poem'. Marvell's line summons up the passage of time, but its place within the poem also dramatizes the passage of time, as it clinches the argument which has been patiently unfolding in the previous lines, and so reminds us that because time can be organized into meaningful human patterns it is not instrinsically waste (*EFGL*, III. 323). Similarly, FitzGerald's borrowed snatch of *In Memoriam* has 'Behind the Veil' returning after the space of twelve quatrains, not because 'faith overleaps the interval', but in order that the phrase can become a figure of the reaches of time which must be experienced before such intimations of immortality can be put to the test. Frederic Harrison remarks that religious writers 'assume the question closed, when they have murmured triumphantly, "Behind the veil, behind the veil"'.[168] It is FitzGerald's skill to open up Tennyson to question by creating, through his repetition of 'Behind the veil', a more measured timespan for the voice, an arch of doubt.

Despite this revisionary echo, within his broader 'per-version' of Omar Khayyám, of what FitzGerald described, scornfully and enviously, as Tennyson's 'poetical machine', it is not possible to reconcile what *Rubáiyát* makes of earlier poems with what Bloom makes of literary influence: 'If the imagination's gift comes necessarily from the perversity of the spirit, then the living labyrinth of literature is built upon the ruin of every impulse most generous in us.'[169] This is a big 'if'. It does not follow from FitzGerald's remoulding of Tennyson that their strongest literary disagreements were built upon the ruins of generous impulses; indeed, it may be that one can disagree this strongly, this generously, only with a friend. In any case, FitzGerald and Tennyson join in thinking of the imagination's 'spirit' as something other than a Bloomian *psyche*, 'a breath of one's own'.[170] This 'spirit' is alcohol and, like a drink, best when shared.

*

In the 'Introduction' to his *Readings in Crabbe*, FitzGerald explained that he had chosen to publish only the edited highlights of his reading, in order 'to attract a reader to an original which ... scarce

---

[168] 'The Soul and Future Life', 623. [169] *AI*, 85.
[170] For Bloom's attempt to fit metaphors of intoxication to his theory, see 'Walter Pater: The Intoxication of Belatedness', *Yale French Studies*, 50 (1974), 163–89. ·

anybody now cares to venture upon in its integrity'.[171] 'Integrity' is a charged word in this period. It is charged by arguments over a future life: the differing emphases which are placed on personal 'integrity' by rival doctrines of Positivist growth and Christian resurrection, or by the financial and contractual bonds which are understood to underwrite social ties.[172] It is further charged by renewed appeals to the aesthetic 'integrity' of long poems, as the established division between 'miscellanies' and 'organic' form is reinforced by an Arnoldian reaction against the baubled excesses of the Spasmodics, who were routinely accused of making 'poetical scrap-books' by smearing a thick paste of commonplace thought across the page, 'with the plums stuck in afterwards'.[173] One side of this last dispute is echoed in FitzGerald's claims that he translated *Agamemnon* by 'one license drawing on another to make all of a piece', or that he joined up the 'little Stories' of *Salámán and Absál*, 'Till, one part drawing on another, the Whole grew to the present form', because in each case the direction of 'drawing on' is poised between one thing beckoning on another, and resorting to it for borrowed credit.[174] However, when FitzGerald set out to make his publications 'all of a piece', it was usually less by tending their organic growth, and more by skilful application of 'Intellect, Scissors & Paste' (*EFGL*, III. 83):

> Some of [Crabbe's] poems I take entire—some half—some only a few stanzas, and these dovetailed together—with a change of a word, or even of a line here and there, to give them logic and fluency ... I am sure I have distilled many pretty little poems out of long dull ones. (*EFGL*, I. 633)

As stated, FitzGerald's editorial principles do not differ significantly from his methods of organizing the scrapbooks and commonplace books to which he devoted so much time and attention, each of which 'dovetailed together' miscellaneous fragments in a way that provided his restless private obsessions with the appearance of a settled taxonomic order.[175] In one notebook of annotated clippings, there is a remark under 'Books': 'It is the advantage of a small book,

---

[171] *EFGW*, VII. 111.

[172] Among the sugary moral fables on one's word as one's bond, see Anon., *Martin & James; or, The Reward of Integrity* (1793, much reprinted into the next century); Mrs Hofland, *Integrity: A Tale* (1823); S. S. J., *Integrity* (1849).

[173] *Eclectic Review*, n.s., 9 (March 1855), 280.

[174] *EFGW*, I. 43; *EFGL*, II. 242.

[175] The ten volumes of scrapbooks presented to Ipswich Musuem by FitzGerald's niece, for example, organize their material into distinct groups of subjects (Vol. I: portraits of

that the author's eye may in a manner be incumbent at once over it all, from the beginning to the end thereof; a cause why they may be more easily corrected.'[176] The allusion to Wordsworth ('incumbent o'er the surface of past time') perfectly captures FitzGerald's intentions in attacking the works of other authors armed with his scissors and paste,[177] because in his eyes the 'beginning' and 'end' of a book extended far beyond its own covers. A poet like Wordsworth, for example, can 'talk big' without producing a weighty volume, because by writing something worth repeating he will be 'taken up into the Life of England' (*EFGL*, II. 12). 'Nameless and dateless Proverbs' carry a similar appeal, as the sort of time-travelling utterances 'which yet "retain life and vigour," and widen into new relations with the widening world', as each one 'gets down into circulation' within a community of speakers.[178] For this reason, FitzGerald argues, a book of literary extracts should not represent bits and pieces taken out of context (the editor as dentist), but the result of steady accumulation and concentration (the editor as distiller); like his literary translations, the physical removal of material from source to commonplace book should shed a text's husk of historical specificity so as to expose its time-travelling core.[179]

Faced with the unpredictable sprawl of 'the widening world', commonplaces showed how the thoughts of writers ever more widely separated in time and space continued to run along parallel lines. The idea achieves its finest expression in *Rubáiyát*, a small poem about the need to keep a sense of proportion, as FitzGerald attempts to provide his quatrains with the sort of epigrammatic stamp which would free them from the local accidents of geography and history. Part of FitzGerald's achievement arises from the present tense in which so much of his poem is framed, which provides the summary judgements of each quatrain with a seal of finality that is forever new. Another part can be traced to the poem's proverbial echoes and borrowings, which FitzGerald incorporates in order to blunt the edges of those ideas and expressions which would mark out *this*

actors and poets; Vol. II: portraits of military officers and noblemen; Vol. III: portraits of politicians and orators; and so on), but all reflect FitzGerald's more general enthusiasm for bringing together people and ideas into orderly clusters.

176 *Trinity*, Add.MSa.10⁵, 8.
177 *The Prelude* (1850 text), IV. 272.
178 *EFGW*, V. 203.
179 See *EFGL*, I. 570.

translation as *his* translation, rather than as the sort of nameless and dateless work which would 'retain life and vigour' as it 'gets down into circulation', with a pressure as invisible and relentless as the circulation of the blood. In particular, FitzGerald translates *Rubáiyát*, but he is also translated by it, as he is taken up into a tradition of thinking about the 'flow' of influence as alcoholic distillation which soaks his poem with more than the 'old familiar juice' of Omar alone.

A. C. Benson tells the story of someone drinking a glass of wine in FitzGerald's company: 'FitzGerald said, with an air of great disgust, "Did you notice how he took up his glass? I am sure he likes it. Bah!" '[180] If accurate, the story is not surprising. As Barthes notes, wine is 'a converting substance, capable of reversing situations and states, and of extracting from objects their opposites—for instance, making a weak man strong, or a silent one talkative'.[181] Within the same mind and voice, as within the same body, wine attracts shifty and reversible attitudes. Thus abstemious in his personal habits, in his letters FitzGerald circles around the association of drink and poetry with the wary compulsion of an addict. He notes approvingly that Goethe needed to be 'got well drunk somehow' before he was inspired, and remarks that his own writing is 'filled on the strength of my one Glass of Porter—all at a heat', as if the imagination's natural home was the liver (*EFGL*, III. 392).[182] Similarly, Burns's 'Go, fetch to me a pint o'wine' is quoted from memory as a verse 'from the heart'; Sádi's merits 'are not strong enough to bear decanting'; La Fontaine is 'too thin a Wine for me'; and 'Carlyle's Wine, so far from weak evaporation, is only grown better by Age, losing some of its former fierceness, and grown mellow without losing Strength' (*EFGL*, I. 444–5; II. 119; III. 550, 545). FitzGerald's own regular decanting of these metaphors proves their continued strength, and makes of wine a further 'spirit', like the blood it sometimes resembles, which links the writer with a revivifying past, because this association of drink and influence circulates in mouths other than his own.

Browning's Balaustion is astonished at her fertility of thought:

> For I have drunk this poem, quenched my thirst,
> Satisfied heart and soul—yet more remains!

---

[180] *Edward FitzGerald*, 176.
[181] Roland Barthes, *Mythologies*, trans. Annette Lavers (1971, repr. 1993), 58.
[182] *EFGL*, II. 511; compare II. 519, III. 604.

Although Dionysus has drained Euripides' version of the Alcestis myth, 'To the last dregs, libation life-blood-like', Browning's simile of the grape implies a transmission both of the work and of the hidden power which produced it: the new writer will give fresh life to Alcestis, to Euripides, and to Balaustion herself, 'As though the cup that gave the wine, gave, too, | The God's prolific giver of the grape'.[183] Her speech sketches a theory of literary influence which readily enacts its own premiss, that 'literary appreciation' entails the growth of a poem along with judgement of its worth. This is not only because it flows on from a free translation of Euripides' *Alcestis* but also because the epitaph chosen for Euripides, '*The Human with his droppings of warm tears*', is taken from 'Wine of Cyprus', EBB's reflections on the wine that's meant for drinking, and 'the wine that's meant for souls':

> Our Euripides, the human,
>   With his droppings of warm tears,
> And his touches of things common
> Till they rose to touch the spheres![184]

'Droppings' is unfortunate, as if EBB needed 'the human' to remind her that Euripides was not a rabbit, but the tears she describes become more touching once it is recognized how they drop into place again in *Balaustion's Adventure*, so making these 'touches' one place where the two poems could meet on common ground.

FitzGerald was not consistently full of good cheer. The confessional narratives of the temperance movement, which warned of the easy slide from falling in with 'jolly companions' to being 'forsaken by friends',[185] find plaintive echoes in his later correspondence with Posh Fletcher, to whom he sent a copy of Cruickshank's 'The Bottle' to warn of the 'one danger—*Drink*—which threatens him', and over whose sorry slips between repentance and second thoughts he was to brood with a prim tenderness which embarrassed others and himself.[186] Indeed, the private timetable of their relationship was largely

[183] *Balaustion's Adventure* (1871), *RBP*, I. 934–5.

[184] *The Poetical Works of Elizabeth Barrett Browning* (1897), 425.

[185] See *Drunkard's Progress*, 56, on attempts made by the temperance movement to exchange the 'jolly companions' of the public house for the sober solidarity of those who had taken the pledge: 'You influence one, and he another, and he another, and they others, until from the impulse given by a single individual, hundreds are brought in' (T. S. Arthur, 'The Experience Meeting' (1842)).

[186] *EFGL*, II. 616; compare III. 210, 237, 241.

structured around public house opening-hours, because although drink removed Fletcher from FitzGerald's benevolent control, the inevitable reconciliations that followed allowed him simultaneously to scold his younger charge and continue to finance his habits, as if guiltily conscious that this sort of friendship, like other bad habits, produced pleasure in direct proportion to the threat of its removal. He is even purse-lipped about Tennyson's 'bottle of wine a day' (*EFGL*, I. 621), although Tennyson's actual drinking habits are less important than his central place in an undergraduate mythology of wine, men, and song which *Rubáiyát* dips into from time to time as a poetic restorative:

> Then said another with a long-drawn Sigh,
> 'My Clay with long oblivion is gone dry:
>   'But, fill me with the old familiar Juice,
> 'Methinks I might recover by-and-bye!'
>
>   (1st edn., LXV)

FitzGerald's choice of 'recover' again squints suspiciously at the vocabulary of temperance tracts, many of which insisted on the strength of the temptation to drink, and the equal strength of the temptation to renounce it while drunk. 'Indeed, indeed, Repentance oft before | I swore—but was I sober when I swore?' (1st edn., LXX): the wobbly internal rhymes smirk at the backslidings of drinkers who had taken the pledge ('Think what I WAS and what I AM', as one popular jingle put it),[187] as the 1860 *Punch* cartoon which FitzGerald preserved (Fig. 2) guys the reformers' equally suspect pieties.[188] However, the association of 'old familiar Juice' and 'recover' also stretches between the private and published worlds of Tennyson and FitzGerald, because one way in which FitzGerald attempts to rewrite, or unwrite, *In Memoriam* is by savouring and retaining in *Rubáiyát* the 'old vintage' and 'old champagne flavour' which he associated with Tennyson's earlier poems.[189]

'After-dinner talk' was the quality FitzGerald aspired to in his *Polonius*, and especially admired in Tennyson's 1832 version of 'The

---

[187] See Harrison, *Drink and the Victorians*, 132.

[188] *Ipswich*, Vol. IX. 39.

[189] *EFGL*, I. 661, 663. In his copy of William Aldis Wright's edition of *The Letters and Literary Remains of Edward FitzGerald* (3 vols., 1889), beside one such passage ('He has written songs to be stuck between the cantos of the Princess, none of them of the old champagne flavour, as I think'), Tennyson wrote '!!!!' (I. 200).

THE PIOUS PUBLIC-HOUSE.

(WHERE YOU MAY GET ADULTERATED BEER AND GIN.)

A Place in which the Great Brewers DON'T see any Particular Harm !

FIG. 2 Cartoon from *Punch* (14 April 1860), preserved by FitzGerald in one of his scrapbooks (*Ipswich*, IX. 39).

Miller's Daughter':[190] 'This Poem, as may be seen is much altered and enlarged from the 1st. Edn. 1833; in some respects, I think, not for

[190] 'Preface', *EFGW*, V. 201.

the better; losing somewhat of the easy character of "Talk over the Walnuts & the Wine." '[191] This is odd, because the lines about after-dinner talking were themselves added in 1842:

> Would God renew me from my birth
> I'd almost live my life again.
> So sweet it seems with thee to walk,
>   And once again to woo thee mine—
> It seems in after-dinner talk
> Across the walnuts and the wine—[192]

'Woo thee mine' dissolves into 'wine', as the first flush of passionate declaration has settled into the comfortable routines of a married couple's 'after-dinner talk'. Similarly, FitzGerald's translation of Omar can sustain 'the "Wine and Walnut" vein of Recollection' beyond their first encounter, because his revisions periodically renew 'Omar himself... as frankly before us as if we were really at Table with him, after the Wine had gone round' (*EFGL*, III. 337).[193]

When *Rubáiyát* begins at cockcrow with 'I heard a Voice within the Tavern cry', this voice belongs in part to Sir William Jones, under whose transcription of a Persian tetrastich FitzGerald wrote 'The Cock of morn does the office of lamentation-making—Matt: V. 30', and in part to Tennyson, whose 'Will Waterproof's Lyrical Monologue' is 'Made at The Cock':[194]

> But for my pleasant hour, 'tis gone;
>   'Tis gone, and let it go.
> 'Tis gone: a thousand such have slipt
>   Away from my embraces,
> And fallen into the dusty crypt
>   Of darkened forms and faces.
>
> Go therefore, thou! thy betters went
>   Long since, and came no more;
> With peals of genial clamour sent
>   From many a tavern-door ... [195]

These are lines describing wine's 'influence on the mind' (l. 12) which FitzGerald claimed would 'outlive' his time (*EFGL*, III. 171). It is also

---

[191] Written in FitzGerald's copy of the 1842 *Poems*, 102.   [192] *TP*, I. 408.
[193] Repr. in Decker (ed.), *Rubáiyát of Omar Khayyám: A Critical Edition*, 66.
[194] FitzGerald's copy of *A Grammar of the Persian Language* (4th edn., 1797), 121.
[195] *TP*, II. 102; FitzGerald kept a draft of ll. 1–20 pasted into his copy of the 1842 *Poems*, part of a letter from Tennyson.

the case that Tennyson's lines came to embody his time, because as the century progressed it became a standard exercise in nostalgia to hark back to the days before the tavern was superseded, in the social life of the better-heeled drinker, by the padded opulence of the gentlemen's club or the anonymous glamour of the hotel. 'As an essential part of the times and the men of whom we have to be most proud', an 1879 article explains, 'we must always look back upon the old tavern life with a lingering indulgent fondness.'[196] FitzGerald's own lines on the tavern-world give this 'lingering' a location and a timeframe, because they revive Tennyson's anxiety that an earlier community of poets is no more, and answer it by joining in a shared rhyme:

> And, as the Cock crew, those who stood before
> The Tavern shouted—'Open then the Door!
> 'You know how little while we have to stay,
> 'And, once departed, may return no more.'
>
> (1st edn., III)

The rhyme 'Door' | 'no more' is a literary commonplace which harks back to a shared past, and so to The Cock tavern as a common place for young poets to meet, as if FitzGerald was rewriting *In Memoriam* in Tennyson's early style in order to show how differently the two of them had aged. However, there is a third voice at work in and between these lines, because both poets brace their lines against the passage from 'genial clamour' to 'dusty crypt' by returning to the same speech from *Hamlet.*

Shakespeare:

FIRST CLOWN: A pestilence on him for a mad rogue! A poured a flagon of Rhenish wine on my head once. This same skull, sir, was Yorick's skull, the King's jester.

HAMLET: This?

FIRST CLOWN: E'en that.

HAMLET: Let me see. Alas, poor Yorick. I knew him, Horatio, a fellow of infinite jest, of most excellent fancy. He hath bore me on his back a thousand times, and now—how abhorred in my imagination it is. My gorge rises at it. Here hung those lips that I have kissed I know not how oft. Where be your gibes now, your gambols, your songs, your flashes of merriment, that were wont to set the table on a roar? Not one now to mock your own grinning? Quite chop-fallen?[197]

---

[196] H. Barton Baker, 'The Old Tavern Life', *Gentlemen's Magazine*, 245 (1879), 755.
[197] V. i. 170–83.

Tennyson, in the 'chop-house':

> I kiss the lips I once have kissed …

FitzGerald:

> I think the Vessel, that with fugitive
> Articulation answer'd, once did live,
>   And merry-make; and the cold Lip I kiss'd
> How many Kisses might it take—and give!
>
> (1st edn., XXXV)

The final question is one to which FitzGerald devoted much of his life to answering, and the fact that it remained largely a rhetorical one in his human relations made the answers all the more central to the 'fugitive Articulation' of his writing. One of his cuttings is taken from Keats's letters:

This is the reason why men who had been bosom friends, ~~on being separated~~ for any number of years meet coldly, neither of them knowing why. The fact is, they are both altered. Men who live together have a silent moulding and influencing power over each other. They inter-assimilate. 'Tis an uneasy thought that in seven years the same hands cannot greet each other again. All this may be obviated by a wilful and dramatic exercise of our minds towards each other.[198]

Writing to George Keats in America, Keats had earlier explained how they could remain present to each other through just such a 'dramatic exercise': 'I shall read a passage of Shakespeare every Sunday at ten o Clock—you read one {a}t the same time and we shall be as near each other as blind bodies can be in the same room.'[199] FitzGerald's decision to cross out 'on being separated' is characteristic of his worry that the more important separations of friends occur in time rather than in space, but *Rubáiyát* shows that he was similarly relieved by the possibility of healing these divisions through something he and Tennyson continued to share: lines from Shakespeare, which would allow them to 'live together' on paper, no matter how estranged they had become in person. In this sense, A. C. Benson was almost right when he claimed that FitzGerald was always sensitive to the 'slight, wistful, fugitive effects' of passing

---

[198] Cutting from *The Academy* (21 July, 1877), 65 (errors uncorrected), *Trinity*, Adv.b.11.2, 49. I discuss this letter in more detail in Ch. 1.

[199] *KL*, II. 5 (16–31 December 1818, 2–4 January 1819).

and past time,[200] missing only how poetry's work of dwelling on the past, of other writers' and its own, can help to articulate the fugitive, making of certain moments the joints around which earlier and later thoughts revolve.

It is when Hamlet jumps into Ophelia's grave and reclaims his past with 'This is I. Hamlet the Dane' that, as Barbara Everett acutely remarks, he 'grows up and grows dead in the same instant'.[201] This earlier speech has its own growing pains, in the appalled returns to 'now' which punctuate its disarray of tenses, the slide of 'bore' into 'abhorred', and a memory of the regular kisses that punctuated Hamlet's childhood which comes in monosyllables—'Here hung those lips that I have kissed I know not how oft'—whose iambic pulse is finally put out of joint on 'not', suddenly returning the speaker to this new, strange, grown-up time. The grave which is no longer Yorick's, and not yet Ophelia's, finally draws together the play's currents of drink and remembrance, as the gravedigger's 'stoup of liquor' loosens his tongue about the drinking games which were possible before Claudius began using drink to lubricate the machinery of the state, and Yorick's presence encourages Hamlet into thoughts which are almost certainly not influenced by Omar's thoughts, but are confluent with them, as he traces the changes which might culminate in Alexander's dust stopping a beer-barrel.

If times have changed for Hamlet, they have also changed for *Hamlet*, whose Victorian readers responded to this imaginative nexus of drink and altered states in their own burlesque rewritings of the play. Old Hamlet, in particular, seems to have inspired writers to notice that 'spirits' is a shared property of alcohol and restless ghosts.[202] The joke is a well-worn period feature of attacks upon spiritualism, as when Dickens's drunk Mr Pecksniff clutches Mrs Todgers's hand in a lurching parody of a seance:

'Has a voice from the grave no influence?' said Mr Pecksniff, with dismal tenderness. 'This is irreligious! My dear creature.'
'Hush!' urged Mrs Todgers. 'Really you mustn't.'
'It's not me,' said Mr Pecksniff. 'Don't suppose it's me: it's the voice; it's her voice.'[203]

---

[200] *Edward FitzGerald*, 192.   [201] *Young Hamlet* (1989), 30.
[202] For early examples of the association of *Hamlet* and drink, see Thomas Trotter, *An Essay on Drunkenness* (1804), 5, and Anon., *Some Enquiries into the Effects of Fermented Liquors* (1814), 'Preface'.
[203] *Martin Chuzzlewit*, ch. 9.

The same joke stretches from John Poole's *Hamlet Travestie* (1810: Hamlet's closet-scene speech is set to the tune 'Drops of Brandy'), through Charles Beckington's *Hamlet the Dane* (1847: Marcellus claims 'I'm a teetotal man', Hamlet asks for 'Oysters and gin', and there is assorted fun at the expense of Ophelia's 'bier'), to Francis Talfourd's *Hamlet Travestie* (1849: the Ghost is poisoned by 'a hearty swig' of gin and water, a music-hall Claudius urges Hamlet to 'Cheer up, and sing us, "Landlord fill the bowl"', and Hamlet's 'How | Unprofitable, beery, flat, and stale, | Seems to me now all that the world thinks ale' works in plugs for a score of popular tipples).[204]

Omar's voice was often heard as *Hamlet*'s ghost: by FitzGerald,[205] by Cowell,[206] and by critics.[207] But it does not follow that this play of restless fathers and uneasy sons dooms either Omar or FitzGerald to the fate of a Bloomian epigone:

Influence is simply a transference of personality, a mode of giving away what is most precious to one's self, and its exercise produces a sense, and, it may be, a reality of loss. Every disciple takes away something from his master.[208]

This is taken from Wilde, and explains more about Wilde's private life than it does about general literary principles. It also ignores how, in human and literary relations alike, a 'transference' can be a willing extension of what is most precious to one's self ('giving away' need not mean 'giving way to'), rather than an unwitting redirection of unsatisfied desires, as FitzGerald took pleasure in claiming and repaying his literary debts by treating his ink as a supply of vital 'spirit' for topping up his original: 'at all Cost, a Thing must *live*: with a transfusion of one's own worse Life if one can't retain the Original's better' (*EFGL*, II. 335).[209] *Rubáiyát* brings *Hamlet* back to life, and so sustains its own life, with the 'transference' of a literary kiss:

[204] Repr. in Stanley Wells (ed.), *Shakespeare Burlesques* (1978), I. 10, 36–7; II. 262, 274, 300; III. 81, 69, 90, 72.

[205] See *EFGL*, II. 305.

[206] Cowell's *Calcutta Review* article argues that Omar spoke 'Like sweet bells jangled, out of tune and harsh', 157.

[207] See, e.g., *Contemporary Review*, 27 (1876), 568.

[208] *AI*, 6.

[209] Compare Dryden on his 'paraphrase' of Virgil (1697): 'Poetry is of so subtile a spirit, that, in pouring out of one language into another, it will all evaporate; and if a new spirit be not added in the transfusion, there will remain nothing but a caput mortuum' (quoted in Lefevere, *Translation, History, Culture*, 104), and FitzGerald on Villon: 'when that old French is turned into a Language least akin to it ... I fancy that what Charm there was must be in great danger of Evaporating' (*EFGL*, IV. 129).

CRESSIDA: In kissing, do you render or receive?
MENELAUS: Both take and give.[210]

Menelaus could be speaking of literary influence. 'To kiss and be kissed', writes Burton in *The Anatomy of Melancholy*, 'is as a burden in a song.'[211] This is more generous than Adam Phillips's suggestion that a kiss represents a silent full-stop to the story of the individual's pyschosexual education, 'the mouth's elegy to itself',[212] as if kissing other people represented nothing more than the failure of our narcissistic longing to kiss ourselves better. It is also a valuable reminder that literature need not be a 'burden' in the way Walter Jackson Bate imagined 'the burden of the past', because singing, like kissing, provides oral pleasures in which we happily confuse where one mouth ends and another begins.

FitzGerald collected drinking-songs. One commonplace book now in Trinity College, Cambridge, still forms the literary equivalent of a public house, FitzGerald's 'tables' as the kind of tables which like-minded souls once sat around to sing 'Let's drink and be merry' or 'Drink with me'.[213] Singing these old tunes could anticipate a theological afterlife which we would taste as well as be absorbed by, as FitzGerald found 'consolation' in Frederick Tennyson's belief that 'men will meet in another world under their own vine and figtree ... and talk over the joys and sorrows of this anterior life ... in cheerful converse, over moderate cups' (*EFGL*, II. 75). Our singing could equally reflect a belief that, after life, nothing of us will be raised but our voices. But then, as Empson pointed out in a note to his poem 'Bacchus', 'Life involves maintaining oneself between contradictions that can't be solved by analysis',[214] and part of this life involves coming to terms with our unresolved speculations over the afterlife. It is FitzGerald's achievement in *Rubáiyát* to find for these living contradictions a lasting imaginative shape.

---

[210] *Troilus and Cressida*, IV. v. 36–7.
[211] Quoted in Adam Phillips, *On Kissing, Tickling, and Being Bored* (1993), 107.
[212] Ibid.
[213] *Trinity*, Add.MSa.8²¹, 67–8; there is another drinking-song in Add.MSa.10¹, 10.
[214] *Collected Poems* (1962), 104–5.

Afterword

CLOV: Do you believe in the life to come?
HAMM: Mine was always that.

Samuel Beckett, *Endgame*

All good things come to an end. The best descriptions of these things can last rather longer. In his essay 'Journées de Lecture', Proust explains why even the most conclusive statements of an author will gain an air of provisionality and speculation in the act of reading:

> ... it is one of the great and wonderful characteristics of good books (which will give us to see the role at once essential yet limited that reading may play in our spiritual lives) that for the author they may be called 'Conclusions' but for the reader 'Incitements'. We feel very strongly that our own wisdom begins where that of the author leaves off, and we would like him to provide us with answers when all he is able to provide us with is desires.[1]

Reading, in Proust's view, is both intrinsically valuable and intrinsically inadequate, 'essential yet limited', because although literature introduces us to new ways of looking at the world, it does not constitute the world; books can awaken us to the life of the mind, but they cannot take its place. This is why a good book, carefully read, is both a fulfilment of and an incitement to imaginative life. It provides a set of pathways for the communication of human minds, but also a set of doorways into those hidden places within our own minds that we would not otherwise have known how to enter. In its end is our beginning.

This can also be true of the way writers read one another. Take T. S. Eliot's description, in 'Little Gidding', of a bomb-site observed during the Blitz:

> Dust in the air suspended
> Marks the place where a story ended.

[1] Repr. in *Against Sainte-Beuve and Other Essays*, trans. John Sturrock (1988), 210.

Dust inbreathed was a house—
The wall, the wainscot and the mouse.[2]

The faded echo of Tennyson's 'Mariana' ('the mouse | Behind the mouldering wainscot shrieked')[3] indicates how, even if this dust marks the end of one life, one human story, we also possess stories which reach out beyond individual lives. Like dust in the air, Tennyson's words circulate to unpredictable effect, but suspended on the page they invite their readers to reconcile local differences of geography and history into the shared life of a poem. Compare the situation of the speaker in Beckett's late work 'Old Earth', who longingly, lingeringly draws out the hope of Tennyson's Tithonus that he will end by creeping into the earth like a lover's embrace:

I come home at nightfall, they take to wing, rise from my little oaktree and whirr away, glutted, into the shadows. I reach up, grasp the bough, pull myself up and go in. Three years in the earth, those the moles don't get, then guzzle guzzle, ten days long, a fortnight, and always the flight at nightfall.[4]

Beckett's speaker hints at something which had also been whisperingly present in Tithonus's voice: a craving to be released into the air, free of the body's dead weight, like the birds he sees whirring away into the shadows. It is a fate which 'Old Earth' holds tantalizingly out of reach. For this speaker, as for Tithonus's Aurora, nightfall is always the time to return home, but never for him to return to the home he wants to settle down in for good. The old earth represents both the final direction of his thoughts and the axis around which they continue to revolve.

Like Eliot's fragmentary extension of 'Mariana', Beckett's brooding recovery of 'Tithonus' responds to Tennyson's habit of leaving his speakers in a strange creative limbo. As Ricks has pointed out, Tennyson's narratives are often awkwardly situated in the gap between the ending we expect for them (Mariana's marriage to Angelo, for example, or Tithonus's grateful transformation into a cricket), and the one which is provided for us; his speakers long to put an end to themselves, but are refused even the satisfaction of a complete story. Beckett's decision to adapt 'Tithonus' to the contours of a later speaker's voice shows how intimately this sort of delayed

[2] *The Complete Poems and Plays of T. S. Eliot*, 192.　　[3] *TP*, I. 209.
[4] 'Old Earth', originally published in French as part of *Pour finir encore et autres foirades* (1976), trans. as *For to End Yet Again and Other Fizzles* (1975, repr. 1999), 53.

finish is bound up with the historical passage of Tennyson's verse. However passionately a figure like Tithonus anticipates his death, he can express this anticipation only through the prolonged lifespan of his voice on the page; so long as Tennyson's poem continues to be read, 'Tithonus', like Tithonus, will be left 'poised, waiting'.[5] The final full-stop of the poem then represents both its formal destination and the aim of its speaker, but the way Tennyson approaches this full-stop transforms it into something less than final: not a halt to ideas, but a startling of them into new postures; not a conclusion, but an incitement.

Not all writers have thought Victorian literature worth this sort of revival. In 1919, Edmund Gosse responded to the casual spite of Lytton Strachey's *Eminent Victorians* by wondering whether historical periods, like the people who live in them, will inevitably wither and die:

> Ages so multiform and redundant and full of blood as the Victorian take a long time to die; they have their surprising recoveries and their uncovenanted convalescences. But even they give up the ghost at length, and are buried hastily with scant reverence. The time has doubtless come when aged mourners must prepare themselves to attend the obsequies of the Victorian Age with as much decency as they can muster.[6]

The tone of this, ambiguously suspended between regret and relief, accurately reflects the mixed feelings which a mourner might experience in attending the funeral of one who, after the pain and humiliation of a lengthy deathbed, has finally been put out of his or her misery, and so put beyond the distress of his or her survivors. But as Gosse also recognizes, with his muffled allusion to *Macbeth* ('who would have thought the old man to have had so much blood in him?'),[7] even what seems to be dead and buried can have unexpected after-effects; like Banquo's ghost, the past can continue to shock the present into acknowledging its unfinished business.

If Goethe was right to think that one proof of genius is its 'posthumous productivity',[8] then the Victorian age has some claim to being as noisily and messily productive since it ended as it was while it lasted. In particular, Victorian ideas of human and literary succes-

---

[5] *Tennyson*, 120.
[6] 'The Agony of the Victorian Age', repr. in *Some Diversions of a Man of Letters* (1919), 337.
[7] V. i. 37–8.
[8] See Richard Holmes, *Coleridge: Darker Reflections* (1998), 561.

sion, ascendancy and sway, have continued to shape later ways of thinking and writing,[9] and so have continued to extend the range of their concerns by proving that the borders between historical periods can be as shifty and porous as the borders between people. Indeed, so many of our lines of thought about human survival extend, or deflect, or cross nineteenth-century lines of thought that more recent attempts to investigate our place in the future, such as Derek Parfit's revision of utilitarian ethics, frequently read like a set of extended footnotes to the questions which Victorian writers approached with such curious and puzzled care. In 1910, Henry James contributed an essay, 'Is There Life After Death?', to a symposium on immortality:

Only because posthumous survival in some other conditions involves what we know, what we have enjoyed and suffered, as our particular personal adventure, does it appeal to us or excite our protest; only because of the *associations* of consciousness do we trouble and consult ourselves—do we wish the latter prolonged and wonder if it may not be indestructible, or decide that we have had enough of it and invoke the conclusion that we have so had it once for all. We pass, I think, through many changes of impression, many shifting estimates, as to the force and value of these associations; and there is no single, there is no decisive sense of them in which, throughout our earthly course, it is easy or needful to rest.[10]

The question mark which follows 'Is There Life After Death?' is one which casts its long shadow back over the Victorian age, and forward into our own age. The fact that James died in 1916 might persuade us that, for him at least, this question has now been answered. The fact that James's 'changes of impression' and 'shifting estimates' remain present to us, in the restless twists and turns of his writing, might also persuade us that, like many of his contemporaries, he continues to provide models for our doubts over whether this is the right question to ask, or whether we are asking it in the right way. The current of Victorian thinking remains live.

[9] Dale Carnegie's *How to Win Friends and Influence People* (1936), for instance, that talismanic successor to Samuel Smiles's *Self-Help*, justifies its examination of 'the fine art of influencing people' with a grateful nod to Herbert Spencer (20–1).

[10] Repr. in F. O. Matthiessen (ed.), *The James Family* (1947), 604.

Bibliography

(This bibliography is limited to books and articles referred to in footnotes. Publication information for frequently cited works is provided in the note on abbreviations at the front of the book.)

Abrams, M. H., *Doing Things with Texts: Essays in Criticism and Critical Theory* (New York, and London: W. W. Norton, 1989).

Ackroyd, P., *Dickens* (London: Sinclair-Stevenson, 1990).

Adams, W. H. D., *Woman's Work and Worth in Girlhood, Maidenhood, and Wifehood* (London: John Hogg, 1880).

—— *The Glass of Fashion* (London: John Hogg, 1881).

—— 'The Poetry of Parody', *The Gentleman's Magazine* (September 1881), 303–29.

Afternoon Lectures on Literature and Art, 4 vols. (London: Bell & Daldy; Dublin: Hodges & Smith, 1864–9).

Aguilar, G., *Home Influence: A Tale for Mothers and Daughters*, 2 vols. (London: R. Groombridge & Sons, 1847).

Allen, M., *Cases of Insanity* (London: George Swire, 1831).

—— *Essay on the Classification of the Insane* (London: John Taylor, n.d.).

Anon., *Martin & James: or, the Reward of Integrity* (Dublin: J. Rice, 1793).

—— *Phrenology, and the Moral Influence of Phrenology* (London: Ackermann & Co., 1835).

—— Review of E. Chadwick, *Report on the Sanitary Condition of the Labouring Population of Great Britain*, *Quarterly Review*, 71 (1843), 417–53.

—— *Some Enquiries into the Effects of Fermented Liquors* (London: J. Johnson & Co., 1814).

—— *The Wives of England* (London: Fisher, Son & Co., 1844).

—— 'Alfred Tennyson', *Hogg's Weekly Instructor*, 148 (25 December 1847), 281–4.

—— 'Our Sanitary Remonstrants', *The Times*, 9 July 1849, 3.

—— 'Dust; or, Ugliness Redeemed', *Household Words*, 16 (13 July 1850), 379–84.

—— Review of Tennyson, *In Memoriam*, *British Quarterly Review*, 12 (August 1850), 291–2.

—— 'Tennyson's *In Memoriam*', *Westminster and Foreign Quarterly Review*, 54 (October 1850), 85–103.

—— 'Influence', *Chambers' Edinburgh Journal*, n.s., 15 (January 1851), 7–9.

——'The Minor Poets of the Day', *The Christian Remembrancer*, n.s., 21 (April 1851), 346–99.

——'Parody', *The Westminster Review*, n.s., 2 (July 1854), 95–115.

——Reports of the Crimean War, *The Times*, 13 November 1854, 6–8, and 14 November 1854, 6–8.

——'Arnold's Poems', *Eclectic Review*, n.s., 9 (March 1855), 276–84.

——'Ticket-of-leave Men', *The Saturday Review*, 14 (30 August 1862), 241–2.

——'The Manners of Posthumous Man', *The Cornhill Magazine*, n.s., 1 (July–December 1883), 214–24.

——'Lapses of Memory', *The Spectator*, 3,571 (5 December 1896), 814–15.

Appignanesi, L., and Forrester, J., *Freud's Women* (London: Weidenfeld & Nicolson, 1992).

Arac, J., *Commissioned Spirits: The Shaping of Social Motion in Dickens, Carlyle, Melville, and Hawthorne* (New Brunswick, NJ: Rutgers University Press, 1979).

Arberry, A. J., *The Romance of the Rubáiyát* (London: George Allen & Unwin, 1959).

Armstrong, I. (ed.), *Victorian Scrutinies: Reviews of Poetry, 1830–1870* (London: Athlone Press, 1972).

Arnold, M., *Matthew Arnold: A Selection of His Poems*, ed. K. Allott (Harmondsworth: Penguin, 1954).

Arthur, T. S., *Six Nights with the Washingtonians: A Series of Temperance Tales* (New York, NY: n.p., 1842).

Ashburner, J., 'Facts in Clairvoyance', *The Zoist*, 6 (1848–9), 96–110.

Austin, A., *Love's Widowhood; And Other Poems* (London: Macmillan & Co., 1889).

Austin, J. L., *How to Do Things with Words*, ed. J. O. Urmson (London: Clarendon Press, 1962).

Babbage, C., *The Ninth Bridgewater Treatise: A Fragment* (London: John Murray, 1837).

Baker, H. B., 'The Old Tavern Life', *Gentleman's Magazine*, 245 (July–December 1879), 741–55.

Baker, W. R., *The Curse of Britain* (London: T. Ward & Co., 1838).

Barcus, J. E. (ed.), *Shelley: The Critical Heritage* (London: Routledge & Kegan Paul, 1975).

Barnes, W., *The Poems of William Barnes*, ed. B. Jones, 2 vols. (London: Centaur Press, 1962).

Barthes, R., *Mythologies*, trans. A. Lavers (London: Cape, 1972, repr. London: Vintage, 1993).

——*A Lover's Discourse*, trans. R. Howard (London: Cape, 1979).

——*On Racine*, trans. R. Howard (New York, NY: Performing Arts Journal Publications, 1983).

Bate, W. J., *John Keats* (Cambridge, Mass.: Belknap Press of Harvard University Press; London: Oxford University Press, 1963).

——*The Burden of the Past and the English Poet* (London: Chatto & Windus, 1971).

Baudelaire, C., *Oeuvres*, 12 vols. (Paris: Bibliothèque de la Pléiade, 1931–50).

Baxendall, M., *Patterns of Intention: On the Historical Explanation of Pictures* (New Haven, Conn.; London: Yale University Press, 1985).

Bayley, J., *An Essay on Hardy* (Cambridge: Cambridge University Press, 1978).

Beckett, S., *Waiting for Godot: A Tragicomedy in Two Acts* (London: Faber & Faber, 1956).

—— *Happy Days* (London: Faber & Faber, 1961).

—— *For to End Yet Again and Other Fizzles* (London: John Calder, 1975, repr. 1999).

—— *Disjecta: Miscellaneous Writings and a Dramatic Fragment*, ed. R. Cohn (London: John Calder, 1983).

Beer, G., *Darwin's Plots: Evolutionary Narrative in Darwin, George Eliot and Nineteenth-Century Fiction* (London: Routledge & Kegan Paul, 1983).

—— *Open Fields: Science in Cultural Encounter* (Oxford: Oxford University Press, 1996).

Bell, C. D., *Unconscious Influence: or, Horace and May* (Edinburgh: W. P. Kennedy, 1855).

Benjamin, W., *Illuminations*, trans. H. Zohn, ed. H. Arendt (London: Cape, 1970).

Bennett, A., *Romantic Poets and the Culture of Posterity* (Cambridge: Cambridge University Press, 1999).

Benson, A. C., *Edward FitzGerald* (London: Macmillan & Co., 1905).

Bickersteth, E. H., *Yesterday, Today, and For Ever* (London: Rivingtons, 1866).

—— *The Shadowed Home, and the Light Beyond* (London: Sampson Low & Co., 1875).

Bickersteth, R., *The Recognition of Friends in Heaven* (London: n.p., 1866).

Blair, C., 'Tennyson and his Friends: Lives and Letters', Ph.D. thesis (Cambridge, 1993).

Blair, J. G., *The Poetic Art of W. H. Auden* (Princeton, NJ: Princeton University Press, 1965).

Bloom, H., 'Walter Pater: The Intoxication of Belatedness', *Yale French Studies*, 50 (1974), 163–89.

—— (ed.), *John Keats* (New York: Chelsea House Publishers, 1985).

Borges, J. L., *Labyrinths*, ed. D. A. Yates and J. E. Irby (Harmondsworth: Penguin, 1970).

Bourdillon, F. W., *Preludes and Romances* (London: G. Allen & Sons, 1908).

Bowers, F., *Textual and Literary Criticism* (Cambridge: Cambridge University Press, 1959).

Bowie, M., *Proust Among the Stars* (London: Harper Collins, 1998).

Bowlby, J., *Attachment and Loss*, 3 vols. (London: Hogarth Press, 1969–80).

Bradley, A. C., *A Commentary on Tennyson's 'In Memoriam'*, 3rd edn. (London: Macmillan & Co., 1910).

Bradley, F. H., *Appearance and Reality* (London: Swan Sonneschein & Co., 1893).

Braudy, L., *The Frenzy of Renown: Fame and its History* (New York and Oxford: Oxford University Press, 1986).

Brereton, Mrs, *Woman's Influence*, 3 vols. (London: T. C. Newby, 1845).

Briggs, A., *Victorian Things* (London: Batsford, 1988).

Brigham, A., *Remarks on the Influence of Mental Cultivation and Mental Excitement upon Health* (Boston, Mass.: Marsh, Capen, & Lyon, 1833).

Brimley, G., *Essays*, ed. W. G. Clark, 3rd edn. (London: Macmillan & Co., 1882).

Brinkley, R., and Hanley, K. (eds.), *Romantic Revisions* (Cambridge: Cambridge University Press, 1996).

Bristow, J. (ed.), *The Victorian Poet: Poetics and Persona* (London: Croom Helm, 1987).

Brodsky, J., *Less Than One: Selected Essays* (New York: Farrar Strauss Giroux, 1986).

Bromwich, D., *Hazlitt: The Mind of a Critic* (New York and Oxford: Oxford University Press, 1983).

Brookfield, F., *The Cambridge Apostles* (London: Sir I. Pitman & Sons, 1906).

Brookfield, J. O., *Influence*, 2 vols. (London: Chapman & Hall, 1871).

'Browne, H.' [H. Ellison], *Stones from the Quarry; or, Moods of the Mind* (London: Provost & Co., 1875).

Browning, E. B., *The Poetical Works of Elizabeth Barrett Browning* (London: Smith, Elder & Co., 1897).

—— *Invisible Friends: The Correspondence of Elizabeth Barrett Barrett and Benjamin Robert Haydon, 1842–1845*, ed. W. B. Pope (Cambridge, Mass.: Harvard University Press, 1972).

—— *Aurora Leigh* [1856], ed. C. Kaplan (London: The Women's Press, 1978).

—— *The Letters of Elizabeth Barrett Browning to Mary Russell Mitford, 1836–1854*, ed. M. B. Raymond and M. R. Sullivan, 3 vols. (Waco, Tex.: Armstrong Browning Library of Baylor University, 1983).

Browning, R., *Letters of Robert Browning Collected by Thomas J. Wise*, ed. T. J. Hood (Port Washington, Wis., and London: Kennikat Press, 1973).

—— *The Poetical Works of Robert Browning*, ed. I. Jack, M. Smith, R. Fowler, R. Inglesfield, S. Hawlin, and T. A. J. Burnett, 8 vols. (Oxford: Clarendon Press, 1983–2001).

—— and Browning, E. B., *The Letters of Robert Browning and Elizabeth Barrett Barrett, 1845–1846*, ed. R. W. B. Browning, 2 vols. (London: Smith, Elder & Co., 1899).

—— *The Brownings: Letters and Poetry*, ed. C. Ricks (Garden City, NY: Doubleday & Company, 1970).

Buchanan, J., *Analogy, Considered as a Guide to Truth, and Applied as an Aid to Truth* (Edinburgh: Johnston, Hunter & Co., 1864).

Buckley, J. H. *The Triumph of Time* (Cambridge, Mass.: Belknap Press of Harvard University Press; London: Oxford University Press, 1967).

Bulwer-Lytton, E., 'The Faults of Recent Poets', *The New Monthly Magazine*, 37 (January 1833), 69–74.

Burgon, J. W., *The Revision Revised* (London: John Murray, 1883).

[Butler, F. K.], 'Tennyson's Poems', *United States Magazine and Democratic Review*, n.s., 14 (January 1844), 62–77.

Butler, J., *The Works of Joseph Butler*, ed. W. E. Gladstone, 3 vols. (Oxford: Clarendon Press, 1896).

Butler, S., *The Way of All Flesh* (London: Grant Richards, 1903, repr. London: J. M. Dent & Sons, 1933).

Bygrave, S., *Coleridge and the Self: Romantic Egotism* (Basingstoke: Macmillan, 1986).

Bynum, C. W., *The Resurrection of the Body in Western Christianity, 200–1336* (New York, NY: Columbia University Press, 1995).

Caird, G. B., *The Language and Imagery of the Bible* (London: Duckworth, 1980).

Cantor, G. N., and Hodge, M. J. S. (eds.), *Conceptions of Ether* (Cambridge: Cambridge University Press, 1981).

Capper, J., 'Important Rubbish', *Household Words*, 11 (19 May 1855), 376–9.

Carey, J., *The Violent Effigy: A Study of Dickens' Imagination* (London: Faber, 1973).

Carlyle, T., *Critical and Miscellaneous Essays*, 5 vols. (London: James Fraser, 1838).

Carnegie, D., *How to Win Friends and Influence People* [1936] rev. edn. (London: Vermilion, 1981, repr. 1999).

Carroll, L., *The Diaries of Lewis Carroll*, ed. R. L. Green, 2 vols. (London: Cassell & Company, 1953).

—— *The Complete Works of Lewis Carroll* (New York: Random House, 1982).

Cashdollar, C. D., *The Transformation of Theology, 1830–1890: Positivism and Protestant Thought in Britain and America* (Princeton, NJ: Princeton University Press, 1989).

Chadwick, E., *Report on the Sanitary Condition of the Labouring Population of Great Britain* [1842], ed. M. W. Flinn (Edinburgh: Edinburgh University Press, 1965).

Chadwick, O., *The Victorian Church*, 2 vols. (London: A. & C. Black, 1966 and 1970).

Chapman, E. R., *A Comtist Lover, and Other Studies* (London: T. Fisher Unwin, 1886).

Chesterton, G. K., *Charles Dickens* (London: Methuen & Co., 1906).

Clare, J., *The Rural Muse*, ed. R. K. R. Thornton (Ashington: Mid Northumberland Arts Group, 1982).

Clayton, J., and Rothstein, E. (eds.), *Influence and Intertextuality in Literary History* (Madison, Wis.; London: University of Wisconsin Press, 1991).

Clodd, E., *Concerning a Pilgrimage to the Grave of Edward FitzGerald* (London: n.p., 1893).

Clouston, T. S., *Disorders of Speech in Insanity* (Edinburgh: Oliver & Boyd, 1876).

Coleridge, S. T., *Biographia Literaria* [1817], ed. J. Shawcross, 2 vols. (Oxford: Clarendon Press, 1907, repr. 1979).

—— *Confessions of an Inquiring Spirit* [1840], ed. H. St J. Hart (London: Adam & Charles Black, 1956).

—— *The Oxford Authors: Samuel Taylor Coleridge*, ed. H. J. Jackson (Oxford and New York: Oxford University Press, 1985).

Collins, J. C., 'A New Study of Tennyson', *The Cornhill Magazine*, 41 (January 1880), 36–50.

—— *Illustrations of Tennyson* (London: Chatto & Windus, 1891).

Collins, W., *The Moonstone: A Romance*, 3 vols. (London: Tinsley Bros., 1868).

Comte, A., *System of Positive Polity*, trans. J. H. Bridges, F. Harrison, E. S. Beesly, and R. Congreve, 4 vols. (London: Longmans, Green & Co., 1875–7).

Conolly, J., *On Some of the Forms of Insanity* (London: Savill & Edwards, 1849).

Connor, S., *Dumbstruck: A Cultural History of Ventriloquism* (New York: Oxford University Press, 2000).

—— (ed.), *Charles Dickens* (London: Longman, 1996).

Cowell, E., 'Persian Poetry', *The Westminster and Foreign Quarterly Review*, 47: 2 (July 1847), 273–308.

—— 'Omar Khayyam, The Astronomer-Poet of Persia', *Calcutta Review*, 30: 60 (June 1858), 149–62.

Cox, S. D., '*The Stranger Within Thee*': *Concepts of the Self in Late Eighteenth-Century Literature* (Pittsburgh, Pa. University of Pittsburgh Press, 1980).

Craft, C., *Another Kind of Love* (Berkeley and London: University of California Press, 1994).

Crews, F., *The Memory Wars: Freud's Legacy in Dispute* (New York: New York Review of Books, 1995).

Cross, J. W., *George Eliot's Life as Related in Her Letters and Journals*, 3 vols. (Edinburgh and London: William Blackwood & Sons, 1885).

Crowley, J. W. (ed.), *Drunkard's Progress: Narratives of Addiction, Despair and Recovery* (Baltimore, Md. and London: Johns Hopkins University Press, 1999).

Culler, J., *The Pursuit of Signs: Semiotics, Literature, Deconstruction* (London: Routledge & Kegan Paul, 1981).

Cunningham, J. W., *Sermons*, 2 vols. (London: J. Hatchard & Son, 1822–4).

Dallas, E. S., *Poetics* (London: Smith, Elder & Co., 1852).

—— *The Gay Science*, 2 vols. (London: Chapman & Hall, 1866).

D'Ambrosio, V-M., *Eliot Possessed: T. S. Eliot and FitzGerald's Rubáiyát* (New York, and London: New York University Press, 1989).

Daniel, S., *Poems, and A Defence of Ryme*, ed. A. C. Sprague (Chicago and London: University of Chicago Press, 1965).

Darwin, C., *The Formation of Vegetable Mould Through the Action of Worms, with Observations on their Habits* (London: John Murray, 1881).

Davidoff, L., and Hall, C., *Family Fortunes: Men and Women of the English Middle Class, 1780–1850* (London: Hutchinson, 1987).

Davis, P., *Memory and Writing from Wordsworth to Lawrence* (Liverpool: Liverpool University Press, 1983).

Dawson, P. M. S., 'Shelley and the *Improvisatore* Sgricci: An Unpublished Review', *Keats–Shelley Memorial Bulletin*, 32 (1981), 22–3.

Delaporte, F., *Disease and Civilisation: The Cholera in Paris, 1832*, trans. A. Goldhammer (Cambridge, Mass. and London: MIT Press, 1986).

De-Shalit, A., *Why Posterity Matters: Environmental Policies and Future Generations* (London: Routledge, 1995).

Desmond, A., and Moore, J., *Darwin* (London: Michael Joseph, 1991).

De Vere, A., Review of Tennyson, *The Princess, Edinburgh Review*, 60 (October 1849), 388–433.

Devlin, D. D., *De Quincey, Wordsworth and the Art of Prose* (London: Macmillan, 1983).

Dickens, C., *The Speeches of Charles Dickens*, ed. K. Fielding (Oxford: Clarendon Press, 1960).

—— *The Letters of Charles Dickens*, ed. M. House, G. Storey, K. Tillotson, K. J. Fielding, N. Burgis, and A. Easson, 11 vols., in progress (Oxford: Clarendon Press, 1965–).

—— *The Uncollected Writings of Charles Dickens: 'Household Words', 1850–1859*, ed. H. Stone, 2 vols. (London: Allen Lane, 1969).

—— *Dickens' Working Notes for His Novels*, ed. H. Stone (Chicago and London: University of Chicago Press, 1987).

Dobell, S., *The Poetical Works of Sydney Dobell*, 2 vols. (London: n. p., 1875).

Dooley, A. C., *Author and Printer in Victorian England* (Charlottesville, Va. and London: University Press of Virginia, 1992).

Douglas, M., *Purity and Danger: An Analysis of the Concepts of Pollution and Taboo* (London: Routledge & Kegan Paul, 1966; repr. London: Ark, 1984).

Dowden, E., *Studies in Literature 1789–1877* (London: C. Kegan Paul & Co., 1878).

Dowling, L., *Hellenism and Homosexuality in Victorian Oxford* (Ithaca, NY and London: Cornell University Press, 1994).

Ebbinghaus, H., *Über das Gedächtnis* (Leipzig: Verlag von Ducker & Humblot, 1885).

'E. F.', 'Memory and Conscience in the Future State', *Universalist and Quarterly Review*, 5 (July 1848), 221–32.

Eich, E., and Birnbaum, I. M., 'Repetition, cuing, and state-dependent memory', *Memory and Cognition*, 10 (1982), 103–14.

Eliot, G., *Adam Bede* [1859], ed. V. Cunningham (Oxford: Oxford University Press, 1996).

—— *The Mill on the Floss* [1860], ed. G. S. Haight (Oxford: Oxford University Press, 1996).

—— *Silas Marner* [1861], ed. T. Cave (Oxford: Oxford University Press, 1996).

—— *Romola* [1862–3], ed. A. Brown (Oxford: Oxford University Press, 1994).

—— *Middlemarch* [1871–2], ed. D. Carroll (Oxford: Oxford University Press, 1998).

—— *Daniel Deronda* [1876], ed. G. Handley (Oxford: Oxford University Press, 1988).

—— *Works of George Eliot*, 24 vols. (Edinburgh and London: William Blackwood & Sons, 1878–85).

—— *The George Eliot Letters*, ed. G. S. Haight, 9 vols. (London: Oxford University Press; New Haven, Conn.: Yale University Press, 1954–78).

—— *The Essays of George Eliot*, ed. T. Pinney (London: Routledge & Kegan Paul, 1963).

Eliot, T. S., *Notes Towards the Definition of Culture* (London: Faber & Faber, 1948; repr. 1962).

—— *On Poetry and Poets* (London: Faber & Faber, 1957).

—— *To Criticize the Critic and Other Writings* (London: Faber & Faber, 1965).

—— *The Complete Poems and Plays of T. S. Eliot* (London: Faber, 1969).

—— *The Waste Land: A Facsimile and Transcript*, ed. V. Eliot (London: Faber & Faber, 1971).

—— *Selected Prose of T. S. Eliot*, ed. F. Kermode (London: Faber, 1975).

—— *Inventions of the March Hare: Poems 1909–1917 by T. S. Eliot*, ed. C. Ricks (London: Faber & Faber, 1996).

Emerson, R. W., *The Early Lectures of Ralph Waldo Emerson*, ed. S. E. Whicher and R. E. Spiller, 3 vols. (Cambridge, Mass.: Harvard University Press, 1959–2).

Empson, W., *Seven Types of Ambiguity* (London: Chatto & Windus, 1930).

—— *Using Biography* (London: Chatto & Windus, 1984).

—— *Argufying: Essays on Literature and Culture*, ed. J. Haffenden (London: Chatto & Windus, 1987).

—— and Pirie, D. (eds.), *Coleridge's Verse: A Selection* (London: Faber, 1972).

Everett, B., *Poets in their Time: Essays on English Poetry from Donne to Larkin* (London: Faber, 1986).

—— *Young Hamlet: Essays on Shakespeare's Tragedies* (Oxford: Clarendon Press, 1989).

Farr, W., *Tenth Annual Report of the Registrar-General of Births, Marriages and Deaths in England* (London: General Register Office, 1847).

Farrar, F. W., *An Essay on the Origin of Language* (London: John Murray, 1860).

—— *Chapters on Language* (London: Longmans, Green, 1865).

Farrar, F. W., *Eternal Hope: Five Sermons* (London: Macmillan & Co., 1878).
—— *The Bible: Its Meaning and Supremacy* (London: Longmans & Co., 1897).
'Field, M.' [K. H. Bradley and E. E. Cooper], *Wild Honey from Various Thyme* (London: T. Fisher Unwin, 1908).
Fite, D., *Harold Bloom: The Rhetoric of Romantic Vision* (Amherst, Mass.: University of Massachusetts Press, 1985).
FitzGerald, E., *Euphranor: A Dialogue on Youth* (London: William Pickering, 1851).
—— *Polonius: A Collection of Wise Saws and Modern Instances* (London: W. Pickering, 1852).
—— *The Letters and Literary Remains of Edward FitzGerald*, ed. W. A. Wright, 3 vols. (London: Macmillan & Co., 1889).
—— *Rubáiyát of Omar Khayyám*, ed. E. D. Ross (London: Golden Cockerel Press, 1938).
—— *Rubáiyát of Omar Khayyám: A Critical Edition*, ed. C. Decker (Charlottesville, Va. and London: University Press of Virginia, 1997).
—— Annotated copy of Sir William Jones's *A Grammar of the Persian Language* (4th edn., 1797, University Library, Cambridge, Adv.c.81.9).
—— Latin paraphrases of the Calcutta transcript of *ROK* (n.d., Trinity College, Cambridge, Add.MSa.6.¹).
—— Rebound and annotated copy of Tennyson's 1830 *Poems, Mostly Lyrical* and 1832 *Poems* (Trinity College Library, Cambridge, Adv.d.25).
—— Annotated copy of Tennyson's 1842 *Poems* (Trinity College Library, Cambridge, Adv.d.26).
—— Annotated copy of Selden's *Table-Talk* (1877 edn., Trinity College Library, Cambridge, Adv.d.11.15).
—— 'Nelly-ad' (n.d., Trinity College Library, Cambridge, Add.MSa.10.²).
—— Collection of Dryden's Prefaces (n.d., Trinity College Library, Cambridge, Adv.d.11.2).
—— Commonplace Books (n.d., Trinity College Library, Cambridge, O.11.12.).
—— Scrapbooks (n.d., 10 vols., Ipswich County Museum).
Flint, K., *The Victorians and the Visual Imagination* (Cambridge: Cambridge University Press, 2000).
Forster, J., *The Life of Charles Dickens*, 2 vols. (London: Chapman & Hall, 1874).
Forster, T., *Observations on the Casual and Periodical Influence of Particular States of the Atmosphere on Human Health and Diseases* (London: T. & G. Underwood, 1817).
—— *A Collection of Letters on Early Education, and its Influence in the Prevention of Crime* (London: Sherwood & Bowyer, 1844).
Foucault, M., *The Order of Things* (London: Tavistock Publications, 1970).
Friedman, A. W., Rossman, C., and Sherzer, D. (eds.), *Beckett Translating | Translating Beckett* (University Park, Pa. and London: Pennsylvania State University Press, 1987).

Froude, J., *Short Stories on Great Subjects*, 3rd edn. (London: Longmans & Co., 1868).

—— *Thomas Carlyle: A History of his Life in London, 1834–1881*, 2 vols. (London: Longmans & Co., 1884).

Frye, N., *Anatomy of Criticism* (Princeton, NJ: Princeton University Press, 1957).

Galton, F., *Inquiries into Human Faculty and its Development* (London: Macmillan & Co., 1883).

Furniss, J. J., *The House of Death* (Dublin: James Duffy, 1860).

Geertz, C., *Local Knowledge: Further Essays in Interpretive Anthropology* (Stanford, Calif.: Stanford University Press, 1983).

Gerard, A., *An Essay on Taste* (Edinburgh: A. Kincaid & J. Bell, 1759).

Gilbert, S. M., and Gubar, S., *The Madwoman in the Attic* (New Haven, Conn. and London: Yale University Press, 1979).

Gissing, G., *Charles Dickens: A Critical Study* (London: The Gresham Publishing Company, 1903).

Glover, J., *I: The Philosophy and Psychology of Personal Identity* (London: Allen Lane, 1988).

Goldberg, M., *Carlyle and Dickens* (Athens, Ga.: University of Georgia Press, 1972).

Gosse, E., *Some Diversions of A Man of Letters* (London: William Heinemann, 1919).

Gould, S. J., *The Mismeasure of Man* (New York and London: Norton, 1981).

Graves, R., *Goodbye to All That* (London: J. Cape, 1929).

Griffiths, E., *The Printed Voice of Victorian Poetry* (Oxford: Clarendon Press, 1989).

—— 'Dryden's Past', *Proceedings of the British Academy*, 84 (1993), 113–49.

—— 'The Disappointment of Christina G. Rossetti', *Essays in Criticism*, 47 (April 1997), 107–42.

Grindrod, R. B., *A Physician's Thoughts on Spiritual Temperance* (Stirling: Drummond's Tract Depot, 1884).

Grünbaum, A., *The Foundations of Psychoanalysis: A Philosophical Critique* (Berkeley, Calif. and London: University of California Press, 1984).

Hair, D. S., *Tennyson's Language* (Toronto: University of Toronto Press, 1991).

Hallam, A. H., *Remains in Verse and Prose of Arthur Henry Hallam*, ed. H. Hallam (Boston, Mass.: Ticknor & Fields, 1863).

Hamilton, W. (ed.), *Parodies of the Works of English and American Authors*, 6 vols. (London: Reeves & Turner, 1884–9).

Hamlin, C., 'Providence and Putrefaction: Victorian Sanitation and the Natural Theology of Health and Disease', *Victorian Studies*, 28: 3 (Spring 1985), 381–411.

Hankins, T. L., and Silverman, R. J., *Instruments and the Imagination* (Princeton, NJ: Princeton University Press, 1995).

Hardy, E. L., *Spaces* (Dorset County Museum MS, n.d.)

—— *Some Recollections by Emma Hardy*, ed. E. Hardy and R. Gittings (London: Oxford University Press, 1961).

—— and Hardy, F., *Letters of Emma and Florence Hardy*, ed. M. Millgate (Oxford: Clarendon Press, 1996).

Hardy, T., *A Pair of Blue Eyes* [1872–3], ed. P. Dalziel (London: Penguin, 1998).

—— *Tess of the D'Urbervilles* [1891], ed. T. Dolin (London: Penguin, 1998).

—— *Jude the Obscure* [1895], ed. D. Taylor (London: Penguin, 1998).

—— *Thomas Hardy's Personal Writings*, ed. H. Orel (London and Melbourne: Macmillan, 1967).

—— *The Personal Notebooks of Thomas Hardy*, ed. R. H. Taylor (London: Macmillan, 1978).

Harrison, B. *Drink and the Victorians* (London: Faber & Faber, 1971).

Harrison, F., 'The Soul and Future Life', *The Nineteenth Century*, 1: 4–5 (June–July 1877), 520–37, 832–56.

Hartley, D., *Observations on Man*, 3 vols. (London: n.p., 1749, repr. London: J. Johnson, 1791).

Haughton, H., Phillips, A., and Summerfield, G. (eds.), *John Clare in Context* (Cambridge: Cambridge University Press, 1994).

Hayman, R., *K: A Biography of Kafka* (London: Weidenfeld and Nicolson, 1981).

Heaney, S., *The Government of the Tongue* (London: Faber, 1988).

Helmholtz, H. von, *Popular Lectures on Scientific Subjects*, trans. E. Atkinson (London: Longman, 1884).

Hill, G., *The Lords of Limit: Essays on Literature and Ideas* (London: Deutsch, 1984).

—— *Collected Poems* (London: Penguin, 1985).

—— *The Enemy's Country: Words, Contexture, and Other Circumstances of Language* (Oxford: Clarendon Press, 1991).

Hofland, B., *Integrity: A Tale* (London: Longman, Hurst, Rees, Orme & Brown, 1823).

Holland, N. N., *Laughing: A Psychology of Humor* (Ithaca and London: Cornell University Press, 1982).

Hollander, J., *The Figure of Echo: A Mode of Allusion in Milton and After* (Berkeley, Calif. and London: University of California Press, 1981).

—— *Melodious Guile: Fictive Pattern in Poetic Language* (New Haven and London: Yale University Press, 1988).

—— (ed.), *Poetics of Influence: Harold Bloom* (New Haven, Conn.: Schwab, 1988).

Holmes, R., *Coleridge: Darker Reflections* (London: HarperCollins, 1998).

Homer, *Odyssey*, trans. A. Pope, ed. M. Mack, 2 vols. (London: Methuen & Co.; New Haven, Conn.: Yale University Press, 1967).

Horace, *Satires, Epistles and Ars Poetica*, ed. H. R. Fairclough (London: Heinemann, 1926).

Horne, P., *Henry James and Revision* (Oxford: Clarendon Press, 1990).

Horne, R. H., *A New Spirit of the Age* (London: Smith, Elder & Co., 1844, repr. 1907).

Hotten, J. C., *Charles Dickens: The Story of his Life* (London: Methuen & Co., 1870).

Houghton, W. E., *The Victorian Frame of Mind, 1830–1870* (New Haven, Conn.: Yale University Press, 1957).

House, H., *The Dickens World*, 2nd edn. (London: Oxford University Press, 1942).

'H. P.', 'The Influence of Externals', *Dublin University Magazine*, 78 (July 1871), 73–86.

Hugo, V., *Correspondance familiale et écrits intimes*, ed. J. Gaudon, S. Gaudon, and B. Leuillot , 2 vols., in progress (Paris: Robert Laffont, 1988–).

Hunt, R., *The Poetry of Science* (London: Reeve, Benham & Reeve, 1848).

Hunter, R., and Macalpine, I., *Three Hundred Years of Psychiatry, 1535–1860* (London: Oxford University Press, 1963).

Hutton, R. H., *Criticisms on Contemporary Thought and Thinkers*, 2 vols. (London: Macmillan & Co., 1894).

——*A Victorian Spectator: Uncollected Writings of R. H. Hutton*, ed. R. Tener and M. Woodfield (Bristol: Bristol Press, 1989).

——T. H. Huxley, Lord Blachford, R. Noel, Lord Seebourne, Canon Barry, W. R. Greg, Revd B. Brown, W. E. Ward, and F. Harrison, 'A Modern "Symposium"', *The Nineteenth Century*, 2 (1877), 329–54.

Hyman, A., *Charles Babbage: Pioneer of the Computer* (Oxford: Oxford University Press, 1982).

Ibsen, H., *Three Plays: The Pillars of the Community, The Wild Duck, Hedda Gabler*, trans. U. Ellis-Fermor (Harmondsworth: Penguin, 1950).

Ioppolo, G., *Revising Shakespeare* (Cambridge, Mass. and London: Harvard University Press, 1991).

Jacob, F., *The Logic of Living Systems: A History of Heredity*, trans. B. E. Spillmann (London: Allen Lane, 1974).

Jalland, P., *Death in the Victorian Family* (Oxford: Oxford University Press, 1996).

James, H., *The Portrait of a Lady* [1881], ed. N. Bradbury (Oxford: Oxford University Press, 1995).

——*The Question of Our Speech* (Boston, Mass. and New York: Houghton Mifflin Co., 1905).

——*Views and Reviews* (Boston, Mass.: Ball Publishing Co., 1908).

——*Ten Short Stories of Henry James* (London: John Lehmann, 1948).

——*Henry James's Literary Criticism*, ed. L. Edel, 2 vols. (New York and Cambridge: Library of America, 1984).

James, H., *The Critical Muse: Selected Literary Criticism*, ed. R. Gard (Harmondsworth: Penguin, 1987).

James, W., *The Principles of Psychology*, 3 vols. (Cambridge, Mass. and London: Harvard University Press, 1981).

Johnson, L., *The Poetical Works of Lionel Johnson* (London: Elkin Matthews, 1915).

Johnson, S., *Essays from the 'Rambler', 'Adventurer', and 'Idler'*, ed. W. J. Bate (New Haven, Conn. and London: Yale University Press, 1968).

Jordan, J. O., and Patten, R. L. (eds.), *Literature in the Marketplace: British Publishing and Reading Practices* (Cambridge: Cambridge University Press, 1995).

'J. S.', 'Illusions of Memory', *Cornhill Magazine*, 41 (January–June 1880), 416–33.

Kant, I., *Lectures on Philosophical Theology*, trans. A. W. Wood and G. M. Clark (Ithaca, NY and London: Cornell University Press, 1978).

Kaplan, F., *Dickens and Mesmerism* (Princeton, NJ: Princeton University Press, 1975).

Karlin, D., *The Courtship of Robert Browning and Elizabeth Barrett* (Oxford: Clarendon Press, 1985).

—— *Browning's Hatreds* (Oxford: Clarendon Press, 1993).

Keats, J., 'Letters of John Keats—II', *The Academy*, 272 (21 July 1877), 65–7.

—— *The Poetical Works and Other Writings of John Keats*, ed. H. Buxton Forman, 8 vols. (New York: C. Scribner's Sons, 1938–9).

Kelley, P., and Coley, B. A., *The Browning Collections: A Reconstruction with Other Memorabilia* (Waco, Tex., New York and Winfield, Kan.: Armstrong Browning Library; Browning Institute; Wedgestone Press, 1984).

Kermode, F., *The Classic* (London: Faber, 1975).

Kingsley, C., 'Poems by Matthew Arnold', *Fraser's Magazine*, 49 (February 1854), 140–9.

—— *Sanitary and Social Lectures and Essays* (London: Macmillan, 1892).

Klein, M., *Envy and Gratitude and Other Works* (London: Hogarth Press, 1975).

—— *Love, Guilt and Reparation and Other Works* (London: Hogarth Press, 1975).

Knights, B., *The Idea of the Clerisy in the Nineteenth Century* (Cambridge: Cambridge University Press, 1978).

Knowles, J., 'Aspects of Tennyson', *The Nineteenth Century*, 33 (1893), 164–88.

Kselman, T. A., *Death and the Afterlife in Modern France* (Princeton, NJ: Princeton University Press, 1993).

LaCapra, D., *Rethinking Intellectual History* (Ithaca, NY, and London: Cornell University Press, 1983).

Larkin, P., *Collected Poems*, ed. A. Thwaite (London: Marvell, 1988).

Leader, Z., *Revision and Romantic Authorship* (Oxford: Clarendon Press, 1996).

Lear, J., *Love and its Place in Nature: A Philosophical Interpretation of Freudian Psychoanalysis* (New York: Farrar, Strauss & Giroux, 1990).

Lecky, W. E. H., *History of the Rise and Influence of the Spirit of Rationalism in Europe*, 2 vols. (London: Longmans, Green, 1865).

Lefevere, A., *Translation, History, Culture: A Sourcebook* (London: Routledge, 1992).

Lewes, G. H., *The Study of Psychology, Its Object, Scope and Method* (London: Trübner & Co., 1879).

Lincoln, A., *Paradise Now and Not Yet* (Cambridge: Cambridge University Press, 1981).

Luckhurst, N., *Science and Structure in Proust's 'A la recherche du temps perdu'* (Oxford: Clarendon Press, 2000).

McDannell, C., and Lang, B., *Heaven: A History* (New Haven and London: Yale University Press, 1988).

McFarland, T., *Originality and Imagination* (Baltimore, Md: Johns Hopkins University Press, 1985).

McManners, J., *Death and the Enlightenment: Changing Attitudes to Death Among Christians and Unbelievers in Eighteenth-Century France* (Oxford: Clarendon Press, 1981).

Macnish, R., *The Anatomy of Drunkenness*, 4th edn. (Glasgow: W. R. M'Phun, 1832).

Main, A. (ed.), *Wise, Witty and Tender Sayings in Prose and Verse Selected from the Works of George Eliot* (Edinburgh and London: William Blackwood & Sons, 1872).

Malet, H. P., *Incidents in the Biography of Dust* (London: Trübner & Co., 1877).

Mandelstam, O., *Selected Essays*, trans. S. Monas (Austin, Tex.: University of Texas Press, 1977).

Manford, A., 'Thomas Hardy's Later Revisions in *A Pair of Blue Eyes*', PBSA, 76: 2 (1982), 209–20.

Mansel, H. L., *Man's Conception of Eternity* (London: J. H. Parker, 1854).

Marsh, J., *Christina Rossetti: A Literary Biography* (London: Jonathan Cape, 1994).

Marshall, D., *The Surprising Effects of Sympathy: Marivaux, Diderot, Rousseau, and Mary Shelley* (Chicago and London: University of Chicago Press, 1988).

Marston, J. W., *Poetry as an Universal Nature* (London: W. Strange, 1838).

Martin, R. B., *Tennyson: The Unquiet Heart* (Oxford: Oxford University Press, 1980).

—— *With Friends Possessed: A Life of Edward FitzGerald* (London: Faber, 1985).

Masson, J., *Freud: The Assault on Truth* (London: Faber, 1984).

Matthiessen, F. O. (ed.), *The James Family* (New York: Alfred A. Knopf, 1948).

Maudsley, H., *The Physiology and Pathology of Mind* (London: Macmillan & Co., 1867).

Maurice, F. D., *Theological Essays* (Cambridge: Macmillan & Co., 1853).

Maurice, F. D., *The Gospel of St John: A Series of Discourses* (Cambridge: Macmillan & Co., 1857).

Maxwell. J. C., 'Molecules', *Nature*, 8 (1873), 437–41.

Mercer, P., *Sympathy and Ethics* (Oxford: Clarendon Press, 1972).

Meynell, V. (ed.), *Friends of a Lifetime: Letters to Sydney Carlyle Cockerell* (London: Jonathan Cape, 1940).

Mill, J. S., *Analysis of the Phenomena of the Human Mind*, 2 vols. (London: Baldwin & Cradock, 1829).

Mill, J. S., *Auguste Comte and Positivism* (London: Trübner, 1865, repr. Ann Arbor, Mich.: Ann Arbor Paperbacks, 1968).

——*Dissertations and Discussions Political, Philosophical and Historical*, 3rd edn., 4 vols. (London: J. W. Parker, 1875)

——*Mill on Bentham and Coleridge*, ed. F. R. Leavis (London: Chatto & Windus, 1950).

——*Essays on Politics and Culture*, ed. G. Himmelfarb (Garden City, NY: Doubleday & Co., 1963).

Miller, J., *Subsequent Performances* (London: Faber, 1986).

Millgate, M., *Thomas Hardy: A biography* (Oxford: Oxford University Press, 1982).

——*Testamentary Acts: Browning, Tennyson, James, Hardy* (Oxford: Clarendon Press, 1992).

Millingen, J. G., *Mind and Matter, Illustrated by Considerations on Hereditary Insanity* (London: n.p., 1847).

Mintz, S., *A Prison of Expectations: The Family in Victorian Culture* (New York and London: New York University Press, 1983).

Mitchell, W. J. T., 'Influence, Autobiography, and Literary History: Rousseau's *Confessions* and Wordsworth's *The Prelude*', *ELH*, 57 (1990), 643–64.

Morgentaler, G., *Dickens and Heredity: When Like Begets Like* (Basingstoke: Macmillan, 2000).

Morley, J., *On Compromise* (London: Chapman & Hall, 1877).

Mullan, J., *Sentiment and Sociability: The Language of Feeling in the Eighteenth Century* (Oxford: Clarendon Press, 1988).

Müller, F. M., *Lectures on the Science of Language* (London: Longman, Green, Longman, Roberts & Green, 1864).

Murphy, S. F. (ed.), *Our Homes, and How to Make Them Healthy* (London: Cassell & Co., 1883–5).

'MWS', 'On Ghosts', *London Magazine*, 9 (March 1824), 253–6.

Naden, C., *The Complete Poetical Works of Constance Naden* (London: Bickers & Son, 1894).

Nagel, T. *Mortal Questions* (London: Cambridge University Press, 1979).

Neville, W. B., *On Insanity* (1837).

Newman, F. W., *The Iliad of Homer Faithfully Translated into Unrhymed English Metre* (London: Walton & Maberly, 1856).

—— *Life after Death? Palinodia* (London and Nottingham: Trubner & Co., 1886)

Newman, J. H., *An Essay on the Development of Christian Doctrine* (London: James Toovey, 1845).

—— *An Essay in Aid of a Grammar of Assent* (London: Burns, Oates & Co., 1870).

—— *Sermons Preached Upon Several Occasions*, 3rd edn. (London: Burns, Oates & Co., 1870).

—— *Autobiographical Writings*, ed. H. Tristram (London and New York: Sheed & Ward, 1956).

Newnham, W., *Essay on Superstition* (London: Hatchard & Son, 1830).

—— *Essay on the Disorders Inherent to Literary Men; and on the Best Means of Preserving Their Health* (London: J. Hatchard & Son, 1836).

—— *The Reciprocal Influence of Body and Mind Considered* (London: J. Hatchard & Son, 1842).

Newton, I., *Opticks*, 2nd edn. (London: W. & J. Innys, 1718).

Nietzsche, F., *Thoughts Out of Season*, trans. A. Collins (Edinburgh and London: J. N. Foulis, 1909).

—— *The Portable Nietzsche*, trans. and ed. W. Kaufmann (London: Chatto & Windus, 1971).

Noel, R., 'Memory and Personal Identity', *The Modern Review*, 4 (1888), 180–7.

Nunokawa, J., *The Afterlife of Property: Domestic Security and the Victorian Novel* (Princeton, NJ: Princeton University Press, 1994).

O'Leary, C. M., 'Memory and its Diseases', *The Catholic World*, 36 (1883), 101–11.

Oppenheim, J., *'Shattered Nerves': Doctors, Patients and Depression in Victorian England* (New York and Oxford: Oxford University Press, 1991).

Parfit, D., *Reasons and Persons* (Oxford: Clarendon Press, 1984, repr. 1987).

Partridge, E. (ed.), *Responsibilities to Future Generations: Environmental Ethics* (Buffalo, NY: Prometheus Books, 1981).

Pasternak, B., *Pasternak on Art and Creativity*, ed. A. Livingstone (Cambridge: Cambridge University Press, 1985).

Pater, W., *Studies in the History of the Renaissance* (London: Macmillan & Co., 1873).

—— *Marius the Epicurean* (London: Macmillan & Co., 1885; 2 vols., 1910).

—— *Appreciations* (London: Macmillan & Co., 1889).

—— *Essays on Literature and Art*, ed. J. Uglow (London: Dent, 1973).

—— *Selected Writings*, ed. H. Bloom (New York: Columbia University Press, 1982).

Patmore, C., *Principle in Art* (London: George Bell & Sons, 1889).

—— *The Poems of Coventry Patmore*, ed. F. Page (London: Oxford University Press, 1949).

Peabody, E., 'Methods of Influence', *The Monthly Religious Magazine*, 11: 1 (January 1854), 1–11.

Phillips, A., *On Kissing, Tickling, and Being Bored* (London: Faber & Faber, 1993).

—— *The Beast in the Nursery* (London: Faber, 1998).

—— *Darwin's Worms* (London: Faber, 1999).

—— *Promises, Promises: Essays on Literature and Psychoanalysis* (London: Faber, 2000).

Pick, D., *Faces of Degeneration: A European Disorder, c.1848–c.1918* (Cambridge: Cambridge University Press, 1989, repr. 1993).

—— *Svengali's Web: The Alien Enchanter in Modern Culture* (New Haven, Conn.: Yale University Press, 2000).

Pollok, R., *The Course of Time: A Poem* (Edinburgh and London: William Blackwood & Sons, 1827, repr. 1857).

Pope, A., *The Correspondence of Alexander Pope*, ed. G. Sherburn, 5 vols. (Oxford: Clarendon Press, 1956).

Postma, J., *Tennyson as Seen by His Parodists* (Amsterdam: H. J. Paris, 1926).

Pound, E., *The Cantos of Ezra Pound* (London: Faber, 1975).

—— *Selected Poems, 1908–1959* (London: Faber, 1975).

Prickett, S., *Words and the Word: Language, Poetics and Biblical Interpretation* (Cambridge: Cambridge University Press, 1986).

Primeau, R. (ed.), *Influx: Essays on Literary Influence* (Port Washington, Wis.: Kennikat Press, 1977).

Proust, M., *Remembrance of Things Past*, trans. C. K. Scott Moncrieff, T. Kilmartin, and A. Mayor, 3 vols. (London: Chatto & Windus, 1981).

—— *On Reading Ruskin*, trans. & ed. J. Autret, W. Burford, and P. J. Wolfe (New Haven, Conn. and London: Yale University Press, 1987).

—— *Against Sainte-Beuve and Other Essays*, trans. J. Sturrock (London: Penguin, 1988).

Rae, S. (ed.), *The Faber Book of Drink, Drinkers and Drinking* (London: Faber, 1991).

Raphael, B., *The Anatomy of Bereavement: A Handbook for the Caring Professions* (London: Hutchinson, 1984).

Rawnsley, H. D., *Memories of the Tennysons* (Glasgow: J. MacLehose & Sons, 1900).

Reade, B. (ed.), *Sexual Heretics: Male Homosexuality in English Literature from 1850–1900* (London: Routledge & Kegan Paul, 1970).

Reid, J., *Essays on Hypochondriasis*, 2nd edn. (London: Longman, Hurst, Rees, Orme & Brown, 1821).

Ribot, T., *Les maladies de la mémoire* (Paris: Germer Baillière et Cie, 1881).

Richardson, J., *Thomas Hardy: The Poetry of Necessity* (Chicago and London: University of Chicago Press, 1977).

Ricks, C., *Tennyson* (London: Macmillan, 1972).

—— *Keats and Embarrassment* (London: Oxford University Press, 1976).

—— *The Force of Poetry* (Oxford: Clarendon Press, 1984).

—— *T. S. Eliot and Prejudice* (London: Faber, 1988, repr. 1994).

—— *Essays in Appreciation* (Oxford: Clarendon Press, 1996).

Robb, G., *Victor Hugo* (London: Picador, 1997).

Robinson, P., *In the Circumstances: About Poems and Poets* (Oxford: Clarendon Press, 1992).

Roscoe, W., *On the Origin and Vicissitudes of Literature, Science, and Art, and their Influence on the Present State of Society* (London: n.p., 1818).

Rose, M., *Authors and Owners: The Invention of Copyright* (Cambridge, Mass. and London: Harvard University Press, 1993).

Rosenberg, J. D., *Carlyle and the Burden of History* (Oxford: Clarendon Press, 1985).

Rossetti, C. G., *The Complete Poems of Christina Rossetti*, ed. R. W. Crump, 3 vols. (Baton Rouge, La.: Louisiana State University Press, 1979–90).

Rossetti, D. G., *The Works of Dante Gabriel Rossetti*, ed. W. M. Rossetti (London: Ellis, 1911).

—— *Letters of D. G. Rossetti*, ed. O. Doughty and J. R. Wahl, 2 vols. (Oxford: Clarendon Press, 1965).

Rossetti, W. M., *Life of John Keats* (London: Walter Scott, 1887)

Rowe, N., *Ulysses* (London: J. Tonson, 1706).

Rowell, G., *Hell and the Victorians* (Oxford: Clarendon Press, 1974).

Ruskin, J., *Collected Works*, ed. E. T. Cook and A. D. O. Wedderburn, 39 vols. (London: George Allen, 1902–12).

Said, E. W., *Orientalism* (London: Routledge & Kegan Paul, 1978).

Saintsbury, G., *A History of English Prosody*, 2nd edn., 3 vols. (London: Macmillan & Co., 1923).

Sanders, A., *Charles Dickens, Resurrectionist* (London: Macmillan 1982).

Saxe, A., 'Influence', *The Universalist Quarterly and General Review*, 47 (1890), 29–41.

Scarry, E., *The Body in Pain: The Making and Unmaking of the World* (New York and Oxford: Oxford University Press, 1985).

Schrödinger, E., *Mind and Matter* (Cambridge: Trinity College Tarner Lectures, 1967)

Schulte, R., and Biguenet, J. (eds.), *Theories of Translation* (Chicago and London: University of Chicago Press, 1992).

Semmel, B., *George Eliot and the Politics of National Inheritance* (New York and Oxford: Oxford University Press, 1994).

Shakespeare, W., *The Works of William Shakespeare*, ed. W. G. Clark and W. A. Wright, 9 vols. (London and Cambridge: Macmillan & Co., 1866).

—— *Hamlet*, ed. H. H. Furness (Philadelphia, Pa.: Lippincott, 1877).

Shannon, E. F., and Ricks, C., ' "The Charge of the Light Brigade": The Creation of a Poem', *Studies in Bibliography*, 38 (1985), 1–44.

Sharp, W., *The Life and Letters of Joseph Severn* (London: Sampson Low & Co., 1892).

Shelley, P. B., *Letters of Percy Bysshe Shelley* (London: Edward Moxon, 1852).

Shelley, P. B., *Shelley's Prose; or, the Trumpet of a Prophecy*, ed. D. L. Clark (New York: New Amsterdam, 1988).

Shuttleworth, S., *George Eliot and Nineteenth-Century Science* (Cambridge: Cambridge University Press, 1984).

—— *Charlotte Brontë and Victorian Psychology* (Cambridge: Cambridge University Press, 1996).

Smiles, S., *Self-Help; With Illustrations of Character and Conduct* (London: John Murray, 1859).

—— *Character* (London: John Murray, 1871, repr. 1888).

—— *Duty* (London: John Murray, 1880).

Smith, A., *Theory of Moral Sentiments* (Edinburgh: A. Kincaid & J. Bell, 1759).

Sontag, S., *A Susan Sontag Reader* (Harmondsworth: Penguin, 1982).

—— *Illness as Metaphor* [1978], repr. in *Illness as Metaphor and Aids and its Metaphors* (London: Penguin, 1991).

Spedding, J., 'Tennyson's Poems', *Edinburgh Review*, 77 (April 1843), 373–91.

Spufford, F., and Uglow, J. (eds.), *Cultural Babbage: Technology, Time and Invention* (London: Faber, 1996).

'S. S. J.', *Integrity; or, The Artist Stanton and his Daughters* (London: n.p., 1849).

Standage, T., *The Victorian Internet: The Remarkable Story of the Telegraph and the Nineteenth Century's Online Pioneers* (London: Wiedenfeld and Nicolson, 1998).

Steiner, G., *After Babel: Aspects of Language and Translation* (London: Oxford University Press, 1975).

Stephen, L., *The Science of Ethics* (London: Smith, Elder & Co., 1882).

Sylvester, J. J., *The Laws of Verse* (London: Longmans, Green & Co., 1870).

Taylor, C. *Sources of the Self: The Making of Modern Identity* (Cambridge: Cambridge University Press, 1989).

Taylor, G., *Reinventing Shakespeare: A Cultural History from the Restoration to the Present* (London: Hogarth, 1989).

Taylor, H., *Philip Van Artevelde: A Dramatic Romance*, 2 vols. (London: Edward Moxon, 1834).

Taylor, I., *Physical Theory of Another Life* (London: William Pickering, 1836).

Tennyson, A., Untitled sonnet, repr. in *Victorian Poetry*, 3 (December 1965), 9.

—— *In Memoriam*, ed. S. Shatto and M. Shaw (Oxford: Clarendon Press, 1982).

—— *Tennyson's 'Maud': A Definitive Edition*, ed. S. Shatto (London: Athlone Press, 1986).

Tennyson, C., *Alfred Tennyson* (London: Macmillan & Co., 1949).

Tennyson, H. (ed.), *Tennyson and his Friends* (London: Macmillan & Co., 1911).

Tennyson, H. (ed.), *Studies in Tennyson* (London: Macmillan, 1981).

'T. H.', 'The Sphere of Human Influence', *The Christian Examiner and Religious Miscellany*, 45: 6 (September 1846), 213–16; 45: 13 (November 1848), 424–7.

Thackeray, W. M., *The Newcomes* [1853–5], ed. D. Pascoe (Harmondsworth: Penguin, 1996).

Thorpe, J., *Principles of Textual Criticism* (San Marino, Calif.: Huntington Library, 1972).

Thwaite, A., *Emily Tennyson: The Poet's Wife* (London: Faber, 1996).

Trench, R. C., *Notes on the Parables of Our Lord* (London: John W. Parker & Son, 1840).

—— *On the Study of Words* (London: John W. Parker & Son, 1851).

—— *English: Past and Present* (London: John W. Parker & Son, 1855).

Trilling, L., *The Liberal Imagination* (London: Secker & Warburg, 1951).

—— *Sincerity and Authenticity* (London: Oxford University Press, 1972).

Trotter, D., *Cooking With Mud: The Idea of Mess in Nineteenth-Century Art and Fiction* (Oxford: Oxford University Press, 2000).

Trotter, T., *An Essay on Drunkenness* (London: Longman, 1804).

—— *A View of the Nervous Temperament* (London: Longman, Hurst, Rees & Orme, 1807).

Tucker, H. F., *Tennyson and the Doom of Romanticism* (Cambridge, Mass. and London: Harvard University Press, 1988).

Turner, C. T., *Collected Sonnets Old and New* (London: Kegan Paul & Co., 1880).

Turner, J. C., *Social Influence* (Milton Keynes: Open University Press, 1991).

Tyndall, J., *Sound* (London: Longmans, Green & Co., 1867).

—— *Fragments of Science for Unscientific People* (London: Longmans, Green & Co., 1871).

Vaughan, C. J., *Revision of the Liturgy: Five Discourses* (Cambridge and London: Macmillan & Co., 1860).

Valéry, P., *Leonardo, Poe, Mallarmé*, trans. M. Cowley and J. R. Lawler (London: Routledge & Kegan Paul, 1972).

—— *The Art of Poetry*, trans. D. Folliot (London: Routledge & Kegan Paul, 1958).

Vaughan, C. J., *Revision of the Liturgy: Five Discourses* (London: Macmillan, 1860).

Venuti, L., *The Translator's Invisibility: A History of Translation* (London: Routledge, 1995).

Verdon, R., 'Forgetfulness', *Mind*, 2: 8 (October 1877), 29–52.

Walker, J., *A Rhyming Dictionary: Answering at the Same Time the Purposes of Spelling, Pronouncing, and Explaining the English Language* [1775], rev. J. Longmuir (London: William Tegg, 1865).

Walzer, M., *Spheres of Justice: A Defence of Pluralism and Equality* (Oxford: Robertson, 1983).

Warnock, M., *Memory* (London: Faber, 1987).

Warren, C. F. S., Letter in *Notes and Queries*, 1, 6th ser. (1880), 523.

Wells, S. (ed.), *Shakespeare Burlesques*, 5 vols. (London: Diploma Press, 1977–8).

Welsh, A., *The City of Dickens* (Oxford: Clarendon Press, 1971).

Wheeler, M., *Heaven, Hell, and the Victorians* (Cambridge: Cambridge University Press, 1994).

Wilde, O., *The Picture of Dorian Gray* [1891], ed. I. Murray (London: Oxford University Press, 1974).

—— *The Artist as Critic: Critical Writings of Oscar Wilde*, ed. R. Ellmann (London: W. H. Allen, 1968).

Williams, B., *Problems of the Self: Philosophical Papers 1956–1972* (Cambridge: Cambridge University Press, 1973).

—— *Moral Luck: Philosophical Papers 1973–1980* (Cambridge: Cambridge University Press, 1981).

—— *Ethics and the Limits of Philosophy* (London: Fontana, 1985, repr. 1993).

Wilson, H. S., 'The Rubáiyát of Omar Khayyam, the Astronomer-Poet of Persia', *Contemporary Review*, 27 (1876), 559–70.

Wimsatt, W. K., 'One Relation of Rhyme to Reason: Alexander Pope', *Modern Language Quarterly*, 5 (1944), 323–38.

Winnicott, D. W., *Through Paediatrics to Psychoanalysis* (London: Hogarth Press and the Institute of Psychoanalysis, 1975).

Winter, A., *Mesmerised: Powers of Mind in Victorian Britain* (Chicago and London: University of Chicago Press, 1998).

Wittgenstein, L., *Philosophical Investigations*, trans. G. E. M. Anscombe, 2nd edn. (Oxford: Basil Blackwell, 1958).

—— *The Blue and Brown Books* (Oxford: Basil Blackwell, 1958).

—— *Remarks on Frazer's 'Golden Bough'*, trans. A. C. Miles, ed. R. Rhees (Retford: Brynmill, 1979).

Wolfson, Susan J., 'Keats Enters History: Autopsy, *Adonais*, and the Fame of Keats', in N. Roe (ed.), *Keats and History* (Oxford: Clarendon Press, 1995).

Woodmansee, M., and Jazsi, P. (eds.), *The Construction of Authorship: Textual Appropriation in Law and Literature* (Durham, NC and London: Duke University Press, 1994).

Woods, G., *A History of Gay Literature: The Male Tradition* (New Haven, Conn. and London: Yale University Press, 1998).

Wordsworth, W., *The Prelude: 1799, 1805, 1850*, ed. J. Wordsworth, M. H. Abrams, and S. Gill (New York and London: Norton, 1979).

—— *The Borderers*, ed. R. Osborn (Ithaca, NY and London: Cornell University Press, 1982).

—— *The Fourteen-Book Prelude*, ed. W. J. B. Owen (Ithaca, NY and London: Cornell University Press, 1985).

Wright, T. R., *The Religion of Humanity: The Impact of Comtean Positivism on Victorian Britain* (Cambridge: Cambridge University Press, 1986).

Wright, W. F., *The Shaping of 'The Dynasts'* (Lincoln, Nebr.: University of Nebraska Press, 1967).

Yeats, W. B., 'Verlaine in 1894', *The Savoy*, 2 (April 1896), 117–19.

Zeller, H., 'A New Approach to the Critical Constitution of Literary Texts', *Studies in Bibliography*, 28 (1975), 231–64.

Index

Printed in the United Kingdom
by Lightning Source UK Ltd.
131823UK00001B/266/A